Personnel Selection
and Productivity

SECOND EDITION

Personnel Selection and Productivity
SECOND EDITION

MARK COOK

JOHN WILEY & SONS

Chichester · New York · Brisbane · Toronto · Singapore

Other Wiley Editorial Offices

John Wiley & Sons, Inc., 605 Third Avenue,
New York, NY 10158-0012, USA

Jacaranda Wiley Ltd, 33 Park Road, Milton,
Queensland 4064, Australia

John Wiley & Sons (Canada) Ltd, 22 Worcester Road,
Rexdale, Ontario M9W 1L1, Canada

John Wiley & Sons (SEA) Pte Ltd, 37 Jalan Pemimpin #05-04,
Block B, Union Industrial Building, Singapore 2057

Library of Congress Cataloging-in-Publication Data

Cook, Mark.
 Personnel selection and productivity / Mark Cook. — 2nd ed.
  p. cm.
 Includes bibliographical references and index.
 ISBN 0-471-94046-1
 1. Employee selection. I. Title.
 HF5549.5.S38C66 1990
 658.3′112 — dc20   93–19468
                                                      CIP

British Library Cataloguing in Publication Data

A catalogue record for this book is available from the British Library

ISBN 0-471-94046-1

Typeset in 10/12pt Palatino from author's disks by Text Processing Department,
John Wiley & Sons Ltd, Chichester
Printed and bound in Great Britain by
Biddles Ltd, Guildford and King's Lynn

Contents

Preface to the First Edition

When I first proposed writing this book I thought it self-evident that personnel selection and productivity are closely linked. Surely an organization that employs poor staff will produce less, or achieve less, than one that finds, keeps and promotes good staff. So it was surprising when several people, including one anonymous reviewer of the book proposal, challenged this assumption, and argued there was no demonstrated link between selection and productivity.

Critics are right, up to a point; there has never been experimental demonstration of the link. The experiment could be made—but might prove very expensive. First create three identical companies. Second, allow company A to select staff using the best techniques available; require company B to fill its vacancies at random (so long as staff have the minimum necessary qualifications); require company C to employ the people company A's selection programme had identified as the least suitable. Then wait a year and see which company is doing best, or—if the results are very clear-cut—which companies are still in business. No such experiment has been performed to my knowledge, although "fair" employment laws in the USA have caused some organizations to adopt personnel policies not far removed from strategy B.

Perhaps critics meant only to say that the outline overlooked other, more important, factors affecting productivity: training, management, labour relations, lighting and ventilation. Or factors the organization can't control: the state of the economy, technical development, foreign competition, political interference. Of course all these affect productivity, but that doesn't prove that—other things being equal—an organization that selects, keeps and promotes good employees won't produce more, or produce better, than one that doesn't.

Within-organization factors affecting productivity are dealt with by the other titles in this series; ones outside the organization, like the state of world trade, fall outside the scope of psychology.

I would like to thank the many people who have helped me prepare this book, in particular those who have commented on earlier drafts, especially Paul Humphries, John MacArthur, Chris Potter, Graham Edwards and Ken Bennett.

Centre for Occupational Research Ltd
10 Woodlands Terrace, Swansea SA1 6BR

Preface to the Second Edition

The five years since the first edition of this title have seen a number of major important developments, such as the rapid development of structured interviewing, the rediscovery of "g" by American psychologists, and Project A, revalidating personality and ability tests for the American military. The last five years have also seen the extension of meta-analysis to several new areas, clarifying the results of large bodies of confusing research, and transforming dispiriting conclusions into more hopeful ones. This is particularly true of personality inventory validity. Another trend that looks promising is the use of job analysis to guide choice of selection test, thereby achieving significantly increased validity. More worrying trends emerge in the literature of fair employment. In the USA, lawyers are pushing hard to re-impose the crippling restrictions of the late 1960's and early 1970's. In the UK, the Commission for Racial Equality seems to want to impose the same restrictions.

Every chapter has been revised to incorporate new research or new ideas. The amount of change reflects therefore the distribution of interesting new research between different selection tests. The chapters on assessment centres, personality tests, interviewing, and work samples have seen extensive alteration. The chapter on biographical methods has seen some alteration. The chapter on references and ratings has seen the least change.

Every chapter has been re-written, even where there isn't so much new research to report. The re-writing is most extensive where students and other users of the first edition have indicated they found the first edition hard to follow. Other changes are made in response to comments by reviewers of the first edition.

Since the first edition appeared, I have become a director of Oxford Psychologists Press Ltd, a publisher of psychological tests, whose products include the California Psychological Inventory, mentioned in Chapter 8, and the Progressive Matrices, mentioned in Chapter 7.

I would like to thank the many people who have helped me prepare this second edition. Firstly I would like to thank the many researchers in the selection area who have generously sent me accounts of research in press or in progress. Secondly I would like to thank the students on the Cardiff Applied

Psychology Masters course whose questions and comments over the last four years have shown me where the first edition needed change. Finally I would like to thank those who have commented on drafts of the first and second editions, especially Christopher Potter, Graham Edwards, Ken Bennett, Stephen Prosser, Wendy Yates, Louise Morris and Maureen Walters.

Mark Cook
March 1993

1 The Value of Good Employees

The best is twice as good as the worst

In an ideal world, two people doing the same job under the same conditions will produce exactly the same amount. In the real world, some employees produce more than others, which poses two questions:

- how much do workers vary in productivity?
- how much are these differences worth?

The short answer to both questions is "a lot". The answer to the first question is that good workers do twice as much work as poor workers. The answer to the second question says the difference in value between a good worker and a poor one is roughly equal to the salary they're paid.

HOW MUCH DOES WORKERS' PRODUCTIVITY VARY?

Clark Hull is better known, to psychologists at least, as an animal learning theorist, but very early in his career he wrote a book on aptitude testing (Hull, 1928), and described ratios of output of best to worst performers in a variety of occupations. The best spoon polishers polished five times as many as the worst. Ratios were less extreme for other occupations—between 1.5 to 1 and 2 to 1 for weaving and shoe-making jobs. (Unfortunately Hull doesn't answer several fascinating questions—how many spoon polishers were studied? and did they polish spoons full time?) Hull was the first psychologist to ask how much workers differ in productivity, and he discovered the principle that should be written in letters of fire on every personnel manager's office wall: *the best is twice as good as the worst.*

Comparing best to worst worker is an index of *range* (see Note 1), so it isn't very informative. Tiffin (1943) drew graphs of the *distribution* (see Note 1) of output for electrical fixture assemblers, for workers who solder the ends of insulated cables, and for 'hosiery loopers', who gather together the loops of thread at the bottom of a stocking to close the opening left in the toe (Figure 1.1).

Tiffin confirmed Hull's finding; the best fixture assembler's output is over twice that of the worst. He also showed that most workers fall between the extremes to form a roughly *normal* distribution (see Note 1) of output. Tiffin checked the effects of practice, and the consistency of differences between workers. Hosiery loopers' output increases after a year's experience, and the range of individual differences narrows, but the best looper still loops twice as many as the worst. The loopers' individual outputs were measured twice in successive weeks, and proved very consistent. More recently Vinchur et al (1991) reported that foundry workers' output is very consistent week by week.

Later work by Rothe (1946) measured differences in output for workers wrapping blocks of butter, for workers hand-dipping chocolates, for coil-winders, and for several samples of machine operators. Differences in output were normally distributed, except in one group of machine operators, where *output norms*—tacit agreements among the workers to limit output—distorted the distribution. Sometimes the structure of work imposes uniformity on output; the best worker on a car assembly line does under 10% more work than the poorest, because both work at the pace of the assembly line itself. The standard deviation of production (SD_p) is a convenient way of summarizing data on output, sales, etc. A standard deviation of the data on Figure 1.1 is the SD_p of hosiery looping.

Hull, Tiffin and Rothe all analyse output in repetitive production work, where it is (relatively) easy to measure. Dorcus & Jones (1950) list a few more occupations where output is fairly easy to measure—typing, accounting machine operation, book-keeping. Selling, too, is usually easy to quantify. Schmidt & Hunter (1983) review all available evidence on range of worker output, with Hull's ratio of best to worst worker. The ratio is very consistent

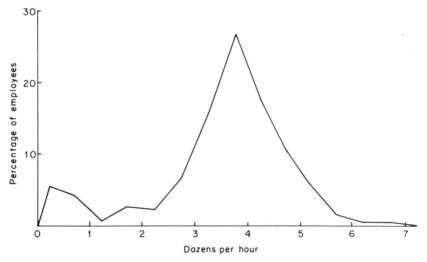

Figure 1.1 Distribution of productivity for 199 hosiery loopers (Tiffin, 1943)

across a wide range of occupations: welders, typists, cashiers, card-punch operators, lathe operators, lampshade manufacturers, sewing machinists, and 'wool pullers'. Schmidt & Hunter define 'best' as the 95th *percentile* (see Figure 1.2) and 'worst' as the 5th percentile; the best 5% of workers usually do twice as much as the worst 5%. If the workers are paid a piece rate, the ratio is slightly compressed—to 1.69/1. Does output increase at the expense of quality? So that workers who do more are no more valuable? Not necessarily—faster key-punch operators and proof machine operators make fewer mistakes.

Not all occupational psychologists try to quantify output; many ask the wider question—Is the employee satisfied? The early work of the (British) National Institute for Industrial Psychology emphasized the worker's "attain-ment of [his/her] self-chosen goal", rather than output as such. The current generation of occupational psychologists are more 'hard-nosed', and hark back to the 1920s, when Bingham defined the successful employee as the one who "does more work, does it better, with less supervision, with less interrup-tion through absence from the job" (Bingham & Freyd, 1926). If the worker is happy, that's nice—for the worker.

Defining productivity in more complex or intangible work poses great problems. Is a good dentist one who fills more teeth per day? Or one who fills fewer because he/she prevents cavities forming? Is a good researcher one who publishes more articles? Or one who makes important discoveries? Who decides a discovery is important? Many occupations have no identifiable output. What defines productivity of lifeboat crew, or ministers of religion, or TV announcers? It's impossible to decide if a selection method works without a *criterion*. Yet it's often very difficult to find a good criterion (Chapter 11).

HOW MUCH IS A PRODUCTIVE WORKER WORTH?

If some workers produce more than others, an employer that succeeds in selecting them will make more money—but how much more? A lot of ingenious effort has gone into putting a cash value on the productive worker. Accountants tried first, and weren't very successful, which left the field to psychologists.

Accountants can, at least in theory, calculate the value of each individual worker: so many units produced, selling at so much each, less the worker's wage costs, and a proportion of the company's overheads. In practice, such calculations have proved very difficult. Roche (1965) tried to quantify the value of individual radial drill operators (and the increase in profits the company might make by selecting new workers using a mechanical compre-hension test). He arrived at an estimate of $0.203 worth per hour increase in output—a 3.7% increase in the company's profits. Even Roche's detailed calculations were criticized (Cronbach & Gleser, 1965) as oversimplified. The drill operators machined a great variety of different components, but the company's figures didn't record output per operator, *per type of component*; pooled estimates had to be used. But if accountants can't put a precise value on an individual production worker's output, how can they hope to do so for a manager, supervisor or personnel director?

For many years, accepted wisdom held that the financial benefit of employing good staff couldn't be directly calculated. Hence the psychologist couldn't tell employers "my selection method can save you so many thousand pounds or dollars per year". (Most psychologists are reluctant to make extravagant claims for their methods, so find it difficult to compete with people who lack their scruples.) The same wisdom made governments and pressure groups think "selection procedures [could] be safely manipulated to achieve other objectives, such as a racially representative workforce" (Schmidt & Hunter, 1981)—because no one could prove that not employing the best people cost the organization money.

Rational Estimates

Recently psychologists have devised a technique for putting a cash value on the people doing any job, no matter how varied and complex its demands, or how indefinable or intangible its end products. *Rational Estimate* (RE) *technique* was invented by two psychologists, Schmidt and Hunter, who argue that people supervising a particular grade of employee "have the best opportunities to observe actual performance and output differences between employees on a day-to-day basis" (Schmidt et al, 1979b). So the best way to put a value on a good employee is simply to ask supervisors to judge the employee's worth.

Rational Estimate technique has two stages: data collection and data analysis. Rational Estimates are collected using these instructions:

> Based on your experience with [widget press supervisors] we would like you to estimate the yearly value to your company of the products and services provided by the average supervisor. Consider the quality and quantity of output typical of the average supervisor and the value of this output.

To make the task easier, the instructions say:

> in placing a cash value on this output, it may help to consider what the cost would be of having an outside firm provide these products and services.

Similar estimates are made for a good supervisor, and for a poor one. "Good" is defined as a supervisor at the 85th percentile, one whose performance is better than 85% of his/her fellows. "Poor" is defined as a supervisor at the 15th percentile, better than only a few other supervisors, and worse than most.

Why 15% and 85%? Because these values correspond roughly to one *standard deviation* (see Note 3) either side of the mean. Therefore assuming the value of supervisors is normally distributed, the three estimates—15th percentile, mean and 85th percentile—can be used to calculate the standard deviation of employee productivity, cryptically referred to as SD_y. The SD_y summarizes the distribution in value to the employer of differences in output between employees (Figure 1.2). SD_y tells the employer how much the workers' work varies in value.

SD_y is a vital term in the equation for estimating the return on a selection program. The smaller SD_y is, the less point there is to putting a lot of effort and expense into selecting staff, because there's less difference in value between good and poor staff. The bigger SD_y is, the greater the difference between good and bad, and the more money can be saved by selecting more productive workers.

After a large number of supervisors and managers have made REs, averages are calculated (stage two). In their first study, Schmidt and Hunter obtained estimates made by 62 supervisors of the value of average and good budget analysts. The mean difference between average and good was $11 327 a year, meaning a good budget analyst is rated as worth $11 000 a year more than an average one. This implies that any selection procedure that increases the proportion of good budget analysts recruited stands to save many thousands of dollars a year.

The study of budget analysts only made estimates for the average and the 85th percentile, which doesn't prove value to the organization is normally distributed. The distribution might be skewed. The difference between average and poor budget analysts might be far less than $11 000, if most analysts

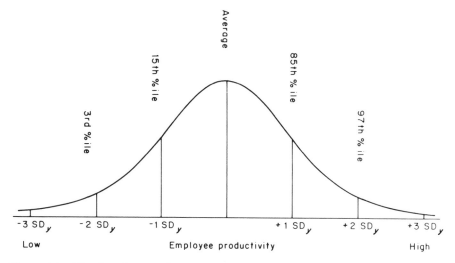

Figure 1.2 The distribution of employee productivity, showing the percentile points used in Rational Estimate Technique to measure it

were much the same with only a few producing outstanding work, or it might be far more than $11 000, if bad budget analysts were disastrously bad. If employee productivity is normally distributed, the difference between average and poor should be about the same as the difference between average and good. The second study by Schmidt and Hunter made REs for good, average and poor computer programmers (Schmidt, Gast-Rosenberg & Hunter, 1980). The differences between average and good, and average and poor, programmers were $10 513 and $9955, respectively; the two estimates don't differ significantly, so they can be averaged to obtain a single estimate for SD_y of just over $10 000. Good programmers are worth over $10 000 more to their employers, each year, so it's clearly worth spending a fraction of that sum to make sure of finding some. (Many employers will cheerfully pay thousands of pounds to advertise for staff, but won't pay a few hundred to assess them.)

Naturally psychologists couldn't wait to apply RE technique to their academic colleagues; Bobko, Shetzer & Russell (1991) report an estimate of SD_y for college professor (university lecturer) of $55 600—although the value varied greatly according to the way it was elicited.

A worker at the 97th percentile of productivity is two standard deviations above the mean (Figure 1.2). If a worker at the 85th percentile is worth £12 000 more than an average worker, a worker at the 97th percentile should be worth twice £12 000, i.e. £24 000, more. Rational Estimates for workers who produce more than do 97% of their peers should differ from REs for the 85th percentile by the same amount as REs for the 85th percentile differ from REs for the average; two studies found that they don't. In both (Bobko, Karren & Parkington, 1983; Burke & Frederick, 1984), the RE for the 97th percentile was lower than predicted. Perhaps there really is an upper limit to what the most productive employee can achieve, imposed by peer pressure or what the organization itself can cope with. Bobko et al disagree, because the distribution of actual sales wasn't "compressed" at the upper end.

Variations on the Rational Estimate theme

US Army tank commanders were unwilling to make REs, saying soldiers' lives and performance in battle weren't describable in dollar terms. Eaton, Wing & Mitchell (1985) devised the *Superior Equivalents Technique*, in which commanders estimate how many tanks with *superior* (85th percentile) crews are the match of a standard company of 17 tanks, with average crews. Estimates converged on a figure of nine. An elite tank company need number only nine to be the match of an average company, neatly confirming Schmidt & Hunter's estimate that the best is twice as good as the worst. Given the price of modern tanks, the US Army could clearly save a fortune if it could be sure of recruiting only superior tank crews. The *Superior Equivalents Technique* is particularly suitable for workers who, while modestly paid themselves, use very expensive equipment.

Cascio (1982) describes a more complex way of calculating differences in productivity: CREPID (Cascio Ramos Estimate of Performance In Dollars). The job is divided into different components (e.g. teaching, research, and administration), the relative importance of each is rated (e.g. equally important), the value of the worker's contribution to each area estimated, multiplied by its weighting, then summed. The CREPID is better suited for jobs with a range of activities that mightn't be done equally efficiently. Weekley et al (1985) find that CREPID gives much lower estimates of SD_y than REs.

Recently Hunter, Schmidt & Judiesch (1990) have summarized data on the ratio of SD_y/X_y. The greater SD_y is, relative to the average of the distribution of value of output (X_y), the more workers vary relative to each other in how valuable they are. For jobs of low complexity, such as welding, delivering post, filing, packing and wrapping, the ratio is low; for highly complex jobs, such as lawyer, doctor and dentist, the ratio is 2.5 times as great. This implies the generalization "the best is twice as good as the worst" holds truer for complex jobs than for simple jobs.

The 40—70% rule

SD_y for budget analysts worked out at 66% of salary; SD_y for computer programmers worked out at 55%. These values prompted Schmidt & Hunter to propose a *rule of thumb*:

> SD_y is between 40% and 70% of salary.

'Best' and 'worst' workers are each one SD_y from the average, so the difference between best and worst is *two* SD_ys. If SD_y is 40—70% of salary, the difference between best and worst is between 80 and 140% of salary, which generates another *rule of thumb*:

> The value of a good employee minus the value of a poor employee is roughly equal to the salary paid for the job.

If salary for the job in question is £15 000, the difference in value between best and worst worker is roughly £15 000 too. (Recall also that 'best' and 'worst', at the 85th percentile and 15th percentile, are far from being the extremes.)

The 'worse than useless' worker?

It's self-evident the average value of each worker's output must exceed average salary; otherwise the organization will lose money, and go out of business or require a subsidy. Schmidt, Hunter & Pearlman (1982) review the evidence, and propose another *rule of thumb*:

> The yearly value of output of the average worker is about twice his/her salary.

Certain combinations of values of the two ratios—productivity/salary and SD_y/salary—have alarming implications for employers. Suppose salary is £10 000. The first rule of thumb implies that SD_y could be as high as £7000 (70% of salary). The second rule of thumb implies average productivity is about £20 000 (twice salary). Consider a worker whose productivity is *three* SD_y below the mean. That worker is worth £20 000 less £7000 × 3, i. e. *minus* £1000 (Figure 1.3). The 'goods and services' he/she provides wouldn't cost anything to buy in from outside, because they aren't worth anything. In fact, that employee actually loses the employer £1000, on top of the cost of his/her salary of £10 000. Two informants in one study (Burke & Frederick, 1984) did value an inferior sales manager at zero dollars, or at *minus* $100 000.

Only one or two in a thousand employees falls three SDs below the mean so, for this employer, 'worse than useless' employees are fortunately scarce. But suppose the productivity/salary ratio were nearer unity. Schmidt, Mack & Hunter (1984) report a ratio of 1.29 for park rangers (average RE $13 530, average salary $10 507). If SD_y were 70% of salary for park rangers, then 7% are 'worth' negative sums to their employer. Could an organization survive a handicap like that? Fortunately later research, including that on park rangers, finds SD_y typically nearer 40% of salary level than 70%, which implies relatively few employees are 'worse than useless'. However, REs still derive from a fairly narrow range of employers; many commentators feel they could nominate organizations where 'worse than useless' workers proliferate.

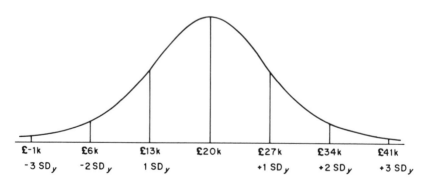

| £-1k | £6k | £13k | £20k | £27k | £34k | £41k |
| -3 SD$_y$ | -2 SD$_y$ | 1 SD$_y$ | | +1 SD$_y$ | +2 SD$_y$ | +3 SD$_y$ |

Figure 1.3   The distribution of employee productivity, where average value is £20 000 and SD$_y$ is £7000

Are Rational Estimates valid?

Some critics think REs are dangerously subjective. Schmidt et al disagree; the instructions specify estimating the cost of employing an outside firm to do the work, which provides a "relatively concrete standard". Furthermore "the idiosyncratic tendencies, biases and random errors of individual judges can be controlled by averaging across a large number of judges". In any case, they argue, cost accounting calculations are often fairly subjective too, involving "many estimates and arbitrary allocations" (Roche, 1965).

Some research indicates REs are valid. Bobko & Karren (1982) compared rational estimates for 92 'telephone counsellors' (a euphemism for insurance salespersons) with counsellors' sales figures. The standard deviation of counsellors' actual sales was \$52 308; SD_y, calculated by RE, was \$56 950. The second study (Ledvinka & Simonet, 1983) used data on insurance claims processed by individual claims supervisors. The average worker processed 5345 claims per year, and the standard deviation of 15 workers' outputs was 1679 claims a year. Differences in productivity were very consistent; one month's figures were nearly identical with another's. Dividing total wage cost by number of claims processed gave an average cost per claim of \$3.30. The number of claims each individual worker processed was then multiplied by \$3.30, to give a dollar estimate of the value of his/her output. The standard deviation of these 15 dollar-estimates is SD_y —measured objectively, not by RE. Objective SD_y was \$5542, which equalled 43% of salary, and confirmed the lower estimate of the 40-70% rule.

However, more recent studies have cast some doubt on the validity of REs. Bobko, Shetzer & Russell (1991) find that relatively minor changes in the wording of the instructions, or the order of presentation (85th percentile estimate then 50th percentile, or vice versa), generate a very wide range of SD_y estimates, from as low as \$29 000, to as high as \$101 000. Another study asked supervisors to explain how they generated REs (Mathieu & Tannenbaum, 1989), and found most—especially the more experienced—based their estimates on salary. This makes some of the *rules of thumb* of Schmidt & Hunter look suspiciously circular. If estimates of SD_y are based on salary, it's not surprising, nor very interesting, to find they're closely related to salary.

A third study by Schmidt & Hunter's group (Judiesch et al, 1992) starts by reporting that many supervisors making REs set their 50th percentile estimate at near average salary for the job, *not* at twice salary—contradicting Schmidt's & Hunter's own 'twice average salary' *rule of thumb*. They then review 11 studies showing that supervisor estimates of SD_p—standard deviation of *production* (output or sales)—agree very well with actual SD_p computed from output or sales data. They conclude by suggesting that SD_y be estimated from SD_p, incorporating an allowance for 'overheads'. The original point of RE technique was that cost accountancy methods couldn't put a value to the individual worker's efforts, yet Schmidt & Hunter now propose using the cost accountants' figures for production and overheads to estimate SD_y because RE technique generates figures that are wrong.

IMPLICATIONS OF RATIONAL ESTIMATE RESEARCH

Rational Estimates calculate the savings made by using effective selection methods, and the cost incurred by not using them. Research on REs reaches some startling conclusions:

1. A 'small' employer, such as the Philadelphia police force (5000 employees), could save $18 million a year by using psychological tests (Schmidt & Hunter, 1981).
2. Dunnette devised a selection program for workers in the US electricity generating industry, and claimed "it does not seem too great a stretch of the imagination to expect a potential annual gain in the neighbourhood of $800 million when these selection procedures are adopted by the [70] companies participating in this research project" (Dunnette, 1982).
3. A 'large' employer—the US Federal Government (4 million employees)— could save $16 billion a year by using psychological tests to select employees. Or, to reverse the perspective, the US Federal Government is losing $16 billion a year by **not** using tests (Schmidt & Hunter, 1981).
4. Critics see a major flaw in the calculations of Schmidt & Hunter. Every company in the country can't employ the 15% best computer programmers or budget analysts; someone has to employ 'the rest'. Good selection can't increase national productivity, only the productivity of employers that use psychological assessment to grab more than their fair share of talent. At present, employers are free to do precisely that. The rest of this book explains *how*.

NOTES

1. *Range and the normal distribution.*   The Astronomer Royal of Belgium in the 19th century, Adolphe Quetelet, plotted a graph of the height of 100 000 French soldiers (Figure 1.4); the soldiers' heights formed a bell-shaped distribution, called the *normal distribution*.

Other naturally occurring measurements, when plotted, also produce a normal distribution: chest diameter, 'vital capacity' (how much air the person can draw into his/her lungs—still a selection requirement for the fire brigade), time it takes to react to a sound, and activity of the autonomic nervous system. (Quetelet's distribution has been estimated for men under 5'2", who weren't in the army because they were too short.)

Range: Quetelet's soldiers varied in height from under 5'2" to over 5'9". A

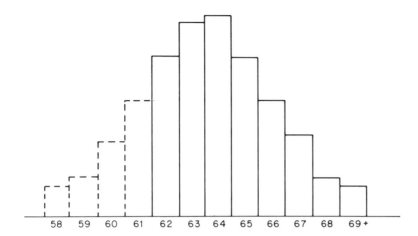

Figure 1.4 Distribution of height, in inches, for nineteenth-century French soldiers. N.B. the distribution has been estimated for men less than 5'2" who weren't accepted as soldiers

statistic summarizing variability is needed. While everyone understands averages, measures of variability are harder to grasp. *Range* is the difference between the tallest and shortest. Range describes extremes, which can be fairly uninformative; the modern *Guinness Book of Records* gives the tallest authentic male height ever recorded as 8'11", and the shortest as 2'2".

2. *Percentile.* Range isn't a very useful statistic, especially to personnel managers who rarely want employees who will feature in the *Guinness Book of Records*. Ways of describing variability in the mass of people between the extremes are more useful. One is the *percentile*. Average male height is now 5'8.5", which is another way of saying 50% of men are as tall as 5'8.5" and 50% are taller. How many men are taller than 6'2"—about 2%. How many men are shorter than 5'6"—some 16%. Percentiles can describe a man's height to someone who doesn't understand feet and inches, by saying "He is taller than 98% of men", or "He is at the 98th *percentile* for height".

3. *Standard deviation.* The standard deviation does two things: it describes how one person compares with another, and it summarizes the variability of the whole distribution. 'Standard deviation' is usually abbreviated to 'SD'.

A distribution is completely summarized by its mean and SD, so long as it is *normal*, i. e. bell-shaped and symmetrical. (Distributions of some 'natural' scores, like height, are normal; distributions of constructed scores, like IQs, are made normal.)

The SD can be used, like the percentile, to describe someone's height, without reference to any particular system of measurement. A man 6'2" high is 2 SDs above the mean. Anyone who understands statistics will know how tall that is, be the local units of height metres, feet and inches, or cubits.

2 Old and New Selection Methods

We've always done it this way

Figure 2.1 summarizes the successive stages of selecting a lecturer (assistant professor) for a British university. The *advertisement* attracts applicants, who complete and return an *application form*. Some applicants' *references* are taken up; the rest are excluded from further consideration. Candidates with satisfactory references are short-listed and invited for *interview*, after which the post is filled. The details vary from university to university, but the basic principle remains: attract as many applicants as possible, then pass them through a series of filters, until the number of candidates equals the number of vacancies.

Advertisement

Most jobs are advertised, locally or nationally. People who answer the advertisement are sent further information about the job, the pay, the conditions and the organization. Many organizations still use recruiting methods dating from times of full employment and labour shortage; they paint a rosy picture of what's really a boring and unpleasant job, because they fear no one will apply otherwise. In the USA, *realistic job previews*—films, brochures, visits—are increasingly used to tell applicants what being, for example, a telephone operator is *really* like: fast-paced, closely supervised, routine to the point of being boring, and solitary except for the occasional unfriendly or 'nasty' customer (Wanous, 1978). The more carefully worded the advertisement and the job description, the fewer unsuitable applicants will apply.

Applicants are sometimes recruited by word of mouth, usually through existing employees, which is cheaper. (A small—7 × 7 cm—advertisement in a British national daily—*The Telegraph* or *The Guardian*—costs over £800.) Besides being cheaper, the 'grapevine' finds employees who stay longer (low *voluntary turnover*), and who are less likely to be dismissed (low *involuntary turnover*) (Breaugh & Mann, 1984; Kirnan, Farley & Geisinger, 1989). People recruited by word of mouth stay longer because they have a clearer idea what the job really involves. But beware: the (British) Commission for Racial Equality may argue employing an all-white workforce's friends is just a subtle way of maintaining an all-white workforce. To date, a high proportion of the Commission's Inquiries have dealt with 'unfair' recruitment.

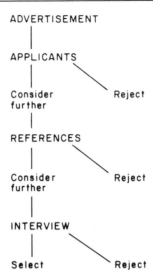

Figure 2.1 Main stages of selecting academic staff in a British university

Table 2.1 Methods used by US employers to find five types of staff; figures are percentages (Bureau of National Affairs, 1979). Reprinted by permission from *Personnel Management*, © 1979 by the Bureau of National Affairs, Inc., 1231 25th Street, NW, Washington, DC 20037, USA

	O/C	P/S	S	P/T	M
Employee referral	92	94	74	68	65
"Walk-ins"	87	92	46	46	40
Newspaper advert	68	88	75	89	82
Radio/TV advert	5	8	2	7	4
Specialist publication advert	12	6	43	75	57
US Employment Service	63	72	34	41	27
Private employment agency	44	11	63	71	75
(employer pays fee)	(31)	(5)	(49)	(48)	(65)
College/university	17	9	48	74	50
Professional Societies	5	19	17	52	36
Head hunters	1	2	2	31	54
Union	1	12	0	3	0

O/C—office clerical; P/S—production/skilled; S—sales; P/T—professional/technical; M—management.

Sometimes people seek jobs, or employers seek staff, through employment agencies—public or private. Some grades of staff are 'head hunted' by *recruitment consultants*. The 'head hunter' advertises without naming the prospective employer, or approaches likely candidates and invites them to apply. Head hunters assess candidates, usually by interview, before deciding whose names to pass on to the employer, which adds yet another stage to assessment. Staff are head hunted when good candidates are in short supply. Occasionally, in tightly unionized jobs, vacancies are filled by the union, not the employer. This practice has little to commend it; seniority, the criterion which unions usually use, doesn't predict productivity (Chapter 6).

Table 2.1 shows (some of) the results of a recent survey of US recruitment methods. Most employers use a combination of methods, and most are willing to consider employee referrals and 'walk-ins'—the person who comes in off the street and asks if they need any widget press operators that day. Employers are less likely to turn to public employment agencies for sales, professional/technical or management vacancies, preferring private agencies or head hunters (Bureau of National Affairs, 1979).

THE 'CLASSIC TRIO'

Most organizations select their staff by the tried and tested trio: *application form, letter of reference* and *interview*.

Application form

The (British) Industrial Society surveyed 50 British application forms; name, address, date of birth, previous employers and reasons for leaving last job are the only universals. Only half ask for age, and only 4% ask the bureaucrat's classic—mother's maiden name. (The British Civil Service sometimes also asks where she was born, to check if the applicant is 'British born of British parents'.) Surprisingly few forms ask about hobbies and leisure interests. Forty percent want to avoid nepotism, and ask if the applicant has any relatives working for the company. Two-thirds ask for an educational history, and 26% about details of membership of professional bodies.

Application forms can be converted into *Weighted Application Blanks* (WABs), by analysing past and present employees for predictors of success, or low turnover, or honesty (Chapter 6). One study found that American female bank clerks who left prematurely tended to be under 25, single, to live at home with a mother who herself works, to have had several jobs, etc. (Robinson, 1972); so American banks that want to recruit employees who will stay longer should avoid employing women with these characteristics. The WAB is economical, effective and difficult to fake. All the items on Robinson's WAB are routine application form questions.

Drawing up the shortlist

In the 1960s, when unemployment in Britain was "nearing half a million", drawing up a shortlist was often difficult because personnel managers were lucky to have as many as five passably good applicants (three of whom didn't show up for the interview anyway). In the 1990s, personnel managers typically face a "mountain of applications" to sift through, which gives researchers a new problem to study: which applications make the short list, and why. Wingrove, Glendinning & Herriot (1984) analyse how personnel managers use information on application forms. In a transport company, 80% of decisions—reject or consider further—can be predicted from nine facts: maths grade (at A level), degree in maths or computer science, work experience in a transport organization, belong to societies related to transport, work experience in computer programming, been on `Insight into Management' course. People who wrote a lot were considered further, as were people who wrote neatly, and people who used "certain [unspecified] keywords". People from certain parts of Britain (also unspecified) were more likely to be rejected.

American research on *application sifting* (Arvey, 1979a) finds women widely discriminated against at short-list stage. Women are also stereotyped as more suitable for some jobs, or for working with other women. Both male and female interviewers are equally biased against women. However, the *size* of the effect was often very small; in one study (Dipboye, Arvey & Terpstra, 1977), preference for male applicants, while statistically significant, was so slight as to be entirely trivial. Arvey found no evidence of discrimination against nonwhites in short listing. Herriot & Wingrove (1984) recorded personnel managers 'thinking aloud' while sifting applications, and heard comments like "Two As and a B at A level, pretty good" (has good exam grades), "Hasn't bothered to read the brochure", or "Oh dear supermarket work every vacation". One in five comments mention 'presentation': "He hasn't written much on this form, and what there is I can't read".

In the USA, application sifting is assisted by *Training & Experience* (T&E) *ratings* (Chapter 10), which seek to quantify applicants' training and experience, instead of relying on possibly arbitrary judgements by the sifter (McDaniel, Schmidt & Hunter, 1988). In Britain, the Commission for Racial Equality recommends application sifting be done by two persons. In the USA, the Equal Employment Opportunities Commission's (EEOC) *Guide to Pre-Employment Inquiries* lists a wide range of potentially objectionable application form questions that could create *adverse impact* on protected minorities, or which aren't *job related*. These include questions about: marital status, children, child care; hair or eye colour; gender; military service or discharge; age; availability over holidays or weekends (which may discourage some religious minorities); height and weight; arrest records. Surveys (Burrington, 1982;) find many, if not nearly all, US application forms make some 'inappropriate' enquiries.

References

Two-thirds of major British employers always take up references; only a handful never do (Robertson & Makin, 1986). In the British public sector—higher education, Health Service, Civil Service—references are taken up before interview. The commercial sector often doesn't take up references until someone has been offered the job, so the reference is little more than a safety check, that the successful candidate really did work for his/her last employer, and that he/she wasn't dismissed for stealing. British references are usually letters saying whatever the referee feels like saying about the candidate, in whatever form he/she feels like saying it. Very few British employers ask for ratings, or for any structured or quantified opinion of the candidate. In the USA employers are more likely to use structured reference forms.

Some employers don't limit themselves to asking people nominated by the applicant what they think of him/her; police and sections of the Civil Service check the applicant's background, associates and even attitudes very thoroughly. Other employers usually haven't the resources or authority to do this, although many gain unofficial access to criminal records by employing former police officers.

Interview

In both public and private sectors the final hurdle is the interview. A 1957 survey in the USA reported that 99% of employers interview job applicants (Ulrich & Trumbo, 1965). A survey by Robertson & Makin of top UK employers, taken from the *Times 1000*, found only one who never interviewed.

BUILDING ON THE CLASSIC TRIO

Psychologists have long known the classic trio isn't very effective. Scott published the first research on the interview in 1915, showing six personnel managers didn't agree about a common set of applicants. Dozens more research studies since have confirmed Scott's conclusions (see Chapter 3). Early research on what one person said about another's personality soon found such opinions highly unreliable. The classic trio's failings prompted both personnel managers and psychologists to look for something better. The various offerings over the years divide into:

(a) psychological tests
(b) group exercises
(c) work sample tests
(d) 'weird and wonderful' measures
(e) miscellaneous

or any combination of these, and the classic trio; long, complicated assessments of a group of applicants are often dignified by the title *assessment centre* (Chapter 9).

(a) Psychological tests

Alfred Binet wrote the first mental ability (MA) test in 1904; it crossed the Atlantic, to become the Stanford–Binet. It wasn't the world's first test of mental ability, but it was the first *general mental ability test*, and the first to be standardized. The Binet tests children individually; personnel selectors test adults in groups. A committee of American psychologists wrote the world's first adult group MA test, to classify recruits to the US Army when America entered the First World War in 1917; 1.7 million recruits were tested. (The British Army didn't use MA tests in the First World War, preferring as Raymond Cattell (1936) said, to "[use] some of the best brains from civilian life to stop bullets in front-line trenches".) The Army Alpha was released for civilian use as the National Intelligence Test, and sold 400 000 copies within 6 months. The Army Beta was a *non-verbal* test for recruits who didn't speak English, or couldn't read; the instructions were given by gesture and example.

General MA tests usually contain a mixture of items—verbal, numerical, and abstract questions. *Aptitude tests* limit themselves to one type of item, and measure a specific ability: mechanical comprehension, spatial relations, clerical speed and accuracy, or ability to program computers. Aptitude tests often correlate (see Note 1) highly with general MA tests, so the distinction between the two isn't always clear.

The *personality questionnaire* also owes its origin to the Great War. By 1917 armies had discovered that many men couldn't stand the stress of continuous battle. The US Army acted on this knowledge, and devised a screening test for men who would crack up so quickly they weren't worth sending to the front line. The Woodworth Personal Data Sheet (PDS) had 116 items, and was surprisingly sophisticated for its day. Questions were excluded if more than 25% of the healthy controls gave the keyed answer, or if the neurotic group didn't give the keyed answer at least twice as often as the controls. The PDS wasn't finished in time to be used in the war, but was released for civilian use, as the Woodworth Psychoneurotic Inventory, and was the ancestor of a long line of tests. Many items from the PDS still give good service in modern questionnaires:

- Do you usually sleep well?
- Do you worry too much about little things?
- Does some particular useless thought keep coming into your mind to bother you?

Other psychological assessments can claim even longer histories. The Utopian reformer Robert Owen used the first known *rating scale* in 1825; children in the New Harmony colony in Indiana were rated on ten 100-point scales of 'courage', 'imagination' or 'excitability'. But it wasn't a paper and pencil measure; Owen's scale was cast in brass, and can still be seen in the New Harmony museum.

Behavioural tests have been used for at least 3000 years. The Book of Judges (Chapter 7, Verses 4–7) tells how Gideon raised an army to "smite" the Midianites, and found he had too many volunteers. He used a simple test of fieldcraft to exclude the inexperienced from his army; he told them to go and take a drink from the nearby river, and selected only those who kept on their guard even while slaking their thirst.

Psychological tests gained acceptance in the USA in the 1920s, and proliferated during the 1930s. Progress was slower in Britain. The National Institute for Industrial Psychology was founded in 1920, and used aptitude tests during the 1920s and 1930s. Studies of selection by psychological tests between 1910 and 1948, reported by Dorcus & Jones (1950), are plotted in Figure 2.2. Test use increased steadily throughout the period in the USA, whereas it started later, grew slower and peaked earlier in Europe and the UK. There was of course a lot of wartime military research in Britain that wasn't published until later, if at all—but so there was in the USA, which didn't halt the growth of civilian testing during the war years. The wartime testing programmes in the USA inspired more civilian test use post-war, whereas UK wartime developments, notably the War Office Selection Board (WOSB), inspired few civilian imitations (except the Civil Service Selection Board, CSSB).

(b) Group exercises

Until 1942, the British Army selected officers by Commanding Officer's recommendation and a panel interview. By 1942 this system was proving ineffective, because the panels didn't like, or couldn't understand, candidates with grammar school education or 'communist' opinions. The War Office Selection Board (WOSB) replaced the panels, and a key element of the WOSB was the *group exercise*—leaderless group discussions, as well as more practical tasks, including the one still featured in British Army officer recruitment ads (building a bridge across a wide gap with short lengths of timber).

Some group tasks were part of a 'cover plan' (Vernon & Parry, 1949) to introduce the measures the psychologists wanted, while persuading the military to accept the new system; Vernon is (?deliberately) vague about which group exercises were "unstandardised and unscoreable, and their diagnostic worth extremely dubious". The WOSB was partly inspired by German military selection methods, which had also used group discussions. It was the model for the British CSSB (Vernon, 1950; Anstey, 1977).

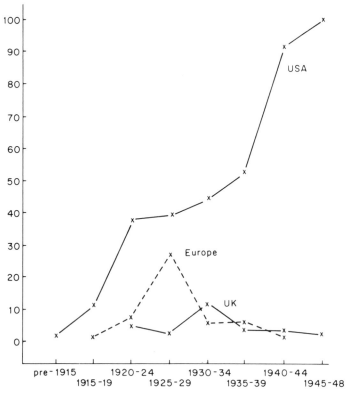

Figure 2.2 Number of studies using psychological tests for personnel selection published in the USA, Europe and the UK, between 1914 and 1948

In the USA, a similar intensive assessment programme, using group discussions alongside many other measures, was used by the Office of Strategic Services (OSS), forerunner of the CIA, to select spies. The OSS programme, and WOSB, eventually inspired the *assessment centre* for evaluating managers, first used by AT&T in 1956; assessment centres are now commonly used in America and Britain, and include a wide range of group exercises. Assessment centres are discussed in greater detail in Chapter 9.

(c) Work sample tests

Most applicants for typing jobs are given a work sample test—they are asked to type something. (Usually a bad work sample test—unstandardized, subjectively scored and fairly uninformative.) In 1913, the Boston streetcar (tramway) system asked Hugo Munsterberg to find a way of reducing the number of accidents, without slowing down the services too much. Munsterberg found some tram drivers were accident prone; (some of) this accident-prone minority were poor at judging speed and closing distance. Munsterburg devised a work sample test, of judgement of closing distances and relative speeds.

Many more work sample tests were devised in the 1920s and 1930s, in Britain and Europe as well as America. Work samples were used very extensively in military selection and classification programs in the Second World War. Work sample tests have two limitations. Because they're samples of work, they're necessarily job specific, so a tramway system needs different work samples for drivers, conductors, inspectors, mechanics, electricians, track maintenance workers, etc. Work samples are more difficult to devise, where the work is diverse or abstract or involves other people. It's much easier to plan work samples for routine production workers than for supervisors and managers. The *in-basket* or *in-tray* exercise is a management work sample test—a dozen letters, memos, and policy documents to read and deal with.

(d) "Weird and wonderful" methods

It's very difficult to select good staff, and quite impossible to make the right choice every time, so most personnel managers are conscious of frequent failures, and always on the look-out for better methods. Some are led astray by extravagant claims for semi-magical methods.

Graphology

"... a hail-fellow-well-met who liked to eat and drink; who might attract women of the class he preyed on by an overwhelming animal charm. I would say in fact he was a latent homosexual ... and passed as a man's man ... capable of conceiving any atrocity and carrying it out in an organised way"—a graphologist's assessment of 'Jack the Ripper', based on what might be one of his letters (Figure 2.3). No one knows who 'Jack' really was, so no one can contradict the graphologist's assessment.

Graphology is widely used in personnel selection in Europe, by 85% of all companies according to Klimoski & Rafaeli (1983). Fewer companies in Britain and the USA use it; Robertson & Makin (1986) report 7–8% of major UK employers 'sometimes' used graphology. If handwriting accurately reflected personality, it would make a very cost-effective selection method, because candidates could be assessed from their application forms. Nor is it obviously absurd to suppose that handwriting reflects personality. However, Klimoski & Rafaeli conclude that all the hard evidence indicates "graphology is not a viable assessment method"; two graphologists independently analysing the same handwriting sample agree very poorly about the writer's personality.

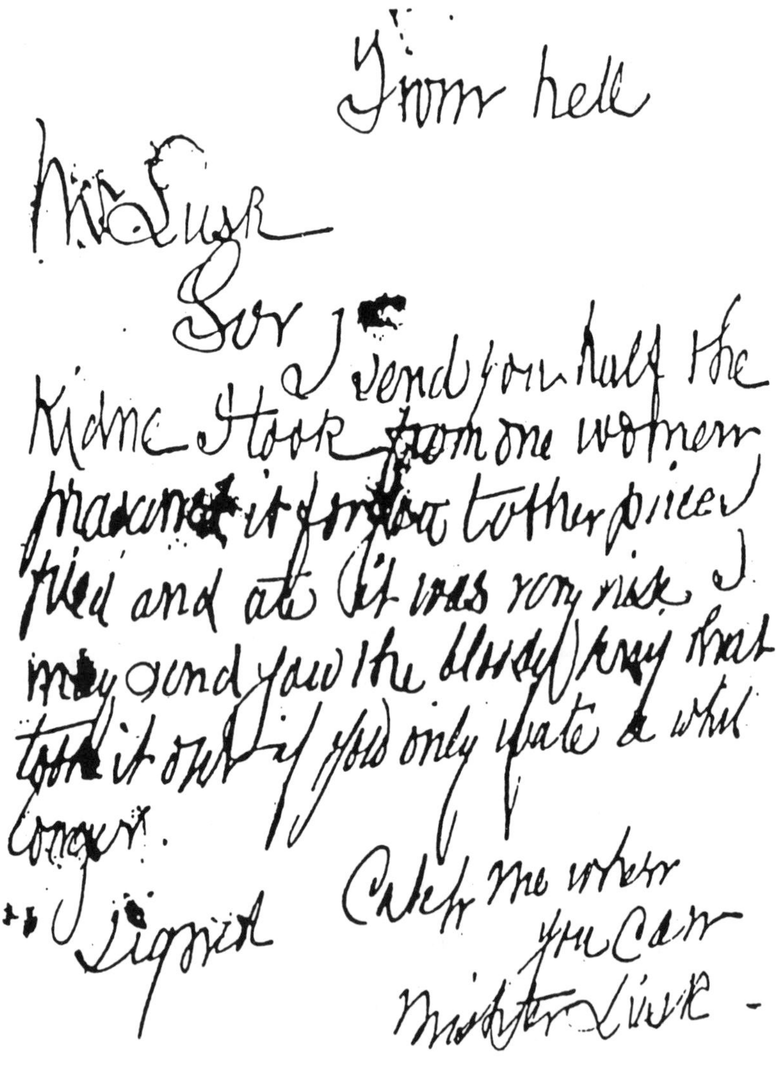

From hell

Mr Lusk
Sor
I send you half the
Kidne I took from one women
prasarved it for you tother piece
I fried and ate it was very nise I
may send you the bloody knif that
took it out if you only wate a whil
longer

signed Catch me when
you Can
Mishter Lusk

Figure 2.3 A letter attributed to 'Jack the Ripper'

Graphologists' ratings of realtors (estate agents) were seen to be completely unrelated to supervisors' ratings and to actual sales figures (Klimoski & Rafaeli, 1983). Graphologists' ratings of insurance salesmen similarly failed to predict their success (Zdep & Weaver, 1967).

Graphologists often ask subjects to write pen pictures of themselves, so the assessment isn't solely based on handwriting. (The *content* of the letter in

Figure 2.3 reveals quite a lot about the writer's mentality.) Neter & Ben-Shakhar (1989) review 17 studies, comparing graphologists and non-graphologists, rating neutral and 'content-laden' scripts. With 'content-laden' scripts, the non-graphologists, who know nothing about analysing handwriting, achieved *better* results than graphologists (0.26 vs 0.21), suggesting they interpreted *what* people wrote, not *how* they wrote it, and interpreted it better than the graphologists. With neutral scripts neither group achieved better than zero validity, suggesting either there's no useful information in handwriting, or that experts don't presently know how to extract it.

Handwriting can be a *sign* or a *sample*. A personnel manager who complains he/she can't read an applicant's writing judges it as a *sample*; legible handwriting may be needed for the job. The graphologist who infers repressed homosexuality from handwriting interprets it as a *sign* of something far removed from putting pen to paper.

Astrology and palmistry

It's not absurd to suppose people reveal their personality in their handwriting—just wrong. It does seem absurd to many people to suppose the sky at the instant of someone's birth could shape their personality. Nevertheless, astrology is taken seriously by some psychologists, and there is evidence of personality differences in people born under different star signs. The difference is fairly basic—more introverts are born in "even-numbered" months—and not very relevant to personnel selection. Bayne (1982) notes that palmistry could make a very good selection device—convenient, cheap, unfakeable—if it worked. Unfortunately it doesn't.

Pseudo-tests

There are a number of these about, or a number of versions of the same one about. It's difficult to be more precise, because the most characteristic feature of the pseudo-test is that it's very wary of psychologists. Pseudo-tests are generally very short, typically a couple of dozen items; they're often checklists of adjectives, or use forced choice—"most like me"/"least like me"; they're often printed in several bright colours; they're complicated to score, and often use 'derived' scores (in which further scores are produced by adding, subtracting, multiplying or dividing the basic scores). Pseudo-tests are usually very expensive, especially as one almost always has to pay handsomely to be trained to use them. Pseudo-tests rarely come with any information about reliability or validity, and are rarely, if ever, mentioned in occupational psychology journals. They tempt personnel managers because they're short, and they're available. Pseudo-tests are generally too short to measure anything, let alone the impressive lists of traits they claim to measure.

Polygraph

The polygraph, also known as the lie detector, was widely used in the USA to check staff who have the opportunity to steal—shop assistants, warehouse staff, bank employees. In 1983, the British Government proposed using the polygraph to 'vet' staff with access to secret information, but eventually abandoned the idea in the face of union opposition. The principle of the polygraph is sound—anxiety causes changes in respiration, pulse and skin conductance—but in practice it has drawbacks, principally a high rate of *false positives* in people who are not lying but are nervous about the test. The polygraph is likely to miss genuine criminals, because they don't see lies as lies, or because they don't respond physically to threat, and might well miss a spy trained to mask physical reactions. Since 1988, use of the polygraph in employment testing in the USA has been prohibited by the Employee Polygraph Protection Act, except for public sector employees. Use of the polygraph is legal (although rare) in Britain; the British Psychological Society disapproves of its use for selection or honesty testing.

Drug-use testing

In the USA, testing applicants for drug use is popular, and controversial. Its advocates point to research in, for example, the US Postal Service (Normand, Salyards & Mahoney, 1990), showing drug use predicts higher absenteeism and higher *involuntary turnover*, the implication being that not employing drug-users will increase productivity. Critics (Guastello, 1992) argue the size of the difference in such studies is minute, accounting for no more than 0.1% of the variation in absence, nowhere near enough to justify the intrusion on the applicant's privacy and civil rights. Acceptability of drug testing depends on 'perceptions of danger' (Murphy, Thornton & Prue, 1991), making it look fair for surgeons, police officers or airline pilots, but not justified for janitors, farmworkers or clerks.

CURRENT SELECTION PRACTICE

In the USA

In 1975, a survey by the American Society of Personnel Administration found 60% of large US employers used psychological tests, whereas only 39% of small employers did. Many employers tested only for clerical jobs. Testing was in decline; three-quarters of employers had cut back their testing programmes since 1970, and 14% intended to drop all testing.

Schmitt et al (1984) review research on selection in North America between

1964 and 1982, and give an interesting analysis of the types of assessment used for six broad classes of work. The WAB was the most commonly reported method. Personality and MA tests were widely used, followed by aptitude tests, peer evaluations, assessment centres, physical tests and job samples. Personality and MA tests are used fairly generally, with some exceptions. Clerical staff are rarely given personality tests, and sales staff are rarely given MA tests [which is odd—Ghiselli (1966a) reports MA tests have good predictive validity for sales]. Assessment centres are used only for management; physical tests are used only for skilled and unskilled labour. The data of Schmitt et al aren't a true survey of recent/current North American practice, since they draw their information solely from articles published in *Personnel Psychology* and *Journal of Applied Psychology*, which describe innovations, but not routine assessment methods. A recent survey of selection methods for US police forces finds they all use background checks and medical examinations; nine out of ten use MA tests; four out of five use tests of physical strength and agility; two out of three use personality tests; and one in three use biographical predictors (Ash, Slora & Britton, 1990).

At least 5000 North American employers use honesty tests, for employees who have access to cash or merchandise. Sackett & Harris (1984) describe these tests—questionnaires of varying lengths from 37 to 158 items—as "largely outside the mainstream of psychological testing"; they are not published by major test publishers, no research on them appears in scientific psychology journals; it's often difficult to get any technical information about them. The validity of *honesty tests* is reviewed in Chapter 8.

In Britain

Surveys of use of psychological tests in Britain have appeared quite regularly (British Psychological Society, 1985); information about other methods is more sketchy (proving that psychologists like measuring things, even themselves). In Britain, management trainees and apprentices are the most frequently tested groups. Engineering and electrical apprentices are particularly likely to face aptitude tests. Personality tests are not often used; they are never used for selecting clerical staff, apprentices or shop floor workers. Graduate trainees are probably Britain's most extensively, and intensively, assessed class of employee—because they're vital to the organization's future? or because they're least likely to complain? Surveys of test use find employers much less likely to test *existing* employees than *prospective* employees, perhaps because present employees have rights, and probably a trade union, whereas applicants haven't. Robertson & Makin (1986) reported that 4% of major UK employers always use personality tests, while 64% never do, and the rest use them sometimes. A similar survey 5 years later (Shackleton & Newell, 1991) found tests had apparently increased in popularity in Britain. Robertson & Makin drew the pessimistic conclusion from their survey of major UK employers that "the frequency of a method's use is inversely related to its known validity".

Surveys also indicate that some assessment methods are more popular with applicants than others (Iles & Robertson, 1989); candidates like work samples and assessment centres, but don't like biodata or peer assessment. In times of high unemployment, employers may feel they can afford to take less notice of candidates' reactions; in times of labour shortage, use of unpopular methods could drive applicants away.

In Europe

Recently several surveys have been reported on Western European and Scandinavian selection practices. All the countries surveyed (Germany, France, The Netherlands, Norway) use the interview more or less routinely. In Germany (Schuler, Frier & Kauffmann, 1991), application form, interview and medical examination are favoured. Methods not widely used include graphology, assessment centres, biodata, personality tests, work samples and tests of MA (except for apprentices). In France (Shackleton & Newell, 1991; Bruchon-Schweitzer & Ferrieux, 1991), graphology joins the interview as a near universal feature. Tests of personality and MA are often used, and projective tests are not uncommon. In-tray exercises and role plays find occasional favour. References are not as widely used; 23% of employers 'never' take them up (compared with only 2% in Britain). Selection in The Netherlands (Altink, Roe & Greuter, 1991) resembles German practice, with interview, application form and medical examination customary, but psychological tests are also very widely used. In Norway (Smith, 1991), the interview is almost always used, psychological tests are occasionally used, while assessment centres, graphology and biodata are rarely or never used.

CONCLUSIONS

Most British organizations still use the classic trio. Many probably still have no doubts about the value of application form, reference and interview. Organizations that haven't heard that the classic trio has its faults probably haven't heard either that application forms, references and interviews can be improved. Which implies a lot of organizations are using old-fashioned, inefficient methods.

Bad personnel selection is often little better than no selection at all, so many organizations in Britain are probably choosing their staff more or less randomly. Schmidt & Hunter (1981) estimate that poor or non-existent selection by the US Federal Government—4 million employees—costs $16 billion a year. Suppose 90% of people employed in Britain are selected more or less randomly, how much does this cost Britain each year? Do they manage things more efficiently in Britain's competitors?

Some organizations in Britain have supplemented the classic trio, although hardly any have abandoned it altogether. Work sample tests have been used since the 1920s, and trainability tests are being adopted. Aptitude tests are quite widely used for apprentices, while MA tests are used for managers and management trainees. Assessment centres have been used by Civil Service and armed services since the 1940s, and have re-crossed the Atlantic back into the commercial sector. Personality testing remains fairly rare. Use of WABs and biodata are even rarer.

What the USA does today, Britain does tomorrow. "Today" and "tomorrow" are years apart—but how many? Suppose Britain is 20–30 years 'behind' the USA: The future in Britain will see MA tests being used very widely in all organizations at all levels. The future will see personality tests used quite widely at supervisory level and above, and WABs used quite widely below. The future will see the demise of the unstructured interview and the free-form reference, and a proliferation of rating systems.

But the future could turn out quite differently. In one important respect Britain is only 10 years 'behind' the USA—in equal opportunity employment legislation. British personnel managers might now be belatedly adopting methods which the law will shortly force them to abandon. By 2003, MA tests could be virtually outlawed, personality tests suspect and WABs unthinkable. Selectors might be forced back onto the classic trio, or forced out of business altogether. Only time—and the efforts of professional bodies like the Institute of Personnel Management and the British Psychological Society—will tell.

NOTE

1. *Correlation.* Height is normally distributed. So is weight. The two also *correlate*; tall people usually weigh more than short people, and heavy people are usually taller than light people. Height and weight are not perfectly correlated; there are plenty of short fat and tall thin exceptions to the rule. (Figure 2.4, page 28).

The correlation coefficient summarizes how closely two measures like height and weight go together. A perfect 'one-to-one' correlation gives a value of +1.00. If two measures are completely unrelated, the correlation is zero, 0.00. Height and weight correlate at about 0.75. Sometimes two measures are inversely or negatively correlated: the older people are, the less fleet of foot they (generally) are.

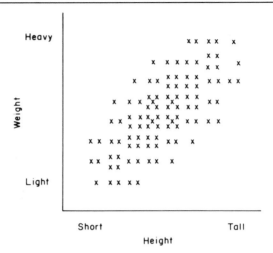

Figure 2.4 Height plotted against weight, showing a positive correlation of 0.75

3 Job Description and Job Analysis

If you don't know where you're going, you'll end up somewhere else

Selectors should always start by deciding what, or who, they are looking for. In Britain, this is often done very inefficiently [but not necessarily very quickly; I once sat through a three-hour discussion of what or who we wanted in a new head of department (chairman), which succeeded only in concluding that we didn't really want a psychoanalyst, but would otherwise like the 'best' candidate; I didn't feel my time had been usefully spent]. American practice, partly under the pressure of 'fair' employment law, has become very much more systematic.

Current British practice recommends selectors to write a *job description* and a *person specification*. Job descriptions start with the job's official title—"Head of Contracts Compliance Unit"—then say how the job fits into the organization—"organizing and leading a team of seven implementing [a London borough] Council's contracts compliance policy"— before listing the job's main duties:

1. devise and implement management control systems and procedures,
2. introduce new technology to the Unit,
3. develop strategies for fighting discrimination, poverty, apartheid, and privatization.

Job descriptions commonly fall into one of two traps. They list every duty—large or small, important or unimportant, frequent or infrequent, routinely easy or very difficult and demanding—without indicating which is which. Secondly, they lapse into a vague, sub-literate 'managementspeak' of "liaising", "resourcing", "monitoring", etc., instead of explaining precisely what the successful applicant will find him/herself doing.

Person specifications also often suffer from vagueness and 'managementspeak'. Having dealt with specifics—must be over 30 and under 45, must have personnel experience and IPM/ASPA (Institute of Personnel Management/American Society for Personnel Administration) membership, must speak Mandarin Chinese—many British person specifications waste time saying the applicant must be keen, well-motivated, energetic, etc., as if any employer were likely to want idle, apathetic, unmotivated employees. American job descriptions are usually focused much more sharply on *KSAs—knowledge, skills, aptitudes*. Ideally, the person specification finishes by saying what selection tests to use, and what—*precisely*—to look for.

Caldwell & O'Reilly (1990) devised a simple system of assessing the fit between person and job, using *Q sorts*. (Q sorting means raters assign statements into a series of categories, from 'most applicable' to 'least applicable', and are required to conform to a roughly normal distribution.) A common set of statements about skills, for example "understanding of the major principles of accounting and bookkeeping and how they are done in the company", was applied to both person characteristics and job requirements. The closer the fit between person and job, in terms of the same statements being applied to both, the better the person's rated job performance and the higher his/her job satisfaction.

The (US) Department of Labor has *Task Analysis Inventories* for collecting job information, under a number of general headings, for example education and training requirements, licensure, certificates, rating, etc., machines and equipment, specializations. The Department of Labor also uses *general educational development* ratings, which assess the level of reasoning, mathematics and language development needed. The lowest point on the *language* scale reads: "recognise meaning of 2,500 (2 or 3 syllable) words ... print simple sentences ... speak simple sentences"; the highest point reads: "read literature ... scientific and technical journals ... write novels, plays, editorials ... converse using the theory, principles and methods of effective and persuasive speaking."

In Britain the *National Vocational Qualifications* (NVQ) scheme analyses jobs in terms of *competencies*. The analysis for health-care assistants lists 35 separate main competencies, such as "assist clients to access and use toilet facilities". The analyses appear to be performed by committee, and are primarily geared to training and to awarding NVQs. They do not generally form a useful framework for assessing candidates for entry to training or employment.

JOB ANALYSIS

Job descriptions and person specifications can be drawn up by a committee in half a day. Job *analysis* is much more ambitious, much more detailed and has many more uses. Some methods require complex statistical analysis.

An example

Krzystofiak, Newman & Anderson (1979) wrote a 754-item Job Analysis Questionnaire (JAQ) for use in a power utility (power station) employing nearly 1900 individuals in 814 different jobs. Employees rated how often they performed nearly 600 tasks, on a five-point scale (never to frequently). Krzystofiak, Newman & Anderson first factor-analysed (Note 1) their data, and extracted 60 factors, representing 60 themes in the work of the 1900 employees. One particular employee's work had six themes (in order of importance):

- personnel administration,
- legal commissions, agencies and hearings,
- staff management,
- training,
- managerial supervision and decision making,
- non-line management.

The sample profile belongs to the company's Administrator of Equal Employment Opportunity. Similar profiles were drawn up for every employee. The profiles have a number of uses:

1. Armed with the knowledge that a particular job has six main themes, one has a much clearer idea of how to recruit and select for it.
2. If one could find a good test of each of the 60 factors, one would have a perfect all-purpose test battery for every one of the 800+ jobs in the plant.
3. Arguments with staff about whose job is more demanding, or deserves more money, can be settled more easily.

Krzystofiak, Newman & Anderson then cluster-analysed their data (Note 2), to sort employees into groups whose jobs were fairly similar. One of their clusters comprised:

- Rate Analyst III,
- Statistical Assistant,
- Research Assistant,
- Affirmative Action Staff Assistant,
- Coordinator, Distribution Service,
- Environmental Coordinator,
- Statistician,
- Power Production Statistician.

These eight jobs had quite a lot in common, but they all came from different departments, so their similarity might easily have been overlooked. Analysis of a matrix of 1700 × 60 ratings was required to uncover this group; human judges are notoriously very bad at interpreting large masses of data. Knowing which posts have a lot in common helps plan training, staff succession, cover for illness, etc.

Collecting information for job analysis

The job analyst tries to understand behaviour at work, so there are as many approaches to job analysis as there are to studying human behaviour itself. Here are nine methods of collecting information about work, arranged in a rough order from the most mechanistic and behaviourist to the most subjective or phenomenological.

1. Film is essential for detailed analysis of motor skills and physical tasks.
2. Written records, of sales, accidents, etc., can be useful.
3. Observation is useful for purely motor jobs, although it may overlook quality of work. Workers react to outsiders with stopwatches and clipboards by working faster (or by going on strike). Observation alone rarely makes sense of higher level jobs.
4. Structured questionnaires, completed by workers and/or supervisors.
5. Diaries are used for jobs with very little structure, like university lecturer (college professor). Diaries are easy to 'fake', consciously or unconsciously.
6. Open-ended questionnaires are more suitable for higher-level jobs with diverse tasks.
7. Interviews take account of things observation can't: plans, intentions, meaning and satisfaction. The person who sees his/her work as 'laying bricks' differs from the person who sees it as 'building a cathedral'. Interviews take time and cost money; it's essential to interview more than one worker. Workers have a vested interest in describing the job as complex and difficult, and themselves as highly skilled and hard-working.
8. Group interviews with workers are more economical, and iron out idiosyncrasies, but just as likely to suffer from the 'vested interest' problem, which may go so far as a conspiracy to misinform.
9. Participation: some psychologists think the only way to understand a job is to do it, or spend as much time as possible alongside someone doing it. Some psychologists researching USAAF flight crew selection in the Second World War went to the lengths of learning to fly themselves.

The trend is increasingly towards structured, 'paper and pencil' methods, in which information is compared with a large database describing dozens or hundreds of jobs.

Ways of analysing information

Having collected information about the work being done, the researcher faces the task of making sense of it; this can be done subjectively, by a committee, or by two types of formal statistical analysis.

Subjective analysis

After spending a month, or a week, or an afternoon, watching people doing the job, or talking to them, the analyst writes down his/her impressions. This is often good enough as the basis for writing a job description, but doesn't really merit the title 'analysis'.

Rational analysis

Official analyses of jobs group them by rational methods, i.e. by committee and consultation. The (US) *Dictionary of Occupational Titles* (DOT) provides detailed descriptions of thousands of jobs, for example:

> Collects, interprets, and applies scientific data to human and animal behavior and mental processes, formulates hypotheses and experimental designs, analyses results using statistics; writes papers describing research; provides therapy and counseling for groups or individuals. Investigates processes of learning and growth, and human interrelationships. Applies psychological techniques to personnel administration and management. May teach college courses.

The DOT's account of a psychologist's work is actually a composite of several types of psychologist—academic, clinical and occupational—few psychologists do everything listed in DOT's description.

Statistical analysis I—factor analysis

Factor analysis correlates scores for different jobs, to find factors of job performance (Note 1). Factor analysis can be misleading; if secretaries make tea, as well as type, typing and tea-making may appear on the same factor, although *rationally* they have little in common.

Statistical analysis II—cluster analysis

Cluster analysis groups jobs according to similarity of ratings (Note 2). Salesmen for 3M ranked sales activities—e.g. "arranging product displays for customers", "entertaining customers"—in order of importance for their particular job (Dunnette & Kirchner, 1959). Sales jobs at 3M divided into five clusters: direct retail contact, jobber and wholesaler contact, retail follow-up and service, industrial selling, and general selling and service. Cluster analysis groups *people*, whereas factor analysis groups *tasks*. Each is useful to the selector, in different ways.

USES OF JOB ANALYSIS

Job analysis has a variety of uses, in selection in particular, and in personnel work in general—so many uses in fact that one wonders how personnel departments ever managed without it. Job analysis is useful at every stage of the selection process, and beyond.

1. *Write selection tests (I)—content validation.* Job analysis allows selectors to write a selection test whose content so closely matches the content of the job that it is *content valid* (Chapter 11), which means it can be used, legally in the USA, without further demonstration of its validity.

2. *Write selection tests (II)—synthetic validation.* Krzystofiak, Newman & Anderson (1979) found 60 factors in power station jobs; if the employer could find an adequate test of each factor, they could *synthesize* a different set of tests for every job, according to the factors involved in each job (Chapter 11).

3. *Write accurate, comprehensive job descriptions.* These help recruit the right applicants, and help recruitment agencies send the right applicants.

4. *Choose selection tests.* A good job analysis identifies the knowledge, skills and abilities needed, allowing the selector to choose the right tests.

5. *Aid interviewer.* If the interviewer knows exactly what the job involves, he/she can concentrate on assessing knowledge, skills and abilities. Otherwise the interview can only assess the candidate *as a person,* which (a) may give poor results and (b) may, in the USA, make it difficult to refute allegations of discrimination (Chapter 12).

6. *Classification.* Assigning new employees to the tasks they are best suited for, assuming they haven't been appointed to a specific job.

7. *Vocational guidance.* Job analysis identifies jobs that are similar in the work done and the attributes needed, so someone interested in job X, where there are presently no vacancies, can be recommended to try jobs Y and Z instead.

8. *Transfer selection tests.* Jobs can be grouped into families, for which the same selection procedure can be used. If jobs are similar, then (1) selection tests for job A can be used for job B, without separate validation, and (2) selection procedures in plant or organization C can be used in plant or organization D, again without separate validation. However, US fair employment legislation may not allow selection procedures to be transferred, without proof that there are no significant differences between jobs. Job analysis can provide the necessary proof.

9. *Criterion development.* The success of selection can't be judged, without a *criterion*—a way of deciding which employees have proved *productive or unproductive.* Detailed analysis of the job makes it easier to distinguish good from bad employees.

10. *Defend selection tests.* In the case of *Arnold* vs *Ballard* a good job analysis allowed an employer to require high-school education—although general

educational requirements are rarely accepted as fair in the USA (Chapters 10 and 12). Job analysis is legally required by the Equal Employment Opportunities Commission (EEOC) in the USA, if the employer needs to use selection methods that differentially exclude women, non-whites, anyone over 40, or the handicapped. The EEOC's Guidelines say: "any method of job analysis may be used if it provides the information required for the specific validation strategy used". The Guidelines don't say how detailed the job analysis has to be.

11. *Rationalize training*. Job analysis can be used to identify jobs with a lot in common, although they may have different titles, which enables employer to rationalize training provision (Sparrow, 1989).

12. *Succession planning*. Job analysis can be used to plan promotions, to find avenues to promote women and non-whites, also to identify employees best able to substitute for absent workers.

13. *Plan performance appraisal systems*. Job analysis can be used to identify the dimensions to be rated in performance appraisal.

SELECTED JOB ANALYSIS TECHNIQUES—AN OVERVIEW

Over the last 20 years, job analysis schemes and inventories have multiplied almost as prolifically as personality inventories. This chapter has space to describe only six or seven of the most widely used, or most important. In general terms, job analysis systems divide into: *job oriented, worker oriented* and *attribute oriented*.

Job-oriented techniques concentrate on what work is accomplished—"install cable pressurization systems", "locating the source of an automobile engine knock"; they are usually check-lists completed by the workers themselves.

Content-oriented techniques are more concerned with what the worker does to accomplish the job—"attention to detail", "use of written materials"; the Position Analysis Questionnaire (PAQ) of McCormick, Jeanneret & Mecham (1972) exemplifies this approach.

Attribute-based techniques describe jobs in terms of traits or aptitudes needed to perform them: good eyesight, verbal fluency, manual dexterity. The PAQ lists attributes, as well as content. Fleishman & Mumford (1991) classifies physical abilities (Chapter 10); psychologists have extensively analysed intellectual abilities (Chapter 7) and biographical factors (Chapter 6).

1. Critical Incident Technique (CIT)

The CIT is the oldest job analysis technique, devised by Flanagan (1954) to analyse failure in flying training during the Second World War. Flanagan found the reasons given for failure too vague to be at all helpful: "lack of inherent flying ability", "poor judgement". Opinions about qualities needed

for success were equally vague: "Too often statements regarding job requirements are merely lists of all the desirable traits of human beings".

Flanagan identified flying's *critical* requirements by asking why, precisely,
men failed flight training. He collected accounts of *critical incidents* which
caused men to be rejected: what led up to the incident, what the man did, what
the consequences were, and whether the man was responsible for them.
Typical incidents included: trying to land on the wrong runway, coming in to
land too high, or coming in to land too fast and running off the end of the
runway.

In modern CIT, hundreds, or even thousands, of accounts are collated to
draw a composite picture of the job's requirements, from which check-lists,
ratings, etc. can be written. Observers are asked for accounts of strikingly
good, as well as bad, performance. The CIT is the basis of *Behaviourally
Anchored Rating Scales* (BARS) (Chapter 5).

2. Repertory Grid Technique (RGT)

The RGT is popular in Britain. Loosely based on *personal construct theory*, it
takes many forms. For example, the informant may be asked to think of a good,
average, and poor worker, then to say which two differ from the third, then
asked to say how (Figure 3.1). In the *grid* in Figure 3.1, the informant says in
the first row that a good ambulance worker can be distinguished from average
and poor by 'commitment', and in the second row that a good ambulance
supervisor can be distinguished from average and poor by 'fairness'. The
informant is usually asked to apply each distinction to *every* person in the grid,
making it possible to calculate the overlap of the *constructs* 'commitment' and
'fairness'. In using RGT for job analysis, one probes the *constructs*, asking the
informant for specific, behavioural examples of 'commitment' (e.g. willing to
stay on after end of shift if there's an emergency call).

3. Position Analysis Questionnaire (PAQ)

The PAQ is *content oriented*, and covers nearly 200 elements, divided into six
main areas (McCormick, Jeanneret & Mecham, 1972). Table 3.1 lists the six
areas, and illustrative elements. Each element is rated, generally for *importance
to the job*, sometimes for *amount of time, noise level, amount of training required*, etc.
Despite its title, the PAQ is not a questionnaire, but a structured interview
schedule. The PAQ is completed by a trained job analyst, who collects
information from workers and supervisors. The analyst does not simply
record what the informant says, but forms his/her own judgement about
importance of elements, etc. The completed PAQ is then analysed by comparing it with a very large American database. The analysis proceeds by a series
of linked stages:

Elements > Sorts	Good ambulance person	Average ambulance person	Poor ambulance person	Good ambulance service supervisor	Average ambulance service supervisor	Poor ambulance service supervisor	Good ambulance service manager	••• Constructs
1	[X]	[ ]	[ ]	X			X	••• *Commitment*
2				[X]	[ ]	[ ]	X	••• *Fairness*
3	[X]			[X]	X		[X]	••• *Calmness*
4			[ ]			[ ]		••••
etc.								••••

Figure 3.1 Repertory Grid Technique used in job analysis. The *elements* are various "role figures" in ambulance work, e.g. good ambulance supervisor. [ ] indicates which three *elements* are used to start each sort

Table 3.1 Position Analysis Questionnaire's (PAQ) six main divisions, and illustrative job elements

PAQ division	Illustrative job elements
1. Information input	Use of written materials Near-visual differentiation (good visual acuity, at short range)
2. Mental process	Level of reasoning in problem solving Coding/decoding
3. Work output	Use of keyboard devices Assembling/disassembling
4. Relationships with other people	Instructing Contacts with public or customers
5. Job context	High temperature Interpersonal conflict
6. Other	Specified work space Amount of job structure

1. Profile of 32 job elements. The original factor analysis of PAQ items identified 32 dimensions, which underlie all forms of work, for example watching things from a distance, being aware of bodily movement and balance, making decisions, dealing with the public, etc. The job element profile can be used to write a job description, plan appraisal and training, and to compare one job with another.

2. Profile of 76 attributes. These are the aptitudes, interests or temperament, the person needs to perform the job elements (McCormick, Jeanneret & Mecham, 1972). Aptitude attributes include: *movement detection*, being able to detect the physical movement of objects and to judge their direction, or *selective attention*, being able to perform a task in the presence of distracting stimuli. Temperament attributes include *empathy*, being able to see things from others' points of view, or *influencing people*, being able to influence others' opinions, attitudes or judgements. The attribute profile provides the selector with a detailed person specification.

3. Recommended psychological tests. The attribute profile leads naturally onto suggestions for tests to assess the attributes. If the job needs an aptitude for *manual dexterity*, the PAQ output suggests using General Aptitude Test Battery (Chapter 7) *place* and *turn* sub-tests (a pegboard test of gross dexterity). Recommendations for tests for interests and temperament are also made, mostly for the Myers Briggs Type Indicator (Chapter 8).

4. Comparable jobs, and remuneration. The job element profile for the job analysed is compared with the extensive PAQ database, to identify other jobs with similar requirements, and to estimate the appropriate salary, in US dollars, for the job analysed. Arvey & Begalla (1975) obtained PAQ ratings for 48 home-makers (housewives), and compared their composite home-maker profile with 1000 other jobs in the PAQ database. The most similar job was police officer, followed by home economist, airport maintenance chief, kitchen helper and fire fighter—all trouble-shooting, emergency-handling jobs. Arvey & Begalla calculate the average salary paid for the 10 jobs most like housewife; that average was $740 a month, at 1968 prices.

The PAQ covers *all* jobs, including unskilled and semi-skilled, but doesn't differentiate very finely at the management/professional level. The Professional and Managerial Position Questionnaire (PMPQ), intended to cover higher level jobs, as yet lacks PAQ's extensive data base.

4. Occupational Analysis Inventory (OAI)

The OAI was developed originally for vocational education and guidance. The OAI is a very long inventory, listing 602 elements, because it's *job-oriented*, whereas the PAQ is *content-oriented*. The OAI also uses factor analysis, yielding 28 factors. Typical factors are:

Electrical/electronic repair maintenance, and operation: radio mechanic, aircraft electrician, communications electrician.

Food preparation: short-order cook, chef, school-lunch supervisor.

Activities requiring coordination, balance, and quickness: fishing vessel's first mate, airplane pilot, brick sorter.

The researchers used the factors to develop a pilot vocational interest inventory, whereas other vocational interest inventories (Chapter 8) use rational classifications of jobs, or factor analysis of questionnaire answers. However, the factor analysis of over 1000 jobs left a lot of variance unaccounted for, implying a lot of tasks are too specific to be grouped in any meaningful way (Cunningham et al, 1983).

5. *J* coefficients

The *J* coefficient, developed by Primoff (1959), uses a 'lens' model (Figure 3.2). *Job elements* are the intermediate steps between *predictors*, and *performance*. The *J* coefficient is calculated from the links between predictors and job elements (R_{xe}), and the links between job elements and performance (R_{ye}), using a complex formula. Predictor × job element links (R_{xe}) are estimated by expert judgements of the relevance of test items for each element. Element × performance links (R_{ye}) can also be estimated by expert judgement, or by *policy capturing*, in which experts make overall judgements based on profiles of estimates, and their decision rules are inferred statistically. The job elements themselves are: *knowledges, skills, abilities* and *other personal characteristics* (KSAOs). Supervisors first list the KSAOs, then rate how important they are.

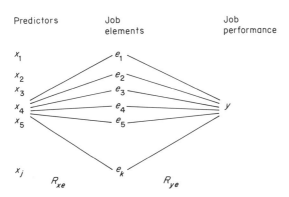

Figure 3.2 The *J* coefficient, showing predictors on the left, performance on the right, with job elements in the middle

6. Job Components Inventory (JCI)

The JCI was developed in Britain (Banks et al, 1983) for jobs requiring limited skill, and it has five principal sections: tools and equipment, perceptual and physical requirements, maths, communication, decision making and responsibility.

7. Physical Abilities Analysis (PAA)

The PAA is a set of nine factors (listed in Table 10.2), each rated on a seven-point *Behaviourally Anchored Rating Scale*. Detailed *physical* job analysis is particularly important when women and the handicapped apply for jobs traditionally done by men and which have physique requirements (Fleishman & Mumford, 1991).

Relative merits of different systems

Levine et al (1983) surveyed experienced job analysts, who found PAQ, J coefficients, Fleishman's PAA, and four other job analysis methods equally useful for selection work, with only Flanagan's CIT getting a poor rating. The PAQ was rated the most practical of the seven schemes, being ready to use 'off the shelf'. Subjects disliked PAQ's "non-job-specific language" and "esoteric terminology". On the other hand, PAQ was cheaper to use. The PAQ's reading difficulty level is very high (Harvey et al, 1988), so less literate staff may find it hard to use. Its output, while very detailed, is not very user-friendly.

Reliability

Job analysis techniques need acceptable inter-observer and intra-observer reliability. McCormick, Jeanneret & Mecham (1972) report acceptable inter-rater reliabilities for PAQ; Banks et al (1983) found JCI ratings by workers and supervisors correlated reasonably for most scales and most jobs. Re-test reliabilities aren't calculated very often for job analysis measures, because they are so long and complicated to complete. Wilson, Harvey & Macy (1990) report that repeating *sections* of the inventory can demonstrate good reliability.

Validity

Research on validity of job analysis faces a familiar dilemma. If results agree with 'common sense', they are dismissed as redundant—'telling us what we already know'; if results don't agree with common sense, they are simply dismissed. Evidence for the validity of job analysis derives from showing its results make sense (technically speaking, *construct* validation—Chapter 11), and from showing that job analysis leads to more accurate selection.

Job analysis should differentiate jobs that differ, but give the same picture of the same job, in different plants or organizations. Banks et al (1983) found JCI ratings distinguished four clerical jobs from four engineering jobs, proving JCI could find a difference where a difference ought to be. Banks et al also showed that JCI ratings were the same for mail-room clerks in different companies, proving JCI didn't find a difference where there shouldn't be one.

Analysis of the work of senior (UK) civil servants found nine factors (Table 3.2), and 13 clusters, which were aggregated into four main groups. Dulewicz & Keenay (1979) sent details of the clusters to the civil servants who contributed the data, and asked if they agreed with the classification, and whether they had been correctly classified. Only 7% thought the classification unsatisfactory, and only 11% disagreed with their personal classification.

From the selector's viewpoint, job analysis has validity, if it results in more accurate selection decisions. Two recent meta-analyses have shown that personality testing (Tett, Jackson & Rothstein, 1991) and structured interviewing (Wiesner & Cronshaw, 1988) achieve higher validity when based on job analysis. In fact, in both cases, job analysis resulted in the highest validity recorded for that selection method. Similar comparisons have yet to be reported for other selection methods.

Ideally, job analysis will give the same account of the job regardless of who contributes the information. In practice, the source of the information does affect ratings of task frequency and importance (Landy & Vasey, 1991). Very experienced police officers report spending less time on traffic work, but more time on non-criminal intervention (answering questions, general social work).

Earlier research had shown that PAQ ratings by experts, supervisors, people doing the job, and students inter-correlated almost perfectly (Smith & Hakel, 1979), which cast some doubt on PAQ's usefulness and validity. If workers or students can analyse jobs, why pay for experts? The students were given only the name of the job, so how could they describe it accurately? Unless PAQ is only measuring stereotyped impressions of jobs, and not really *analysing* them? However, Cornelius, DeNisi & Blencoe (1984) were able to show that the more the students knew about the job, the better their PAQ ratings agreed with the experts', which confirms PAQ's validity. Furthermore, very high levels of student—expert agreement are partly an artefact, based on PAQ's *does not apply* ratings; everyone knows that college professors (university lecturers) don't use powered hand tools as part of their job. When *does not apply* ratings were excluded from the analysis, agreement between students and experts was further reduced. These results imply PAQ genuinely analyses jobs, and isn't just a complicated way of measuring stereotypes.

Some critics (Barrett, 1992) think job analysis as generally practised is fundamentally misguided. Asking workers what abilities they need to do their

Table 3.2 Factors in senior (UK) Civil Service jobs (Dulewicz and Keenay, 1979) (Reproduced by permission)

1. *Personnel.* Organizing the work of one's staff, supervising and appraising them. Training and lecturing to staff. Selecting, and giving careers guidance, to staff. Consulting and negotiating with Staff Associations. Knowledge of a wide range of personnel management techniques.

2. *Resource utilization.* Knowing how to manage projects/programmes and how to plan /evaluate the utilisation of resources. Planning computer operations and knowledge of computer data preparation.

3. *Finance.* Knowledge of financial parliamentary procedures and of financial disciplines and techniques—accountancy, economics, investment appraisal and cost-benefit analysis.

4. *Figure-work.* Carrying out numerical calculations. Assimilating and making inferences from statistical information. Knowledge of descriptive and analytical statistical techniques.

5. *Foreign.* Consulting and negotiating with representatives from foreign governments, etc. Speaking foreign languages.

6. *Local government.* Consulting or negotiating with representatives of local authorities. Knowledge of local government constitution, procedures and finance, and of social studies.

7. *Contracts.* Consulting or negotiating with representatives of local authorities and industry, and specialists. Knowledge of legislative parliamentary procedures and law.

8. *Parliamentary.* Advising ministers. Writing explanatory briefs on policy, speeches and answers to Parliamentary Questions. Knowledge of legislative parliamentary procedures and law.

9. *Generalist.* Consulting and negotiating with other senior civil servants. Acting as a committee member or chairman. Assimilating critically and commenting on written material. Writing persuasive expositions to colleagues. Writing instructions and other authoritative communications.

work is like asking sick or injured people to diagnose their own illnesses. Analysing a job and identifying its skills is a job for the expert, not the layperson. Barrett (1992) cites Baehr & Orban's unpublished job analysis for bus drivers. Bus drivers listed fast reaction time and alert senses as essential for their work. Common sense would probably agree with them, but research doesn't: reaction time and visual acuity are in reality unrelated to effectiveness as a bus driver. Many job analysis systems collect their information from supervisors, not workers, which may not reduce the force of Barrett's criticism.

There is no reason to suppose supervisors are any better able to decide what characteristics workers really need to function effectively.

USING JOB ANALYSIS TO SELECT WORKERS

Analysis by PAQ of the job of plastics injection-moulding setter in a British plant identified seven attributes needed in workers (Table 3.3). Sparrow et al (1982) recommended an appropriate test for each attribute: Raven's Standard Progressive Matrices for intelligence, a standard eye chart read at 30 cm for acuity etc. Sparrow's work illustrates the use of job analysis first to generate a person specification, then choose appropriate selection tests.

Table 3.3 Job analysis by Position Analysis Questionnaire and choice of tests, for the job of plastic injection moulding setter (Sparrow et al, 1982)

Attribute	Test
Long-term memory	Wechsler Memory Scale
Intelligence	Standard Progressive Matrices
Short-term memory	Wechsler Memory Scale
Near visual acuity	Eye chart at 30 cm
Perceptual speed	Thurstone Perceptual Speed Test
Convergent thinking	Standard Progressive Matrices
Mechanical ability	Birkbeck Mechanical Comprehension Test

More ambitiously, job analysis systems have been linked to aptitude batteries. For example Mecham (cited in McCormick, DeNisi & Shaw, 1979) analysed 163 jobs for which both *General Aptitude Test Battery* (GATB) and PAQ data were available, and then asked two questions:

1. Does the PAQ profile for a job correlate with the GATB profile for the same job? If PAQ says the job needs *spatial ability*, do people doing the job tend to have high *spatial ability* scores on GATB?

2. Does the PAQ profile for a job correlate with GATB profile *validity* for the same job? If PAQ says the job needs *spatial ability*, do people with high *spatial ability* scores on GATB perform the job better?

The answer to both questions was Yes. The correlation between PAQ profile and GATB profile across jobs was 0.71. The correlation between PAQ profile and GATB validity across jobs was lower, but still positive—0.43. This research implies each job needs a particular set of attributes, that can be identified by PAQ, and then assessed by GATB. Similar research by Cunningham (cited by Pearlman, Schmidt & Hunter, 1980) using the *Differential Aptitude Test* (DAT) and OAI, was less successful, possibly because the samples were too small.

However the work of Schmidt, Hunter and Pearlman, reviewed in greater detail in Chapter 7, suggests analysis of jobs might not need to be very detailed, for selection purposes. US Army jobs needed only to be grouped into very broad categories—clerical, general technical, electronics, etc.—to achieve good predictive validity. Pearlman, Schmidt & Hunter (1980) concluded that deciding a job is 'clerical' was all the job analysis needed to choose tests which predicted productivity. (One should bear in bear that during the 1970s and 1980s the Schmidt—Hunter—Pearlman group developed the view that *all* jobs in the USA could be selected for by a combination of general mental ability and dexterity, which clearly doesn't leave much scope for detailed job analysis in guiding choice of test.)

Even if Pearlman's conclusions are correct, it would probably be difficult to act on them at present. Deciding a job is 'clerical', and using a 'clerical' test for selection, may satisfy common sense, and may be good enough for Pearlman et al, but it won't satisfy the EEOC, if there are complaints about the composition of the workforce. The full detail and complexity of PAQ may be needed to prove that a clerical job really is clerical. Similarly, an American employer who has proved that GATB selects wool-pullers in Plant A, and wants to use GATB to select wool-pullers in Plant B, may have to analyse both wool-pulling jobs to prove they really are the same.

CONCLUSIONS

Job analysis contributes to selecting more productive workers by identifying the main themes in the job, and the attributes needed in successful workers. Two meta-analyses find that job analysis maximizes selection test validity. PAQ ratings predict fairly accurately what profiles of abilities will be found in people doing different jobs, and how valid GATB subtests will be, providing the selector with a coherent theoretical framework to choosing tests.

Like the interview, job analysis serves a wide range of other personnel functions, besides selection, making it a key central feature of any human resource strategy.

It's probably no exaggeration to say job analysis is vital in personnel practice in the USA. American employers, ever conscious of fair employment agencies, usually find they can't have too much information about work and workers so enormously detailed, complexly analysed inventories like PAQ are often a godsend.

NOTES

1. Factor analysis. Table 3.4 shows correlations between performance on eight typical school subjects, in a large sample. (A table of correlations between every pair of a set of measures is called a correlation *matrix*.)

The correlations between English Language, English Literature, French and German are all fairly high; people who are good at one tend to be good at the others. Similarly the correlations between Maths, Physics, Chemistry and Biology are fairly high. However correlations between subjects in the two sets of four—for example English Literature x Physics—are much lower. All of which suggests that people who are good at one language tend to be good at another, while people who are good at one science are good at another. There are *eight* school subjects, but only *two* underlying abilities.

Clear groupings in small sets of correlations can be seen by inspection. Larger sets of less clear correlations can only be interpreted by *factor analysis*, which calculates how many *factors* are needed to account for the observed correlations. Two factors account for performance in the eight school subjects. Fleishman's analysis of dozens of measures of physical strength and activity shows that nine factors are needed.

2. Cluster analysis. In the study by Krzystofiak, Newman & Anderson, each of 1710 workers who completed the JAQ has a profile on 60 factors, giving a 1710 × 60 (= 102 600) matrix. One could check through this by hand/eye, to pick out people with similar profiles, but this would be very tedious, and very inaccurate. Cluster analysis calculates *intersubject distance* (D^2) for every possible pair of profiles, where D^2 is the sum of the squared differences between the 60 pairs of scores. The pair whose D^2 is lowest have the most similar profiles of 60 scores. Cluster analysis then seeks the person with most similar profile to the composite of the first two subjects, and adds that in, and so on.

Table 3.4   (Fictitious) correlations between school subject marks

	Maths	Physics	Chemistry	Biology	English	French	German
Maths							
Physics	0. 67						
Chemistry	0.76	0.55					
Biology	0.60	0 .61	0 .70				
English	0.33	0 .23	0.25	0.21			
French	0.23	0 .31	0.30	0.15	0.77		
German	0.11	0.21	0 .22	0.14	0.80	0.67	
English literature	0.33	0 .23	0 .24	0.55	0.45	0.56	0.69

Garwood, Anderson & Greengart (1991) note that different cluster analysis methods generate different solutions, and suggest users ought to understand what the analysis is doing, although since nearly all cluster analysis is done by computer packages, this could be difficult to achieve in practice.

4 The Interview

I know one when I see one

I described the interview that got me my job at the University College of Swansea (UCS) as "assembly of a dozen or so people, with no experience or training in selection and no idea what they're looking for, ask[ing] whatever questions come into their heads" (Cook, 1979). Only one of the dozen was a psychologist, and he an expert on colour vision rather than selection or the fields I was being employed to teach.

I describe interview practices at UCS not, or not solely, to mock them, but to make an important point. Research on the interview describes a very small tip of a very large iceberg. The small tip is what employers who are willing to be researched on do when the researcher is watching. The rest of the iceberg is the other 200 million interviews conducted each year in the USA and UK. Some of these interviews may be as good as the best the researcher sees; rumour, anecdote and one's own experience suggest many aren't. One hears of personnel managers who judge applicants by the look of the back of their neck while they're standing at attention, or by the manager's dog's reaction, or by the ratio of hat size to shoe size, but these employers aren't likely to invite psychologists to study their activities. Interviews vary widely. They can be as short as 3 minutes, or as long as 2 hours. The public sector in Britain favours the 'panel' interview, in which the candidate faces five, 10 or even 20 interviewers. In campus recruitment, the 'milk round', candidates often go through a series of interviews. Robertson & Makin's (1986) survey of major British employers, from the *Times 1000*, reports that small panel interviews (two or three interviewers) were slightly more popular than one-to-one interviews, while large panels weren't favoured. Some interviewers are psychologists or psychiatrists; some are personnel managers; some are line managers; a lot are nobody in particular. Robertson & Makin's survey shows line managers and personnel specialists usually interview in British industry. Sometimes the interviewer is friendly and tries to establish rapport; sometimes the interviewer makes the applicant try to sell him/her something; sometimes the interviewer tries stress methods; quite often he/she has no particular strategy. The armed services favour psychiatric screening, which Ulrich & Trumbo (1965) think could prove useful in industry, "in the light of evidence that a majority of dismissals are for reasons of interpersonal inadequacies and maladjustments".

Bad interviews are legion, and they are clearly a waste of time. They also cost a lot of money—over a billion dollars a year in the US according to Hakel (1982). The question is whether a good interviewer, asking sensible questions, listening to the answers, attaching the right weight to each of them, can out-perform other selection methods, or can add anything to them, or can even do better than sticking a pin in the list of applicants.

What defines a *useful* selection method? A good selection method is *reliable*; it gives a consistent account of the person being assessed. A good selection method is *valid*; it selects good applicants and rejects bad ones. A good selection method is *cost-effective*; it saves the employer more in increased output than it costs to use. (Psychologists call cost-effectiveness *utility*; see Chapter 13).

A *reliable* measure gives consistent results. Physical measurements are usually so reliable their consistency is taken for granted. Subjective measures like interview assessments aren't so consistent. At their worst they may be so inconsistent that they convey no information at all. Reliability is usually measured by the correlation between two sets of measures. If two interviewers each rate 50 applicants, the correlation between their ratings estimates *inter-rater reliability*, a.k.a. *inter-observer* or *inter-judge reliability*. If two interviewers don't agree in their ratings, one of them must be wrong, but which? Compar-ing the same interviewer's ratings on separate occasions estimates *intra-rater reliability*. Interviews are moderately reliable; inter-interviewer reliability coefficients range from 0.62 to 0.90; "with a few exceptions ... lower than usually accepted for devices used for individual prediction" (Ulrich & Trumbo, 1965). Interviewers also agree with themselves if they re-rate candidates (Mayfield, 1964).

Interviewers share a stereotype of the good applicant, which ensures they agree but not necessarily that they're accurate. Canadian Army interviewers agreed very well on the 'ideal officer', using 120 items derived from previous interviews (Sydiaha, 1961). Interviewers also share a stereotype of an effective salesperson: sociable, supportive of others, dominant, attention seeking, ambitious, independent, approval seeking, orderly, aggressive, persistent, willing to promote (Jackson et al, 1982). Dedrick & Dobbins (1991) report interviewers stereotype older employees as less employable, motivated, pro-ductive, creative, etc. But while interviewers collectively agree what they're looking for, each individual interviewer's own stereotype may have idiosyn-cratic elements. Some interviewers see "is presently active in eight outside organizations" as a very good sign, while others see it as a very bad sign (Mayfield & Carlson, 1966).

VALIDITY

Doubts about the value of interviewing date from an early study by Hollingworth, in 1922, of 12 sales managers who interviewed 57 would-be salesmen, and generated some spectacular disagreements. Since 1922, dozens of researches on interview validity have been reported. A typical *validation* study collects two sets of data: *predictor* and *criterion*. Interviewer ratings form the predictor, while some index of productivity forms the criterion (Chapter 11). Figure 4.1 presents some *fictitious*, but not untypical, data for 100 interview candidates. Note that the interviewer's opinion of the candidates has to be quantified, as does candidates' productivity. The researcher then computes a *correlation* between predictor and criterion data, which is the *validity coefficient*; in the fictitious data of Figure 4.1, the correlation is 0.10, showing there is positive, but very small, relationship between interview rating and productivity. Different types of validity are discussed in Chapter 11; so are different types of criterion.

Research on the interview has been reviewed increasingly frequently since 1949 (Wagner, 1949; Mayfield, 1964; Ulrich & Trumbo, 1965; Wright, 1969; Schmitt, 1976; Arvey, 1979a; Hakel, 1982; Reilly & Chao, 1982; Wiesner & Cronshaw, 1988; Harris, 1989). Most earlier reviews concluded interviews weren't a very good way of choosing productive workers and rejecting unproductive ones. Ulrich & Trumbo (1965) reported validity coefficients of less than 0.50 to be the rule, and validities of less than 0.30 very common.

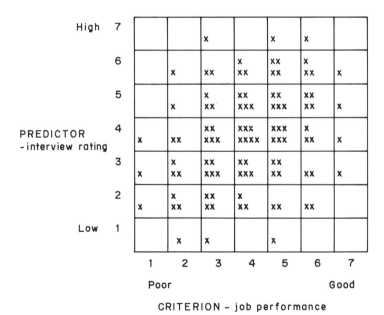

Figure 4.1   A typical validation study. Data on *predictor* (interview rating) and *criterion* (job performance) are collected and plotted for 100 persons; a correlation calculated between predictor and criterion scores has the value 0.10

However, earlier reviews were *narrative* reviews, meaning authors didn't use any formal quantitative means of summarizing the research reviewed. The human mind, however expert or impartial, is not very good at summarizing large bodies of complex numerical information. Narrative reviews are often confusing; Meehl (1978) dismisses them as a 'tabular asterisks game', because the reviewer often draws up a summary table, awarding each study "*" for a difference or correlation significant at the 5% level, "**" for the 1% level, and so on. Narrative reviews often fail to enlighten because, for example, for the hypothesis that interviews predict job performance, 10 studies will confirm the hypothesis, 10 studies will reject it, and 10 will be inconclusive. At their worst, narrative reviews are like projective tests; reviewers read into the research whatever conclusions they want to find.

Meta-analytic reviews

Meta-analysis pools the results of many different researches, to produce a single estimate of overall *effect size*. In selection research this means an estimate of the correlation between predictor and criterion. Dunnette (1972) analysed 30 interview validity coefficients for the American petroleum industry, and found a very low average validity (0.13); only 25% of validity coefficients exceeded 0.21. Two other small-scale meta-analytic reviews in the early 1980s reported similar results. Reilly & Chao (1982) analysed 12 validity studies, eight of them unpublished, and calculated a low average validity coefficient (0.19) against supervisor ratings. Hunter & Hunter (1984) pooled 10 studies, about which they say very little except that none were included in Reilly's & Chao's analysis, and obtained a similarly low average validity (0.11).

Two larger meta-analyses (McDaniel et al, 1987; Wiesner & Cronshaw, 1988) obtain more positive results. McDaniel et al report an overall validity of 0.22 for interviews in the US public sector. Wiesner & Cronshaw analyse 150 validities, from research in Germany, France, Israel as well as the USA, and report an *overall* validity of 0.26. As Wiesner & Cronshaw remark, the interview may not be quite such a poor predictor as generations of occupational psychologists have assumed. However, 0.26 is probably an overestimate of the validity of the typical interview as observed in Britain. The review by Wiesner & Cronshaw showed unstructured one-to-one interviews achieve a validity of only 0.11. Board or panel interviews achieve better results—0.21. McDaniel et al report that job-related interviews, which assess training, experience and interests, achieve better results than 'psychological' interviews, which try to assess personality.

Reasons for poor validity

Most validity studies pool data from a number of interviewers, thereby mixing good, bad and indifferent interviewers. One early study (Ghiselli, 1966a) and several more recent ones (Dougherty, Ebert & Callender, 1986; Zedeck, Tziner & Middlestadt, 1983) suggest some interviewers are much more successful than others. Pooling data from many interviewers also risks the results being obscured by known errors in subjective ratings, such *leniency* (or *level*). Some interviewers mark everyone generously, others mark everyone harshly. If the criterion ratings are generous, the harsh interviewer will appear consistently much further 'out' than the generous rater. The harsh interviewer may be less accurate, or may be using the rating scale differently. Sophisticated analyses can correct for this problem; Dreher, Ash & Hancock (1988) argue many studies use crude analyses and underestimate interview validity.

Criterion reliability

Validity coefficients are low because the interview is trying to predict the unpredictable. The interviewer's judgement is compared with a *criterion* that defines a good employee. Supervisor ratings, the most commonly used criterion, have limited reliability (around 0.60); one supervisor agrees only moderately well with another supervisor. A selection test can't have a validity coefficient higher than the square root of the reliability of the criterion, so a study using supervisor ratings can't achieve a validity higher than $\sqrt{0.60}$, i.e. 0.77. Validity coefficients can be corrected for criterion unreliability; correction raised the estimate by Hunter & Hunter for the interview validity from 0.11 to 0.14.

Range restriction

Validity coefficients are low because *range* is *restricted*. Validity should ideally be calculated from a sample of *applicants*, but usually has to be estimated from a sample of *successful* applicants. Few organizations can afford to employ every applicant, or to employ people judged unsuitable, simply to allow psychologists to calculate better estimates of validity. Nearly all research settles for correlating interview ratings with success, *within the minority of selected applicants*. Figure 4.2 shows the effect on the validity coefficient. If only the top 20% are employed, a (potentially) large correlation is greatly reduced, because none of the unsuccessful applicants contribute criterion data.

Validity coefficients can be corrected for restricted range, which increased Hunter's & Hunter's (1984) estimate of interview validity from 0.14 to 0.22. Reilly & Chao (1982) report a very similar corrected value (0.23). Wiesner & Cronshaw (1988) also correct for restricted range and criterion reliability, and report corrected validities of 0.47 for all interviews, 0.20 for unstructured one-to-one interviews, and 0.37 for unstructured panel interviews. (The corrections were made as part of *validity generalization analysis*, which is described fully in Chapter 7.)

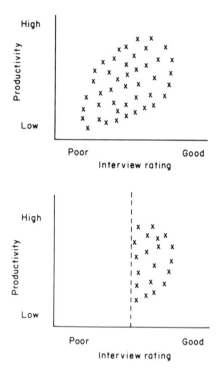

Figure 4.2 Restriction of range. In the lower distribution, everyone with a lower interview rating has been excluded from the analysis (necessarily, because they weren't employed, so their productivity can't be known). A very low correlation results. The upper distribution shows the results that would have been obtained, if everyone was employed, regardless of interview rating

What does a correlation of 0.20 mean? Figure 4.1 shows the relationship between interview rating and job proficiency is slight. Another way of interpreting a correlation is to calculate how much *variance* it accounts for, by squaring it. A rating of a candidate by an unstructured one-to-one interview explains only 1% ($0.10^2 = 0.01$) of the variance in later success in the job; the other 99% of employee effectiveness remains accounted for. Figure 4.3 shows that even large correlations, e.g. 0.60, account for less than half the variance in the relationship.

The limited proportion of variance accounted for by even the 'best' validity coefficients is often cited by critics of psychological testing or the whole selection enterprise. The largest correlations obtainable in practice (0.50—0.60) account for only a quarter to a third of the variance in performance. But is it realistic to expect more than this? Performance at work is influenced by a host of other factors—management, organizational climate, co-workers,

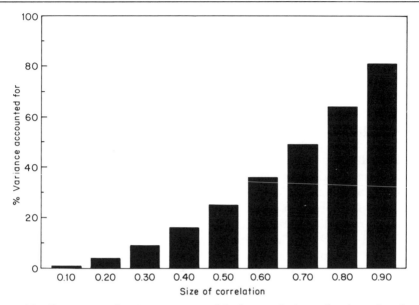

Figure 4.3 Proportion of variance accounted for by correlations of various sizes from 0.10 to 0.90

economic climate, the working environment—besides the assessable characteristics of the individual worker. In psychological research, correlations of
0.80 or 0.90, which the 'variance accounted for' argument implies tests ought
to have, rarely happen, unless the researcher is doing something trivial like
correlating a measure with a thinly disguised version of itself.

Incremental validity

'Credentials' alone predict success in graduate psychology training with only
moderate validity; an interview increased validity, but a battery of tests—
without an interview—did rather better. Anderson (1960) found a 30-minute
interview greatly improved decisions about graduate psychologists based on
college grades and tests. However, neither of two long interviews added
anything to 'credentials' and test data when selecting clinical psychologists
(Kelly & Fiske, 1951). Success in clinical psychology proved very hard to
predict accurately by any means.

Qualities that can be accurately estimated by interview

Intelligence can be judged fairly accurately in the interview. It used to be
said—correctly—that tests should be used to measure intelligence, because

tests are more consistent, more accurate, and therefore fairer. Intelligence tests are quicker—because every applicant can be tested at once—and cheaper. But intelligence tests have fallen foul of fair employment laws in the USA, so an employer who wants to assess intelligence, but doesn't want to use tests, could make a reasonable approximation by interview. Snedden (1930) devised an interview that purposely used 'high-level vocabulary', like "stamina" or "pertinacity"; interview assessments achieved a very high correlation with test intelligence. (However, interviews are legally 'tests' under fair employment law, so a vocabulary test thinly disguised as an interview might be challenged.)

Rundquist (1947) asked what can the interview assess that other methods can't, and answered 'social interaction'—ability to get on well with others and create a good impression. A panel interview, designed to be stressful, achieved very high reliability, and correlated moderately well with ratings of overall efficiency by brother officers, in a very large sample of US Naval officers.

Ulrich & Trumbo (1965) identify the other question the interview can answer as "What is the applicant's motivation to work?"; analysis of selection of US Naval officer cadets found the interview best at assessing career motivation. AT&T's management follow-up study later confirmed that interviews were best at assessing 'career passivity'—no strong need to advance, willingness to wait, and desire for job security (Grant & Bray, 1969).

Interviews are often used to assess what's variously referred to as 'organizational fit', 'chemistry', or 'the right type'. Often this is just a code word for the interviewer's prejudices or reluctance to explain him/herself. However, it can refer to legitimate organization-specific requirements, which the interview could be used to assess. Rynes & Gerhart (1990) report that interviewers from the same organization agreed about candidates' 'fit', showing the concept wasn't idiosyncratic. However 'fit' couldn't be related to objective data such as *grade-point average*, but was related to appearance, which suggests an irrational element.

Gifford, Ng & Wilkinson (1985) found motivation couldn't be assessed in the interview, whereas social skill could be, up to a point. Gifford used a *lens model* (Figure 4.4) to explain why interviewers could assess social skill, but not motivation. Social skill is *visible* in the interview; candidates who rated themselves socially skilled smiled more, gestured more, and said more; the more the candidate smiled, gestured and spoke, the higher the interviewer's rating of social skill. Motivation too is visible in the interview; highly motivated candidates dressed more formally, and leaned back more during the interview. But interviewers didn't base assessments of motivation on dress and posture; they rated as highly motivated candidates who smiled, gestured and said more—behaviour which didn't relate to motivation—which is why interviewers' assessments of motivation were inaccurate. Gifford's interviewers could have judged motivation if they'd used the right cues; but suppose

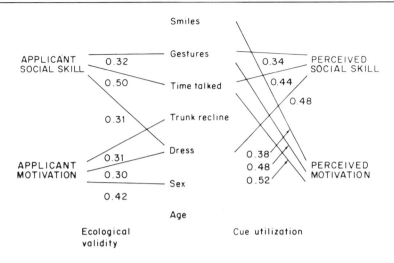

Figure 4.4 The "lens" model, showing the link between interviewee's personality (motivation and social skill) and interview behaviour, and the link between interview behaviour and interviewer rating (Gifford, Ng & Wilkinson, 1985) (Reproduced by permission)

they'd been asked to judge something that wasn't reflected in the candidates' behaviour? Clearly their task would be impossible.

REAL AND IDEAL INTERVIEWS

Interview models

Books on how to interview, and schemes for improving interviewing abound— generally unsupported by any proof that they work. Multi-point interviews *plans* are many; the (UK) Engineering Industry Training Board recommends a *six-point plan* for interviewing apprentices: general personal questions, educational questions, engineering questions, motivational questions, supply information, questions from candidates. Anstey (1977) gives detailed advice on panel interviews. The best number is three, including chairman; larger boards are uneconomic and cumbersome, while even numbered boards may be deadlocked in a vote. An interview for a specialist might follow the sequence:

> *Chairman*—8 minutes on present job, education and career to date, and reasons for wanting the job.
> *Internal specialist*—10 minutes on qualifications and experience for the specific post.
> *Outside specialist*—10 minutes on qualifications and experience in general.

Chairman—5 minutes on interests and leisure pursuits.
Final review—including opportunity for candidate to add information and ask questions.

Knatz & Inwald (1983) discuss highly specialized interviews for screening police officers who might break under stress; the interviewer should set a fast pace, asking leading questions, 'when did you stop beating your wife?' questions, and surprise questions ("when was the last time you were in a fist fight?"). The interviewer looks for excessive fearfulness, phobias, uncontrolled impulsivity, inability to handle hostility, as well as overt psychoses, alcoholism, etc.

A lot of interviews remain very haphazard; Keenan & Wedderburn (1980) found that some 'milk round' (campus recruitment) interviewers "failed to use an interview guide or any form of structured format".

The interview in practice

How long do selection interviews last? What do interviewers ask about? How much information does the candidate supply? What do interviewees think about interviews and interviewers? While the literature on interview reliability and validity is vast, information about what actually goes on in interviews remains sketchy. Some research has *debriefed* students after 'milk round' (campus recruitment) interviews, questioning interviewers about their aims and methods. American graduate recruiters ask about extra-curricular activities, whereas British interviewers are more interested in academic work, and knowledge of job and company (Keenan & Wedderburn, 1980; Taylor & Sniezek, 1984). Interviewers often ask a lot of factual, biographical questions, which are likely to be redundant because the answer's on the application form. Interviewers often 'lead' the candidate, which is usually a mistake.

Interviewers don't agree among themselves which are the most important topics, nor is there a high "level of agreement between recruiters' importance ratings and applicant's reports of interview content" (Taylor & Sniezek, 1984). Interviewers discuss different topics with successive candidates (Keenan & Wedderburn, 1980). Applicants expect interviewers to tell them more about the job, while interviewers expect applicants to say more about themselves, about their reasons for applying for the job, and about the company (Herriot & Rothwell; 1983). Interviewees describe interviews as generally superficial and easy to deal with.

'Hard' information about what happens in interviews is scarcer. Several studies find interviewers talk more than candidates (Mayfield, 1964), which is obviously undesirable since they're supposed to be getting information, not giving it. Content analysis of interviews shows the interviewer decides how long the interview should last, while the interviewee determines how many questions are asked (by the length of his/her answers). 'Non-directive' open-ended questions get more information out of the interviewee. Applicants who talk more are more likely to be selected (Anderson, 1960; Tullar, 1989). Is this because applicants who talk more improve their chances? Or because interviewers encourage applicants they like to say more?

Non-verbal behaviour in the interview

Several studies have shown that successful candidates look the interviewer in the eye more, smile more, gesture more, move their head more (shaking and nodding), and generally both look and sound more friendly and enthusiastic (Imada & Hakel, 1977). It doesn't follow of course that smiling, looking, etc. *causes* the candidate's success; the candidate may look, smile, etc. more because he/she feels—rightly—the interview is going well. Research on 'milk round' interviews (Anderson & Shackleton, 1990) finds that candidates who make more eye contact, more positive facial expressions, etc., are rated as more interesting, relaxed, strong, etc., besides being more likely to be accepted. Rasmussen (1984) reports the effect of non-verbal behaviour depends on *what* the candidate is saying. If candidates are giving the interviewer job-related information, more accompanying non-verbal behaviour gets them a better interview rating, but if candidates aren't giving the interviewer job-related information, a lot of accompanying 'non-verbals' gets them a lower rating.

IMPROVING THE INTERVIEW

The traditional interview, especially as practised in Britain, has very limited validity, which implies personnel departments should be thinking in terms of replacing it by more accurate methods. But people expect to be interviewed, and feel cheated if they aren't. Hakel (1982) says "most people have faith in the process. The interview is the place to 'put your best foot forward' ... 'If you can just get in to see the interviewer you can tell your whole story'". Interviews *look* fair, especially when they are large and elaborate; many organizations' rules require them to interview five candidates even when they already know who they want.

Given the interview is here to stay, what can be done to improve it?

(a) Select interviewers

Vernon & Parry (1949) found one naval recruiting assistant who made much better decisions than the Royal Navy's test battery, which usually far outperformed interviewers. Ghiselli (1966a) also found one interviewer—

himself—whose accuracy in selecting 275 stockbrokers over 17 years yielded a personal validity coefficient of 0.51 (corrected for restricted range). Other research (Zedeck, Tziner & Middlestadt, 1983; Dougherty, Ebert & Callender, 1986) confirms that different interviewers' decisions differ widely in accuracy. But selecting the selectors creates problems. Research on the 'good judge of others' (Cook, 1979) has generally failed to find such a person. Judging people accurately isn't a generalized ability; people who are good at rating traits aren't necessarily good at rating someone's vocabulary. This implies Vernon's & Parry's recruiting assistant may have been a 'fluke', who wouldn't be so accurate if her task changed, or even with her next batch of recruits. If there's no generalized trait of being good at summing up other people, there's no simple way of finding good judges. Social intelligence tests and 'empathy' scales haven't proved very useful. A 'track record' of good judgements is presently the only sure way of finding a good interviewer, so an organization that thinks it has one should hang on to him/her.

(b) Train interviewers

Training schemes abound. Interviewers can be warned of common sources of bias and inaccuracy, and be taught how to use rating scales efficiently. Training makes ratings more reliable (Wright, Carter & Fowler, 1967), improves accuracy of observation of behaviour (Spool, 1978), and can change interviewers' style of questioning (Mayfield, 1964). Maurer & Fay (1988), however, report that short interview training schemes achieve little. Orpen (1985) found interviewers trained in traditional interview techniques still achieved near zero validity predicting supervisor ratings and sales. Campion & Campion (1987) report that interview training taught interviewers the 'right' answers to questions about interviewing, but didn't change the way they completed interview evaluations.

(c) Tell interviewers what to look for

Interviewers can assess the applicant's social skill and motivation, but can't predict if he/she can fly an aircraft. More specifically, research can supply the interviewer with a list of points to cover. Vernon & Parry (1949) list proven 'contraindications' for military responsibility: poor work record, inability to give an intelligible account of present job, hypochondria, preference at school for handiwork/athletics/geography over maths/science, underachievement at school. Interviewers working from a good job description agree with each other better, pay less attention to irrelevant information and are less likely to make up their minds too quickly. Interviewing without a job description is risky under current US law (Arvey, 1979a). *Structured interviews* (see later) based on job analysis achieve significantly higher validity.

(d) Listen to the candidates

The average interviewer isn't very good at answering questions about what happened, immediately after the interview (Carlson, 1967); more experienced interviewers are more accurate, as are ones who use a structured interview guide. Anstey (1977) thinks 'effective listening' the hallmark of a good interview. Effective listening goes beyond merely staying awake: "One should note not so much what the candidate has said ... as what one has learnt from it", not whether he/she is in favour of the EEC but whether his/her arguments are sound and well presented. People who remember what someone looked like, said and did are better at predicting what that person will do in the future (Cline, 1964).

(e) Use the information efficiently

No one knows how many facts the typical interviewer collects in the typical interview, but it presumably runs into double figures. (Janz (1982) recorded an average of 17 answers in a 30-minute interview.) Some facts will point one way, some the other. People are generally very bad at interpreting inconsistent information; they ignore or distort information that doesn't fit their overall impression. Tullar, Mullins & Caldwell (1979) found that interviewers who rejected a candidate said he/she didn't look them in the eye, while interviewers who accepted the same candidate thought he/she did. Interviewers should list all the facts about the candidate, preferably as they emerge, decide which way each points, and calculate a score. More important facts can be given greater weight.

STRUCTURED INTERVIEWS

The biggest improvement to the interview is *structured interviewing*, which has developed rapidly since 1980. Structured interviewing does *not* mean following the 'seven-point plan', or agreeing who asks what before the interview starts. That is no more than good interviewing practice. Structured interview systems structure every part of the interview. The interviewers' judgements are structured by rating scales, checklists, etc. The interviewers' questions are structured too, often to the point of being tightly scripted. Structured interviewing systems start with a detailed *job analysis*, which ensures the questions and judgements are job-related. Structured interview systems largely deprive interviewers of their traditional autonomy.

Hovland & Wonderlic first proposed a standardized interview in 1939, taking the Terman—Binet intelligence test as their model. Their form covers work history, family history, social history and personal history. Some questions are answered by the applicant, others by the interviewer: "Does the applicant indicate a sincere interest and attitude towards his work?" The form proved quite successful and predicted quite well which employees were later dismissed.

Another early structured system was McMurray's *patterned interview*. McMurray (1947) reported very high validity coefficients (as high as 0.68) for three samples of factory workers, perhaps because the interview ratings weren't used in the selection, so there was no restriction of range. McMurray's interview lists not only questions for the interviewer to ask—"What plans do you have for your children?"—but questions for the interviewer to *answer*, about the candidate's reply—"Do dependants provide adequate motivation?" McMurray's *patterned interview* was designed to measure personality traits which makes its high predictive validity all the more surprising.

There are several structured interview systems in current use: Situational Interviews (Latham et al, 1980), Patterned Behaviour Description Interview (Janz, 1982), Comprehensive Structured Interview (Campion, Pursell & Brown, 1988), Structured Behavioural Interview (Motowidlo et al, 1992).

Situational Interviews

Situational Interviews (Latham et al, 1980) are developed from *critical incidents* (Chapter 3) of particularly effective or ineffective behaviour:

> The employee was devoted to his family. He had only been married for 18 months. He used whatever excuse he could to stay at home. One day the fellow's baby got a cold. His wife had a hangnail or something on her toe. He didn't come to work. He didn't even phone in.

The incidents are re-written as questions:

> Your spouse and two teenage children are sick in bed with a cold. There are no friends or relatives available to look in on them. Your shift starts in 3 hours. What would you do in this situation?

The company supervisors who describe the incidents also agree 'benchmark' answers for good, average and poor workers:

> I'd stay home—my spouse and family come first. [Poor]
> I'd phone my supervisor and explain my situation. [Average]
> Since they only have colds, I'd come to work. [Good]

At the interview, the questions are read out, the candidate replies and is rated against the benchmarks. The Situational Interview is very reliable, and predicts supervisor ratings of overall effectiveness in sawmill workers very well. Weekley & Gier (1987) report a high correlation (0.45) with sales figures in retail jewellery salespersons. Latham argues the structured interview is also fair because it deals with very specific behaviour, of proven direct relevance; it avoids mention of legally risky abstractions like abilities or dispositions.

Patterned Behaviour Description Interviews

Patterned Behaviour Description Interviews (Janz, 1982) also start by analysing the job with *critical incidents*, and end by rating the applicant's responses, but place more emphasis on what happens in between—questioning and recording. The Patterned Behaviour interviewer plays a more active role than the situational interviewer, being "trained to redirect [applicants] when their responses strayed from or evaded the question". The Patterned Behaviour Interview looks *back*, focusing on actual behaviour that occurred in the past; a typical question reads:

> Balancing the cash bag is always the bottom line for a cashier position, but bags can't always balance. Tell me about the time your experience helped you discover why your bag didn't balance.

Patterned Behaviour interviewing achieves higher validity than conventional interviews (Janz, 1982; Orpen, 1985).

Comprehensive Structured Interviews

Comprehensive Structured Interviews (Campion, Pursell & Brown, 1988) have four sections: job knowledge, job simulation, worker requirements, and situational. Job knowledge covers questions like: "When putting a piece of machinery back together after cleaning it, why would you clean all the parts first?" Job simulation means questions like "Many of the jobs require the operation of a forklift. Please read this [90-word] fork-lift procedure aloud". Worker requirements are assessed by questions like: "Some jobs require climbing ladders to a height of a five-story building and going out on a catwalk to work. Give us your feelings about performing a task such as this." The fourth section uses the same Situational Interview technique as Latham et al.

As in the Situational Interview, no attempt is made to probe or follow up; the emphasis is on consistency of administration. Campion et al (1988) report excellent reliability (0.88) and validity (0.56) for entry-level paper-mill workers; the interview performed as well as tests of reading, maths, and mechanical reasoning.

Structured Behavioural Interviews

Structural Behavioural Interview technique was devised for a consortium of American telecommunications companies (Motowidlo et al, 1992). Like other structured interview techniques it's based on *critical incidents*. This approach gives interviewers a more active role; they are directed to ask supplementary probing questions. Research finds audio and transcript forms have the same validity, suggesting non-verbal behaviours don't play much part in ratings.

Validity of structured interviews

Authors of structured interview methods usually report very high validities— but often from very small samples. However, reviews of interview validity confirm that structured interviews achieve far better results that conventional interviews. The overall interview validity estimate (0.47, corrected for re- stricted range and unreliability) made by Wiesner & Cronshaw (1988) divides into 0.31 for unstructured interviews, and 0.62 for structured interviews. The review by McDaniel et al (1987) of US public sector interviews finds a smaller difference: 0.45 for structured, 0.36 for unstructured, again fully corrected. Wiesner & Cronshaw's analysis finds structured interviews perform equally well, whether there is one interviewer or several. However structured inter- views based on formal job analysis do achieve better results—0.87, corrected for restricted range and criterion unreliability.

Very structured interviews, such Latham's Situational Interviews, blur the distinction between interview and paper and pencil test. Why not read the questions to a group of interviewees, or even print them as a questionnaire?— unless the raters attend to the interviewee's manner when rating his answers (Latham doesn't say). Comprehensive Structured Interviews correlate so highly with aptitude tests—a multiple correlation of 0.75—as to suggest they are really disguised tests of mental ability (Campion, Pursell & Brown, 1988). Structured Behavioural Interviews, on the other hand, show little or no correlation with mental ability (Motowidlo et al, 1992). German research (Schuler, 1989) reports large correlations between structured interview ratings and scores on the California Psychological Inventory, suggesting structured interviews may also be operating as disguised personality tests. Disguising tests of mental ability or personality as structured interviews may make them more acceptable to candidates and fair employment agencies, but is otherwise expensive and inefficient.

HOW THE INTERVIEWER REACHES A DECISION

Ideally the interviewer will listen carefully to everything the candidate says, and reach a wise decision based on all the information available. In reality, research has documented a number of ways in which the interviewer does not operate ideally.

(a) Interviewers make their minds up before the interview

Interviewers usually have some information about candidates before the interview starts, from CV, application form, etc. Research reaches conflicting conclusions about how much weight interviewers place on such data. Several studies suggest little attention is paid to what the application reveals about qualifications, experience, background, etc (Raza & Carpenter, 1987; Graves & Powell, 1988). However, a meta-analysis of 19 studies (Olian, Schwab & Haberfeld, 1988) reports that qualifications accounted for 35% of the variance in selection decisions.

(b) Interviewers make up their minds quickly

Springbett (1958) reports that interviewers make up their minds after only 4 minutes of a 15-minute interview, although his methodology was not very subtle (Buckley & Eder, 1988). Tucker & Rowe (1977) found interviewers accepted or rejected after an average of 9 minutes. Surprisingly, interviewers who *hadn't* seen the interviewee's application form took exactly as long as ones who did know his/her background, which implies that factual information didn't play a very big role in the interviewers' decisions. What happens in these 4–9 minutes? Experienced employment counsellors take longer to decide, the better the applicant (Tullar, Mullins & Caldwell, 1979).

(c) The interviewer forms a first impression

Ratings of application blank and candidate's appearance predicted final ratings for 85 or 88% of candidates (Springbett, 1958). Advice to 'be on time and dress smartly' is obviously sound. Male interviewers react against scent or aftershave, regardless of sex of applicant; female interviewers favour it, also regardless of sex of applicant (Baron, 1983). Female applicants for management positions create the best impression by being conventionally but not severely dressed (Forsythe, Drake & Cox, 1985). But beware—order effects are notoriously fickle. Interviewers normally rely on first impressions, but if they're asked to make a series of ratings they rely more on 'last impressions' (Farr, 1973)—so a structured interview system might not over-weight first impressions.

Moreover, research doesn't always find first impressions count (McDonald & Hakel, 1985); interviewers saw good and bad résumés, which created a first impression, then chose which 10 of a list of 30 questions to ask. Contrary to expectations, interviewers didn't choose negative questions—"What course did you have most problems with at school"—when interviewing 'poor' candidates. Nor did interviewers ignore candidates' answers, even though they contradicted the first impression; if a 'bad' resume candidate gave 'good' answers, he/she got a *good* final rating.

(d) The interviewer looks for reasons to reject

Springbett (1958) found just one bad rating was sufficient to reject 90% of candidates. Bad news shifts interviewers' ratings more readily than good news. Hollman (1972) argues interviewers pay *too little* attention to the candidate's *good* points, not *too much* to his/her *bad* points. Interviewers are more sensitive to bad news, because they get more criticism for hiring poor workers—who remain visible—than for rejecting good ones, who necessarily remain an unknown quantity. Looking for reasons to reject is a rational strategy if the organization has plenty of good applicants.

(e) The interviewer relies on an implicit personality theory

Andrews (1922) describes an interviewer who hired a salesman, who proved a disaster, and for ever after wouldn't employ anyone who'd ever sold adding machines. Why not? Because the disastrous salesman has previously sold adding machines. The interviewer reasoned:

> People who sell adding machines are terrible salesmen.
>
> This candidate formerly sold adding machines.
>
> Therefore he will be a terrible salesman.

Andrews's interviewer's reasoning is obviously at fault; someone must be good at selling adding machines.

COMPLEX JUDGEMENT IN THE INTERVIEW

Defenders of the interview argue that a good interviewer can see patterns in the information, that pre-set, mechanistic methods, like check-lists and *Weighted Application Blanks* (WABs), miss. Thorndike argued many years ago that the value of technical skill *interacts* with general intelligence multiplicatively. Skill—say with a paint brush—is invaluable in a genius, but useless in a stupid person. A mechanistic assessment that gives points to each separately ignores the relation between them. In selecting sonar operators in the Second World War, selectors initially gave marks for general intelligence, mechanical comprehension and tone discrimination, added them up, and selected applicants whose total exceeded the pass-mark. This allowed an applicant whose ear was poor to compensate through the other tests; unfortunately intelligence or mechanical comprehension can't help a sonar operator who is tone deaf. A good interviewer's judgement can help him/her avoid such silly mistakes.

However, research casts considerable doubt on the interviewer's claim to be doing something so mysterious and complex that no other method can replace him/her. Research shows:

1. human experts never perform better than a system,
2. human experts don't use information as complexly as they claim, and
3. 'models' of experts are better than experts.

1. Expert vs system

Nearly 40 years ago, Meehl (1954) reviewed 20 studies comparing 'mechanical' systems with human experts, and concluded that system always predicted as well as expert, often better. Expert never did better than system. Three of the 20 studies were of personnel selection, for the US Navy or Coast Guards. Research since 1954 hasn't disproved Meehl's conclusion. Reilly & Chao (1982) review six studies in which experts, usually psychologists, used test data to rate applicants, and in which the ratings (not the test scores) were used to predict potential, sales, tenure, income or survival. Experts did fairly poorly overall, achieving a mean validity well below that achieved by the tests themselves. Of particular interest is a study by Roose & Dougherty (1976), which compared directly experts' opinion based on tests, biography and interview, with multiple regressions (Note 1) calculated from the same data. Regressions predicted productivity far better than experts.

2. Does the expert use information complexly?

Experts like to think "combining [of information] is done intuitively ... hypotheses and constructs are generated during the course of the analysis ... and the process is mediated by an individual's judgment and reflection" (Gough, 1962). Some experts make a positive virtue of not being able to explain how they reach their judgments citing 'nose', 'ear' 'eye', 'gut' or 'hunch'. Research suggests, however, that most interviewers have a moderate degree of insight into their own decision processes (Stumpf & London, 1981).

Research on how experts make decisions mostly uses the *analysis of variance (ANOVA) paradigm*. The researcher constructs sets of cases in which information is systematically varied, asks experts to assess each case, then deduces how the experts reached their decisions. If the expert 'passes' one set of cases and 'fails' another, and the only feature distinguishing the two sets is exam results, it follows that the expert's decisions are based on exam grades and exam grades alone. Experts claim they don't think as simplistically as this; they say they use *configurations*, for example exam grades are important in young candidates but not for people over 30—an *interaction* of age and grades. Experts like the layperson to credit them with very complex decisions: pass candidates with good exam grades (1), unless they're mature students (2), but then not if they have low IQ (3), or if they had the opportunity to study (4) but didn't use it (5), unless of course they're housewives (6)—a six-way interaction.

Studies using ANOVA find that experts rarely use configurations, even simple ones like "exam grades count for younger but not for older candidates". Most of their decisions fit a *linear additive* model: superior exam grades—plus point; good vocabulary—plus point; young—plus point; keen—plus point; giving a total of four plus points. Hiring decisions based on academic standing, experience and interests, showed little or no evidence of complexity (Hakel, Dobmeyer & Dunnette, 1970). Choice of secretary based on five cues also yielded no evidence of complex decisions (Valenzi & Andrews, 1971). Professional interviewers rating paper candidates gave extra low ratings for the combination of poor oral communication and poor interpersonal skills, but otherwise made little use of interactions in six cues (Graves & Karren, 1992). One study found evidence of personnel managers using cues complexly, but not wisely; Hitt & Barr (1989) report that 'managers ... make different attributions when comparing a Black, 45-year-old woman with 10 years of experience and a master's degree with a White, 35-year-old man with 10 years of experience and a master's degree'. Irrelevant, 'forbidden' cues—race and sex—were used complexly more than relevant cues such as experience and education. Personnel managers join an illustrious company: doctors, nurses, psychologists, radiologists, prison governors, social workers. All claim to make very sophisticated judgements; all show little evidence of actually doing so. Only one class of expert really does make complex configural decisions— the stockbroker.

3. A 'model' of the expert is better than the expert

Studies using ANOVA can construct a model of the expert's thought processes, which model can then be used to make a fresh batch of decisions. The results are unexpected: the model performs better than the expert it was derived from. The model never has 'off-days'; it always performs as well as the expert's best performance. An organization could preserve the wisdom of its best personnel manager, by constructing a model of his/her decisions, and continue to 'use' him/her after he/she had left. However, Dougherty, Ebert & Callender, (1986) report that while models of poor interviewers were better than the interviewers themselves, the same wasn't true for a *good* interviewer. 'Cross-modelling' showed a model of the accurate interviewer improved on one inaccurate interviewer, but not on the other.

Constructing a model could prove humiliating for the expert, if his/her decisions turn out to be so inconsistent or so simplistic that they're not worth modelling. Miner (1970) found interviewers influenced by only three of 19 aspects of the candidate: height, weight and having been an officer in the armed services. Dawes (1971) found the decisions of medical school admissions committees could be forecast fairly accurately from candidates' admission test scores and college grades. However, it's unlikely this information—

already over 30 years old—will prevent the highly paid staff of medical schools wasting their time discussing candidates. Cook's Law states:

> The more important the selection decision, the more man hours must be spent arriving at it.

In ANOVA studies, 'cut and dried' information is used, like exam grades, which are easily analysed statistically. Forty years ago, Meehl (1954) pointed out it's a waste of time using an expert interviewer to do things a clerk or a WAB can do. Very often the interviewer can't be replaced by a system, because the interview is needed to define the problem. The psychiatrist seeing a new patient starts with an open mind about symptoms and diagnosis; similarly the personnel manager, wearing a welfare or industrial relations hat, may need to interview to formulate the problem. But selection interviews should always have a clear goal, and shouldn't be allowed to turn into 'fishing expeditions'.

ERROR AND BIAS IN THE INTERVIEW

The more the interviewer likes the candidate, the more likely the interviewer is to make an offer (Anderson & Shackleton, 1989). Liking may of course be based on job-related competence, but it may equally well arise from irrational biases.

(a) Are interviewers biased against minorities?

Hakel says the interview is "far more susceptible to bias, error ... than is testing or the statistical use of biographical information"; in fact "if one's intent is to discriminate against the members of one group ... the simplest way to do so is through the employment interview". Earlier research on application sifting (Arvey, 1979a) found consistent bias against women. However, if other, more relevant, information is provided, less notice is taken of gender (Tosi & Einbender, 1985). More recent researches have sometimes found bias *in favour of* women (Elliott, 1981; Arvey et al, 1987). Harris (1989) concludes that "More recent evidence indicates that females typically do not receive lower ratings in the employment interview". Several studies have reported age bias in interview decisions (Arvey et al, 1987; Avolio & Barrett, 1987; Raza & Carpenter, 1987).

Interviewers may have stereotypes that bias their decisions. Cecil, Paul & Olins, (1973) listed the characteristics seen as desirable in male and female applicants for a white-collar job. The ideal male candidate can change his mind readily, is persuasive, can take a lot of pressure, is highly motivated and aggressive; the ideal female candidate has a pleasant voice, excellent clerical skills, excellent computational skills, expresses herself well, is immaculate in dress and person, and is a high-school graduate.

(b) Physical attractiveness

An extensive body of research, dating back to 1965, shows that people agree fairly well on who is physically attractive, and that being 'good looking' confers a wide range of social advantages. Dipboye, Arvey & Terpstra (1977) found assessors strongly biased by physical attractiveness; being good looking was worth two rank positions in 12. Like most physical attractiveness effects, it operated regardless of gender, being as strong for males rating males, as for males rating females. Research on physical attractiveness is easy to do in the USA, where college yearbooks form a source of professional quality, standard format photos of entire graduating classes of 1980 or 1970 or 1960, whose attractiveness *then* can be linked to their career *since*. Dickey-Bryant et al (1986) used this technique on American army officers, and found a correlation between physical attractiveness and success in military academy, but only in those men who were still in the army 14 years later. They interpret this as a *survival* effect: 'persons fitting the attractiveness—ability mold are more likely to remain active in the organisation'. Cash, Gillen & Burns, (1977) report effect of physical attractiveness interacts with job type. In stereotypically masculine jobs, attractiveness only benefits males; in stereotypically female jobs, attractiveness only benefits females; only for 'gender neutral' jobs is physical attractiveness advantageous to both males and females. Other studies report the effect of physical attractiveness, while detectable, is slight; Morrow et al (1990) found the attractiveness of a photo attached to a 'paper person' accounted for only 1—2% of the variance in ratings.

(c) Clones and mirror images

Do interviewers look for 'clones ' or 'mirror images'? People generally do prefer others who share their outlook and background, but research on interviewer—candidate similarity has mixed results (Schmitt, 1976). Some interviewers are biased in favour of candidates like themselves, others aren't. Similar applicants *are* rated more competent, *aren't* more likely to be offered a post, but *are* offered a higher salary if employed.

(d) Are interviewers biased by the previous candidate?

The two preceding candidates can exert a massive biasing effect on interviewers—but only if they haven't been warned (Wexley et al, 1972). Warning them reduces the 'contrast effect' considerably, while a week's training virtually eliminates it. Other studies, however, have either found no contrast effects, or ones so tiny as to be quite unimportant (Schmitt, 1976).

LAW AND FAIRNESS

The interview has largely escaped the legal problems that beset psychological tests in the USA, even though it is the easiest way of all to discriminate, consciously or unconsciously.

Until recently, the interview could only fall foul of US fair employment laws, if those complaining could prove deliberate discrimination. So long as employers avoided gross mistakes, the interview was relatively 'safe'. Questions that aren't clearly *job-related* should be avoided; this can exclude a surprising range of topics: marital status, home ownership, criminal record, military discharge, pregnancy, citizenship, spouse and family. Interviews are easier to defend legally if they are based on good job descriptions, if interviewers are carefully selected and trained, and if panels are used, not individual interviewers. In Britain, the Equal Opportunities Commission's *Code of Practice* says "questions posed during interviews [should] relate **only** to the requirements of the job. Where it is necessary to discuss personal circumstances and their effect upon ability to do the job, this should be done in a neutral manner, equally applicable to all applicants".

In 1988, the case of *Watson* vs *Ft Worth Bank & Trust* opened the way for interview decisions in the USA to be challenged under the *adverse impact* principle (Barrett, 1990). If disproportionately fewer women or minorities are selected or promoted, the employer then has to prove the test is valid. This makes life much more difficult for the employer, because adverse impact is much easier to prove than deliberate discrimination, and proving a selection test valid is much more difficult than finding ways of criticising it. The *Watson* vs *Ft Worth Bank* decision may make interviewing much less popular in the USA.

CONCLUSIONS

Psychologists have always branded the interview as a low- or zero-validity selection method. Recent reviews suggest they're both right and wrong. They're right, because traditional, one-to-one, unstructured interviews do have low validity. They're wrong, because structured interviews can achieve very high validity, although in the process many have almost ceased to be recognizable as interviews. Structured interviews are also 'safer' legally.

Some interviewers are more successful than others. The traditional interview is probably better at assessing some characteristics than others; social skill, mental ability and career motivation may be more accurately assessed. The traditional interview is also subject to many biases, some of which, notably gender bias, constitute discrimination.

The selection interview serves other purposes—to answer the applicant's questions, to 'sell' the organization, to clarify gaps in the applicant's CV, or to negotiate terms of employment.

NOTE

1. Multiple regression. A correlation (Note 1, Chapter 2) describes the relationship between *two* variables, for example predictor and criterion. Often the selector has several predictors: a set of test scores, a number of interview ratings, etc. A *multiple regression*, denoted by R, takes account of intercorrelations between predictors. A multiple regression summarizes the information in a set of ratings, or a set of tests.

The multiple regression also identifies redundancy in a set of ratings or tests. Suppose four interview ratings all predict productivity quite well: 0.40, 0.45, 0.42, 0.45. If each rating provides independent information, the combination of the four would give a very much better prediction than any one of the four. If the four ratings are highly intercorrelated—as is much more likely—the prediction from all four combined will not be much better than the prediction from any individual rating.

Selection research shows that adding new tests to a selection battery soon brings diminishing returns; adding new tests after the third or fourth rarely increases R by a significant or worthwhile amount.

5 References and Ratings

The eye of the beholder

Interviews allow the applicant to speak for him/herself, on the principle that 'the best way of finding out about someone is to ask them'. References and ratings work on a different principle: that the best way of finding out about someone is to ask someone who knows him/her well—former employers, school teachers, colleagues or fellow trainees. The standard US book on references argues: "Reference givers who have closely and frequently observed an applicant performing a job similar to the job being applied for can provide the most potentially useful information" (Levine & Rudolph, 1977). References are the traditional approach to finding out what others think of the applicant, part of the classic trio. Ratings try to get more systematic and useful information from the same source.

REFERENCES

Known in the USA as: 'letter of recommendation', 'recommendation form', 'referee report', 'voucher' or 'perif', in Britain, they are generally called 'references' or even 'a character'. References are usually written, although people in a hurry, or who don't want to commit themselves, may use the telephone. Virtually all American employers take up references on new employees (Muchinsky, 1979); three-quarters of US companies felt selection could suffer if references couldn't be checked. However, not one company had investigated the effectiveness of references.

References are used (a) to check accuracy of information given by applicants, and (b) to predict success on the job. Forty-eight percent of American employers use references only to check accuracy; the rest hope to learn something new about the candidate. Of these, 20% (of the total) use the reference to search for negative information. Most employers want information about personality—cooperativeness, honesty and social adjustment. This makes sense. Personality is *typical behaviour*—how the person behaves routinely, when he/she isn't making a special effort. Typical behaviour is less accessible to selectors, because it's easy for applicants to make a special effort for the duration of most selection tests, whereas previous employers or teachers have seen the candidate all day every day, perhaps for years, and can report how he/she usually behaves and what he/she is like on 'off days'.

References may be structured—questions, checklists, ratings—or unstructured—"Tell me what you think of [John Smith] in your own words"—or a mixture of both. In Britain the completely unstructured reference is still very widely used. Sixty years ago American occupational psychologists recommended it be replaced by a list of specific questions, and some simple five-point ratings:

1. [Mr Henry B Smith] states that he was in your employ from [Jan 1 1928] to [Mar 16 1932] as a [machinist]. Is this correct?
2. He states that he left your employ because [he was anxious to attend day school and could not do it in your employ]. Is this true. If not, why did he leave?
3. Did he have any habits to which you objected? If so, what?

  (a) *powers of application.* exceptionally industrious [] industrious [] performs work assigned [] shiftless [] lazy [].
  (b) *popularity.* very popular [] good mixer [] average [] exclusive [] unpopular [].

American industry listened; 51% of American employers use structured reference reports, in which the most useful questions were "Would you re-employ?", "How long did the person work for you?" and "Why did he/she leave?" (Mosel & Goheen, 1958).

There isn't much published research on the reference, which is odd, given the vehemence with which most occupational psychologists condemn it. There are two studies of the unstructured reference, and half a dozen studies of rating format references (Muchinsky, 1979). Baxter et al (1981) searched medical school files to find 20 cases where the same two referees had written references for the same two applicants (Figure 5.1). If references are useful, what referee A says about applicant X ought to resemble what referee B says about applicant X. Analysis of the qualities listed in the letters—intelligent,

	Candidate X		Candidate Y
		A	
Referee A		g	
		r	
		e	
	Idiosyncratic	e	Way of describing people
		m	
		e	
Referee B		n	
		t	

Figure 5.1 Schematic representation of the study by Baxter et al (1981) letters of reference

reserved, unimaginative, etc.—revealed a different, and much less encouraging, pattern. What referee A said about applicant X didn't resemble what referee B said about applicant X, but did resemble what referee A said about applicant Y. Each referee had his/her own idiosyncratic way of describing people, which came through no matter who he/she was describing. The free-form reference tells you more about its author than about its subject.

Peres & Garcia (1962) analysed 625 reference letters for engineering applicants, and found most used generalized trait descriptions, and didn't describe specific behaviour. Factor analysis found five factors that distinguished good from poor candidates: mental agility, vigour, dependability/reliability, 'urbanity', and co-operation/consideration. Good engineer applicants got favourable ratings on mental agility, vigour and dependability; poor applicants were 'damned with faint praise' as 'urbane' (talkative, cultured, poised) or 'co-operative'.

Reliability

American research suggests references are unreliable. Most research compares one referee with another and finds they agree poorly or not at all, which creates problems for employers: which—if either—is right? Referees agreed very poorly about applicants for (US) Civil Service jobs, for 80% of correlations were lower than 0.40; references given by supervisors bore no relation to references given by acquaintances, while references by supervisors and co-workers (who both see the applicant at work) agreed only very moderately (Mosel & Goheen, 1959). Reilly & Chao (1982) cite an unpublished study by Sharon showing references for would-be judges were very unreliable. Another unpublished study by Bartlett & Goldstein found raters agreed whether a reference was favourable or not, but that different referees didn't agree about the same applicant.

The (UK) Civil Service Selection Board (CSSB) uses five or six references, covering school, college, armed services and former employers, and "take[s] them very seriously" (Wilson, 1948). Thirteen CSSB staff achieved very high inter-rater reliability in assessments of candidates based on references alone. The CSSB finds references reliable, in sharp distinction to most American research; it used five or six references, not two or three, which may increase reliability. Or perhaps CSSB panels understand the reference's private language, or perhaps they can pick out and discount 'rogue' references.

Validity

Mosel & Goheen report several investigations of the Employment Recommendation Questionnaire (ERQ), a structured reference request form written by the US Civil Service, and widely used by private industry in America. The ERQ covers:

1. *Occupational ability*: skill, carefulness, industry, efficiency.
2. *Character and reputation.*
3. "Is the applicant specially qualified in any particular branch of trade in which he seeks employment?"
4. "Would you employ him in a position of the kinds he seeks?"
5. "Has the applicant ever been discharged from any employment to your knowledge? If yes, Why?"

Mosel & Goheen (1958) analyse ERQ data for US Federal civil servants and military personnel. The US Civil Service normally uses ERQ data 'clinically', i. e. unsystematically. Mosel & Goheen quantified ERQs and correlated them with supervisor ratings. For some occupations, ERQ had zero validity: carpenters, painters, motor mechanics, ordnancemen. For other occupations, ERQ achieved very limited validity, represented by correlations of 0.20—0.30: machinist, radio mechanic and forklift truck driver. Sample sizes were, however, small—50–100. The ERQ ratings didn't correlate at all with *Training and Experience* ratings, in which experienced examiners rate the applicant's skills as listed on his/her application. Mosel & Goheen also compared ERQs with *qualification investigations,* in which US Civil Service investigators interview between three and six people who know the applicant—a sort of oral reference. For three occupations—economist, budget examiner and training officer—the two sources of information agreed moderately well. The persons interviewed included some of the people who had written the ERQs. Browning (1968) compared reference ratings of teachers with criterion ratings of teaching performance by headteachers. The correlations were generally very low, across 11 categories of referee (median 0.13).

Attempts to improve the reference have had mixed results. Carroll & Nash (1972) used a forced-choice reference rating form. Items in each pair of items are equated for social desirability, but only one statement predicted job success:

- has many worthwhile ideas
- completes all assignments
- always works fast
- requires little supervision

Scores predicted performance ratings 4 months after hire quite well in university clerical workers. Reilly & Chao (1982) cite unpublished studies by Rhea, on structured reference forms for US Navy officer cadets. Rhea devised a novel technique, in which references are *empirically keyed* to performance ratings (and cross-validated). Rhea didn't take what referees said at face value, but correlated each item with performance ratings, intending to use only those items that actually predicted performance. Unfortunately these items didn't prove numerous enough for the method to be successful. Reilly & Chao also cite an unpublished study by Bartlett & Goldstein, showing telephone reference checks had very limited ability to predict *voluntary* and *involuntary termination* in airport workers. Few workers left, and even fewer were sacked, making it inherently difficult to predict which. Summarizing all available US data, Reilly & Chao conclude reference checks give poor predictions of supervisor ratings (r = 0.18) and turnover (r = 0.08).

Hunter & Hunter's (1984) review calculated mean validity of reference checks for four criteria:

supervisor ratings	0.26	(10 coefficients)
training grades	0.23	(1 coefficient)
promotion	0.16	(3 coefficients)
tenure	0.27	(2 coefficients)

Hunter & Hunter give no details of the studies analysed, but inspection of their Table 8 shows some were also included in the analysis by Reilly & Chao. Hunter & Hunter quote higher average validities for the reference than Reilly & Chao, because they correct for criterion unreliability. The reference check achieves fourth place in the 'final league table' of Hunter & Hunter—behind mental ability tests, job tryouts and biodata. This fourth place is only provisional because Hunter & Hunter found relatively few studies of reference validity. Neither review includes British data on reference validity for the CSSB and Admiralty Selection Board.

UK Research

Candidates for Royal Naval officer college are rated by headteacher on seven scales. Reference ratings were correlated with ratings of *leadership* and *general conduct*, an examination mark, and the two combined. All seven ratings combined predicted *total mark* moderately well. Ratings of leadership were best predicted by headteacher's rating of *sporting and extra-curricular activities*, while exam mark was best predicted by rating of *application to studies* (Jones & Harrison, 1982). Jones & Harrison think these results are quite promising; the overall (corrected) predictive validity of headteacher's report equals that reported for psychological tests predicting training grades (Ghiselli, 1966b). Jones & Harrison find the prediction of leadership and conduct "particularly encouraging", given how difficult these are to measure by any other test. Jones & Harrison don't expect such good results every time; headteachers are more likely (than, say, former employers) to write careful, *critical* references, because they know they will be writing Naval College references for future pupils, and because their own credibility is at stake. Anstey (1966) reports an interesting finding. The British Foreign Office recruited 150 entrants to the

Diplomatic Service between 1948 and 1959, including eight who had poor references from school or college. On follow up in 1963, six of these eight were found to have poor, or very poor, performance reports, suggesting the Foreign Office were unwise to decide to ignore their references.

Apart from Carroll & Nash's forced-choice method, references haven't proved very promising. At their very best—naval officer cadets—they do as well as intelligence tests. But references do have one great advantage—they're very cheap, because someone else does all the work, and doesn't expect to be paid.

Pollyanna effect

A very early (1923) survey, described by Moore (1942), found most reference writers said (a) they always gave the employee the benefit of the doubt, (b) they only said good things about him/her, and (c) they didn't point out his/her failings. In some circles it's considered bad form to write a bad reference; one should either refuse to act as referee, or hint as strongly as necessary that one doesn't feel able to write anything very flattering. If referees are reluctant to say anything unkind, references will clearly prove a poor source of information. They will have very limited predictive validity, because their range (of favourableness) will be very restricted. Research confirms this pessimistic conclusion. Mosel & Goheen found ERQ ratings highly skewed, with 'outstanding' or 'good' opinions greatly out-numbering 'satisfactory' or 'poor' opinions. Candidates were hardly ever rated 'poor'. Nearly all (97.5%) referees said 'Yes' to "Would you employ him?", while 99.1% said 'No' to "Has the applicant ever been discharged?". However Mosel & Goheen were studying *successful* applicants, so perhaps this isn't surprising. Jones & Harrison (1982) analysed ratings given to **all** applicants for Dartmouth Naval College; the average mark was well above the midpoint of the scale, and marks below the midpoint were rarely given. Carroll & Nash (1972), however, disagree. They wrote a forced-choice reference questionnaire that contained only positive statements, and found a high proportion of subjects complained of being deprived of the opportunity to say anything negative about the applicants. Perhaps this is a case of only wanting something when you can't have it.

RATINGS

American personnel practice uses ratings a lot, far more than British personnel work. In personnel selection, ratings can be used as the *predictor*, but are more often used as the *criterion*. Ratings used as *predictor*, in selection, are usually made by external referees (see earlier), or by the candidate's peers. *Criterion* ratings are usually made by supervisor or manager. Ratings are used for regular performance appraisals in American industry, so they're big business.

Performance appraisals often determine promotion, salary, even survival, so rating systems come under keen scrutiny. Ratings are prone to systematic errors:

(a) Halo. First described in 1907, halo means ratings on different dimensions aren't independent. The employee rated punctual is also rated ambitious, smart, able and conscientious. However, one can't infer halo simply because ratings on different dimensions correlate; the attributes might 'really' go together ('true halo'). Cooper (1981) reviews attempts to control 'halo' and concludes they are only partly successful. It's usually a mistake to multiply rating scales, because factor analysis (see Note 1, Chapter 3) almost always shows a large number of ratings reduce to a fairly small number of factors.

(b) Leniency. Reluctance to give poor ratings, which pervasively affects referees' ratings (see earlier).

(c) Central tendency. Using the middle points of the scale, and avoiding the extremes. This is particularly irritating to the researcher because it reduces variance and restricts correlations.

Attempts to reduce halo, leniency and central tendency divide into varying the format of ratings, and training raters to use the scales 'properly'. Rating formats have multiplied over the last 20—30 years. Landy & Farr (1980) suggest calling a moratorium on writing new formats, because they aren't solving any problems, except how to fill the pages of *Journal of Applied Psychology* and *Personnel Psychology*. The *graphic rating scale* is the conventional rating scale format:

efficient  inefficient

Different formats vary the number of scale points, supply adverbs—'very', 'fairly', 'slightly', etc.—for each point, etc. The dimensions to be rated are often very vague: 'quality', 'demeanor', 'production', 'organization'. American psychologists call these *motherhood* traits; they sound warm and comforting, but are almost impossible to define.

The *Behaviourally Anchored Rating Scale* (BARS) format tries to make each point of the scale more meaningful to the rater, to make ratings less arbitrary, and so to reduce halo, leniency and central tendency. Writing a BARS proceeds by four stages.

1. Choose the dimensions. The supervisors who will make the ratings meet, for a day or half a day, to identify what to rate. They are encouraged to avoid *motherhood* concepts. Israeli tank commanders listed five dimensions for tank crews: *efficiency* with which weaponry is operated, *effort, proficiency in maintenance, proficiency in manouevre* and *teamwork* (Shapira & Shirom, 1980).

2. List examples of good, average, and poor work. The same supervisors, working individually, write descriptions of *critical incidents* (Chapter 3) of good, bad and average performance. Up to 900 incidents may be described. The incidents are sifted, to exclude duplicates, ones that are too vague, and ones raters couldn't observe.

3. Sort the items. Supervisors work through the revised list of incidents, and assign each to one of the dimensions listed in stage 1. Incidents that aren't assigned to the same dimension by 75% of supervisors are discarded.

4. Scale the incidents. Supervisors scale incidents that survive stage 3, on a seven-point scale. If the standard deviation (see Note 3, Chapter 1) of supervisors' ratings exceeds 1.5, the incident is discarded, because supervisors don't agree well enough on its weighting.

The BARS is now ready to use, having taken 2–3 days to complete. Up to 30 supervisors contribute data, so BARS writing is expensive. Figure 5.2 illustrates a typical BARS. Behaviourally Anchored Rating Scales are claimed to reduce halo and leniency, and to increase inter-rater agreement. Shapira & Shirom (1980) found correlations between different BARSs to be fairly low, suggesting raters weren't just rating the same thing five times under different

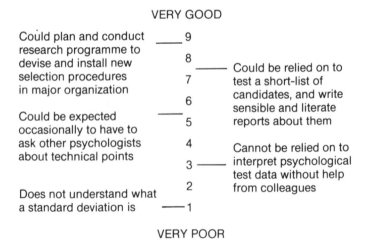

Figure 5.2   An (invented) example of Behaviourally Anchored Rating Scale (BARS) for an occupational psychologist

headings. Other authors are sceptical about the BARS's advantages over simpler rating formats (Borman, 1979). Because BARSs are highly specific, a new set has to be developed for each job.

Training schemes

Borman (1979) reviews a number of training schemes and describes his own. Training aims to reduce *halo* and *leniency*, without reducing accuracy. Borman's training consisted of group discussion of actual ratings, led by a trainer who pointed out inaccuracies and examples of halo and leniency errors. Another study (Pursell, Dossett & Latham, 1980) initially found five psychological tests failed to predict supervisor ratings of electricians; after the supervisors had been trained to reduce rating error, test validity increased dramatically. However, Warmke & Billings (1979) found the effects of training short lived; practice ratings made at the end of the training course were better, but 'real' ratings by senior nurses 2 months after training still showed halo.

PEER ASSESSMENTS

Research dating back to the 1920s finds that people are surprisingly good at predicting who among their peers will succeed, and surprisingly honest too. Even when they know their opinions will help determine who gets selected or promoted, people say (fairly) willingly what they think of each other, and are (relatively) uninfluenced by who they like and dislike.

Sometimes rating scales are used, sometimes forced choice formats. In *peer nomination* each subject nominates the best or worst performers in the group, usually in order of effectiveness or ineffectiveness. In *peer ranking*, each subject rank orders the whole group from best to worst. Subjects don't usually judge themselves. Peer assessments don't work well unless the group numbers at least 10. Ratings and rankings describe everyone, whereas nominations ignore the middle of the distribution; between a quarter and half the candidates might receive no nominations at all. This doesn't matter if the selectors want the best 10%, or want to screen out unacceptable candidates. Love (1981) found nominations and ranking were more reliable and had higher predictive validity than ratings. Peer *nominations* achieve very high reliabilities—generally in the region of 0.80—because only extremes are included (Kane & Lawler, 1978). Nominations achieve high reliability after a very short time, and regardless of whether they are used for research, or 'for real'. Army basic training squads are re-shuffled after 4 weeks, but once the groups have settled down, peer assessments retain their predictive validity, even though different peers are making them.

Military research

The US and Israeli armed services have researched peer assessments extensively. Early research (Williams & Leavitt, 1947) found peer ratings of US Marine officers to correlate well with combat ratings; peer ratings were "a more valid predictor both of success in officer candidate school and of combat performance than several objective tests". A series of studies by Hollander (1965) found peer evaluations of global potential in officer candidates correlated fairly well with effectiveness ratings as regular officers, that peer nominations were very reliable, and that they achieved good predictive validity within as little as 3 weeks. Recent Israeli research (Amir, Kovarsky & Sharan, 1970; Tziner & Dolan, 1982) reports very high correlations between peer evaluations and admission to officer school, in large male and female samples. Peer assessments had higher predictive validity than almost any other test, including intelligence tests, interview rating, and rating by commanding officer. Reviews (Lewin & Zwany, 1976) of US Army and Navy research finds correlations centring in the region of 0.20 and 0.30. In military research, validity proves equally good whether ratings are collected for research purposes or for actual selection. Peer assessment has been most popular in the armed services—whose subjects are less likely (or less able) to complain. Peer ratings are unpopular if used *administratively*, i.e. to make decisions about promotion, etc. Love (1981) found peer assessments unpopular with policemen, who thought that they were unfair, inaccurate and shouldn't be used for deciding who to promote. McEvoy & Buller (1987) report peer ratings are more acceptable if used to 'develop' staff rather than to select them.

Civilian research

Peer nominations of insurance agents predicted appraisals of managerial effectiveness quite well (Mayfield, 1970). Peer ratings distinguish middle managers who get promoted from ones who don't (Roadman, 1964). Most data were collected for research purposes, but Mayfield's subjects were told the data were to be used *administratively*. Peer assessments have also been used to predict sales performance (Waters & Waters, 1970); McBain's (1970) research implies peer assessments could predict accident rate in truck (HGV) drivers. Kraut (1975) found peer ratings of *impact* predicted future advancement, but not performance appraisal ratings. This suggests peer ratings, like the assessment centre (Chapter 9), may measure whose 'face fits' better than they predict productivity. Peer nominations retain their validity for long periods—up to 3 years (Hollander, 1965). Reilly & Chao (1982) review peer evaluations for MBA graduates, managers, life insurance agents, sales staff, pharmaceutical scientists and secretaries, and calculate average validities for three criteria:

training	0.31
promotion	0.51
performance ratings	0.37

Friendship

Personnel managers usually dismiss peer assessments on the grounds they will prove little more than popularity contests; researchers disagree. Hollander found subjects had on average three friends, but nominated only one as a leader. Love (1981) found friendship didn't bias the relationship between peer assessment and criterion rating. On the other hand, Waters & Waters (1970) found nominations among friends had no predictive validity, whereas nominations among enemies or neutral groups did, which implies friendship distorts judgements. However, Waters & Waters's subjects were salesmen, for whom avoiding being disliked by others arguably genuinely increases productivity.

'Negative' nominations—who is "selfish" or "overbearing"—are more idiosyncratic, and more likely to be biased by dislike. Nominations of five most effective had good predictive validity, whereas nominations of five least effective had none (Kaufman & Johnson, 1974). Negative nominations caused resentment; candidates described them graphically as being asked to "cut their buddy's throat".

Summary

Kane & Lawler (1978) analyse 19 studies and conclude peer *nominations* achieve an average validity of 0.43; military studies achieve higher validities than civilian studies. However, Kane & Lawler calculate these medians from the *best validity* achieved in each study, not from *all validities* reported. Peer nominations predict objective criteria—graduation, promotion, survival—better than supervisor ratings. Nominations for specific criteria—will make a good officer—are more accurate than nominations for vague criteria—"extravert", "emotional". Kane & Lawler conclude nominations are best used for predicting leadership. Kane & Lawler also conclude peer *ratings* are less valid than nominations probably because everyone is rated, not just the highly visible extremes. Validity is equally good for civilian and military studies. Hunter & Hunter (1984) calculate a new *meta-analysis* (pooling the results of a large number of separate researches) for peer ratings, against three criteria:

supervisor ratings	0.49
training grades	0.36
promotion	0.49

In Hunter's & Hunter's review of *alternative tests* (alternative to ability tests), peer ratings are clearly superior to other alternatives: biodata, reference checks, college grades or interview. Hunter & Hunter place peer ratings third measures in order of suitability for promotion decisions, but don't list it as a predictor for initial selection. The *validity generalization analysis* of Schmitt et al (1984) (see Chapter 7), of 31 validity coefficients for supervisor/peer assessments, mostly of managers, found a mean validity of 0.43, the highest of any of eight classes of predictor.

Why are peer assessments such good predictors? Mumford (1983) discusses several theories:

(a) Friendship. Popular people get good peer evaluations and promotion. This is not necessarily mere bias, if making oneself liked is part of the job.

(b) Consensus. Traditional references rely on two or three opinions, where peer assessments use half a dozen or more. Multiple assessors cancel out each others' errors.

(c) No place to hide. In military research, the group is together, 24 hours a day, faced with all sorts of challenges—physical, mental, emotional—so they get to know each other very well, and can't keep anything hidden. Amir, Kovarsky & Sharan, (1970) argue peer assessments work, because soldiers know what's needed in an officer and because they know their own survival may one day depend on being led by the right person.

Usefulness

Peer assessment is very cheap. The selectors get between 10 and 100 expert opinions about each subject, entirely free. Peer assessments generally have good validity, sometimes very good. Peer assessment has two big disadvantages. It's unpopular, and it presupposes applicants spend long enough together to get to know each other really well, both of which effectively limit it to predicting promotability in uniformed, disciplined services. Kane & Lawler question whether peer assessments often add any *new* information; Hollander found peer nominations correlated very highly with pre-flight training grade, so they didn't contribute any unique variance. (No other study has considered this issue.)

In practice, peer assessments aren't used very widely, if at all, to make routine selection or promotion decisions. Probably no one really believes peer assessment will work if used, and *known to be used*, within an organization year in, year out. Hughes, Dunn & Baxter (1956) describe how a *biodata* completely lost its initial high validity in 3 years' field use, because candidates, with the connivance of field managers, 'bent' their answers to fit. The same fate might befall peer assessments if used routinely.

'FAIRNESS' AND THE LAW

Defamation and privacy

Employers often assume references and ratings aren't covered by the usual law of libel. This isn't necessarily true, although surveys show few American employers have faced litigation over references. Nevertheless, many play safe, and restrict themselves to saying the person was employed by them from time A to time B, without offering opinions of any sort. Unstructured references allow a skilful writer to 'damn with faint praise', and an experienced recipient to 'read between the lines'—so long as they both speak the same private language. In the USA, the Buckley Amendment gives post-secondary students the right to see what referees have written about them. As a consequence, either selectors require students to sign statements relinquishing their rights under the Act, or referees write bland, unhelpful references (Shaffer, Mays & Etheridge, 1976).

Selectors in the USA now face *negligent hiring claims* (Ryan & Lasek, 1991) if an employee attacks a customer. In theory, a good reference check could help identify such risks, so long as it isn't defamatory.

Fairness

The reference is legally a 'test', which can differentially exclude minorities, and so be challenged. In the case of *EEOC* v *National Academy of Sciences* a non-white female refused a job on the basis of a bad reference claimed the reference check had adverse impact on non-whites and wasn't job-related. Both claims were dismissed. In *Rutherford* v *American Bank of Commerce*, a reference that mentioned the employee had filed a charge of sex discrimination was ruled unlawful.

Peer ratings haven't been legally challenged as a selection test. Peer assessments demonstrated some racial bias in earlier research (Cox & Krumboltz, 1958), in which Black and White alike rated their own race higher. A later study by Schmidt & Johnson (1973) found no racial bias in peer ratings—but then, as Kane & Lawler point out, the data of Schmidt & Johnson data were collected during a programme to improve race relations. Bias in peer assessment is small enough to have little practical significance, and can probably be removed by training (Mumford, 1983).

SUMMARY

References are traditionally dismissed by occupational psychologists, even though there hasn't been all that much research on them. Most research that has been reported finds references are unreliable, and have little or no validity.

However, some British research reaches different conclusions. References can be useful if the referee is careful, and concerned for his/her future credibility. A composite of six references, in place of the usual two, may be more reliable. References 'digested' by a panel may be more useful. (But the British research that supports these more optimistic conclusions is limited, sketchily reported, many years old, and in urgent need of replication.)

Peer ratings by contrast have consistently very high validity—in a very limited setting. Peer assessments are only feasible where the candidates already know each other well, and where the assessor has considerable power over them. Even then, peer assessments are rarely used 'for real'. However, peer assessments prove the principle behind references is sound: people who know the candidate can describe him/her well. There is information to be gained, if selectors can go about it the right way.

6 Weighted Application Blanks and Biodata

"Did you ever build a model airplane that flew?"

Over 60 years ago, Goldsmith (1922) devised an ingenious new solution to an old problem: selecting people who could endure selling life insurance. He took 50 good, 50 poor and 50 middling salesmen from a larger sample of 502, and analysed their application forms. Age, marital status, education, (current) occupation, previous experience (of selling insurance), belonging to clubs, whether the candidate was applying for full- or part-time selling, whether the candidate himself had life insurance, and *whether* (not *what*) candidate replied to question "What amount of insurance are you confident of placing each month?", collectively distinguished good from average and average from bad. Binary items—married/single—were scored +1/-1. Scoring age was more complicated:

    -2 for 18–20
    -1 for 21–22
     0 for 23–24
    +1 for 25–27
    +2 for 28–29
    +3 for 30–40
    +1 for 41–50
     0 for 51–60
     1 for over 60

Education was scored in the same asymmetric curvilinear way: 8 years scores +1, through 12 years scores +3, down to 16 years scores +2. Low scorers in Goldsmith's sample almost all failed as insurance salesmen; the small minority of high scorers formed half of a slightly larger minority who succeeded at selling life insurance (Figure 6.1).

Goldsmith had turned the conventional application form into a Weighted Application Blank (WAB). (The idea was first mooted as long ago as 1894.) The WAB works on the principle "the best predictor of future behaviour is past

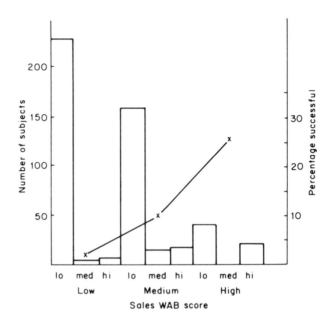

Figure 6.1 The first published Weighted Application Blank (WAB) (Goldsmith, 1922). The proportion of successful life insurance salesmen is much higher in high scoring applicants

behaviour", and the easiest way of measuring past behaviour is what the applicant writes on his/her application form. The principle is familiar to anyone with motor insurance. The insurance company knows from experience what sort of person has more accidents, and charges them higher premiums. People who drive sports cars, people who live in London, people who run bars—all are poorer risks. Insurers don't rely on common sense, which might well convince them that young drivers, with faster reflexes, will be safer; they rely on experience, which shows young drivers by and large are a menace. If insurers can calculate premiums from occupation, age and address, perhaps personnel managers can use application forms as a convenient but very powerful way of selecting employees. Viteles (1932) devised a seven-item WAB for taxi drivers, which rejected 60% of the poorest drivers, while rejecting only 22% of the best, *after* they had been screened by mental ability tests.

By end of the 1930s the WAB technique was well developed; ready-made tables had been drawn up for WAB construction. Table 6.1 illustrates one of 88 WAB items from Mitchell & Klimoski's (1982) study of trainee realtors (estate agents). Columns 1 and 2 show successful realtors are more likely to own their own home, and less likely to rent a flat or live with relatives. Column 3

Table 6.1   A sample WAB item, from Mitchell & Klimoski (1982)

Do you:	Licensed %	Unlicensed %	Difference	Weight
Own your own home?	81	60	21	5
Rent home?	3	5	-2	-1
Rent apartment?	9	25	-16	-4
Live with relatives?	5	10	-5	-2

compares the percentages. Column 4 assigns a scoring weight, from Strong's (1926) Tables; larger percentage differences get higher weights. The 'home' item weight is added to the weights from 87 other items, and a cut-off point chosen to maximize efficiency of selection. Finally the WAB is *cross-validated* on a second *hold-out* sample. A WAB derived from sample A will usually *shrink* when used on sample B, because some items 'predict' within sample A by chance, and don't work for sample B.

Construction of WAB is entirely empirical, *mindlessly* empirical in the eyes of its critics: "The procedure is raw empiricism in the extreme, the 'score' is the most heterogeneous value imaginable, representing a highly complex and usually unravelled network of information" (Guion, 1965b). It doesn't matter *why* an item differentiates successful estate agents from unsuccessful—only that it *does*. (Although one might argue an estate agent who hasn't succeeded in buying his/her own house can't be very good at his/her job.)

Some WAB items are familiar to personnel managers: (absence of) 'job-hopping', being born locally, being referred by existing employee, owning a home, being married, belonging to clubs and organizations, playing sports or physical games. Others are less obvious—coming from rural or small town home; some make sense when you know they work, but need a very devious mind to predict—"doesn't want a relative contacted in case of emergency", as a predictor of employee theft; some are bizarre—no middle initial given (employee theft again). Physique often gets included; scoring systems usually prefer average height and weight to extremes.

Department store staff and clerical turnover

The classic WAB was often used to select department store staff. Mosel (1952) compared the best and worst saleswomen in a large department store, and found the ideal saleswoman was: between 35 and 54 years old, had 13—16 years formal education, had over 5 years' selling experience, weighed over 160 pounds, had worked on her *next to last* job for *under* 5 years, lived in a boarding house, had worked on her *last* job for *over* 5 years, had her principal previous experience as a 'minor executive', was between 4'11" and 5'2" high, had between one and three dependants, was widowed, and had lost no time from work during the last 2 years (in order of predictive validity). It's particularly difficult to explain why the ideal saleswoman stayed a long time in her *last* job but left her *next to last* job more quickly.

Weighted Application Blanks are also often used to predict clerical turnover. Buel (1964) compared female clerks who left within 9 months with those who stayed longer, to find 16 differentiating items. Buel cross-validated his blank on two hold-out samples, and found a high correlation. Soon after, the company moved from city centre to suburb, which meant many more clerks were needed, and also that three of the 16 items ceased to be relevant. The WAB still achieved a reasonable validity.

Pea-canners and oil company executives

Weighted Application Blanks have been used for very humble jobs. The Green Giant Co. found its seasonal pea- and corn-canners often inexplicably left within a few days of starting work, causing the company great inconvenience and expense. Dunnette & Maetzold (1955) devised a WAB to reduce turnover: "the typically stable Green Giant production worker lives [locally], has a telephone, is married and has no children, is not a veteran [not an ex-serviceman], is either young (under 25) or old (over 55), weighs more than 150 pounds but less than 175, has obtained more than ten years education, has worked for Green Giant, will be available for work until the end of summer, and prefers field work to inside work". The WAB was only used for male applicants; female employees didn't present a turnover problem.

This profile retained its predictive validity over three successive years, and into three other Green Giant canning factories, but it didn't work for non-seasonal cannery workers. Scott & Johnson (1967) found permanent workers' turnover predicted by the regression equation:

$$\text{Tenure} = 0.30\,(\text{age}) + 8.82\,(\text{sex}) - 0.69\,(\text{miles from plant}) + 5.29\,(\text{type of residence}) + 2.66\,(\text{children}) + 1.08\,(\text{years on last job}) - 1.99$$

where female = 1; male = 0; living with parents, or in a room (bedsit) = 0; living in own home = 1.

Permanent cannery workers who stay the course have family and domestic responsibilities (and tend to be women), whereas the profile for seasonal workers identifies young college students, or semi-retired people, both wanting a short-term job.

At the other extreme, Laurent (1962) used a biographical survey to predict managerial success in Standard Oil of New Jersey. The survey was double checked, and any item that reflected age or experience, not effectiveness, eliminated. Successful executives were good in college, pursue leadership opportunities, and see themselves as forceful, dominant, assertive and strong.

Military WABs

In selection of pilots in the Second World War, a single biographical question turned out to predict success almost as well as all the elaborate batteries put together: 'Did you ever build a model airplane that flew?' The US Navy presently uses a very short WAB, combined with tests of mental ability, to select recruits (Sands, 1978; Booth, McNally & Berry, 1978). The Navy WAB covers only: years' schooling completed, expulsions or suspensions from school, age at enlistment, and existence of 'primary dependents'. Using a huge sample (N = 68,616), the researchers calculated an *odds for effectiveness* (OFE) table, which allows recruiting office staff to read off 'survival' probability of applicants with particular combinations of age, dependents, education and ability.

Large sample size helps US Navy researchers find an apparently genuine interaction between age at enlistment and education. Men with 12 or more years education were equally successful whether aged over or under 19, whereas less well-educated men were more successful if aged 19 or over, which implies poorly educated 17- and 18-year-olds should be asked to come back when they're 19 (Hoiberg & Pugh, 1978). One of the few recorded examples of WAB technology in Britain is a set of four, keyed to different criteria, used to select naval officers (Drakeley, Herriott & Jones, 1988).

BIODATA

The classic WAB is invisible, and unfakeable. It's invisible because the applicant expects to complete an application blank. It's unfakeable because most of the items could be verified independently, if the employer could afford the time and expense. (Some can: it's called *positive vetting*.) The classic WAB has tended to be supplanted since the 1960s, by *biodata*, a.k.a. *Biographical Inventory*. Biodata uses questionnaire format with multiple choice answers:

How old was your father when you were born?

1. About 20.
2. About 25.
3. About 30.
4. About 35.
5. I don't know.

Biodata items divide into 'hard', which are verifiable but also often intrusive, and 'soft' which cause less offence but are easier to fake. Mael (1991) notes some items are *controllable*, while others aren't; one chooses one's hobbies but not one's parents' social class. Biodata in the US public sector and military tend to avoid non-controllable items, as making the biodata harder to defend against criticism. Kleiman & Faley (1990) find that items asking about present behaviour prove as successful as items asking about past behaviour, and suggest they will prove more acceptable.

Biodata items have been derived from a number of sources. Russell et al (1990) use *retrospective life experience essays*, in which Naval Academy students describe a group effort, an accomplishment at school, a disappointment and a stressful event. Miner (1971) stated specific hypotheses about 'eliteness motivation', e. g. that status-conscious Americans will serve (as officers of course) in the Navy or Air Force, but not in the Army. Many studies use the *Catalog of Life History Items* by Glennon, Albright and Owens (1963), which lists 484 biographical items. The questionnaire format of biodata loses the invisibility of the WAB. Smith et al (1961) used the *Catalog* to predict research creativity in scientists (using supervisor ratings and patentable ideas as criteria). On cross-validation, the 22 item Biographical Inventory of Research and Scientific Talent achieved good validity for both criteria. Umeda & Frey (1974) used the *Catalog* to try to construct a biodata predictor for ministers of religion. They were unusually *un*successful; only two items had predictive value: ministers who 'heard the call' later in life were more successful, and ministers who supported themselves as theology students were more successful. Miner (1971) reports successful management consultants show 'eliteness motivation' in their biography: small private school, small private college, prestige business school, Navy or Air Force but not Army, commissioned rank, and better off or better educated than father.

Biodata have been used successfully to predict success as sales/research engineer, oil industry research scientist, pharmaceutical industry researcher, bus driver, custodial officer and police officer (Reilly & Chao, 1982). Schmitt et al (1984) found biodata used for professional, clerical, sales, skilled labour and unskilled labour. Biodata were used most frequently for selecting sales staff, least often for managerial occupations.

Rational or empirical construction?

Purely empirical WABs offend psychologists who like to feel they have a theory. They aren't happy knowing canary breeders make dishonest employees; they want to know *why*. Ideally they want to *predict* that canary breeders will make dishonest employees. Critics of pure empiricism also argue a WAB with a foundation of theory is more likely to hold up over time, and across different employers. The *rational* school of WAB construction doesn't go in for very elaborate theories. Indeed, by the standards of personality research, their efforts too are mindless empiricism, for they generally rely on correlation and factor analysis to discover structure in biographical information. They "attempt to quantify composites of items that measure an interpretable set of constructs", and to discover "psychologically meaningful personal history variables" (Mitchell & Klimoski, 1982).

Matteson (1978) proposed item analysis of biographical data to find sets of closely related facts; his target was a group of four items homogeneous in item content and highly correlated. Analysis of 75 items in successful and unsuccessful applicants for oil refinery maintenance and construction work produced 12 keys. Each key contains at least six items, so scores are more reliable, and less likely to capitalize on chance. Matteson predicts such keys will suffer less *shrinkage* and be more *transportable*.

Owens takes this idea a stage further, and uses biodata to *classify* people. Scores on his Biographical Questionnaire are factor-analysed, yielding 13 factors for men and 15 for women. The factor scores are then cluster-analysed (Note 2 in Chapter 3), to group people with common patterns of prior experience (Owens & Schoenfeldt, 1979). Different sub-groups had different profiles on mental ability, personality, and interest tests (which *hadn't* been used in the cluster analysis). For example, the group of female *active, conventional social leaders*, who score high on biodata factors of *social leadership* and *athletic participation*, but low on *negative emotions*, also scored high on tendermindedness, social–religious conformity, interest in physical goals, extraversion, and the *social service* and *sales–managerial* scales of the Strong Interest Inventory (SII), but low on its human and hard science interests.

Brush & Owens (1979) classified oil company employees into 18 subgroups, and then compared unskilled employees in *bio-group* 5 (higher *personal values* and very high *trade skills, interest* and *experience*) with those in bio-group 6 (low on *family relationships* and very low on *achievement motivation, self confidence* and *personal values*). Bio-group 5 members had lower termination rates, which implies the company could reduce turnover by selecting bio-group 5 subjects, and rejecting bio-group 6. Owens (1976) describes similar unpublished studies on salesmen and oil company executives: Taylor found most salesmen came from only three (of nine) biodata groups (one-time *college athletes, college politicians* and *hard workers*); Pinto found biodata group membership predicted survival as a salesman in two large samples, with astonishing power (0.66). Owens (1976) suggests biodata groups could be used for selection, classification and career counselling.

Mitchell & Klimoski (1982) compare predictive validity of *rationally* and *empirically* constructed biodata inventories. The rational inventory factoranalysed rating format items "Own your own home/Rent home/Rent apartment/Live with relative", to yield six factors, for example:

> *Economic establishment*: financially established and secure, most likely married, tending to be older, active in community and civic affairs, socially ascendant,

professional knowledge and contacts beyond what would be expected in a younger person.

The empirical inventory used classic WAB methodology, scoring the items by Strong's (1926) Tables, and summing the weights from all 87 items to give a single index. Mitchell & Klimoski predicted that empirical biodata will give better results with the original sample, but will cross-validate less well. Their predictions were correct, up to a point:

1 The empirical measure gives much better results on the original sample.
2 The rational measure doesn't shrink at all.
3 But the empirical measure still gives better results on the cross-validation sample, even after shrinkage.

Most modern researches use a mixture of classic WAB and biodata. They're also generally much more reticent about item content, so it's often unclear how much of each they include. (Early studies published their WABs in full, presumably quite confident that pea-canners or shop assistants didn't read *Journal of Applied Psychology*, and couldn't discover the right answers to give.) The success of the classic WAB depends on the general public never suspecting application forms have any but the usual bureaucratic purpose.

The fine distinction between biodata and personality inventory

Many 'biographical' items look remarkably like personality inventory items. What is the conceptual difference between personality inventory questions, like those listed in Chapter 8, and biodata questions?

1. Biodata questions allow a *definite* answer, whereas personality questions often don't. Most biodata questions could be answered by someone who knows the respondent well. Most biodata questions could be argued about sensibly, which many personality questions can't be.

2. Personality inventory questions are *carefully phrased*, to elicit a rapid, unthinking reply, whereas biodata items often sound quite clumsy in their desire to specify precisely the information they want, for example:

    With regard to personal appearance, as compared with the appearance of my friends, I think that:

    (a) Most of my friends make a better appearance.
    (b) I am equal to most of them in appearance.
    (c) I am better than most of them in appearance.
    (d) I don't feel strongly one way or the other.

In a personality inventory this would read more like:

"I am fairly happy about the way I look   TRUE   FALSE."

3. Personality inventories have *fixed keys*, whereas biodata items are re-keyed for each selection task. [However, just to confuse the issue, the American insurance industry's *Aptitude Index Battery* has included questions from personality inventories, empirically keyed like WAB items. Personality questions lost their validity faster than biographical questions (Thayer, 1977).]

The distinction between personality inventory and biodata inventory is often so fine that one wonders if the choice of title reflects the authors' outlook, or their perception of what's acceptable in their organization, not a real difference.

In Britain, WABs and biodata aren't used much. Robertson & Makin's (1986) survey found 5% of major British employers using biodata for selection. The (UK) Civil Service Commission are writing a biodata inventory for Income Tax inspectors. British Airways use one for cabin crew. Source documents, like the Glennon et al *Catalog* of biodata items, are virtually unobtainable in Britain.

VALIDITY

It's vital to distinguish between the *original* sample, on which WAB or biodata inventory is constructed, and *cross-validation* or *hold-out* samples. Validity can only be calculated from the *cross-validation* sample. A WAB or biodata inventory that hasn't been cross-validated shouldn't be used for selection. Cureton (1950) calls un-cross-validated coefficients "baloney coefficients". Biodata and WABs are particularly likely to shrink on cross-validation, because they are purely empirical, not to say arbitrary, and can easily capitalize on chance differences between the original samples. Several studies report validity shrinks so fast the inventory ceases to have any predictive validity within a few years, and it has to be re-written, with new scoring weights (Roach, 1971).

Several reviews of WAB and biodata validity have reported impressively good results. Dunnette's (1972) meta-analysis of biographical inventories reported validity (0.34), comparable with perceptual speed and psychomotor tests, but not quite as good as general intelligence tests, job knowledge tests or job tryouts. Owens (1976) summarized 72 studies and found biodata had good predictive validity for success in selling (mostly insurance), high level talent or creativity, and credit risk. Muchinsky & Tuttle (1979) review 16 studies using WABs or biodata to predict turnover, and found significant, cross-validated results in most cases, for a range of occupations: sales assistants, route salesmen, professional workers clerical workers, and Dunnette's pea-pickers. Guion & Gottier (1965) found 'personal history data' had consistently better validity than personality inventories, and had usually been cross-validated (unlike personality inventories).

Reilly & Chao (1982) reviewed published and unpublished American research, and found Biographical Inventories the best alternative predictor, with an average validity of 0.38. Table 6.2 shows the effectiveness of biodata in predicting five criteria, for six classes of occupation. Biodata are particularly effective in predicting clerical tenure. (The value of 0.62 for Sales × Productivity derives from only one study, with a small sample.)

Vineberg & Joyner's (1982) review of military research found WABs predicted global ratings of performance fairly poorly and predicted ratings of suitability only a little better. Hunter & Hunter (1984) argue that 'suitability' may really mean the applicant's 'face fits', which might or might not indicate he/she is more effective. Schmitt et al (1984) review research published between 1964 and 1982, covering some of the same ground as Reilly & Chao. The weighted average of 99 validity coefficients was 0.24, definitely poorer than assessment centres, work samples, peer ratings, but definitely better than personality inventories. Biodata were used to predict:

performance ratings	0.32
turnover	0.21
achievement/grades	0.23
status change	0.33
wages	0.53
productivity	0.20

The high correlation with wages, based on seven samples and 1544 subjects, is unexplained.

Hunter & Hunter (1984) review biodata research, using *validity generalization analysis* to arrive at a single estimate of biodata validity, based on pooled samples of 4000–10 000, for four criteria:

supervisor ratings	0.37
promotion	0.26
training success	0.30
tenure	0.26

(*Validity generalization analysis* corrects for restriction of range, criterion reliability and sampling error, to give an estimate of the best the measure can achieve. Chapter 7 gives fuller details.) Note that WABs predicted supervisor ratings better than training grades, a reversal of the usual pattern. In Hunter's & Hunter's final league table of selection methods, biodata came third, after ability tests and job tryouts. However Hunter & Hunter only included 12 validity coefficients in their analysis. Mael & Schwartz (1991) devised a

Table 6.2 Summary of validity for biodata (Reilly & Chao, 1982) (Reproduced by permission)

Occupation	Criteria					
	Tenure	Training	Ratings	Productivity	Salary	Average for Occupation
Military	.30(3;4684)	.39(3;569)	.25(3;990)	NA	NA	.30(9;6243)
Clerical	.52(6;553)	NA	NA	NA	NA	.52(6;553)
Management	NA	NA	.40(4;2504)	NA	.23(3;320)	.38(7;2824)
Other non-management	.14(2;327)	NA	NA	NA	NA	.14(2;327)
Sales	NA	NA	.40(4;146)	.62(1;98)	NA	.50(5;244)
Scientific/engineering	.50(2;157)	NA	.32(4;360)	.43(5;563)	.43(4;360)	.41(15;1440)
Average for criteria	.32(13;5721)	.39(3;569)	.36(15;4000)	.46(6;661)	.34(7;680)	.35(44;11 631)

Note—The number of coefficients and total sample size are shown in parentheses.

biodata keyed to the US military's new personality inventory, Assessment of Background and Life Experience (ABLE), and find the biodata achieves *incremental validity* over ABLE and mental ability tests, in predicting leadership ratings.

Validity generalization and transportability

Validity isn't the only criterion of a good selection test; *cost* and *practicality* matter too. A test that can be introduced ready made into any selection procedure is cheaper and more practical than one that has to be specially written, or re-written, for every new employer. Ability tests (Chapter 7) are *transportable* or *generalizable*, as well as being good predictors of productivity. Biodata and WABs aren't so versatile. An unpublished study by Kirkpatrick (Owens, 1976) re-tested Chamber of Commerce managers after 5 years, using a different criterion, and found the WAB keys held up well. Laurent (1970) found that a biodata inventory that predicted managerial effectiveness in New Jersey travelled to Norway, Denmark and The Netherlands, survived translation, and still retained good predictive validity. (Translating biodata inventories can be difficult; education systems differ from country to country, so "How many O levels did you pass?" means nothing outside Britain.) Other research finds WABs and biodata *don't* 'travel well'; they tend to be specific to the organization they were developed in. They tend even to be specific to the criterion they were developed against; a WAB that predicts supervisor ratings doesn't predict tenure, and vice versa (Tucker, Cline & Schmitt, 1967).

The best data on transportability comes from the *Aptitude Index Battery* (AIB), a biodata inventory used by the North American insurance industry. Brown (1981) analysed AIB data, for 12 453 insurance salesmen from 12 large US life insurance companies. A *validity generalization analysis* showed the AIB's mean true validity coefficient was 0.26, and that 62% of the variation between validity in the 12 companies could be accounted for by sources of error—differences in range restriction, sample size and criterion reliability. This means (a) AIB was valid for all 12 insurance companies, but also (b) that it is genuinely more valid for some than for others. Brown divided the companies into group A, who recruited through press adverts and agencies, and group B who recruited by personal contacts. Group B had higher average production levels, and selected more people with high AIB scores. Brown compared AIB validities in the two groups, and found it higher for group B companies.

Rothstein et al (1990) hypothesize that biodata don't travel well because they are usually keyed inside one single organization, making them too parochial. The *Supervisory Profile Record* (SPR) derives from no less than 39 organizations, and proves to have highly generalizable validity, being unaffected by organization, sex, race, supervisory experience, social class or education. The SPR achieved a mean *true validity* of 0.29. However, the same analysis finds the SPR correlates 0.50 with mental ability tests, and gives only slight incremental validity on MA tests alone. A new US Federal Government selection battery for college graduate entrants includes biodata, and finds its validity generalizes well across different occupations and government agencies (Gandy et al, 1989).

Biodata sometimes lose predictive power because they're misused. Hughes, Dunn & Baxter (1956) wrote a new form of AIB which worked well while it was still experimental, but lost its validity as soon as it was used for actual hiring (Figure 6.2). Field managers scored the forms and were supposed to use them to reject unsuitable applicants; instead they guided favoured applicants into giving the 'right' answers. In 1954, far more applicants reported they owned $7000 life insurance, $7000 'just happening' to be the border between one and two points. Since 1969, field managers have only been told if applicants pass or fail AIB, to prevent them 'stretching a point' for favoured borderline candidates. Clearly the scoring of any WAB must be kept secret. But if WABs risk losing their predictive power once their very existence gets known, they could never be used on a really large scale, for example to screen out unsuitable applicants for driving licences.

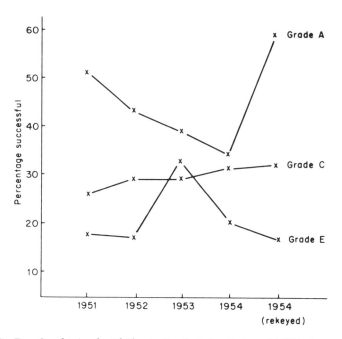

Figure 6.2 Results obtained with the Aptitude Index Battery (AIB) between 1951 and 1954. High and low grades converge, as the test's scoring is "leaked". Predictive validity is regained, and the grades diverge again, when the AIB is re-keyed in 1954. Data from Hughes, Dunn and Baxter (1956)

Validity of specific cues

Early WAB research occasionally gave some very contradictory results. Owning one's own home is generally a 'good' sign, but wasn't for Mosel's shop saleswomen, where the most efficient lived in boarding houses. Are there any biographical pointers that have fairly general predictive validity?

Experience . Although experience has very moderate predictive validity for supervisor ratings, it has zero validity for training grades (Hunter & Hunter, 1984). Arvey, McGowan & Horgan (1981) review half a dozen studies, and conclude there's little evidence experience predicts productivity. General experience, in supervising people, or selling, has no predictive validity. Research on air-traffic controllers finds experience was only useful when it's directly and specifically relevant; having used a radio or flown an aircraft doesn't predict efficiency as an air-traffic controller, but experience of instrument flying does.

Seniority. How long the person has been working there, is often used to decide who gets promoted: 'Buggins's turn'. Unions, in Britain and America, often insist it should be the sole criterion. Seniority almost always plays a big part in deciding who is 'released' when the workforce has to be reduced: "Last in first out". There's no reason to expect seniority to be related to efficiency, and not much research on the link; Gordon & Fitzgibbons (1982) find seniority quite unrelated to efficiency in female sewing machine operators.

Age. Hunter & Hunter reviewed over 500 validity coefficients, and found age alone has zero validity as a predictor, whether the criterion is supervisor rating or training grade. Age does predict turnover; younger employees are more likely to leave (Muchinsky & Tuttle, 1979). Age can distort WAB/biodata scoring; older people tend to have more dependants and higher living expenses, and to belong to more organizations than younger people (Thayer, 1977), so a WAB/biodata using age-related items for subjects with diverse ages could give misleading results. Some tests, including AIB, have different norms for different ages. Hunter & Hunter note that age does predict 'survival' in US Navy recruits. Vineberg & Joyner (1982) confirm that age predicts performance ratings and suitability ratings, in the US armed services. These military data obviously cover a very narrow age range.

Consortium WABS

Biodata and WABs suffer 'decay of validity' over time, and need revising every few years. They also need very large samples—preferably 400–1000. They haven't in the past proved transportable from one organization to another, or even from part of a single organization to another part. These problems are interlinked; any test devised on a small sample is less likely to work somewhere else. The answer for organizations that don't employ vast numbers is the *consortium WAB/biodata*.

The AIB has been used by the (US) Life Insurance Marketing & Research Association since the 1930s, and dates in part back to 1919 (Thayer, 1977). It is a composite measure: biographical items, including dependants, employment history, educational level, financial status, membership of organizations, etc., as well as personality and interest items. It is now called the *Career Profile System*. Figure 6.3 shows success closely related to AIB score, and also shows how few succeed in insurance, even from the highest score bands (Brown, 1979). The AIB predicts failure very well (Thayer, 1977); low scorers rarely succeed. It predicts success less well; many high scorers nevertheless fail to survive. Figure 6.4 shows schematically the distribution of AIB scores against the composite survival and sales criterion. Essentially, the AIB is a screening test, that eliminates potential failures but doesn't necessarily identify successes. It has been re-written and re-scored a dozen times, but retains some continuity. Brown (1978) claims the 1933 keys still worked in 1969, showing the AIB's validity doesn't decay over time; Hunter & Hunter (1984) disagree and say validity of the 1933 key had shrunk badly by 1939, and had virtually vanished by 1969.

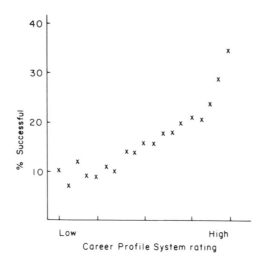

Figure 6.3 Predictive validity of the Career Profile System (CPS), the successor to Aptitude Index Battery (AIB), showing that the higher the CPS score, the greater the proportion of applicants who 'survive'. Data from Thayer (1977)

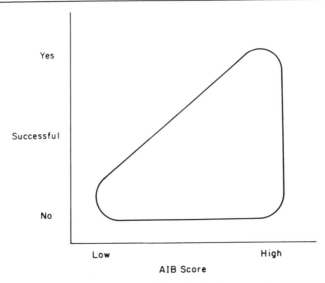

Figure 6.4 Schematic representation of the relation between Aptitude Index Battery (AIB) score and success in selling insurance. A low score means the applicant will fail, but a high score doesn't mean he/she will necessarily succeed

Fakeability

A lot of psychologists tend to grow restless when fakeability of measures is discussed, either because they object to the assumption that people don't tell the truth or perhaps because they don't like to admit most selectors in the last analysis can't do very much about being lied to. Faking *does* matter. Computer programmers have a saying "Garbage In—Garbage Out": if the information going in one end of a selection process is incorrect, the decision coming out the other end hasn't much chance of being accurate.

The traditional WAB can only be faked if the subject deliberately lies. Research gives conflicting accounts of how often people do this. Keating, Patterson & Stone (1950) report near perfect correlations between what applicant and previous employer said. On the other hand, Goldstein (1971) checked information given by applicants for a nursing aide post against what previous employers said, and found major discrepancies. Half the sample overestimated how long they had worked for their previous employer. Overstating previous salary, and describing part-time work as full time were also common. More seriously, a quarter gave reasons for leaving their last job that the employer didn't agree with, and no less than 17% listed as their last employer someone who denied ever having employed them. Moore (1942) noted that recruits to US Army during the First World War gave very unreliable accounts of their skills. Only 6% who claimed a trade really knew it, while 30% + were totally inexperienced in "trade bluffers". Owens (1976) is right to say more research is needed on the accuracy of WAB and biodata information.

Biodata inventories are more like personality inventories. They can be deliberately faked—sometimes called *gross faking*. They can suffer from the natural desire of subjects to present themselves in a favourable light—*social desirability*. Klein & Owens (1965) studied fakeability of biodata used to predict research creativity, and found students could double their chance of 'passing' one key, and increase their pass rate on a second. However, subjects *instructed* to fake good distort their answers far more than job applicants (Becker & Colquitt, 1992), so the deliberate faking experiment isn't a good model to use. Schrader & Osburn (1977) told half their subjects the inventory included a lie-detection scale (which it didn't). Subjects improved their scores in both conditions, but faked less when warned there was a lie scale. An unpublished study by Larsen (Owens, 1976) found answers to questions about past behaviour less fakeable than self-evaluations. Becker & Colquitt (1992) report that only three items, of 25, were answered differently by job applicants; these items were less historical, objective and verifiable.

Kluger, Reilly & Russell (1991) reports that subjects pretending to be job applicants give socially desirable responses to biodata, creating a large shift in their scores, when a simple linear scoring system is used, but not when more complex scoring systems are used. Of 184 items used to select police officers (Cascio, 1975), 17 were verifiable, of which only two showed a substantial discrepancy: age when first married and number of full-time jobs held prior to the present. Shaffer, Saunders & Owens (1986) compared items on Owen's Biographical Questionnaire with a parallel questionnaire completed by the subjects' parents.

'FAIRNESS' AND THE LAW

Rosenbaum (1976) found one predictor of employee theft that he didn't have much hesitation in not using—being non-white. Other ways of discriminating against protected groups are subtler; having a Detroit (city centre, as opposed to suburban) address distinguishes thieves from non-thieves (Pace & Schoenfeldt, 1977), but also tends to distinguish white from non-white, much as a Brixton or Handsworth address might in Britain. An early biodata for predicting administrative ability in scientists (Travers, 1951) appeared to show its *absence* went with a big city, retail merchant family background; on closer inspection it turned out the criterion ratings were biased by anti-semitism, so the biodata was actually distinguishing Jewish from other scientists.

If WAB/biodata items are linked to race, sex or age, they may exclude these protected minorities disproportionately, and give rise to claims of *adverse impact* (Chapter 12). However, biodata studies reviewed by Reilly & Chao didn't by and large create adverse impact for ethnic minorities. No adverse impact was found in studies of bus drivers, clerical staff, army recruits, supervisors. Scores on a biodata inventory of creativity were completely uncorrelated with race (Owens, 1976). Cascio (1976) found a WAB predicted turnover in white and non-white female clerical workers equally accurately. The combination of Supervisory Profile Record and MA test, while predicting only slightly better than the MA tests alone, creates less adverse impact (Rothstein et al, 1990).

While biodata inventories seem more or less colour blind, they do sometimes distinguish male and female. Biodata for US Navy recruits need different predictors for male and female (Sands, 1978). Nevo (1976) found different predictors were needed to predict male and female promotion in the Israeli army. The American insurance industry's AIB can be used for male and female, but has to be scored differently. On the other hand, Ritchie & Boehm (1977) developed a biodata inventory for AT&T managers, which achieved equally good cross-validity for women and men; Ritchie & Boehm conclude "the same kinds of experiences and interests that characterise successful managers of one sex are also predictive of success for the other".

If a selection procedure does create *adverse impact*, the employer must prove it's a valid predictor of effective performance. Pace & Schoenfeldt (1977) suggest WABs/biodata are necessarily valid, "since they are in fact derived in such a way as to assure it". A cross-validated WAB necessarily has *predictive* validity. But WABs and biodata often lack *face* validity; they look arbitrary, so a good lawyer will have a field-day asking the employer to explain the connection between not using a middle initial and theft. Robertson & Smith (1989) found applicants greatly disliked biodata inventories, and thought them both inaccurate and unfair, which suggests strongly biodata measures are much more likely to be challenged than, for example, interviews.

As a whole, WABs/biodata inventories don't seem to create too much adverse impact—but many of their component items are likely to prove inherently objectionable to fair employment agencies: age (if over 40), arrest record, convictions, height and weight, marital status, home ownership, etc. The Equal Opportunities Commission in Britain doesn't approve of any requirement that "inhibits applicants from one sex or from married persons". Mitchell & Klimoski (1982) say

> Items such as age, sex, and marital status may in fact be challenged by the courts if such items are included in inventories for the purpose of personnel selection. In that event, whatever gains in predictive power to be derived through the inclusion of these items must be weighed against the possible expense of legal defense.

But if no one notices them, or realizes their purpose ...

Class. Social class pervades WAB and biodata questions: owns an automobile, owns own home, lives in suburbs, finished high school, persons/room ratio at home, father's occupation, mother's occupation, father's education, etc. Parental occupation, which appears in most WABs, is often used by researchers to *define* a person's social class. It's not against the law, even in the USA, to discriminate on grounds of social class. But it's potentially risky, for two reasons:

1. On both sides of the Atlantic being non-white tends to mean being poor, so indices of class are often also indices of race.
2. On both sides of the Atlantic, an enterprising journalist or politician could make considerable capital attacking a selection process that looks both capriciously arbitrary, and blatantly biased in favour of middle-class applicants.

CONCLUSIONS

Biodata inventories and WABs have a number of disadvantages. They don't seem to 'travel' all that well, certainly not as well as ability tests. This makes them expensive, because each employer has to write and validate their own WAB/biodata. Biodata/WABs haven't attracted a lot of criticism, but could prove hard to defend if claims of 'unfairness' were to be made.

On the other hand, WABs/biodata are cheaper than other custom made tests, for example work samples, because they're paper and pencil, and because employer's records can be used to provide instant validation *and* cross-validation.

Biodata/WABs can be faked, but a true WAB is hard to fake, because the information can be checked—at a price. A true WAB is also proof against faking because the applicant doesn't realize the test is a test. The true WAB is *invisible*. From another perspective, however, invisibility is a major weakness. The invisible WAB pre-supposes public ignorance of its very existence. What worked for pea-canners in rural America 30–40 years ago may not survive in an age of freedom of information and investigative journalism.

The biographical inventory has to be taken seriously, because it achieves consistently good results—but it's profoundly unsatisfactory in two, linked, respects. The distinction between biodata inventories and personality inventories is hard to discern (except that biodata inventories achieve better results). Most personality inventories reflect a *theory* of personality, whereas biodata inventories are almost completely atheoretical. Owens has made a start trying to understand biodata, but they mostly remain mindlessly empirical: a set of answers that can predict an outcome. No one knows why.

7 Tests of Mental Ability

"We know much less than we have proven"
[Glass, 1976]

This book is easier to write in 1993 than in 1978; this chapter would have been very depressing to write 15 years ago, and would have become hopelessly out of date very quickly. Fifteen years ago, most people, even many occupational psychologists, were inclined to write off tests of mental ability (MA) as having little or no value in predicting productivity. New research, and re-analysis of older research, has shown most people, and many occupational psychologists, were wrong.

OVERVIEW OF MENTAL ABILITY TESTS

In the 90 years since the first tests of MA appeared, they have diversified into a number of forms, used for different purposes, and reflecting different approaches. Children and the mentally disturbed are tested *individually*; selectors usually test people in *groups*. US psychologists favour *multiple aptitude batteries*, sets of six to 12 tests that yield a profile of abilities; British psychologists traditionally prefer tests of *general intelligence* or *general mental ability*, which yield a single score. Some tests of general MA use mostly *verbal* items, while some use mostly *non-verbal* items—numerical, diagrammatic or abstract. Mental ability tests produce *raw scores*, which must be converted to *standard scores*; several systems are used:

(a) Mental age. This was used by the earliest MA tests; a person with a mental age of 5 does as well on the test as the typical 5-year-old. The mental age system only works for children, because mental growth tapers off after age 16.

(b) Intelligence quotient. The IQ was originally calculated by dividing mental age by actual (chronological) age, and multiplying by 100; this type of IQ is no longer used. IQ is now a standard score, in which mean is set at 100, and standard deviation at 15 (Figure 7.1).

(c) Percentiles (see Note 2, page 11). These are used by most MA tests, for example, Differential Aptitude Test, Progressive Matrices, Watson Glaser Critical Thinking Appraisal, and Graduate Managerial Assessment.

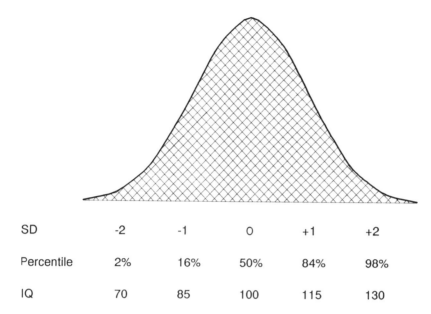

SD	-2	-1	0	+1	+2
Percentile	2%	16%	50%	84%	98%
IQ	70	85	100	115	130

Figure 7.1 The distribution of intelligence about a mean of 100, with SD of 15

Nowadays, IQs are avoided because they give a spurious impression of precision. No one thinks the difference between IQs of 117 and 118 amounts to much; but what about the difference between 115 and 120? A simple formula based on re-test reliability and standard deviation of test scores allows *error of measurement* to be calculated. An IQ test with a re-test reliability of 0.90 has an error of measurement of five IQ points, meaning one in three re-tests will vary by five *or more* points.

Differential aptitude batteries

As far back as 1928, Hull argued that profiles of specific abilities will predict work performance better than tests of general MA, since when American psychology has preferred multiple aptitude batteries. The earliest was Thurstone's Primary Mental Abilities, which measured seven separate mental abilities: verbal, reasoning, number, spatial, perceptual speed, memory, and word fluency. The most important aptitude battery is the General Aptitude Test Battery (GATB), which has been used by the US Employment Service (USES) for career placements since 1948. The GATB measures nine abilities with 12 tests (Table 7.1). It has a very large database; its manual (US Department of Labor, 1970) reports 515 validity studies on a very wide range of jobs.

Table 7.1 General Aptitude Test Battery, which measures nine abilities, using eight paper-and-pencil and four apparatus tests (Reproduced by permission of US Employment Service)

	Ability	Test
G	General	Vocabulary, 3D space, arithmetic reasoning
V	Verbal	Vocabulary
N	Numerical	Computation, arithmetic reasoning
S	Spatial	3D space
P	Form perception	Tool matching, form matching
Q	Clerical perception	Name comparison
K	Motor co-ordination	Mark making
F	Finger dexterity	Assemble, disassemble
M	Manual dexterity	Place, turn

Another widely used aptitude battery is the Differential Aptitude Test (DAT) which measures seven abilities: verbal reasoning, numerical ability, abstract reasoning, clerical speed and accuracy, mechanical reasoning, space relations, spelling and language usage. The US military has used several generations of aptitude battery: Army General Classification Test (AGCT), Army Classification Battery (ACB), Armed Forces Qualification Test (AFQT), and Armed Services Vocational Aptitude Battery (ASVAB). Guilford (1967) proposes a complex 120-factor model of mental abilities, which includes a range of *social intelligence* tests that look promising for personnel work, perhaps even for selecting selectors, but which aren't very widely used. Guilford's 120 factors also include tests of *divergent thinking*, or creativity.

Differential aptitude batteries can be difficult to interpret, because the difference between two scores contains *two* sources of error. Suppose a test produces verbal and numerical subscores, each with a reliability of 0.90; differences up to six or seven IQ points will be found in two out of three retests, and differences up to 12 or 14 in one in three. Some tests, e.g. DAT, use specially designed profile sheets that allow the significance of differences to be checked easily.

Aptitude tests and achievement tests

Most aptitude tests are paper-and-pencil tests but some require apparatus; some of those currently available include the General Clerical Test, Bennett Mechanical Comprehension Test (MCT), Engineering Selection Test Battery (UK), Computer Programmer Aptitude Battery, and Crawford Small Parts

Dexterity Tests (an apparatus test). Aptitude tests often correlate fairly highly with general MA tests; for example the Bennett MCT correlates around 0.60 with tests of general MA.

Aptitude tests measure what a person *could* learn, *achievement tests* what a person *has* learnt. (In practice, the distinction isn't always so clear.) British employers usually rely on professional qualifications, completed apprenticeships, or diplomas, but not achievement tests. In the USA, Short Occupational Knowledge Tests are available for a range of occupations: auto [motor] mechanic, electricians, machinists, plumbers, secretaries, etc. Achievement tests are also known as *job knowledge* or *trade* tests.

Computerised and biological testing

Everyone who completes Graduate and Managerial Assessment—Numerical has 30 minutes to answer the same 33 questions, whether they can't answer a single one, or whether they get them all right in 10 minutes [fairly unlikely—the graduate (college) normative data for 600 subjects includes no one who got all 33 right]. By contrast, computerized testing can be tailored to the individual's performance. If the subject does well, the questions get harder; if the subject does poorly, questions get easier, until the subject reaches his/her own limit. Individual tests, like the Binet, have always had this flexibility; if the cost of computers falls below the cost of testing time, it may become economic for group testing. The US Army has devised a Computerized Adaptive Screening Test which screens recruits in a third of the time, with a third of the items of the paper-and-pencil form (Sands & Gade, 1983). Computerization also makes scoring and interpretation of tests far faster, and far more detailed (Vale, Keller & Bentz, 1986). Early doubts about comparability of paper-and-pencil and computerized testing were soon laid to rest; for example, Silver & Bennett (1987) show computerized and paper forms of the Minnesota Clerical Test correlate as highly as the paper form correlates with itself.

Researches reported since the beginning of the 1980s claim that biological measures of MA correlate well with conventional paper-and-pencil tests. Biological measures include *averaged evoked potential* in the cerebral cortex, and speed of neural transmission in specific pathways. Biological measures have great promise (Matarazzo, 1992); they do not depend on the subject's motivation nor on what he/she has learned in the past.

THE VALIDITY OF MENTAL ABILITY TESTS

In 1918, Link published a validation study of munitions workers using a battery of nine MA tests. Some tests predicted hourly output well; the Woodworth Wells Cancellation Test correlated well (0.63) with a month's production figures for 52 shell inspectors. Link probably published the first validity coefficient. Since 1918, thousands of similar studies have been reported, for a vast range of occupations. Early validation research is summarized by Dorcus & Jones (1950), who give brief abstracts of 426 many and varied studies; research during the 1950s is reviewed by Super & Crites (1962).

However by the 1960s, disillusion with MA testing for personnel selection had begun to develop, through distrust of the very idea of individual differences in mental ability, and the apparent failure of tests to predict anything successfully. In 1969 Arthur Jensen published his *Harvard Educational Review* article "How Much Can We Boost IQ and Scholastic Achievement", which stated the evidence on heritability of MA more forcefully than people in the USA were used to, or cared for. The original researches were then read carefully, for the first time in years, and their defects noted. Burt's research on heritability proved not just badly done; substantial parts of it were fraudulent. Over-inclusive thinking then caused many people to assert all research on heritability was suspect, or even that MA tests in general had been discredited. Actually, just one of many studies of heritability of MA was invalid, and heritability has little relevance to the use of tests in selection.

Towards the end of the 1960s some critics (Mischel, 1968) began talking about the "0.30 barrier", arguing that tests never correlate at more than 0.30 with any outcome, because psychological tests are founded on a fundamentally incorrect model, of broad internal dispositions that don't really exist. If there isn't any such thing as 'intelligence' or 'personality', it isn't surprising that tests of either fail to predict very much.

The late 1960s also saw the birth of the notion of 'competencies', as an alternative to tests of MA. McClelland (1973) argued MA tests didn't predict occupational success, and were unfair on minorities. Neither claim is correct, but both were widely cited in the media, and in introductory psychology texts (Barrett & Depinet, 1991). A 'competency' is "a motive, skill, aspect of one's self-image or social role, or a body of knowledge". McClelland proposed assessing them by a variation of *critical incident technique*, in which people describe three incidents when they felt particularly effective, and three when they felt especially ineffective. Competency testing hasn't developed from a vague feeling of 'we ought to be doing something different' into a usable method of assessing something that predicts useful outcomes.

Meta-analysis

Some attempts during the 1960s to summarize validation research used the *narrative review*/"tabular asterisks" approach: "*" for a result significant at the 5% level, "**" for the 1% level, etc. Lent, Aurbach & Levin (1971) exemplify this approach, by calculating 'Significance Batting Averages'; if a test–criterion correlation achieved significance at the "$p < 0.05$" level, it scored a 'hit'.

Aptitude tests scored hits in 75% of published studies, whereas personality measures achieved only 10–27% hit rates.

Meta-analysis pools studies to yield an estimate of effect size based on a sample of thousands, not tens (Glass, 1976). Variations in design and analysis of researches usually make pooling difficult, but most validation studies report correlations and sample size, so comparison across studies is possible. Ghiselli (1966b, 1973) reports meta-analyses of validation research; his analysis weights each validity coefficient by its sample size, then calculates an average (median) for each test × job pair. Figure 7.2 presents distributions of validity coefficients for four test × job pairs.

Dunnette (1972) meta-analysed data on the validity of MA tests for four broad classes of jobs in the American petroleum industry. The resulting median validities are not high, mostly in the 0.20–0.30 range. However, some MA tests achieved better results; the ACB achieved a median validity of 0.51, while the Wonderlic Personnel Test (see Chapter 12) achieved a median validity of 0.43.

Ghiselli (1959) found reviewing the literature depressing:

> A confirmed pessimist at best, even I was surprised at the variation in findings concerning a particular test applied to workers on a particular job. We certainly never expected the repetition of an investigation to give the same results as the original. But we never anticipated them to be worlds apart.

Ghiselli's and Dunnette's distributions of validity coefficients had generally low averages—around 0.30. Critics were quick to argue that a correlation of 0.30 explains only 9% of the variance in productivity, leaving 91% unaccounted for. Is it worth using tests that appear to contribute so little information, especially when they were beginning to meet difficulties with fair employment laws. Critics overlooked Ghiselli's reminder that:

> Averages of validity coefficients ... are distorted by the fact that reliability of tests and criteria varies from one investigation to another. Furthermore ... the workers used differ in range of talent, so that in cases of extensive restriction there is marked attenuation of the validity coefficient. Errors of these sorts ... are likely to reduce the magnitude of the average validity coefficient. Therefore the trends in validity coefficients to be reported here may well be underestimates.

Two questions were asked: "Why are these average observed validity coefficients so low? and why is considerable variability observed between similar predictor—criterion pairings?" (Burke, 1984). Two linked answers were given during the 1960s and early 1970s: *moderator variables* and *situational specificity*.

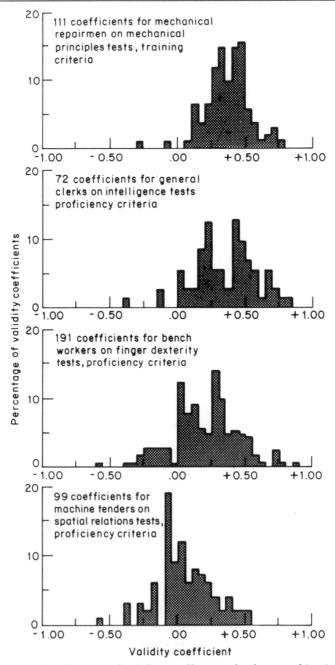

Figure 7.2 Four distributions of validity coefficients, for four combinations of test, and criterion (Ghiselli, 1966b). (Reprinted by permission of John Wiley & Sons, Inc.)

Moderator variables

The test–criterion correlation is *moderated* by some third factor. *Perceptual speed* may correlate well with clerical proficiency where work is routine and fast, but poorly or not at all where work is more varied and less rushed. Pace and complexity moderate predictive validity of *perceptual speed*. (The example is *fictional*.) Supposed moderator variables include: "organisational climate, management philosophy or leadership style, geographical location; changes in technology, product, or job tasks over time; age; socioeconomic status; and applicant pool composition" (Schmidt, Hunter & Pearlman, 1981). Moderator variables are likely to be 'found' where the number of studies being reviewed is small; the handful that manage to achieve significance may chance to have some feature in common.

Situational specificity

A more pessimistic hypothesis, developed as the search for moderators failed to find them reliably. The moderator is the 'undifferentiated situation'. So many factors affect test validity so complexly that it's impossible to construct a model that predicts validity in any particular setting. The right tests for a particular job, in a particular organization, can only be found by trial and error—the *local validation study*. Reviewers are more likely to conclude validity is situationally specific when validation studies are many, because chance moderator variables are less likely to be 'found'. (Their existence in nevertheless presumed; Hunter & Hunter (1984) note that reviewers always piously conclude "Further research is needed to find out what these moderator variables are".) Schmidt & Hunter (1978) conclude that "personnel psychologists have a strong tendency, maybe even a psychological need, to interpret error variance as true variance".

Job analysis (Chapter 3) enables the psychologist to choose the tests most likely to predict productivity. Note the contradiction inherent in believing in both situational specificity *and* the value of job analysis. If test–criterion relationships are so complex that no one can predict the outcome, what is the point of analysing the job? The only logical strategy is a comprehensive, all-purpose test battery—the 'shot-gun' approach.

VALIDITY GENERALIZATION

Meta-analysis makes some sense of validation studies, but still leaves a fairly confused and depressing picture, because it fails to take account of the limits of the typical validity study. *Validity generalization analysis* (VGA) goes one step further, and addresses two questions:

Question 1: Why do validity coefficients *vary so much*?
Question 2: Why do validity coefficients vary about such a *low mean*?

The answers to both questions lie in four limitations of the conventional validity study:

1. Sampling error,
2. Restricted range,
3. Criterion reliability,
4. Test reliability.

(1) Sampling error

The biggest limitation in validation research is *sampling error*. The typical validity study tests a fairly small sample; Lent, Aurbach & Levin (1971) report an average (median) sample size of 68 in a survey of 406 studies. The *law of large numbers* states that *large* random samples will be highly representative of the population from which they're drawn. The *fallacy of small numbers* holds that *small* random samples are also representative of the population from which they're drawn; they are not. Correlations calculated on small samples vary a lot. Bender & Loveless (1958) selected shorthand typists, using the same five tests, for four successive years. Tests that 'worked' one year didn't 'work' the next; the Minnesota Clerical (Names) Test correlated significantly with proficiency the first year, but not for the next two, then achieved significance again in the fourth year. Perhaps each year's cohort of applicants differed, or perhaps the job changed subtly. Or more likely the answer is in the sample sizes: 39, 41, 41 and 49—far too small to produce stable correlations.

Schmidt et al (1985b) demonstrate conclusively how small sample correlations vary in the absence of any possible real cause. They randomly divided a large sample ($N = 1455$) of US Postal Service letter sorters into smaller groups. The validity coefficient of a clerical test for the whole sample was 0.22. Figure 7.3 shows the distribution of validity coefficients for 63 pseudo-samples of 68 each (the median sample size in validation studies reviewed by Lent, Aurbach & Levin 1971). Values ranged from -0.03 to 0.48; less than a third of the coefficients were statistically significant. The validity coefficients in Figure 7.3 only vary because of sampling error, which shows how misleading correlations calculated on small samples are, and shows that 68 is a small sample—-too small. If 63 correlations from pseudo-samples—in Figure 7.3—can vary so much just by chance, perhaps 72 'real' correlations in Ghiselli's clerical samples in Figure 7.2 can vary as much for the same reason.

Hartigan & Wigdor (1989) classify the 515 GATB validity studies by sample size, and show that the smaller the N, the wider the distribution of validity coefficients.

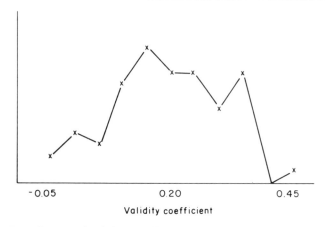

Figure 7.3 Distribution of validity coefficients for 63 "pseudo-samples", each of 68, drawn randomly from a larger sample of 1455. Data from Schmidt *et al* (1985b)

Every statistics text warns researchers of sampling error in the correlation coefficient; why do these warnings go unheeded? Why have psychologists "effectively denied the real role of sampling error in small samples" (Schmidt & Hunter, 1984) so that "By reading error variance like tea leaves, they have conjured up visions of complexity"? Expedience, perhaps. US Government and military psychologists have ready access to very large captive samples; psychologists selling local validation studies in the private sector must often settle for $N = 68$, or starve. Schmidt, Mack & Hunter (1984) liken faith in the local validity study to "checking the accuracy of the powerful telescopes used in astronomy by looking at the night sky with the naked eye".

Sampling error explains why validity coefficients vary a lot—because sample sizes are too small—but not why validity coefficients are generally low.

(2) Restricted range

The second limitation of the typical validity study is *restricted range* (see Figure 4.1). An *ideal* validation study tests every applicant, *employs* every applicant, and obtains criterion data from every applicant. During the Second World War, the US Air Force did put an unselected sample of 1143 men through pilot training, enabling Flanagan (1946) to calculate validity of the test battery without restriction of range. The failure rate was high, 77%, but so was the correlation between test scores and success, 0.64. Flanagan's study shows how well MA tests can work, under ideal conditions. Few other employers can afford to test and employ large unselected intakes, so the personnel researcher usually has to compromise, and calculate validity from the restricted range of *successful* applicants. This excludes people with low scores on the predictor, and necessarily reduces the validity coefficient. Restriction of range varies from one study to another. If the employer employs only one in five applicants and relies solely on the test score, range will be greatly restricted; if the employer employs two out of three applicants and prefers interview impression to test score, range of test scores will not be greatly restricted.

Restricted range can account for both variability of validity coefficient (because restriction varies from study to study), and their generally low mean (because restriction limits validity).

(3) Criterion reliability

Every validity study needs a criterion—a quantifiable index of successful work performance (Chapter 11). Whatever criterion is used will be *unreliable* to a greater or lesser extent. An unreliable criterion is difficult to predict. The most widely used criterion—supervisor rating—has poor reliability; one supervisor's rating of a worker agrees poorly with a second supervisor's rating. Schmidt's & Hunter's (1984) estimate of the reliability of the supervisor rating criterion is 0.60. The next most widely used criterion—training grades— is more reliable; Schmidt & Hunter estimate its average reliability at 0.80.

Criterion reliability varies from one validity study to another; variations in criterion reliability will cause variations in the validity coefficients, which cannot exceed the square root of criterion reliability. Suppose the criterion in study A has a reliability of 0.75, while the criterion in study B achieved a reliability of only 0.45 (because the criterion raters in study B weren't as careful, or as observant, or as keen to help the researcher as those in study A). Validity in Study B can't exceed $\sqrt{0.45}$, i. e. 0.67, whereas in Study A it could be as high as $\sqrt{0.75}$, i. e. 0.86.

Criterion unreliability can account for both variability of validity coefficients (because unreliability varies from study to study), and their generally low mean (because criterion unreliability limits validity).

(4) Test reliability

Validity is limited by test reliability, which also varies from study to study, contributing a fourth source of variation in validity coefficients.

Test unreliability can account for both the variability of validity coefficients (because unreliability varies from study to study), and for their generally low mean (because test unreliability limits validity).

Critics say it's pointless estimating how much more accurate selection would be if tests were perfectly reliable—because no test is perfectly reliable. Validity is necessarily limited by test reliability. For most purposes, including routine selection, this is true. However, researchers testing a theory of quantitative ability and job satisfaction can regard both as *constructs* that could ideally be measured perfectly reliably, and can legitimately correct for reliability of both before calculating the true correlation between the two (Hunter, Schmidt & Pearlman, 1982).

Question 1: Why do validity coefficients vary so much?

All four limitations of the typical validity study increase error variance in validity coefficients. All four limitations themselves *vary* from study to study, meaning the highest validity coefficient possible also *varies*. Suppose the four sources of error in validity were sufficient to *explain all the variation about the mean*. So that, in a series of ideal validation studies, the validity coefficient will always be the same. *Validity generalization analysis* estimates how much variance in a sample of validity coefficients the four sources of error could account for, then compares this estimate with the actual variance to see if there's any *residual variance* left to explain. Sampling error can (usually) be calculated. Variations in range restriction and test and criterion reliability can sometimes be calculated, if the authors of the study give details; otherwise they are estimated. Pearlman, Schmidt & Hunter (1980) give computational details.

Residual variance is the variance:

that would be observed among uncorrected ("observed") correlations across a large number of studies if:

1. N were infinite in each study;
2. criterion reliability were held constant *at its mean value*;
3. range restriction were held constant *at its mean value*; and
4. test reliability were held constant *at its mean value*.
   [Schmidt et al, 1979]

Zero residual variance means there's no variance left when the four sources of error have been subtracted. There is no true variation in validity. Validity is the same in every study included in the analysis. Validity only *appears* to vary because it isn't measured accurately. If residual variance is zero, the hypothesis of *situational specificity* can be rejected.

Table 7.2 applies VGA to four sets of Ghiselli's data (Figure 7.2). Column 6 of Table 7.2 shows that between 54% and 90% of the *observed* variance in validity can be accounted for by the four artefacts. In research on testing repair men with tests of mechanical principles, 90% of the variation in size of correlations can be explained by the four limitations, suggesting the correlation doesn't 'really' vary much. In research on testing bench workers with finger-dexterity tests, however, only half the variation in size of correlation can be explained by the four limitations, which suggests the correlation does 'really' vary.

Table 7.2   Validity generalization analysis of the data of Figure 7.2. Based on data given by Schmidt & Hunter (1977)

Job	Ability	1	2	3	4	5	6	7	8	9
Mechanical repair man	Mechanical principles	114	0.39	0.2 1	0.19	0.02	90	0.78	0.75	0.70
Bench worker	Finger dexterity	191	0.25	0.26	0.14	0.12	54	0.39	0.24	-0.04
Clerk	Intelligence	72	0.36	0.26	0.17	0.09	65	0.67	0.50	0.40
Machine tender	Spatial relations	99	0.11	0.22	0.12	0.10	54	0.05	-0.03	-0.30

Column I gives the number of validity coefficients analysed (not the number of subjects): column 2 lists the raw median validity coefficient calculated by Ghiselli.

Column 3 lists the actual SD of the validity coefficients averaged in column 2; column 4 lists the estimate derived from validity generalization analysis of the size of SD that known artefacts could produce; column 5 lists the difference between columns 4 and 3, which is residual variance; column 6 lists what percentage proportion of observed variance could be accounted for by the artefacts.

Column 7 lists estimated mean true validity.

Column 8 lists 90% credibility values; column 9 lists 97.5% credibility values.

Credibility values

If there is residual variance, so situational specificity can't be rejected, validity can still be generalized, using *credibility values*, which calculate the value in the estimated true validity distribution above which 90% of true validities lie. Suppose true validity is 0.52, and the SD of the distribution of true validity is 0.148 (Figure 7.4). Ten percent of a normal distribution lies 1.28 SDs below the

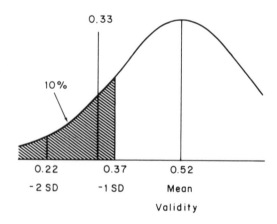

Figure 7.4   Credibility values for validity coefficients. Mean true validity is 0.52, and its SD is 0.148. In such a distribution, 10% of observed validity coefficients are below $r=0.33$, so the 90% credibility value is 0.33

mean, so the value above which 90% of true validity coefficients lie is 0.52 -1.28 × 0.148 = 0.33. This implies the test can be used with a nine in 10 chance of achieving a true validity of at least 0.33. Column 8 of Table 7.2 gives 90% credibility values for the four test × job pairs. Values for mechanical comprehension in repair men and general intelligence in clerks are high; the value for bench workers is lower. Linn, Harnisch & Dunbar (1981) note yet another rule of thumb: "90% credibility values are of about the same magnitude as the average observed [i.e. uncorrected] correlation". If the 90% credibility value exceeds zero, selectors can use the test with a reasonable (nine in 10) certainty it will predict something.

Question 2: Why do validity coefficients vary about such a low mean?

The traditional validity study underestimates validity, because range is restricted, and the criterion is unreliable. A VGA corrects mean validity for criterion unreliability and restricted range, to find *estimated mean true validity*. (This is not a new idea; both corrections were discussed, and sometimes made, long before VGA first appeared.) Column 7 of Table 7.2 gives *estimated mean true validity* for Ghiselli's four sets of data. Corrected estimates of mean validity, with one exception, are far higher than the uncorrected estimates presented by Ghiselli (Schmidt & Hunter, 1977). As a *rule of thumb*, VGAs find true validity is twice the uncorrected mean validity coefficient. The exception—spatial relations tests in machine tenders—shows that if validity is zero, twice zero still equals zero.

APPLICATIONS OF VALIDITY GENERALIZATION

Schmidt's & Hunter's (1977) first VGA showed how limited or non-existent situational specificity was in four of Ghiselli's numerous test × job validity distributions. Subsequent work explores the full potential of VGAs.

Computer programmers and law enforcement officers

The Programmer Aptitude Test (PAT) achieves a very high *true validity*—0.73 for job proficiency, and 0.91 for training grades (Schmidt, Gast-Rosenberg & Hunter, 1979). The PAT, which is no longer available, consisted of number series, figure analogy and arithmetic reasoning items; effectively it is a non-verbal MA test, which implies another such could serve the same purpose. By contrast, VGA for law enforcement officers finds true validity is low—no more than 0.27; Hirsch, Northrop & Schmidt (1986) think criteria for law enforcement work are particularly problematic.

Validity generalization—General Aptitude Test Battery

In 1980, the US Department of Labor contracted Hunter to re-analyse the GATB database. Hunter (1986) concluded that GATB's nine sub-tests were not all needed for US Employment Service (USES) placements. Only two scores—g (general intelligence) and *psychomotor ability* (dexterity and co-ordination)—were needed to place Americans into all 12 000 jobs listed in the *Dictionary of Occupational Titles* i.e. into just about every job in the USA. Jobs needed only to be categorized into five broad levels of complexity; more complex jobs needed more g, while less complex jobs needed more dexterity. Hartigan & Wigdor (1989) suggest dexterity is required only for jobs at the lowest of the five levels. The two scores and five levels of complexity system was known as VG–GATB system (VG standing for validity generalization). Hunter claimed that if VG–GATB were used for all four million USES placements each year, US national productivity could increase by $79 billion. In practice, VG–GATB was adopted by only a minority of USES offices, and was shelved in 1986 after fair employment problems (Chapter 12).

Project A

During the 1980s, the American armed services carried out the world's largest and most expensive validation study, Project A, to re-validate ASVAB against five new composite criteria (McHenry et al, 1990). Project A data show that 'core job performance' (*technical proficiency* and *general soldiering proficiency*) in nine Military Occupational Specialities is best predicted by general MA, which achieves a true validity of 0.65 and 0.69. The other three criteria—*effort and leadership, personal discipline, fitness and military bearing*—are better predicted by personality measures (Chapter 8).

The job families argument

The situational specificity and local validity arguments held that every job was different, and so needed different selection tests. Using VGA makes it easy to test this hypothesis. If genuinely different jobs are grouped together in a VGA, then true residual variance will be found, indicating test validity varies according to job type. Conversely, if grouping jobs together in a VGA does not result in true residual variance, then those jobs do not 'really' differ, in terms of how to select for them.

The hypothesis was first tested in a large hierarchical family of clerical jobs (Pearlman, Schmidt & Hunter, 1980): secretaries in different organizations (a single job); secretaries, shorthand-typists, typists, filing clerks and mailing room staff (a family of clerical jobs); cashiers and tellers, shipping clerks, telephone operators, and transportation service clerks (members of the five different clerical families). The VGA found no true residual variance, disproving the specificity hypothesis and indicating the same tests can be used to select for all clerical jobs. Subsequently, similar analyses have been reported for several large sets of US military and public sector data.

Army trades

The ACB's nine sub-tests have been validated for 35 very different army jobs, ranging from radar repair, through welder, dental laboratory technician, clerk, cook, to military policeman. The VGA does find reliable differences in ACB sub-test validities between military jobs—but the differences are too small to have any practical use (Schmidt & Hunter, 1978). In other words the ACB predicts productivity equally well for any of the 35 trades—generalizable validity indeed!

Technicians and apprentices

Trattner (1985) reports very little information is lost by using the same test battery for 23 diverse 'semi-professional' occupations; the savings in time and cost are of course considerable. Similarly, Northrop (1985) reports the same set of tests can be used for selecting 74 different types of apprentice, without losing information. The US Government and armed services employ a wide range of technicians and aides, including such varied specialities as: meteorological technician, geodetic technician, nuclear medical technician, pathology technician; the 24 jobs fell into two broad categories—health, and science/ engineering. Lilienthal & Pearlman (1983) conclude the same tests can be used to select for all 24 jobs with equal validity.

IMPLICATIONS OF VALIDITY GENERALIZATION ANALYSIS

Validity generalization analysis has a number of very important implications, and completely changes the selector's perspective on a number of issues.

(1) Mental ability tests can break the '0.30 barrier'

Critics have argued that the 'typical validity coefficient', of 0.30, accounts for less than 10% of the variation in employee effectiveness—insufficient to justify using tests, especially when they create 'fairness' problems. Hunter & Hunter (1984) re-analyse Ghiselli's data (Figure 7.2), and conclude *mean true validity* is much higher than 0.30. Table 7.3 shows general intelligence has higher validity for some classes of job, while psychomotor tests have higher validity for others. Validity of general intelligence and psychomotor tests tend to be inversely related across the nine groups of jobs, so the multiple correlation of all three tests is fairly constant at around 0.50, which accounts for 25% of the variation in employee effectiveness.

Table 7.3 Re-analysis by Hunter & Hunter (1984) of Ghiselli's (1966b) summary of validity coefficients for nine broad classes of job, and three ability factors

	General ability	Perceptual speed	Psycho-motor	All three combined
Manager	53	43	26	53
Clerk	54	46	29	55
Salesperson	61	40	29	62
Protective professions	42	37	26	43
Service jobs	48	20	27	49
Trades and crafts	46	43	34	50
Elementary industrial	37	37	40	47
Vehicle operator	28	31	44	46
Sales clerk	27	22	17	28

(2) Mental ability tests are transportable

If the hypothesis of *situational specificity* is rejected, tests become *transportable*, and can be used without a local validity study. If GATB selects good clerical workers in Washington DC, it can also select good clerical workers in Boston, San Francisco, and very probably in London. In the USA, fair employment *guidelines* (Chapter 12) still favour local validation studies, although some courts have accepted that tests are transportable (Schmidt, Mack & Hunter, 1984).

(3) Moderator variables are not that important

Faced with inconsistent results, researchers start a "well intentioned search for moderator variables" (Pearlman, 1984)—and 'find' them. If enough researchers conduct enough studies of the moderating effect of organizational climate on the validity of the Watson Glaser Critical Thinking Appraisal for department store managers, then a lucky few will find results significant at the 5% level—about 1 in 20 is Pearlman's estimate. Having found a moderator, "any investigators worth their salt (or up for tenure) ... will publish a new model or theory".

(4) Job analyses aren't absolutely essential

Pearlman, Schmidt & Hunter (1980) report MA tests predict productivity equally well throughout a large hierarchical family of clerical jobs, which implies job analysis need be no more elaborate than categorizing the job as 'clerical'. (This doesn't mean all job analyses are redundant; Chapter 3 lists many other uses, besides guiding choice of measures in selection.)

(5) Mental ability tests can be used off the shelf

For many years, no self-respecting occupational psychologist committed him/herself to advising an employer "the best tests for this job are X, Y, and Z". Instead the psychologist always recommended a local validation study. But the local validation study can rarely include enough subjects to give a meaningful estimate of the test's validity. So might not the psychologist's experience, or knowledge of the literature on test validity, enable him/her to select an appropriate test? Schmidt et al (1983) asked 20 occupational psychologists to predict the validity of six sub-tests of the Navy Basic Test Battery for nine navy jobs. They then compared estimates with the actual (but unpublished) validities based on samples of 3000 to 14 000. The *pooled* judgement of any four experts gave a fairly accurate estimate of validity, as accurate as could be obtained by actually testing a sample of 173 subjects. In other words, asking four experts what test to use gives as good an answer as actually doing a local validation study on a sizeable sample. It's also much quicker, and much cheaper.

(6) Mental ability tests work for minorities

The hypothesis of *single group validity* states that tests work for white Americans, but not for non-white. The hypothesis of *differential validity* states that tests are more valid for whites than non-whites. Both hypotheses are tested by comparing correlations for whites and non-whites, and finding the 'white' correlation higher than the 'non-white'. Chapter 12 reviews research in greater detail, and concludes there's no evidence for single group validity or differential validity, which implies tests can be used equally well for whites and non-whites.

(7) Mental ability tests are useful at all occupational levels

Hunter and Hunter's (1984) re-analysis of Ghiselli's (1966b) database concludes the combination of general intelligence, perceptual ability and psychomotor validity achieves true validities higher than 0.40 for all classes of work, except sales clerks. Hunter & Hunter's analysis of the 515 studies of the earlier GATB database reports true validity of around 0.30 even for the least complex jobs.

'g' OR APTITUDE BATTERY?

In theory, differential aptitude testing should give more accurate predictions, on the assumption that each job requires a different profile of abilities; accountants need to be numerate, architects need good spatial ability, lawyers need good verbal reasoning ability, etc. During the late 1980s some American psychologists rediscovered 'g', and started asking themselves whether ploughing through the whole of the GATB or ASVAB added much to their predictions.

Thorndike (1986) analysed three large sets of data: DAT predicting school grades, ACB predicting training grades in 35 military specialities, and GATB data for many occupations. In each, he compared the predictive power of the whole profile with the predictive power of a single general score derived from the whole battery. In the former, a different combination of weightings of scores was used for each outcome or job; in the latter the same method of combining the various scores was used throughout. Thorndike concluded that the gain from using differential weighting was small (for DAT and ACB) or non-existent (for GATB). Treating GATB like a single, very long test of general MA, scored and weighted in exactly the same way for every occupation listed in the GATB Manual, predicted proficiency as well as using differently weighted combinations for each job.

Ree & Earles (1991) analysed how well ASVAB data for 78 041 US Air Force personnel doing 82 different jobs predicted training grades. The ASVAB's 10 tests include

> some seemingly specific measures of automotive knowledge, shop information, word knowledge, reading, mathematics, mechanical principles, electronic and scientific facts, as well as clerical speed, yet its predictive power was derived from psychometric g. The training courses prepared students for seemingly different job performance, such as handling police dogs, clerical filing, jet engine repair, administering injections, and fire fighting, yet a universal set of weights across all jobs was as good as a unique set of weights for each job.

Hunter (1986) argues the American preference for aptitude batteries, and sets of weights carefully tailored to specific jobs, may be another exercise in trying to read meaning into error variance. A single study may 'find'—by chance—that sub-tests A, C and F predict success in a particular job; the finding, however, won't replicate, and won't survive a VGA.

Criticisms of the 'g' hypothesis take two lines; some argue that specific abilities are required for some jobs. Recent research provides two examples of specific abilities that predict success in work, with 'g' held constant. Trainee military pilots with poor visuospatial ability tend to fail pilot training, regardless of 'g' (Gordon & Leighty, 1988). Fuel-tanker drivers with poor selective attention make more mistakes, holding Progressive Matrices scores constant (Arthur, Barrett & Doverspike, 1990).

Other critics argue that very broad analyses covering the entire range of MA and of work aren't detailed enough to detect true differential profile validities. Baehr & Orban (1989) point out that Hunter's levels of complexity analysis lumps all 'managers' together, at the highest level; they cite data showing technical specialists and general managers, while equal in 'g', differ markedly in speeded word fluency and visual closure flexibility. Thorndike's analysis of US Air Force pilot training data finds that 'g' gives almost as good a prediction as a profile in an *unselected* intake—but not in the usual pilot intakes, where pre-screening had weeded out those with lower 'g'. Where all candidates are generally bright, the contribution of specific abilities can reveal itself. In the selected intakes, weighting gave much better prediction than an unweighted sum—0.48 against 0.38.

CRITICISMS OF VALIDITY GENERALIZATION

Callender & Osburn (1980) find an error in the original VGA of Schmidt & Hunter, and develop their own equations by computer simulation. Hunter, Schmidt & Pearlman, (1982) see "only trivial differences between [their] equations and the independent equations of Callender & Osburn". Burke (1984) reviews six sets of equations for VGA. Schmidt, Ones & Hunter (1992) give a good review of statistical criticisms of VGA.

Reporting bias

Journals are notoriously reluctant to publish 'insignificant' results, so perhaps published studies are a biased sample of validity research. Mean validities, whether *raw* or *true*, may be gross overestimates. However, most VGAs include unpublished studies, and make careful enquiries to locate them. The VGAs reported by the Schmidt–Hunter–Pearlman group use US Government or military research, which tests whole, large populations. Other validity data are drawn from *Personnel Psychology's Validity Information Exchange* (VIE), whose policy was to publish all validity information regardless of statistical significance. Recently, VIE has been revived as the *Test Validity Yearbook*.

It's also possible to calculate the likelihood of unreported studies that may change conclusions about test validity. The File Drawer statistic "allows one to calculate the number of unreported studies in researchers' file drawers, all with null results, that would be needed to bring the overall p level for reported studies down to the .05 level of significance" (Burke, 1984). Callender & Osburn (1981) report File Drawer values for their VGA of petroleum industry employees; between 482 and 2010 unreported studies with insignificant results are needed to exist to reduce to insignificance the pooled estimate of validity based on 25–38 reported studies. Callender & Osburn aren't likely not to know about over 400 validity studies in the petroleum industry, and it's very unlikely there could be 2000 unreported researches in a fairly centralized industry. Ashworth et al (1992), however, suggest File Drawer is overly optimistic; their proposed replacement—Null-K—gives much smaller estimates of the number of unincluded studies needed to nullify published VGAs.

Restricted range

Range is restricted when the SD of the sample is less than the SD of the population. In selection validity studies, this usually means comparing the SD of successful applicants with the SD of all actual *or potential* applicants. Critics claim it's often difficult to define the 'population' or decide who are 'potential applicants'. In his VGA of the GATB database, Hunter defined the population as the general average of all the subjects in all 515 GATB validity studies, i.e. he compared the SD of each occupational group with the SD of a (rough) cross-section of all employed Americans. This generates sample/population ratios of the order of 0.80, correcting for which multiplies validity coefficients by 1.25. Hartigan & Wigdor (1989) find Hunter's analysis "troubling", because "Intuitively we tend to think ... highly educated people tend not to apply for minimum wage jobs". Hartigan & Wigdor go perhaps to the other extreme; because they couldn't decide what population to compare any particular GATB sample with, they don't correct for restricted range at all.

Overgenerous assumptions

VGA makes assumptions about criterion reliability. The size of the assumption directly affects the resulting size of the corrected true validity coefficient. Assuming reliability of the supervisor rating criterion averages 0.60—as Hunter's group do—increases estimated validity by 29%. Hartigan & Wigdor prefer a more conservative assumption, that supervisor rating reliability averages 0.80, which increases raw-to-true validity by only 12%. The most recent review by Rothstein et al (1990) favours Hunter, suggesting 0.60 if anything *over*estimates the reliability of supervisor ratings. Correcting for criterion unreliability creates the worrying paradox that the *less* reliable the criterion, the *higher* the *true validity* becomes.

Re-analysis of GATB data

Hartigan & Wigdor re-analyse the GATB database, and reach quite different conclusions. They assume criterion reliability is 0.80, not 0.60. They do not correct for restricted range, because they do not know what population SD to use. These more conservative assumptions increase validity by only 12%, whereas Hunter's more generous assumptions increased it by 40%. Furthermore Hartigan & Wigdor start from a different, *lower*, average raw validity. They use an extended GATB database, of 755 studies, in which the later studies show consistently lower validity than the earlier studies used in Hunter's VGA. The combined effect of these three differences is to place their estimate of GATB's true validity at only 0.22, compared with Hunter's 0.47. A correlation of 0.47 explains 22% of the variance in job performance, while a correlation of 0.22 explains only 5%. The smaller GATB's true validity, the less loss to American national productivity results from not using it, and the more scope there is for using personnel selection for other ends, such as ensuring securing a representative workforce.

Too many assumptions?

Validity generalization analyses estimate distributions of unreliability and range restriction, because neither are reported in most validation studies. Only sampling error can be calculated, because validity studies always report sample size. Schmidt and Hunter argue sampling error accounts for 90% of the random variation in validity, and propose *bare bones* VGA, a conservative procedure that corrects validity variance for sampling error only, and needs make no assumptions about test or criterion reliability or range restriction. Bare bones VGA of the PAT increased *residual SD* by a trivial amount (Schmidt, Gast-Rosenberg & Hunter, 1980), which implies that sampling error matters most when assessing true validity of a selection test. Hirsch, Northrop & Schmidt (1986) tried another approach; they found data on test and criterion reliability and range restriction for enough studies to *calculate* their effects. *Calculated* variance contributed by the four artefacts accounted for 79% of observed variance, whereas *estimated* artefacts accounted for only 72.5%, showing the assumptions are if anything conservative.

True restriction of criterion range

Range might be restricted on the test (predictor) or the criterion, or both. If a test is used to select, clearly the range of test scores will be restricted; if the test has any validity, then criterion scores will also be restricted, because the test will exclude some poor performers. This is an artefact, and leads to a genuine underestimate of the test's validity, a fact recognized long before VGA was devised. Suppose, however, criterion scores are restricted for some other reason, not because less proficient workers aren't available to be included in the analysis. *Restrictiveness of organizational climate* means work is highly standardized, and employees are allowed little autonomy, because management doesn't trust them (James et al, 1992); such a climate tends to iron out individual differences in job performance. Hence everyone performs at the same mediocre level, range is restricted and test validity is reduced.

Correcting for restricted range isn't appropriate, because the restriction is inherent to the way the organization works, not a practical problem of data collection.

WHY MENTAL ABILITY TESTS PREDICT PRODUCTIVITY

Personnel psychology often bemoans its lack of theory, and sometimes tries to make good the perceived deficiency. Mental ability testing has never pretended to any systematic theory. Binet's first test was written to screen out educationally subnormal children, and derived its items from the convenient fact that older children can solve problems younger ones can't. Ever since, MA tests have mostly been written for particular practical purposes, not as part of a general theory of human mental abilities.

(1) Occupational differences in mental ability level

American Army conscripts in the Second World War were tested with the AGCT, and classified according to their peacetime occupations (Harrell & Harrell, 1945). Occupations with low average MA included miner, farm worker, lumberjack and teamster; occupations with high average level included accountant, personnel clerk, and students of medicine or mechanical and electrical engineering. Similar data are included in the GATB database, and described in the GATB manual; the occupations with the lowest average general MA were tomato peeler, mushroom inspector and battery loader, while the three with the highest were mathematician, general practitioner and programmer. However, the AGCT and GATB data merely show that people presently in various jobs have different general MA levels, which doesn't prove they *need* general MA to perform successfully.

Sociologists argue that any apparent link between occupation and MA is a creation of the class system. Better-off children get better educations, so do better on MA tests, which are in any case heavily biased towards the better off; better-off children go on to get better-paid jobs. There is no true link between MA and job proficiency: "the great majority of all jobs can be learned through practice by almost any literate person" (Collins, 1979). Tests, psychological or educational, are merely class-laden rationing mechanisms.

(2) Threshold hypothesis

A widely held 'common sense' view holds that, above a certain minimum level, most people are capable of most jobs. All that tests can accomplish is to screen out an unfortunate minority of incompetents (who probably lack 'common sense', not intelligence). This view implies a threshold or step in the relation between test scores and job proficiency. Thus Mls (1935) found a clear break in truck-driving proficiency (people either could or couldn't), which happened at approximately IQ 80. Any Czech soldier with an IQ over 80 was equally proficient at truck driving, while all those whose IQ fell below 80 were equally unfit to be trusted with an army vehicle. The model used by most psychologists and testers by contrast assumes *linearity*, that proficiency increases as test score increases, throughout the entire range of test scores. The threshold vs linearity issue has important 'fair' employment implications. Linearity implies candidates should be placed in a strict rank order, on the predictor, and selected in that order, because the higher the predictor score, the better their job performance. The threshold hypothesis by contrast allows scope for *minority quotas*, without reducing overall efficiency.

However cut-offs as clear as the IQ of 80 chosen by Mls are rare, and several large analyses of test data suggest test × proficiency relationships are generally linear. Some analyses rely on statistical tests of non-linearity in very large GATB × proficiency data sets (Hawk, 1970; Coward & Sackett, 1990), which find no evidence of significant non-linear relationships. Other researchers have computed correlations between test and proficiency separately for different levels of test scores (Waldman & Avolio, 1989), and found high, average and low GATB scores predict performance equally well, whereas the threshold hypothesis predicts differences.

The linearity of test × outcome relationships justifies selectors using strict rank ordering of candidates but doesn't answer a question selectors are often asked: is this/any candidate appointable? In other words, what is the minimum level of MA necessary to function in this job? Appointing someone below this level might cross the *threshold of organizational embarrassment*, if that person's performance proved grossly deficient. Gottfredson (1988) states that only 10–20% of the general population have enough general MA to achieve 'minimally acceptable performance' as a physician, whereas 80% have enough to function as a licensed practical nurse (state-enrolled nurse). Unfortunately she gives no information about how she derives these estimates.

The commonest approach to setting cut-offs is *distribution-based*; do not appoint anyone who falls in the bottom one-third of existing post-holders, or the lowest 25%, or more than one SD below the mean, etc. Matarazzo (1972) reports that "few" high-level executives, physicians and "professionals" have IQs below 115. This approach requires a good database of existing employees, and looks very arbitrary. The *contrasting groups* method (Darlington & Stauffer, 1966) nominates groups of definitely satisfactory and unsatisfactory employees, and hopes to find a cut-off that clearly distinguishes them. The *Angoff* method goes through the test item by item, and asks a panel of experts to estimate the probability that a barely competent person could answer each item correctly; the cut-off is set at the average of these estimated probabilities. This is much more systematic—but only suitable for very specific job-knowledge tests, and quite inapplicable to tests of general MA.

Strictly speaking the idea of a fixed cut-off is simplistic, because the relationship between test score and performance is linear, and probabilistic;

the *lower* the test score, the *poorer* the person's performance is *likely* to be. Selectors should think in terms of an *expectancy table*, showing the range of performance indices expected at each level of test score (Figure 7.5). The decision to appoint a particular candidate depends primarily on his/her expected level of performance, but also on the state of the labour market, how desperate the organization is to fill the vacancy, etc. Part of the problem, in Britain at any rate, is that the organization often has no reliable, quantitative information to enter into the 'performance' side of the expectancy table. They have no appraisal system, or keep no systematic records of staff performance, so can only think in simplistic terms like 'appointable/unappointable'.

(3) Necessary but not sufficient

Herrnstein (1973) argues MA is *necessary but not sufficient* for productivity. Table 7.4 shows few accountants had IQs more than 15 points below the accountant average, whereas quite a few lumberjacks had IQs well *over* their average of 85. Assuming the latter hadn't always wanted to be lumberjacks, the data imply they couldn't or didn't use their MA to find more prestigious work. Research that shows personality tests have *incremental validity* (Chapter 8) over MA tests confirms Herrnstein's hypothesis.

Test score	Appraisal rating				
	Very poor	Poor	Average	Good	Very good
Very good	7	15	20	37	21
Good	6	20	32	31	11
Average	11	18	44	20	7
Poor	13	36	33	15	3
Very poor	26	31	23	18	2

Figure 7.5 An expectancy table, showing the probability (%) of persons with test scores, ranging from very good to very poor, receiving appraisal ratings, ranging from very good to very poor; the probability, based on a large sample of existing and former post holders, of a person with a *very poor* test score obtaining an appraisal rating of *very good* is 2%

Table 7.4 Average IQs of accountants and lumberjacks conscripted into the US Army during the Second World War, and 10th and 90th percentiles

	10th percentile	Median	90th percentile
Accountants	114	129	143
Lumberjacks	60	85	116

(4) Mental ability, job knowledge and productivity

Recent research uses *path analysis* to explore why MA tests predict productivity so well, in such a wide range of jobs. (*Path analysis* is essentially a correlational analysis in which the investigator is prepared to make some assumptions about direction of cause.) Hunter (1983) found *general MA* didn't correlate directly with supervisor ratings, but did correlate with *job knowledge* and *work-sample* performance, which in turn correlated with supervisor ratings (Figure 7.6). An intelligent person learns quickly what he/she needs to know to do the job (job knowledge), and he/she learns how to do the job well (work sample), which causes supervisors to rate him/her highly. Acquisition of knowledge is the more important path between general MA and good ratings, although there is some direct contribution of general MA to work-sample performance. More intelligent people are better workers primarily because they learn more quickly what the job is about. In high-level work, this may mean learning scientific method, scientific techniques and a large body of knowledge. In low-level work it may mean only learning where to find the raw materials, what to do with them and where to put the finished product.

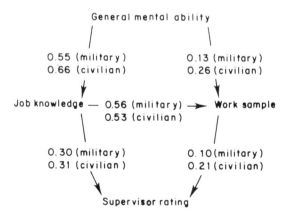

Figure 7.6 The relationships between general mental ability, supervisor ratings, job knowledge and work-sample performance, in civilian and military samples (Hunter, 1983) (Reproduced by permission of Lawrence Erlbaum Associates, Inc., Publishers)

Hunter (1983) reports the paths between general MA, work sample and supervisor ratings are weaker in military samples than in civilian ones. He suggests this reflects military emphasis on training and drill. Soldiers aren't left to work things out for themselves, or to devise their own ways of doing things; performance reflects training more than individual differences in MA. Borman et al (1991) replicate Hunter's analysis with 4362 subjects in nine Military Occupational Specialities, and suggest the paths can be simplified to:

general mental ability > job knowledge > work sample > supervisor rating.

The more intelligent person learns the job quicker, so does better on the work sample, so gets a better supervisor rating.

CONCLUSIONS

Validity generalization analysis has proved again what psychologists really always knew: tests of MA predict productivity very well. For a vast range of jobs, the more able worker produces more. The predictive validity of MA tests, for virtually all work, doesn't really need any further demonstration, although the American legal system (Chapter 12) is likely to continue demanding such proof. What is worth researching, and has been neglected for over 80 years, is *why* MA predicts efficiency so well. Knowing *why* may produce better tests, and may eventually satisfy the tests' critics.

Validity generalization analysis proves something psychologists didn't know before, or were reluctant to admit. Tests can be used off the shelf; it isn't really necessary to analyse the job in great detail, nor to conduct a local validation study, to know that MA tests will select more productive workers.

Some other tests can predict as well as MA tests, but none are so cheap, nor so universally valuable. Assessment centres (Chapter 9) are expensive; work samples (Chapter 10) are necessarily specific to the job, which makes them expensive also; peer assessments (Chapter 5) are unpopular and impractical.

The value of MA tests has been well known since the 1920s, so why were so many people so eager to write them off? Why has it been necessary to invent a new way of analysing selection research, just to prove MA tests are worth using? There is the irrelevant (for selection purposes) issue of heredity. There is also the problem of *adverse impact* (Chapter 12). Humphreys (1986) suggests the answer lies in *regression to the mean*, the fact that bright parents tend *on average* to have less bright children; this creates a vested interest in middle-class parents against using MA tests for educational and occupational selection.

8 Tests of Personality

Total awareness of bottom line vitality

Ghiselli's (1966b) review of test validity lists mental ability (MA) as the best single predictor of selling ability. This always surprises personnel managers who say "Surely personality is more important". Advertisements for sales staff, from the lowest level to the highest, list the traits essential for selling: commitment, enthusiasm, smartness, discipline, dynamism, flair, drive, resilience, acumen, self-motivation. "Self-starting" is a phrase much in vogue. One advert for sales manager created a series of bizarre, even indecent, images by specifying "thrusters—pro-active and professional in interpersonal skills—with total awareness of bottom line vitality" (but neglected to say what the product was).

Defining personality

Everyone agrees the right personality is essential for selling. Then the *disagree-ments* start. First, define personality. The layperson usually means social presence—"Jill has a lot of personality"; personnel managers often mean the same. Psychologists' definitions are broader. Cattell (1965) defines it as: "that which permits a prediction of what a person will do in a given situation". Cronbach's (1984) definition is a little narrower: "one's habits and usual style, but also ... abilities to play roles". Allport (1937) defines personality as "the dynamic organisation within the individual of those psychophysical systems that determine his unique adjustment to his environment". Personality traits are "neuropsychic system[s] ... with the capacity to render many stimuli functionally equivalent, and to initiate and guide consistent (equivalent) forms of adaptive and expressive behaviour". Traits are mechanisms within the individual that shape how he/she reacts to classes of event and occasion. Most occupational psychologists adopt, explicitly or implicitly, the trait model. A trait summarizes past behaviour and predicts future behaviour. A few psychologists prefer 'dustbowl empiricism', and reduce traits to scores that derive from personality tests and which might predict productivity.

Is there anything there to define? In the late 1960s, many psychologists began to question the very existence of personality. Mischel (1968) reviewed evidence, much of it by no means new, that seemed to show that behaviour wasn't consistent enough to make general statements about personality meaningful. Take the trait of honesty, which so many reference requests ask about. Hartshorne's & May's Character Education Inquiry, in the late 1920s (Hartshorne & May, 1928), found seven sets of measures of honesty virtually uncorrelated, so it's meaningless to describe someone as "honest" unless one specifies when, where, with what, with whom. Mischel reviews similar evidence for other traits that often feature in job descriptions: extraversion, punctuality, curiosity, persistence, attitude to authority.

Personality theorists argue Hartshorne's & May's tests of honesty, while very ingenious, were single-item tests, so it isn't surprising they intercorrelated poorly. Single-item tests are inherently unreliable, and unlikely to predict anything. One question from an intelligence test wouldn't predict anything, so why should a single-item honesty test prove any more successful? Epstein (1979) averaged measures of extraversion, forgetfulness, mood and carefulness across 6 days, and found he got stable, useful measures.

Recently, Kenny & Zaccaro (1983) re-analysed data on leadership, long regarded as the classic non-trait. Leadership research uses a *rotation* paradigm, in which groups of people are re-combined, and emerging patterns of leadership studied. Conventional wisdom (among social psychologists) held that leadership wasn't an individual trait, but a *role* anyone could assume. Kenny & Zaccaro's re-analysis finds individual identity accounts for 49–82% variance in leadership in rotation studies, and they conclude there *are* leaders. Earlier research found leadership correlates very modestly with intelligence, dominance and adjustment. The correlations are small (0.15–0.25), but arguably not completely useless (Chapter 13). To adapt a remark first made about schizophrenia, if personality is a myth, it's a myth with a genetic component. Research finds scores on many inventories to be heritable; people are born predisposed to be anxious, introvert, or aggressive (Cook, 1993).

Measuring personality

Layperson and personnel manager alike express scorn at most personality measures: "But surely *that* doesn't really measure personality?" Personality measures divide into:

1. *Observation.*   The Thought Police in Orwell's *1984* could watch everyone all the time. "You had to live ... in the assumption that every sound you made was overheard, and, except in darkness, every movement scrutinized". Personnel managers can only observe a limited, carefully edited performance, lasting between the 30 minutes of a typical interview and the 3 days of a long *assessment centre*. Nor can they observe applicants' thoughts and feelings.

2. *Situational tests.* Waiting for behaviour to occur naturally is very time-consuming; the situational test saves time by contriving an occasion for significant behaviour. Hartshorne & May (1928) gave children opportunities to cheat, take money, lie about their strength, etc. The War Office Selection Board uses *command tasks* which give candidates opportunity to demonstrate leadership.

3. *Questionnaire/inventory.* Observation is time-consuming; it can easily take 15 minutes to observe a single act by a single person. One short cut is the questionnaire or inventory; instead of watching the person to see if he/she talks to strangers, one asks "Are you afraid of talking to strangers?" Questionnaires are very economical; in 15 minutes one can ask 100 questions to as many people as one can assemble. The questions can tap thoughts and feelings, as well as behaviour: "Do you often long for excitement?", "Are you sometimes troubled by unusual thoughts?" (Questionnaires are justified as a quick and easy substitute for observation, but historically their true origin lies in the medical interview.)

4. *Ratings, check-lists.* Another short cut is to ask someone who knows the subject well to describe them: references, ratings, check-lists (Chapter 5).

5. *Projective tests.* People react to being observed, and may not tell the truth about themselves or others; projective tests are supposed to bypass these defences, and make people reveal their personality despite themselves.

6. *Miscellaneous.* This includes Kelly's (1955) *role repertory grid* ('rep grid'), and *self-characterizations.*

Different theories of personality (Cook, 1993) favour different approaches to measurement. Psychoanalysis relies on dreams and free associations. Motive/need theories favour projective tests. Trait theory accepts questionnaires and inventories. Behaviourists prefer behavioural measures, such as work samples. Phenomenal approaches use Repertory Grids, and self-characterizations. In practice, distinctions are blurred; questionnaires are used to test all sorts of personality theory, even psychoanalytic. Questionnaire measurements of different traits often correlate very highly; similarly ratings of different traits often correlate very highly. This effect—called *method variance*—means assessors should ideally measure every trait by two *different* types of measure—*multi-trait multi-method measurement*—but it's not always possible in practice.

PERSONALITY INVENTORIES

Personality questionnaires, or inventories, are what most people think of as 'personality tests'. The first, the Woodworth Personal Data Sheet (PDS), was written in 1917, since when hundreds more have been devised. Inventories use various formats, differing ways of choosing the questions to ask, and different ways of deciding what aspects of personality to measure.

Most use *endorsement* items:

My eyes are always cold.	True	False
My parents are older than me.	True	False
Do you trust psychologists?	Yes	No

Endorsement format is quicker and easier for subjects, but encourages *response sets*: consistently agreeing, consistently disagreeing, being consistently evasive or non-committal (by checking '?'). Kline (1976) says "on careful reflection, many [endorsement items] are unanswerable, although they evoke an immediate natural response."

Forced-choice format equates the attractiveness of the alternatives, to try to limit faking:

Would you rather be Dr Crippen or Jack the Ripper?

The Edwards Personal Preference Schedule uses forced-choice format, to measure 15 human motives. Forced-choice format needs more thought and takes longer. Cattell (1986) thinks it creates "cumulative antipathy". The Crippen/Ripper example, said to come from a real inventory, shows why; it offers subjects a difficult and unpleasant choice: *either* a poisoner *or* a maniac, and both long dead. Forced choice also *creates* correlations between the scales, which can give very misleading results (see page 147).

Rating format is used less frequently:

I run around screaming if I cannot find something

never 5 4 3 2 1 always

Keying and validation

The way the items are chosen distinguishes a list of questions thrown together, like an "Is your Partner a Good Lover?" quiz in a magazine, from a proper personality test. A proper personality test is *validated*, and *standardized*. There are four main ways of validating personality tests.

1. Acceptance. People accept the test's results. Stagner (1958) gave personnel managers a personality test, pretended to score it, then handed each manager a profile; all were convinced the test had described them perfectly, even though Stagner gave *every* manager the *same* interpretation. People are very ready to be taken in by all-purpose personality profiles, the so-called *Barnum effect*, so long as the profile's not too harsh—people often indignantly reject the less flattering parts of California Psychological Inventory (CPI) reports.

2. *Content.* The inventory looks plausible. The first personality inventory, Woodworth's Personal Data Sheet (PDS), gathered questions from lists of neurotic and psychotic symptoms in textbooks and from discussions with psychiatrists, to ensure item *content* was plausible and relevant. The first stage in writing any inventory is choosing the questions, but a good inventory doesn't leave it there. The second stage, deciding which questions to keep, uses factorial or empirical validation.

3. *Factorial.* The questions hang together. The author of the inventory chooses questions that relate to a common theme, and tests his/her hunch by correlation and factor analysis. Questions that don't fit are discarded. If the questions measure two things, the scale may have to be split. Cattell's (1965) research is the most ambitious use of factorial validation.

4. *Empirical.* The questions are included because they predict. The inventory is *empirically keyed* using *criterion groups*. The questions may be very diverse, and the link between the question and what it measures may be obscure. In theory, questions might appear totally irrelevant; playing tiddly-winks every Sunday afternoon might help identify mass murderers. In practice, items on the Minnesota Multiphasic Personality Inventory (MMPI) Psychopathic Deviance scale (the nearest thing to a mass murderer scale) aren't that subtle; they consist mostly of expressions of fondness for hurting people, or disregard for law or social norms.

Answers to inventory questions are *signs*, not *samples*; the psychologist wants an answer to "I sleep pretty soundly most nights" for what he/she can *infer* from it. If the psychologist wanted precise information about the subject's sleep patterns, he/she wouldn't use vague phrases like "pretty well" or "most nights". Empirical keying can produce inventories that are almost completely atheoretical, that postulate no traits, drives, complexes, etc., but simply generate scores that predict outcomes. The best example is the Strong Interest Inventory; biodata inventories (Chapter 6) use the same approach. Some recent inventories, like the Hogan Personality Inventory, use *homogeneous item composites (HICs)*, short, highly coherent sub-scales.

Different inventories measure different numbers of traits; the Eysenck Personality Inventory measures only two, while the Occupational Personality Questionnaire (OPQ) Concept model measures 30. Many inventories use *factor analysis* (see Note 1, in Chapter 3) to set the number of traits measured, but do not necessarily achieve consensus. Cattell found 16 personality factors

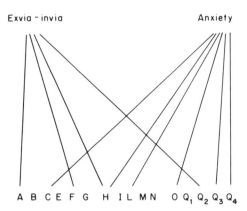

Figure 8.1 Higher order factors, 'exvia–invia' and anxiety, in Cattell's 16 personality factors

(PFs), Guilford (1959) found 10, and Eysenck (1953) finds as few as two. However there isn't necessarily any real disagreement between Eysenck and Cattell. Cattell's 16 factors intercorrelate to some extent; factor analysis of the factors reveals *higher-order factors*—exvia–invia and anxiety—which resemble Eysenck's extraversion and neuroticism (Figure 8.1). Sixteen scores look more useful than two or three, and 16PF is much more widely used for selection than Eysenck's measures. Critics argue the 16PF is too short to measure 16 factors reliably, and that it's *over-factored*: some of the factors don't appear in every analysis, and may not really exist. Recently the idea of the 'big five' personality dimensions (Table 8.2) has been widely canvassed.

Interpreting inventory scores

A raw score on a personality inventory, like a raw score on a MA test, is meaningless; it must be related to a population—people in general, bank managers, bus drivers, students, etc. Several variations on the *standard score* theme are used (Figure 8.2). Many inventories use *T scores*, in which the mean is set at 50, and the standard deviation at 10. Cattell's 16PF uses *sten* scores, and Guilford's inventories use *C scores*; the two systems differ only in detail from *T* scores.

Standard scores also allow *profiles* of scores to be plotted and interpreted. Figure 8.3 shows a CPI profile sheet. Each of 20 raw scores is converted into a *T* score, using a conversion chart printed on the profile sheet. All 20 scores are now on a common scale, defined by the mean and SD of the male standardization data. In Figure 8.3, the score for *Do(minance)* is the highest, at 1.5 SDs above the mean. The score for *So(cialization)* on the other hand is nearly 3 SDs below

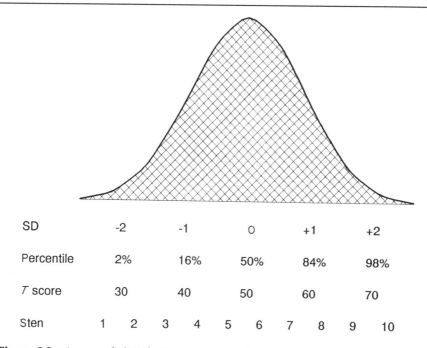

SD	-2	-1	O	+1	+2
Percentile	2%	16%	50%	84%	98%
T score	30	40	50	60	70
Sten	1 2 3	4 5	6 7	8 9	10

Figure 8.2 A normal distribution of personality test scores, illustrating *T* scores and stens

the mean, indicating a person with a very low level of social maturity, integrity and rectitude. The combination, in Figure 8.3, of someone very keen to exert influence on others, but lacking any maturity or moral standards, suggests someone liable to lapse into dishonesty. (The profile in Figure 8.3 belongs to a person who ran a 'dating agency' which was accused of taking money and failing to provide a worthwhile service in exchange.) Profiles of this type, used for 16PF, Guilford Zimmerman Temperament Survey (GZTS), CPI, etc., are a neat, quick way of presenting the data but encourage over-interpretation. The reliability of individual scales may be low; the difference between two unreliable scores is doubly unreliable, so the difference between points on a CPI or 16PF profile has to be quite large to merit interpretation. For example, on 16PF Forms A and B, a difference of two stens between Factor A *affectothymia* and Factor B *intelligence* falls well within the error of measurement. Only a difference of four stens can be confidently taken as 'real'. There are only 10 stens in all, so only very gross differences within 16PF profiles can be safely interpreted. The difference between *dominance* and *socialization*, in Figure 8.3, covers four whole SDs, or eight stens, and is large enough to interpret with some confidence.

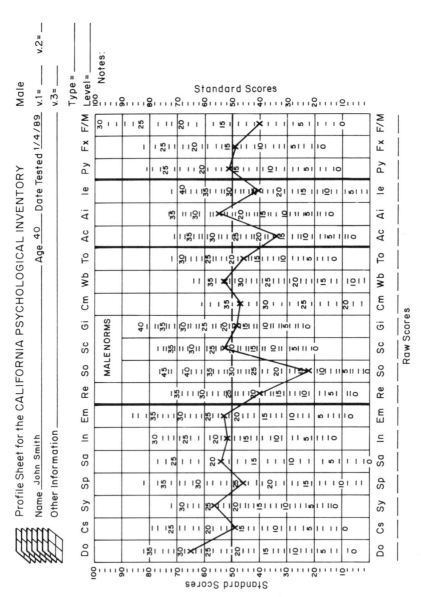

Figure 8.3 California Psychological Inventory profile sheet, with profile of "John Smith" plotted. (Modified and reproduced by special permission of the Publisher, Consulting Psychologists Press, Inc., Palo Alto, CA 94303, from *Profile Form for the California Psychological Inventory* by Harrison G. Gough. Copyright 1986 by Consulting Psychologists Press, Inc. All rights reserved. Further reproduction is prohibited without the Publisher's written consent)

Some inventories contain *infrequency keys*—sets of questions, where most subjects say 'true' or most say 'false'. People answering at random are as likely to give the infrequent answer as the frequent one, so accumulate a high infrequency score, which means they're answering carelessly, or don't understand the procedure, or don't speak English very well, or are being deliberately unco-operative.

SURVEY OF (SOME) INVENTORIES

Woodworth's PDS was written too late to be used in the First World War, but created so much interest that several hundred inventories were in use in the USA by 1935. Most were fairly bad, so people soon became wary of them. Inventories are listed and reviewed in the *Mental Measurements Yearbooks* (MMYs) (Buros, 1970); *MMY* reviews discuss size and adequacy of standardization sample, reliability, validity and whether the manual is any good; *MMY* reviews are very critical even of major tests.

Major inventories like CPI or 16PF are used for clinical diagnosis, career guidance and counselling, as well as for selection. Large new inventories are hard to launch because so much is invested in existing ones; Gough lists nearly 800 books, chapters or papers on the CPI. Nearly all major inventories originate in the USA, because no one else has the money, access to large populations, or general acceptance of the inventory's value. Nevertheless, personality inventories haven't been used, even in the USA, on anything like the scale of MA tests, which may be why they haven't proved so reliable and accurate. (On the other hand, perhaps people don't use them, precisely *because* they're less reliable and accurate.)

Most inventories can be administered, scored, and interpreted by computer (Fowler, 1985). Computer administration is twice as fast as paper-and-pencil testing; computer scoring is 50 times faster. Fowler reports that 80% of subjects preferred computer administration, while none preferred the paper form (which isn't surprising, given that most answer sheets are designed to be read by scoring machines, not people); he concludes that "fear of computing is a malady that affects professionals much more than their patients". Computer interpretation can be faster still.

Minnesota Multiphasic Personality Inventory (MMPI)

The first major multi-score inventory, dating from the late 1930s, MMPI asks 550 questions, answered *true*, *false*, or *?*, and measures nine psychiatric syndromes. The MMPI was the first inventory to be empirically keyed against (not very large) clinical groups. It can be used for screening but is rather long and offends some subjects by asking intrusive questions. It is the classic inventory everyone criticizes—"long and inefficient", "dimensions used ...

relics of an antiquated psychiatry" (Cronbach, 1984)—but goes on using, because they're used to it or can't find anything better.

Cattell's 16PF

Cattell's 16PF measures 16 personality *source traits*, derived from factor analysis. Cattell originally referred to his factors by letter and neologism, to emphasize his factor analysis yielded an entirely new account of human personality, but soon had to compromise and give 'plain English' descriptions. Factor H was originally called *parmia*, meaning parasympathetic autonomic nervous system strength, which later became *venturesome–shy*. In the UK 16PF is very popular, partly because tradition allows non-psychologist personnel managers to be trained to use it. It is also used by 38% of UK occupational psychologists, not necessarily for selection, and not necessarily without reservations. Parry (1959) says 16PF was considered for inclusion in the Civil Service Selection Board (CSSB), but was rejected, because there are only 10 or 13 questions measuring each factor, although "a reliable paper test with less than 20 items is almost unknown". The 16PF has four forms; forms A and B are parallel long forms, each asking 187 questions. Forms C and D are parallel short forms, each asking 105 questions. Critics say forms A and B are too short in the first place, making a shorter form undesirable. The 16PF is widely criticized for poor reliability—"correlations between forms (even pairs of forms) are so low that data gathered with one form or pair of forms may simply not be generalisable to all forms" (Buros, 1970). The 16PF manual (Cattell, Eber & Tatsuoka, 1970) gives *specification equations* for over 50 occupations. The equation for psychiatric technicians reads:

rated performance = $0.12A + 0.31C - 0.12E + 0.19G + 0.16H - 0.19M - 0.12O$
$- 0.19Q1 + 0.19Q3 - 0.12Q4 + 4.07.$

People who make good aides in psychiatric hospitals have high scores on factors A, C, G, H and Q3, and low scores on factors E, M, O, Q1 and Q4. Cattell says:

> The emphasis on emotional stability, superego strength, and self-sentiment development is to be expected in an occupation requiring calm, objective, and considerate treatment of irrationality in others. It is interesting to note also that high ... H is also favourable, presumably meaning a sympathetic autonomic nervous system which can take disturbing impacts without over-reacting.

Specification equations can be very misleading if they are calculated on small samples; they should be cross-validated on a second sample before they're used for selection. Most of the specification equations in the 16PF handbook don't appear to have been cross-validated, and should be viewed with caution.

Guilford Zimmerman Temperament Survey (GZTS)

The GZTS was developed factorially from inter-correlations between answers to inventory questions. (Whereas Cattell's factors were first calculated from inter-correlations of ratings.) The GZTS asks 300 questions, to measure 10 factors, asking 30 questions for each factor. Interpretation of GZTS emphasizes interactions between scales. A high score on Emotional Stability (E) is desirable if accompanied by *high* General Activity (G); but high E with *low* G means the subject is likely to be sluggish, lazy and phlegmatic. Like 16PF, GZTS isn't all that reliable, but high reliabilities for individual scales are essential for reliable interpretation of differences between scales.

California Psychological Inventory (CPI)

The CPI includes 462 endorsement format questions, to measure 22 traits (Table 8.1). All 22 scales are written so that high scores are 'good' scores; Gough (1969) regards the average of all 22 scores as an index of the individual's social and intellectual efficiency. The CPI contains about half the MMPI—the less intrusive questions—and is often called the "sane man's MMPI" (Megargee, 1972). Despite its derivation from MMPI, the CPI hasn't seen the same proliferation of special scales. Instead Gough prefers to devise new indices using regressions. *Type A* (coronary heart disease prone) personality can be estimated using the formula:

$$44.93 + 0.22Do + 0.62Sa + 0.32Sc - 0.35Re - 0.39So - 0.39Ai - 0.26Fx$$

The CPI has larger and better normative samples than MMPI. Its main defect is redundancy; the scales inter-correlate quite highly.

Strong Interest Inventory (SII)

The SII (formerly Strong Campbell Interest Inventory or Strong Vocational Interest Blank) was first written in 1920s, and has been through seven editions. The core of SII is the 209 *Occupational Interest Scales*, which compare subjects' answers with keys derived from *criterion groups* of people successful in various vocations. Critics say SII's occupational keying is mindless empiricism: "[tests like SII] have no psychological meaning. Practically, they are useful; theoretically they are almost valueless" (Kline, 1976). Kline also thinks SII redundant: "we would probably do as well to ask our clients 'What are you interested in?' as to give them the elaborate ritual of the SVIB!" [It's] "really an elaborate and technically wonderful steam hammer with which to crack an egg." However, SII also contains scales based on factor and cluster analysis: 23 *Basic Interest Scales*, and six *General Occupational Themes*: Realistic, Investigative, Artistic, Social, Enterprising, and Conventional. The General Occupational Themes

Table 8.1 Scales of the California Psychological Inventory, with brief descriptions of high and low scores, in occupational setting

Scale		Brief Description	
		Low score	High score
Do	Dominance	Non-assertive	Enjoys leadership
Cs	Capacity for Status	Not seeking major challenges	Seeks increased status
Sy	Sociability	Private person	Outgoing and sociable
Sp	Social Presence	Doesn't seek limelight	Enjoys being centre stage
Sa	Self-acceptance	Lacks self-confidence	Has self-confidence
In	Independence	Needs reassurance	Self-reliant
Em	Empathy	Poor at reading others	Good at reading others
Re	Responsibility	Careless with details	Conscientious, dependable
So	Socialization	Questioning, rebellious	Conforms readily
Sc	Self-Control	Impulsive, outspoken	Thinks before acting or speaking
Gi	Good Impression	Unconcerned about others' opinion	Careful to present favourable image
Cm	Communality	(Gives many unusual responses)	(Gives few unusual responses)
Wb	Well-being	Poor morale	Enjoys good morale
To	Tolerance	Suspicious, untrusting	Accepts others regardless of background
Ac	Achievement via Conformance	Uncomfortable fitting into a system	Likes working within a system
Ai	Achievement via Independence	Reluctant to take initiative	Likes autonomy and using initiative
Ie	Intellectual Efficiency	Prefers concrete to abstract	Enjoys intellectual challenge
Py	Psychological Mindedness	Uninterested in others' motives	Interested in others' motives
Fx	Flexibility	Wary of new ideas	Welcomes new ideas
Fe	Femininity/Masculinity	Tough-minded, insensitive	Tender-minded, sensitive

derive partly from factor analysis, and represent six types of people, each suited for a very general class of work.

Occupational Personality Questionnaires (OPQ)

A family of nine inventories, varying in *length*, and *format*. The longest versions measure 30 *Concepts*; the shorter *Factor*, *Octagon* and *Pentagon* versions measure 17, eight and five higher-order factors derived from the 30 Concepts (Figure 8.4). The OPQ uses three formats: endorsement, forced choice, and five-point rating from *strongly agree* to *strongly disagree*. The manual recommends pairs of formats be used. A meta-analysis of 20 OPQ studies (Robertson & Kinder, 1993) report (uncorrected) validities for individual scales ranging from 0.08 to 0.25, and for composites of several scales ranging from 0.09 to 0.33, according to the criterion used. Some forms of OPQ use forced-choice format, and have been criticized for creating problems of *inter-dependence* of scores (see page 147). The OPQ illustrates the expense of launching major new inventories; to recover their R & D costs, the publishers (Saville & Holdsworth Ltd) have to charge OPQ users an annual licence fee of £1350 (on top of the cost of materials and training).

OPQ FACTOR MODEL	OCTAGON MODEL	PENTAGON MODEL
PEOPLE		
Influence	Assertive	
Social confidence		
Empathy	Empathy	Extroversion
Gregarious	Gregarious	
Social desirability		
COGNITIVE STYLE		
Imaginative	Abstract	Abstract
Conservative		
Planful	Methodical	Methodical
Detail conscious		
EMOTIONS		
Relaxed	Relaxed	Emotional
Phlegmatic		stability
Optimistic	Self-controlled	
VIGOUR		
Contesting		
Active	Vigorous	Vigorous
Decisive		

Figure 8.4 The three forms of Occupational Personality Questionnaires: factors, Octagon and Pentagon, which measure 15, 8 and 5 traits (Saville and Holdsworth Ltd, 1985) (Reproduced by permission)

Assessment of Background and Life Experiences (ABLE)

Assessment of Background and Life Experiences was written for the US armed forces as part of Project A. It has 205 items, and measures six temperament constructs: Surgency, Adjustment, Agreeableness, Dependability, Intellectance, Affiliation. It also has four control scales: Random Responding, Social Desirability, Poor Impression and Self-knowledge (Hough et al, 1990).

GENERAL VALUE OF INVENTORIES

Personality inventories are less reliable than tests of mental ability. A good inventory will normally achieve re-test reliabilities of at least 0.80. This level of reliability is consistent with individual profiles, or parts of profiles, changing considerably over fairly short periods of time. Changes exceeding 0.5 SD, i.e. five T points, or one whole sten (Figure 8.2), may be expected to occur in one in three re-tests with a typical inventory. Changes exceeding 1 SD, i.e. 10 T points, or two whole stens, may be expected to occur in one in 20 re-tests. On the other hand, inventories have shown impressive long term stability. Strong (1955) reports high median re-test correlations (0.75) in SII profiles over 22 years; "those who had interests most similar to engineer, lawyer, or minister on the first occasion were ones who had scores most similar to those criterion groups on the second occasion". Similarly, Helson & Moane (1987) report long-term stability of CPI scores in women tested at ages 21, 28 and 43.

A recent meta-analysis (Schuerger, Zarrella & Hotz, 1989) finds measures of extroversion are more reliable than measures of anxiety, over intervals of up to 6 years. Another study suggests intelligence moderates reliability of personality measures. Inventories completed by low scorers on the Wonderlic Personnel Tests are much less reliable (Stone, Stone & Gueutal, 1990), because low scorers left out more questions or couldn't understand them.

Faking

Most inventories are fairly transparent. No one applying for a sales job is likely to say *true* to "I don't much like talking to strangers", nor is someone trying to join the police likely to agree that he/she has "pretty undesirable acquaintances". Faking good isn't a problem with ability tests; the only ways to get a high score on Raven's Progressive Matrices are to work out the correct answers, or cheat.

Faking may be deliberate lying, or half-conscious distortion. An inventory necessarily measures the individual's self-concept which, in well-adjusted people, is usually fairly favourable. Cronbach (1984) likens a completed inventory to a 'statesman's diary': "the image the man wished to leave in history", "the reputation the subject would like to have". Personality inventories are generally fakeable. If subjects are instructed to complete an inventory, giving the answers they think will maximize their chances of getting a job they really wanted, the resulting profiles are consistently more favourable than profiles from the same persons completed as an anonymous practical class exercise.

But do real applicants fake inventories? The GZTS profiles completed by job applicants are 'better' than profiles completed by people seeking counselling or taking part in research (Herzberg, 1954), but nowhere near as 'good' as faked good profiles. This implies real applicants are relatively honest, compared with subjects in fake-good studies. Dunnette et al (1962) estimated one in seven applicants for sales jobs faked, and even they faked less than subjects in fake-good studies. People already employed fake less than applicants (which means tests validated on existing staff may not work so well for applicants). Hough et al (1990) analysed the moderating effect of faking good on ABLE, using very large samples, and found faking good doesn't reduce validity. Ones, et al (undated) reach similar conclusions in their analysis of 'integrity' tests.

There are many lines of defence against faking:

1. *Rapport*   The tester can try to persuade the subjects it's not in their interests to fake, because getting a job for which one's personality isn't really suited will ultimately cause unhappiness, failure, etc. This argument may have limited appeal to those who haven't any job, ideal or otherwise.

2. *Faking verboten*   At the other extreme, military testers have been known to warn their subjects that faking, if detected, will be severely punished.

3. *Subtle questions*   "Do you like meeting strangers" is clearly a crass question when selecting a door-to-door salesman. Is it possible to find subtler questions? Authors of empirically keyed inventories like to think so. Gough argues many CPI items are too subtle to be faked easily; "There are times when I act like a coward" is keyed *true* for Dominance, because, Gough argues, dominant people can admit to feeling fear occasionally. Critics say inventory questions can be divided into the unsubtle that work, and the subtle that don't.

4. *Control keys*   Many inventories contain *lie scales*, more politely known as *social desirability* scales. Lie scales are lists of answers that deny common faults, or claim uncommon virtues, or both. A high score alerts the test user to the possibility of less than total candour. The CPI's lie scale is called Good impression (Gi); when subjects are instructed to 'fake good' on the CPI, 95% of the faked profiles include Gi scores over 60. However, lie scales aren't always all that subtle. Subjects who know the Eysenck Personality Inventory has extraversion, neuroticism and lie questions can tell which is which (Power & MacRae, 1971). But do naive subjects know about lie scales?

5. Correcting for defensiveness A high lie score reveals the subject's answers can't be trusted, which is clearly worth knowing. However, the assessor is then left without an interpretable personality profile. The MMPI's *K* key measures defensiveness, then seeks to correct the profile by adding varying proportions of *K*. Cattell (1986) suggests inventories need a *distortion matrix*, of different sets of corrections for different purposes: counselling, selection, clinical diagnosis, military screening, etc. Cronbach (1984) is sceptical: "if the subject lies to the tester there is no way to convert the lies into truth".

6. Forced choice Choice format questions can be equated for desirability, so the subject must choose between pairs of equally flattering or unflattering statements:

> I am very good at making friends with people,
> I am respected by all my colleagues.
>
> I lose my temper occasionally,
> I am sometimes late for appointments.

Forced-choice format has several snags. It's slower, and people don't like it. It also creates *inter-dependence* between scales (see page 147). Forced-choice format is supposed to prevent faking, but doesn't always succeed. The forced-choice format Edwards Personal Preference Schedule (EPPS) is still fakeable, because pairing questions for *general* desirability doesn't make them equally desirable for every *specific* purpose.

7. Change the questionnaire's format Cattell's Motivation Analysis Test uses several novel question formats, some of which are probably quite hard to fake. The *Information* sub-test consists of factual questions, with verifiable answers, and works on the principle that people know more about things that matter to them. An aggressive person is more likely to know which of the following *isn't* a type of firearm: Gatling, Sterling, Gresley, Enfield, FN. The *Estimates* sub-test includes a mix of objective questions, such the quarantine period after rabies, and subjective questions, such as the relative importance of money and sex appeal. Cattell assumes peoples' needs shape the replies they give, so a person motivated by fear thinks quarantine periods *are* longer, because he/she thinks they *ought* to be longer.

8. Don't use questionnaires There are other ways of assessing personality: projective tests, behavioural tests, ratings and check-lists, observations, biodata, and assessment centres.

9. Accept the inevitable Elliott (1981) suggests faking good shows the applicant knows what's expected, whereas the person who produces an honest but bad profile either doesn't know what's expected at work, or isn't prepared to deliver. Faked responses on the Gordon Personal Inventory correlate quite well with clerical performance, whereas scores corrected for faking have no predictive value.

Forced choice and inter-dependence

Forced-choice format creates *inter-dependence* between scales, which can make interpretation difficult. Consider the Allport–Vernon–Lindzey Study of Values (AVL). On the AVL, the six scores must total 180; the test's instructions advise using this as a check on scoring accuracy. If all six scores must total 180, the person who wants to express a strong preference for one value must express less interest in one or more others; it's impossible to get six very high scores, or to get six very low scores.

Several authors (Johnson, Wood & Blinkhorn, 1988; Cook, 1992) have pointed out that inter-dependence in forced-choice questionnaires makes it impossible to use them *normatively*. The typical forced-choice measure can conclude that a person is more interested in dominating others than in helping others (an *ipsative* comparison). Forced-choice measures can't usually conclude that person A is more interested in dominating others than is person B— but the latter is the comparison selectors usually want to make. Using forced-choice questionaires to compare people or groups can give very misleading results. Comparing senior and middle managers, AVL data appear to show senior managers less interested in *religious* values (Grimsley & Jarrett, 1973). Are senior managers really less religious? Or is it their lowest priority, which they're willing to give up, to make room for a stronger interest in some other value—theoretical, economic, social, political, aesthetic? But which?

USING INVENTORIES IN PERSONNEL SELECTION

Inventories answer three main questions:

1. Has the applicant the right personality for the job?
2. Will he/she be any good at the job?
3. Is there anything wrong with him/her?

Questions 1 and 2 look very similar, but differ subtly. Question 1 is answered by comparing bank managers with people in general; question 2 is answered by comparing *good* and *poor* bank managers. Question 1 uses the survival or gravitational criterion of success; people *gravitate* to jobs they can do well, and then *survive*, so anyone who has been a bank manager for 10 years must be reasonably good at it. But suppose there are jobs where no one is ever sacked, or even criticized, for inefficiency? Survival then proves nothing.

Question 1: the right personality?

Miller (1976) is conscious of a "strong demand from personnel officers, or their managing directors, ... for a profile involving all of the traits assessed by the questionnaire". Employers want a book of perfect personality profiles for manager, salesman, engineer, computer programmer, etc. Manuals for some tests meet this demand; 16PF and CPI manuals both give norms for different occupations. The 16PF handbook (Cattell, Eber & Tatsuoka, 1970) suggests matching applicants to profiles. For some occupations, the handbook gives detailed *specification equations*; for others it suggests which scales should be above average, and which below: for example, naval officer cadets are "able (B+), rather adventurous (E+, H+), and active (F+) ... with practical realism (I–, M–, N+) and have good control mechanisms (C+, Q3+)".

Figure 8.5 shows a composite CPI profile, for an occupational group showing how it deviates from *men in general*. Security-van crewmen score below average on Capacity for Status, Responsibility, Tolerance, both forms of Achievement, Intellectual Efficiency, and Empathy.

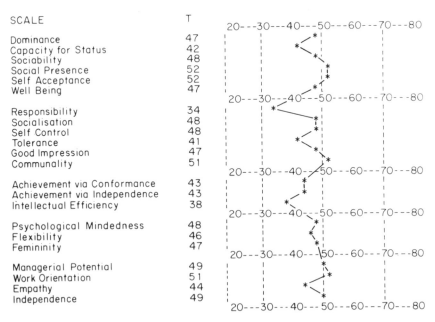

Figure 8.5 Composite CPI profile for 30 security van crewmen. (Modified and reproduced by special permission of the Publisher, Consulting Psychologists Press, Inc., Palo Alto, CA 94303, from *Profile Form for the California Psychological Inventory* by Harrison G. Gough. Copyright 1986 by Consulting Psychologists Press, Inc. All rights reserved. Further reproduction is prohibited without the Publisher's written consent.)

The *perfect profile* approach has several limitations.

(a) The sample sizes for occupational profiles in 16PF's manual range from 18 to 1707, with a median of 90, which probably isn't big enough.
(b) Cross-validation information is rarely available. Ideally, a perfect profile for a cost accountant will be based on two or more large, separate, samples.
(c) The perfect profile is an average, about which scores vary a lot.
(d) Most perfect profiles derive from people doing the job, taking no account of how well they do it, nor how happy they are.
(e) The perfect profile may show how well the person has adapted to the job's demands, not how well people with that profile will fit the job.

The SII's Occupational Interest Scales are based entirely on gravitation and survival. The SII occupational samples are drawn from people who have been in their work at least 3 years, and who have achieved some success, most typically in the form of membership of their professional body. Personnel managers, for example, were all members of the American Society for Personnel Administration. The SII scores predict career choice and satisfaction very accurately; Strong (1955) reports an 18-year follow up of Stanford students. Those with A ratings (interests very similar) for a profession had a 3.6 to 1 chance of entering that profession, whereas students with C ratings (interests very dissimilar) had a 5 to 1 chance of *not* entering that profession. Students who had entered careers their interests suited them for were happier in their work.

Recent research on personality (Cook, 1993), and attitudes (Keller et al, 1992) suggests a large heritable element in both, which could be interpreted as implying that some people are temperamentally better suited to certain kinds of work.

Question 2: will he/she be successful?

Many researches have used inventories to predict creativity, effective management or just 'success'.

Creativity

A battery of seven inventories predicted creativity in architects, with varying success (Hall & MacKinnon, 1969). The CPI did fairly well, achieving a cross validated multiple correlation of 0.47. The SII did very well—achieving a cross-validated multiple correlation over 57 scales of 0.55. Other personality measures—Gough Adjective Check List (ACL), Myers Briggs Type Indicator, FIRO-B, and AVL—also achieved moderately high cross-validated multiple correlations. Only the MMPI failed to predict creativity.

Effective management

Mahoney, Jerdee & Nash (1960) divided 468 managers into two parallel sets of effective and ineffective. The managers were tested with CPI, SII, Wonderlic Personnel Test, and a Biodata Inventory; cut-off points that distinguished effective from ineffective were calculated on one sample, then cross-validated on a second. The effective manager is:

> somewhat more intelligent than the 'less effective' manager; his vocational interests are more similar to the interests of sales managers, purchasing agents, and manufacturing company presidents; and they are less similar to the interests of men engaged in biological sciences and technical crafts ... he tends to be more aggressive, persuasive, and self-reliant; he has had more educational training and was more active in sports and hobbies as a young man; and his wife also has had more educational training and worked less after marriage.

Success

In Stanford MBAs 5 years after graduation, GZTS Ascendance predicts higher income (Harrell, 1972); the difference is fairly small—corresponding to a correlation of roughly 0.20. In MBAs working for *large* firms (1000+ employees), GZTS Social Interest and General Energy and MMPI Mania also predicted success. Harrell thinks success in large firms requires high, almost manic, energy levels. [However, VGAs of ability tests (Chapter 7) make one wary of suggesting organizational climate 'moderates' predictive validity, on the strength of just one study.] Baehr & Orban (1989) report a similar study, using personality and MA tests to predict salary in 800 line managers, salespersons, professionals (engineers, architects) and technical experts (programmers, analysts). The personality measures achieved incremental validity over the MA tests, for line and sales managers, less so for professionals, and not at all for technical experts.

Fighter pilots and clerical workers

The Eysenck Personality Inventory (EPI) has 57 items, measuring extraversion and neuroticism. The EPI was written to test Eysenck's experimental and biological theory of personality, not for personnel testing. Nevertheless Bartram & Dale (1982) found men who failed flying training were less stable and more introvert. The correlations weren't very large, but EPI takes only 10 minutes to complete, and pilot training is extremely expensive, so any increase in predictive validity is worth having. Eysenck's personality theory generates many predictions with direct relevance for work. He predicts extroverts lack persistence in repetitive tasks, which in turn implies they will be bored by routine clerical work; Sterns et al (1983) found extroverts less satisfied in clerical jobs, and Cooper & Payne (1967) found extroverts tended to leave jobs sooner.

Assessment of Background and Life Experiences

ABLE is validated against five criteria, in very large samples of seven or eight thousand soldiers (Hough et al, 1990; McHenry et al 1990). The ABLE scales predict three composite criteria (*effort and leadership, personal discipline, physical fitness and military bearing*), but not the other two (*technical proficiency* or *general soldiering proficiency*); the correlations are modest—in the region of 0.10 and 0.20—but have not been corrected for criterion reliability or restricted range. Furthermore, ABLE contributes *incremental validity*, predicting aspects of soldiers' performance that weren't predicted by MA tests. The sample size was large enough to check various factors that might plausibly be thought to lower ABLE's validity: faking good, malingering, or lack of self-knowledge. The data showed none of these factors reduced correlations between ABLE scores and the five criteria. Only one 'test-taking attitude' lowered ABLE's validity—careless responding.

Unskilled workers

Inventories like 16PF and CPI are too long and difficult for unskilled workers; Johnson, Messe & Crano (1984) describe a short inventory designed specifically for low-income workers. The Work Opinion Questionnaire has only 35 items, all fairly short—"Supervisors are too bossy", "If something goes wrong on the job, I get blamed". Scores correlate moderately well with supervisor ratings.

Honeymoon period

Helmreich, Sawin & Carsrud (1986) reported that inventory measures of *commitment to work* only correlated with performance in telephone reservation clerks *after* the first 3 months. The first 3 months was the 'honeymoon period' when new staff were still trying hard all the time; only after the honeymoon was over did personality differences emerge, as some new staff started following output norms, or making less effort.

Summaries of validity of personality inventories

Earlier reviews (Guion & Gottier, 1965; Lent, Aurbach & Levin, 1971; Dunnette, 1972; Ghiselli, 1973) generally make depressing reading—low correlations and insignificant differences being the usual outcome. No measure stands out as better or worse. Most studies use small samples. Dunnette (1972) meta-analysed 134 validity coefficients for the American petroleum industry. Interest and personality inventories both achieved near zero median validity; however, the best 25% of coefficients for personality tests exceeded 0.37, suggesting perhaps tests can predict productivity if used properly. Ghiselli (1973) calculated pooled validities across eight broad classes of job, for training and proficiency criteria; validity averaged at or below 0.20 for most jobs, but reached 0.30 for executives and sales staff (as high as MA tests). Personality and interest tests were rarely used for industrial workers, and weren't very widely used for trades and crafts workers.

Recently four *meta-analytic* reviews have been calculated, three of them also using *validity generalization analysis* (Hough, 1988, in press; Barrick & Mount, 1991; Tett, Jackson & Rothstein, 1991; Ones et al, in press). Two reviews use the 'big five' framework, while a third (Hough) uses an extended form of it. The fourth review (Ones et al, undated) analyses 'integrity' tests, which measure one of the 'big five'—honesty. Three reviews show that a general *job proficiency* criterion is poorly predicted by personality tests (Table 8.2); even making

Table 8.2 Four meta-analyses of personality test validity, using the "big five" categorization of personality. The outcome predicted is job proficiency.

	Corrected validity			Raw validity		
	B&M	Tett	Ones	B&M	Tett	Hough
'Big five'						
extroversion	10	16		06	10	
ascendancy						10
sociability						00
adjustment	07	22		04	15	09
agreeableness	06	33		04	22	05
conscientiousness	23	18	41	13	12	08
openness	- 03	27		- 02	18	01
Hough's three extra scales						
achievement						15
locus control						11
masculinity						08

B&M — Barrick & Mount (1991; data from Table 2), values based on between 82 and 124 correlations, and total pooled sample of between 14 236 and 19 511; correlations are corrected for restricted range, criterion reliability and *test reliability*.

Ones — Ones et al (in press; data from Table 8), value based on 23 correlations and 7550 subjects; correlations are corrected for restricted range, and criterion reliability.

Tett — Tett et al (1991; data from Table 5), based on between 4 and 15 correlations, and between 280 and 2302 subjects. Corrected validity corrected for criterion reliability and test reliability, but not restricted range.

Hough — Hough (1992; data from Table 3), based on between 15 and 274 correlations, and between 2811 and 65 876 subjects. Hough's correlations are not corrected for unreliability of test or criterion, nor for restricted range.

every possible allowance, for restricted range, unreliability, etc, personality inventories mostly couldn't even reach the 0.30 barrier, let alone break it. The fourth analysis reports that 'integrity' tests achieve good *true validity* (0.41) against a supervisor rating criterion. Barrick & Mount's average validities are lower than those of Tett et al, because the latter ignored sign when averaging correlations, whereas Barrick's & Mount's analysis averaged -0.20 and 0.20 to give 0.00, which clearly tends to depress average validity. (Whereas the correlation between MA tests and job performance is always positive, the relationship between personality and performance isn't necessarily; extraversion might be an asset in some jobs, such as selling, but a liability in others, such as lighthouse keeper.) The average validities obtained by Tett et al for the 'big five' are higher, because they include only studies that stated a hypothesis about personality and job proficiency. Neither difference between the two analyses explains why Tett et al find *openness* and *agreeableness* achieve higher validities, whereas Barrick & Mount find *conscientiousness* achieves the highest validity. Ones et al (in press) note that Tett et al include only published studies, which may be biased towards 'more positive' results; they also argue that the meta-analysis of Tett et al contains errors of interpretation.

The VGA of Tett et al identifies finds several moderators of personality test validity. Validity is higher when the experimenter is testing a hypothesis about personality and work performance, rather than firing a shotgun full of scales; Ones et al (in press) argue however that many researchers 'find' hypotheses, after they have found significant correlations. Tett et al report validity is higher still (0.38) when job analysis is used to select the tests, almost justifying the 0.40 estimate for inventory validity optimistically quoted in some quarters. Barrick & Mount find one occupational difference; extraversion predicts success in sales and management but not in other occupations. Tett et al, however, find no occupational differences.

Hough's meta-analysis was conducted as part of Project A, and reaches several important conclusions.

1. Hough started with the 'big five', but found it useful to split extroversion into *ascendancy* and *sociability*. She also found some personality traits, which didn't fit into the 'big five', had much higher validity, leading her to conclude the 'big five' is an unhelpful over-simplification.

2. Hough's (1988) meta-analysis distinguishes six other criteria besides *job proficiency*, including *training success, commendable behaviour, non-delinquency* and *non-substance abuse. Commendable behaviour* is defined as "letters of recommendation, letters of reprimand, disciplinary actions, demotions, involuntary terminations, ratings of effort, hard work". *Delinquency* means actual theft, conviction or imprisonment; *substance abuse* means drink and drugs. While inventories generally failed to predict the *job*

proficiency criterion, they could predict *commendable behaviour* and *non-substance abuse* moderately well (0.20–0.39), and *non-delinquency* very well (up to 0.52). Ones et al confirm this, finding a *true validity* of 0.32 for *counterproductive behaviours*, defined as breaking rules, being disciplined, being dismissed for theft, being rated as disruptive by supervisor.

3. Hough (1988) compared 37 different inventories, and concluded some predicted much better than others. The "best all-round inventory" was the CPI, which achieved *uncorrected* correlations as high as 0.64 with *non-delinquency* (Table 8.3). The CPI also predicted *commendable behaviours* and drink and drug problems in the workplace very well. Many of the other 36 inventories included in Hough's meta-analysis succeeded in predicting very little.

Question 3: Is there anything wrong with him/her?

Personality inventories can be used like the driving test: not to select the best, but to exclude the unacceptable. Honesty testing is used on a very large scale in the USA. Employees are also screened for (mal)*adjustment*. Screening for *burnout* is becoming popular in some professions.

Adjustment

Anderson's (1929) survey of staff at Macy's department store in New York found 20% employees fell into the "problem" category—can't learn, suffer chronic ill-health, are in constant trouble with fellow-employees, can't adjust satisfactorily to their work. A survey of over 1000 British workers found 20–30% suffering some measurable level of neurosis (Culpin & Smith, 1930). These figures may seem improbably high, but are confirmed by *community surveys* of mental health; if psychologists go out looking for maladjusted people, instead of waiting for them to be referred, one in five is the typical ratio they discover. Anderson used a clinical interview—time-consuming, and expensive. Culpin & Smith used interviews and the McDougall–Schuster Dotting Task: subjects try to make marks in small circles on a paper disk that rotates faster and faster, which requires good motor control, good attention and freedom from panic. Good performers had fewer neurotic symptoms.

In the USA, 42 States screen to identify people who are emotionally or psychologically unfit for police work. The MMPI is the favourite test, with CPI, EPPS and 16PF the runners up. Hargrave & Hiatt (1989) compared 45 'problem' police officers with 45 matched controls, who had all completed CPI on joining the force. The problem group had lower Socialization, Self-control, Well-being and Tolerance, indicating they tended to greater impulsivity, risk-taking, intolerance and willingness to break the rules. Problem officers were much more likely to have scores more than one SD below the general average.

Officials in the American nuclear power industry were able to list over 150 cases of 'disturbing behaviour' in nuclear power plant operators. Psychologists advised the industry to test all operators on hiring with MMPI and CPI, and to re-test periodically (Dunnette et al, 1981, cited in Cronbach, 1984). Dunnette thought MMPI 4-9 *types* likely to be a risk—because they are prone to "argumentative hostility" and "impulsive action".

Table 8.3 Meta-analysis of the validity of scales of the California Psychological Inventory, against five criteria (Hough, 1988)

	JOB	TRN	COM	NDL	NSA
Dominance	—	—	30	38	—
Capacity for status	—	—	—	39	—
Sociability	—	—	—	25	—
Social presence	—	—	—	29	—
Self-acceptance	—	—	—	20	—
Well-being	—	—	—	35	—
Responsibility	—	—	44	56	32
Socialization	—	—	32*	64*	41
Self-control	—	—	—	20	24
Tolerance	—	—	—	48	—
Good impression	—	—	—	—	—
Communality	—	—	—	—	—
Achievement via conformance	—	—	—	43	26
Achievement via independence	—	21	33	42	- 27
Intellectual efficiency	—	—	—	46	- 23
Psychological mindedness	—	—	—	—	—
Flexibility	—	—	—	—	—
Femininity/masculinity	—	—	—	—	—
N correlations/N subjects		9/1160	2/4144 *4/4318	2/5918 *7/15851	2/148

JOB	—	overall job proficiency; technical proficiency, advancement.
TRN	—	training grades and ratings.
COM	—	commendable behaviours: reprimands, disciplinary, dismissals, demotions.
NDL	—	non-delinquency: theft, offences, imprisonment.
NSA	—	non-substance abuse: drugs, alcohol consumed, addiction.

* except for these values.

Burnout

People in some professions—counsellors, police officers, teachers, child care workers, nurses, lawyers—experience "emotional exhaustion resulting from chronic tension and stress in people helping work" (Meier, 1984). *Burnout* is caused by lack of reward and encouragement, frequent 'punishment', and the feeling that one has no control over whether people are pleased or displeased with one's work. Burnout can be assessed by Maslach Burnout Inventory. Cynics note that burnout seems to occur almost exclusively in the public sector; 'burned out' managers and salesmen, if such exist, are dismissed.

Military screening

Very large numbers of US service men were screened during the Second World War; Ellis & Conrad (1948) describe MMPI and shorter inventories as "sieves separating the recruits into ... those who had to be screened further by a clinician ... and those who needed no further screening". Some studies reported very high correlations between inventory scores and adjustment—as high as 0.80. Other studies reported cutting points of amazing efficiency— anyone scoring over 25 on the Cornell Selectee Index "invariably fell into the category of severe psychoneurotics" while anyone with a Cornell score under 15 "could almost as readily be accepted for employment".

   Some military screening results *were* too good to be true. Many studies suffered *criterion contamination*, which means the psychiatrist making the diagnosis knew the man's test score. Faking was less likely in military testing, because many men didn't *want* to get good scores, because many weren't intelligent enough to fake, and because the military could issue dire threats about what would happen to anyone who was found to have given untrue answers. Military testing reached men other test programmes never saw: "unemployables, tramps, loafers, 'bums', alcoholics, frank neurotics", so it suffered an unusual statistical problem—*excessive* (as opposed to *restricted*) *range*. There's a *wider* range of individual differences in conscript samples than in typical applicant samples, so the test can correlate better. It's useful to know how a test performs on a complete cross-section of American men, but not all that relevant to civilian employers who aren't interested in screening out people who'd never apply anyway, or wouldn't get past the receptionist if they did.

   Callan (1972) describes a more recent US military screening, again using the MMPI (in a slightly unorthodox way; groups of 200 men at a time listened to the questions being played by a tape recorder over a public address system— answering 'by numbers'?). Callan first wrote a key that predicted discharge, absence without leave, malingering and disciplinary problem, then cross-validated it on 3328 recruits. Table 8.4 shows his best results (he tried several scoring methods). Callan—unlike Ellis & Conrad—didn't think screening cost-effective, because it wrongly turned away more good candidates (*false positives*) than it detected genuine problem cases (*true positives*).

Table 8.4 Best results achieved (on cross-validation) by Callan's (1972) military delinquency Minnesota Multiphasic Personality Inventory (MMPI) key

MMPI key's prediction	Outcome	
	Problem	Not problem
Problem	80 (True positive)	156 (False positive)
Not problem	232 (False negative)	2860 (True negative)

Honesty testing

Questionnaires are widely used in the USA to screen out staff thought more likely to steal money or goods (Sackett & Harris, 1984; Ones et al, in press). Some are 'mainstream' personality tests, published by major psychological test publishers. Many other honesty or 'integrity' tests are written and published by organizations who specialize in that type of testing specifically. Honesty tests have gained extra popularity since 1988 when use of the polygraph was restricted. Ones et al (undated) were able to find 665 validity coefficients, across 576 460 subjects, for their VGA. Honesty testing is most popular in the retail sector. Honesty tests use various approaches: indirect questions that assume dishonest people see crime as more frequent, or see crime as easier, or questions that present dishonesty as meriting less punishment, or as more easily justified (by low wages, etc.).

Honesty tests have been validated against polygraph assessments, or by comparisons of convicted criminals and control subjects. One study reported high correlations between honesty scores and how often the employee's till was more than $5 short. Another study correlated honesty scores with the amount collected by paid charity collectors, on the assumption low takings meant the collector was helping him/herself. However, many honesty tests are 'validated' by including questions asking subjects to admit past dishonesty, and using these questions as 'criterion' for the rest of the measure. This is obviously a very weak form of validation. Some validation, however, does use more solid criteria, such as supervisor rating, or externally measured behaviour; the VGA reported by Ones et al concludes honesty tests predict both general *job proficiency*, and *counterproductive behaviours* very well. Mainstream psychological tests and specialist honesty tests perform equally well.

Honesty testing, like the polygraph before it, generates a high rate of *false positives*—about one in four.

Employee *reliability* is broader concept than honesty; it covers "counterproductive acts such as: theft, drug and alcohol abuse, lying, insubordination, vandalism, sabotage, absenteeism and assaultive actions". Hogan & Hogan (1989) describe an inventory, based on *homogeneous item composites*, and report 13 concurrent validation studies against very varied organizational delinquency criteria: injuries, rated attitude and sales figures.

Problems in personality screening

The value of screening depends on:

(a)   Whether it's accurate.
(b)   *Base rate*—what proportion of applicants are maladjusted, dishonest or indisciplined. In Callan's data, the base rate was only 9%, whereas in the earlier surveys by Anderson (1929) and Culpin & Smith (1930) it was nearer 30%. The lower the base rate, i.e. the less frequent the problem is, the less successful any screening programme will be.
(c)   *Selection ratio*—what proportion of applicants are accepted. Screening, like any selection exercise, works better when there are lots of applicants to choose from.
(d)   How serious are the consequences of a *miss*. A dishonest sales assistant is less of a threat than an unstable armed police officer.
(e)   What happens to positives—*true* or *false*. In US military screenings, all positives were seen by a psychiatrist, so weren't necessarily lost.

Some critics think the existence of *false positives* a strong argument for not using honesty tests, because a false positive means an honest person wrongly accused of dishonesty. False positives will always happen, because no test will ever be perfectly valid. A less radical argument suggests screening tests shouldn't be used if the false positive rate exceeds the *true positive* rate, i.e. if someone who 'fails' the test is more likely to be honest than dishonest. Martin & Terris (1991) argue the false positive issue is irrelevant; if the test has any validity, then using it will benefit the organization by excluding some dishonest persons. They also argue that *not* screening in reality creates a higher false positive rate; *not* screening implies accepting more dishonest persons, thereby excluding some honest individuals who might otherwise have got the job. On this argument screening, by and large, benefits honest applicants. Guastello & Rieke (1991) disagree with Martin & Terris; a *false positive* on an honesty test means labelling someone dishonest when he/she is not, and abridging that person's civil rights by implicitly accusing them of theft but denying them any opportunity to answer. Sackett & Harris suggest it's not unreasonable to reject *applicants* on the strength of honesty tests, given that all selection is imperfect and that all job applicants face rejections. They argue equally strongly it would be wrong to use honesty tests on *established employees*.

INVENTORIES AND THE LAW

Inventories have come in for surprisingly little criticism—given their generally poor validity, and the ease with which they can be ridiculed. The Psychological Corporation's (1978) review of 'fair' employment cases between 1968 and 1977 mentions only one case, from 112, in which a personality test—16PF—featured.

Sex differences

The SII originally had separate male and female forms, appropriately printed on pink and blue paper. The questions were merged into a common form in 1966, but SII still retains different scoring keys for the Occupational Interest scales. Virtually every occupation has a pair of separate male and female keys. Great effort has gone into finding samples of female farmers and male beauticians, etc. Other vocational interest inventories prefer to devise *common* keys for male and female soldiers, travel agents, bus drivers, etc., partly to simplify scoring and interpretation, partly to head off criticism about gender discrimination. Hansen (1976) argues it's unrealistic to seek common keys at present, because men and women doing the same job often do it for different reasons and have different outlooks; male pharmacists are typically entrepreneurs, whereas female pharmacists have a more scientific interest in their work. Common scoring keys eliminate questions that create sex differences, which shortens the scoring key, and reduces its reliability.

Privacy

Inventories were criticized for invasion of privacy during the 1960s. The US Senate voted that "no [guidance] program shall provide for the conduct of any test ... to elicit information dealing with the personality, environment, home life, parental or family relationships, economic status, or sociological and psychological problems of the pupil tested". It must be very difficult to 'guide' someone without being allowed to learn anything about their background, personality or problems.

The use of MMPI to assess ability to withstand stress in fire fighters was challenged as an invasion of privacy, but was ruled acceptable "in the public interest". Similarly, the right of law enforcement agencies to use psychological tests has also been upheld; in fact in one case the plaintiff won substantial damages when a police officer shot and crippled his wife, because the officer *hadn't* been screened.

Negligent hiring

In 1979 the Avis car-rental company were sued when an employee raped a customer, and was subsequently found to have previous convictions for similar offences. Avis should, it was claimed, have found out that the man was dangerous. Avis lost the case, since when negligent hiring claims have become common in the USA (Ryan & Lasek, 1991). How can employers foresee crimes employees might commit against customers? Personality tests or biodata could screen out some potentially dangerous persons, but only at the expense of a high false positive rate.

ALTERNATIVES TO THE INVENTORY

"Across the front of each test and each manual, there should be stamped in large, red letters (preferably letters which will glow in the stygian darkness of the personality measurement field) the word EXPERIMENTAL" (Gustad, 1956). Everyone agrees inventories have limitations, but what can replace them?

Projective tests

Projective tests assume everything a person does, says, writes, thinks, paints or even dreams reflects his/her personality. If people don't know they are revealing their personalities, they can't censor themselves and consciously or unconsciously 'fake good'. Projective tests are even more numerous and vastly more varied than questionnaires/inventories. Kinslinger's (1966) review covers six tests widely used in US personnel research:

- Rorschach (and several variants),
- Thematic Apperception Test (TAT) and variants, including Vocational Apperception Test,
- Worthington Personal History,
- sentence completion tests,
- Tomkins–Horn Picture Arrangement Test,
- Rosenzweig Picture Frustration Study.

Rorschach

Subjects describe what they see in a set of inkblots. The Rorschach is classically scored by deciding if the response is based on detail or the whole blot, on colour or form, etc. Multiple-choice scoring has also been used. Rorschach scores are very poor at differentiating physical scientists, technicians, biologists, anthropologists, psychologists and artists. Other studies reviewed by Kinslinger found Rorschach unable to distinguish production engineers, research engineers, lab technicians and administrators. Rorschach is similarly unable to predict success at work. Early studies, described by Dorcus & Jones (1950), thought TAT and Rorschach the ideal way to predict turnover or accident proneness in tram (streetcar) drivers in Southern California; neither test predicted anything. Kelly & Fiske's (1950) study found Rorschach scores unable to predict success in clinical psychology. Other studies reviewed by Kinslinger similarly failed to find Rorschach reliably predicted any aspect of productivity.

Thematic Apperception Test (TAT)

A set of pictures carefully chosen both for their suggestive content and their vagueness is used. The subject describes "what led up to the event shown in the picture, what is happening, what the characters are thinking and feeling, and what the outcome will be". The subject 'projects' into the story his/her own "dominant drives, emotions, sentiments, complexes and conflicts".

Much research with TAT has used it to assess *need for achievement (nAch)* (Chapter 11). Rodger (1959) found 'route' salesmen, tested by Rorschach and TAT, showed "markedly rigid personality structures and personality impoverishment"; the salesmen had no strongly held opinions of their own, but were skilled at taking the lead from what others thought; they were materially oriented, to the point of being "less inhibited by concepts of right and wrong"; their relations with others were superficial, to the point of "conceal[ing] distrust behind a facade of congeniality".

Tomkins—Horn Picture Arrangement Test (PAT)

Sets of three pictures, which can be arranged in various sequences, are used. If the subject chooses a sequence that ends with the hero in others' company, the choice scores for *general sociophilia*. Critics say the test has too many scoring keys, many of which are too short. Miner (1971) used the PAT for selecting management consultants, concurrently validated against management ratings. The PAT showed successful consultants are drawn to authority figures, don't want to be alone when away from work, prefer physically close relationships and move towards supportive relationships. They can act independently, want to be with more powerful people and don't want to be with peers. The results make sense, given that management consultants spend a lot of time with bosses of large companies. A composite PAT score correlated very well with success.

Sentence completion tests

These are more structured, and easier to score, but not necessarily very subtle:

> My last boss was ...
> I don't like people who ...

The Rotter Incomplete Sentences Test has some scope for screening out disturbed persons. The Miner Sentence Completion Scale is written for selecting managers; it measures: attitude to authority, competitive motivation, masculine role, etc. According to Miner, the test can predict promotion in marketing and other managers (Miner, 1978). AT&T's Management Progress Study used two-sentence completion tests, and the TAT, from which composite scores were drawn by a clinical psychologist. The projective tests predicted salary increase less successfully than assessment-centre ratings.

Worthington Personal History Blank (WPHB)

This is a specially designed four-page application form, that gives the applicant the fullest scope for revealing his/her personality. The space for name is just that—a space, with no indication whether to put surname first, use full initials, titles or whatever. An applicant who wrote "Jonathan Jasper Jones Jnr" stood out because men usually use initials; exceptions tend to be "young men who haven't yet made their way in the world" (Spencer & Worthington, 1952). Early research suggested the WPHB was very promising; *qualitative* scoring predicted output in factory workers very well. Other studies, described by Kinslinger, found the WPHB could predict supervisory potential, and characterize workers in ways supervisors and managers agreed with. Owens, however, found the WPHB of little value (Clark & Owens, 1954). Owens went on to develop biodata methods (Chapter 6)—the exact opposite of the WPHB. The WPHB is intentionally open-ended and subjectively scored, whereas WABs and biodata are highly structured and quantitatively scored.

Miscellaneous tests

Personal construct theory (Cook, 1993) argues the way people see or *construe* the world, and people in it, determines how they act, so assessment of *personal constructs* is central to understanding people. Personal construct theory (Kelly, 1955) provides two ways of assessing personal constructs: *self-characterization*, and the *Role Repertory Grid test ('rep test')*. The self-characterization is a sketch written, in the third person, as if by a close, sympathetic friend; Kelly (1955) thinks it a good way of finding out about someone.

The *Repertory Grid*, as originally conceived by Kelly, is an elaborate procedure, in which:

1. The subject writes the initials of people filling significant *roles* in his/her life: e.g father, mother, spouse, teacher, boss, etc.
2. The subject *sorts* three roles, e.g. self, father, mother, stating which one differs from the other two, e.g. self and father differ from mother.
3. The subject names the *construct* used to sort the three roles, e.g. male/female.
4. The subject applies the construct to the other roles, i.e. saying which are male, which female.
5. The subject repeats steps 2–4 a number of times for different sets of three roles.

The *rep test* reveals how the subject groups people, what concepts he/she uses to group them, and how many independent ways of understanding others the subject has. The *rep test* has been very popular, especially in Britain, but has never proved to predict much, including productivity.

CONCLUSIONS

'Personality test' means, in practice, personality *inventory*; other methods are generally cumbersome and ineffective.

Research on validity of inventories was for a long time very disappointing. The earlier narrative reviews found validity coefficients very inconsistent, but tending to be small. Recent meta-analyses, however, begin to paint a more positive picture. Inventories have some predictive validity, especially for motivational, 'will do' rather than 'can do', aspects of performance. This validity is incremental, adding to the validity of MA tests. Some inventories give better results than others: the CPI, ABLE, and integrity tests emerge with credit from the recent meta-analyses.

The best estimates of inventory validity (CPI, ABLE, etc.) suggests they can perform as well (c. 0.40) as *Weighted Application Blanks* and *Biodata* (Chapter 6), or *assessment centres* (Chapter 9).

9 Assessment Centres

Does your face fit?

An assessment centre (AC) isn't a place; it's a method. It's not a cut-and-dried copyright method, like the Wonderlic Personnel Test, or McMurray's Programmed Interview; it's a very broad class of method. Assessment centres were invented simultaneously both sides of the Atlantic: War Office Selection Board (WOSB) in Britain, and Office of Strategic Services (OSS) programme in the USA.

Before 1943, the British Army selected its officers by conventional, *short* tests: recommendation, and interview. The most striking feature of WOSB was *length*, so it became known as the 'country-house weekend'. Candidates were assessed by a variety of methods. Tests included group discussions and group tasks, such as planning how to escape over an electrified wire entanglement. Typical topics for discussion included: "Is saluting a waste of time?" The WOSB included group exercises, "to assess the subject's ability to get on with and influence his colleagues, to display qualities of spontaneous leadership and to think and produce ideas in a real life situation" (Parry, 1959). Group discussions and group exercises have remained a key feature of ACs since. The WOSB assessors included: board president, visiting member, psychiatrist and military testing officer.

In the USA, psychologists led by Henry Murray were advising the OSS, forerunner of the CIA, how to select agents to be dropped behind enemy lines, collect intelligence, and return it to Headquarters. Murray's team identified nine dimensions to effective spying: practical intelligence, emotional stability, leadership, physical ability, propaganda skills, maintenance of cover, etc. 'Maintenance of cover' required each candidate to pretend to be someone else throughout the assessment—"to have been born where he wasn't, to have been educated in institutions other than those he attended, to have been engaged in work or profession not his own, and to live now in a place that was not his true residence" (Mackinnon, 1977). The OSS programme must be unique in regarding systematic lying as a virtue.

The first modern, peacetime AC was AT&T's Management Progress Study (MPS). The MPS included a business game, leaderless group discussion, a 25-item in-basket test, a two-hour interview, an autobiographical essay and personal history questionnaire, projective tests, personality inventories, a Q sort (a variant on the inventory, in which the subject sorts cards, on which inventory type statements are typed, into a forced distribution), and a high level intelligence test. The programme included far more individual tasks and psychological tests than most American ACs. So did the UK Civil Service Selection Board (CSSB), which in its earliest form included 17 mental ability tests. The original MPS assessed over 400 candidates, who were followed up 5–7 years later; AC ratings predicted success in management with an accuracy that came as a welcome surprise to psychologists who were finding most other methods so fallible they were hardly worth using (Bray & Grant, 1966). AT&T now run ACs on a very large scale, with 50 centres passing 10 000 candidates a year.

Since the 1960s, ACs have become very popular in North America; over 1000 organizations were using them by the mid-1970s, including a high proportion of public bodies. Britain has been slower to adopt ACs, and current interest in British industry owes its inspiration more to US practice than to WOSB and CSSB. A survey of Institute of Personnel Management (IPM) members in 1973 found only a handful (4%) used ACs. By 1986, over 20% of top UK employers were using ACs to select at least some managers (Robertson & Makin, 1986). In Britain ACs are mostly used for selection, whereas in North America they're used more for development—deciding who to promote, and what training people need.

THE PRESENT SHAPE OF ASSESSMENT CENTRES

Assessment centres work on the principle of *multi-trait multi-method* assessment. Any single assessment method may give misleading results; some people 'interview well', while others are 'good at tests'. Whereas a person who shows ability to influence in both interview and inventory is more likely 'really' to be able to influence others. The *key* feature of the true AC is the *dimension × assessment method matrix* (Figure 9.1). Having decided what *dimensions* of work performance are to be assessed, the AC planners select or devise *at least two, qualitatively different methods of assessing* each dimension. In Figure 9.1, *ability to influence* is assessed by group exercise *and* personality inventory, while *numerical ability* is assessed by financial case study *and* timed numerical reasoning test. An AC that doesn't have a matrix plan like that in Figure 9.1 isn't a real AC, just a superstitious imitation of one. Unfortunately one all too often encounters people whose idea of an AC is any old collection of tests and exercises, begged, borrowed or stolen, included because they're available, not because they're accurate measures of important dimensions of work performance.

Assessing candidates in groups has several inherent advantages. It allows group psychological testing, which saves time. It creates group dynamics,

COMPONENTS	DIMENSIONS			
	Influence	Numerical ability	Strategic vision	etc.
Group exercise "Future"		▨		
Group exercise "Manufacturer"	▨		▨	
Mental ability (numerical)	▨		▨	
Personality inventory		▨		
etc.				

Figure 9.1 The dimension × component matrix underlying every assessment centre. The dimension *influence* is assessed by group exercise "Future" and the personality inventory

which allow aspects of the individual to be studied that can't be measured by other means. People may *describe* themselves as dominant and forceful on their application form or when completing a personality inventory, but can they *actually* dominate a group and persuade others to accept their views? Purists argue every group is unique, so no two ACs are comparable; recombining candidates in differing sub-sets for different exercises meets this criticism, up to a point.

The length and intensity of some ACs can get behind the "front" the candidates present, to give a clearer idea what they are really like. Sociologists will argue the distinction between a 'front' and what 'someone's really like' is false. Everyone, everywhere, is playing a role. But some roles are easier to play than others, and some can only be played for a short time. Many people can bluff their way through a half-hour interview; acting the part of a good manager for 2 or 3 days is more of a test.

COMPONENTS OF THE ASSESSMENT CENTRE

An AC includes whatever assessment methods are needed to each dimension twice. Sometimes the measures can be taken 'off the shelf'; sometimes they are devised specially. Assessment Centres use both *group* and *individual* exercises.

Group exercises

Group exercises further divide into *assigned role* and *unassigned role* exercises.

1. *Assigned role exercises*   In these, each person has an individual brief,

competing for a share of a single budget, or trying to push his/her candidate for a job. Assigned role exercises are often used to assess negotiating skills, persuasiveness and ability to compromise. Military ACs often use *command exercises*, simulating the task of controlling a group of men solving a practical problem. The OSS programme included the famous 'Buster' and 'Kippy' command task, in which candidates tried to erect a prefabricated structure, using two specially selected and trained 'assistants', one aggressive, critical and insulting, the other sluggish and incompetent.

2. *Unassigned role exercises*   These involve exercises such as running a simulated business, in which decisions must be made rapidly, with incomplete information, under constantly changing conditions. Unassigned role exercises are often used to assess tolerance of uncertainty, tolerance of stress and flexibility. The *unassigned role* category also includes leaderless group discussions.

3. *Team exercises*   In these, half the group collectively advocates one side of a case, and the other half takes the opposing viewpoint. Team exercises are often used to assess negotiating skill, teamwork, analytical skill, and problem-solving ability.

Individual exercises

These divide into:

1. *In-basket (or in-tray) exercises*   These are often used to assess planning, organizing, quality of decisions, decisiveness, management control and delegation (Chapter 10). Candidates can be interviewed about their actions and asked to account for them.

2. *Irate customer/employee*   The candidate handles a visit or phone call from a dissatisfied customer, or from an employee with a grievance. This type of role play is often used to assess communication, listening and interpersonal skills. The OSS programme included an exercise in which the candidate tried to explain why he had been found in Government offices late at night searching secret files, and was searchingly cross-examined by a trial lawyer.

3. *Sales presentation*   The candidate tries to sell goods/services to an assessor briefed to be challenging, sceptical, unsure the product is necessary etc.

Surveys shows the in-tray exercise, the business game and the leaderless group are used in nearly all ACs, whereas interviews and psychological tests were included in only two-thirds.

Assessors' conference

Most elements of the AC—group exercises, role plays, in-tray exercises, simulation—are rated by assessors, who are usually line managers. The final stage of the AC is the assessors' conference, when all information about each candidate is collated (Figure 9.2). The assessors resolve disagreements in ratings of group exercises, in-trays, etc., then review all the ratings in the matrix, to determine a final set of ratings for each candidate. The final ratings define the candidate's *development needs* in a developmental AC, or who is successful in a selection AC. American ACs often use the AT&T model, in which assessors only observe and record behaviour during the AC, but don't make any evaluations until after all exercises are complete, when assessors

Centre for Occupational Research Ltd
Assessment Centre for Health Service Management
Candidate Summary Rating form

CANDIDATE   RECOMMENDATION:

DIMENSION	UIN	UFG	VIS	INF	AWA	ENG	TIM
Personality (CPI)	XXX	XXX					
Ability (GMA-N)	XXX		XXX	XXX	XXX	XXX	
tests (GMA-V)		XXX	XXX	XXX	XXX	XXX	XXX
In-tray exercise		XXX		XXX			
Group ("access")	XXX	XXX			XXX	XXX	XXX
exercises ("home")			XXX		XXX		
Presentation	XXX	XXX	XXX			XXX	
SUM							
AVERAGE							
FINAL							
	UIN	UFG	VIS	INF	AWA	ENG	TIM

UIN understanding information   AWA awareness of others
UFG understanding figures   ENG energy
VIS strategic vision   TIM time management
INF influence

Figure 9.2 Example of summary sheet used to record assessment centre data for one person

share observations and rate candidates. The assessors' conference can last many hours, and on average takes a third of the total time of the AC as a whole. American AC practice emphasizes the importance of the assessors achieving consensus after discussing the candidates (Cohen, 1978). Sackett & Wilson (1982) refer to "Abundant anecdotal evidence of vice-presidents serving as assessors and exerting considerable influence on consensus decisions"; research on conformity, not to mention common sense, suggest such anecdotes reflect reality.

Other researchers have analysed how the conference generates its final ratings. Sackett & Wilson (1982) found a simple two-stage decision rule predicted 94.5% of all consensus decisions. If three assessors (of four) agree on a rating, that value is taken as final; otherwise the mean of assessors' ratings, rounded to the nearest whole number, is taken as final. This implies the consensus discussion may often be redundant. Several subsequent analyses conclude that mechanical generation of final ratings gives much the same results as the conference method, is equally valid and of course saves a lot of very expensive management time (Pynes et al, 1988). Sackett & Wilson suggest the "disassembled assessment center", in which assessors never meet, but separately view and rate videotapes of AC exercises.

Another study suggests the assessors' conference sometimes fails to make the best use of the wealth of information collected during the AC. In Britain, ACs used for selecting senior police officers contain 13 components: leaderless group discussion, committee exercise, written 'appreciation', drafting a letter, peer nomination, mental ability tests and a panel interview. The assessors' conference use the 13 components to generate an *overall assessment rating* (OAR), which decides who is promoted, and is validated against five criteria. Feltham (1988b) analysed the AC data statistically and found only four, of the 13, components were needed to predict the five criteria. Moreover, a weighted average of the four successful predictors predicted the criteria *better* than the OAR. This clearly implies the assessors' conference is not doing an efficient job of processing the information the AC generates, and that their discussion ought to be complemented by a statistical analysis of the data.

These researches suggest the assessors' conference could be replaced by a simple numerical model, achieving greater accuracy, and saving a lot of time. This is unlikely to happen; Jones et al (1991) think it unlikely anyone would agree to act as assessor if the AC used a formula or model to reach decisions—but without line managers to act as assessors, the AC risks losing much of its credibility. Moreover Cook's Law—"The more important the decision, the more time must be taken, or must *be seen to be taken*, to reach it"—implies discussion will never be abandoned or replaced. The final AC summary form often has some missing data; what happens if Candidate X missed some of the tests or one of the exercises? Jagacinski's (1991) study suggest missing values cause assessors to give a poorer overall rating.

RELIABILITY OF ASSESSMENT CENTRES

Reliability is a complex issue, in research on ACs. One can calculate the reliability of the entire process, of its component parts, or of the ratings made by assessors. Wilson (1948) quotes a fairly good retest reliability for CSSB as a whole, apparently based on candidates who exercised their right to try CSSB twice. Morris (1949) gives details of two re-test reliability studies with WOSB. In the first, two parallel WOSBs were set up specifically to test inter-WOSB agreement, and two batches of candidates attended both WOSBs. There were "major disagreements" over 25% of candidates. In the second study, two parallel Boards simultaneously but independently observed and evaluated the same 200 candidates, but didn't communicate with each other at all; the parallel WOSBs agreed very well overall, as did their respective Presidents, psychiatrists, psychologists and Military Testing Officers.

Later Moses (1973) compared 85 candidates who attended long and short ACs and were evaluated by different staff. Overall ratings from the two ACs correlated well. Ratings on parallel dimensions were also highly correlated. A complex procedure like an AC can't be replicated as precisely as an ability test or even an interview. Cohen & Sands (1978) list some of the factors that are hard to control: assessor/candidate acquaintance, assessors' consensus discussions, the way instructions for exercises are given. The group dynamic aspect of the AC makes an exactly parallel replication impossible.

Ratings of group discussions achieve fair to good inter-rater reliability; Hinrichs & Haanpera (1976) review 12 studies, and find generally good agreement, in the short term, although agreement after 8 years was very much lower. Jones (1981) reports fair inter-rater reliabilities, for ratings of naval officer candidates by trained naval officers. Overall judgements made *after* discussing the candidates achieved higher inter-rater reliabilities. Schmitt (1977) also found inter-rater reliabilities higher after raters had discussed ratings. Inter-rater reliability in ACs takes many forms, some less reliable than others; for example ratings of the same persons in two different groups, with different tasks and different sets of other people, achieve reliabilities in the range 0.35–0.62. Global ratings of how people perform overall in an exercise are more reliable than ratings of specific aspects of performance (Gatewood, Thornton & Hennessey, 1990), which implies assessors may not be operating the way the logic of the AC method implies they should.

VALIDITY OF ASSESSMENT CENTRES

Assessment centres achieve impressively good predictive validity, which accounts for their popularity, and justifies their cost. AT&T's MPS assessed 123 new college hires and 144 non-graduate first level managers. On follow-up, 8 years later, the MPS had identified 82% of the college group and 75% of the non-graduates who had reached middle management (Table 9.1).

Table 9.1   Results of the AT&T Management Progress Study

Assessment centre ratings	Achieved management rank			
	N	1st line	2nd line	Middle
College hires				
potential middle manager	62	1	30	31
not potential middle manager	63	7	49	7
Non-college hires				
potential middle manager	41	3	23	15
not potential middle manager	103	61	37	5
All combined				
potential middle manager	103	4	53	46
not potential middle manager	166	68	86	12

The AC achieved a predictive validity of 0.44 for college educated and 0.71 for non-college educated subjects. The AC also identified 88% of the college group and 95% of the others who didn't reach middle manager level. The AC identified successful and unsuccessful managers equally accurately (Bray & Grant, 1966). Toplis (1975) thinks validity of the MPS varied markedly from year to year, but may be falling into the *fallacy of small numbers*. Some AT&T research has used very large samples. An unpublished study by Moses (cited in Byham, 1971) followed up 5943 assessees, and found AC rating correlated well with promotion—but promotions *weren't* made in ignorance of AC results, in contrast to the original MPS.

Reviews and meta-analyses

Byham (1971) reviewed 22 AC validity studies, and found 15 positive, with only one negative result (the rest were inconclusive). Campbell & Bray's (1967) study, across four Bell telephone companies, divided candidates into 'acceptable', 'questionable', and 'unacceptable'—but all were promoted to first-level management anyway. While the AC had some predictive validity, it also proved to have a high *false negative* rate; 46% of 'unacceptable' candidates nevertheless succeeded as first level managers. False negatives matter more in promotion than in selection. A rejected applicant can apply elsewhere, whereas an employee turned down for promotion he/she really merits stays in the organization, and may start getting resentful.

Later reviews (Cohen, Moses & Byham, 1974; Schmitt et al, 1984; Gaugler et al, 1987) distinguish between different criteria of success: performance ratings, promotion, rated potential for further promotion, achievement/grades, status change, wages (Table 9.2). Hunter & Hunter (1984) correct the median of Cohen et al for performance ratings for attenuation, increasing it to 0.43, which is the value they quote in their 'final league table' for promotion decisions. In that league table ACs come last, below work sample tests, ability composites, peer ratings, behavioural consistency experience ratings and job knowledge tests. However, the range from best to worst was very small: 0.54 to 0.43; all methods of deciding who to promote are fairly successful. Hunter & Hunter found too few researches using ACs for initial selection to calculate their place in that league table. British data, especially from CSSB, suggests ACs have good predictive validity in selection also. Schmitt et al corrected for sampling error, but not for criterion reliability. Their estimate for *true validity* of ACs predicting performance ratings is exactly the same as Hunter's & Hunter's (0.43). The two analyses overlap to some extent, but Schmitt et al include only studies published in *Journal of Applied Psychology* and *Personnel Psychology*, whereas the review by Cohen et al (which Hunter & Hunter re-analysed) included many unpublished researches.

The third review (Gaugler et al, 1987) is a *validity generalization analysis* (VGA) covering 50 studies; the authors report a median raw validity of 0.29, and estimated true validity of 0.37. Where the criterion was *rated potential*, validity was higher, as in earlier reviews. The VGA uncovered several factors that moderate AC validity, as well as finding that several other factors that might be thought to affect validity did not in fact do so. Assessment centre

Table 9.2 Summary of four analyses of assessment centre validity. Data from Cohen et al (1974), Hunter & Hunter (1984), Schmitt et al (1984), and Gaugler et al (1987)

| | Reviewer | | | |
	Cohen	Hunter	Schmitt	Gaugler
Criterion				
Performance	0.33	0.43	0.43	0.37
Promotion	0.40		0.41	0.36
"Potential"	0.63			0.53
Achievement			0.31	
Wages			0.24	
Training				0.35

validity was higher when a larger number of assessment devices were used—but wasn't affected by the ratio of candidates to assessors, the amount of assessor training, or how long the assessors spent integrating the information. Assessment centre validity was increased by using psychologists, not managers, as assessors, and by using peer evaluations. Also, AC validity was higher, when more female candidates were included.

British assessment centre validation research

Civil Service Selection Board (UK)

The most senior ranks of the UK Civil Service have been selected since 1945 by CSSB: group discussion, written 'appreciation' of a problem, committee exercise, 'individual problem', short talk, interview and second group discussion, as well as an extensive battery of MA tests. Vernon (1950) reported predictive validity data for successful applicants, after 2 years, using supervisor ratings as criterion. The CSSB was highly selective—only one in 15 were accepted—so Vernon corrected for restricted range. Table 9.3 shows CSSB achieved good predictive validity. The correlations listed in Table 9.3 are not independent, but *cumulative*, representing validity after assessors had seen each exercise. Anstey (1977) continued to follow up Vernon's sample, until the mid 1970s, when many were nearing retirement. Using achieved rank as criterion, Anstey reported an eventual predictive validity, after 30 years, that was amazingly good (0.66, corrected for restricted range). Anstey admits achieved rank and CSSB ratings aren't independent, so *criterion contamination* could exist, but argues that CSSB rating wouldn't influence opinion for more

Table 9.3 Predictive validity of the Civil Service Selection Board, and its components, after 2 years (Vernon, 1956) (Reproduced by permission)

	Observer	Psychologist	Chairman
First discussion	0.26	0.34	0.36
Appreciation	—	—	0.31
Committee	0.42	0.34	0.41
Individual problem	0.35	0.36	0.42
Short talk	0.40	—	0.47
Interview	0.42	0.42	0.48
Second discussion	0.32	—	—
Final mark	0.44	0.49	0.49

than 2 or 3 years, after which "departments would have formed their own opinions". All but 21 of 301 CSSB graduates in Anstey's analysis achieved Assistant Secretary rank, showing they made the grade as senior Civil Servants; only three left because of "definite inefficiency".

Admiralty Interview Board

Royal Navy officers are selected by individual and group command tasks, group discussions, short talks, interviews, and an extensive battery of mental ability tests. Gardner & Williams (1973) review the Board's first 25 years, and find the Board's mark correlated modestly (0.14–0.22, uncorrected for restricted range or criterion reliability) with three speed of promotion criteria. Adding exam grades for maths, physics and English to the Board rating increased the correlations slightly.

The War Office Selection Board revisited

The Regular Commissions Board presently selects British Army officers (Dobson & Williams, 1989); its validity is assessed against Annual Confidential Reports, plus two training grades. The results from 567 candidates appear to show validity varies by service arm, but VGA shows it doesn't vary reliably. Candidates are very highly self-selected; they come predominantly from public (private) schools, and from military families, and had always wanted to become army officers. Corrected validities average 0.30–0.40.

Police officers

Assessment centres, described as 'extended interviews', are used for selecting senior officers (Feltham, 1988b). Validity is very disappointing; assessors' conference rating correlates at best 0.18 (uncorrected) with supervisor rating and training criteria, although Feltham's re-analysis (see earlier) suggests more efficient use of the information could have achieved better results. American research using ACs, for entry-level police officer selection, also gets poor results (Pynes & Bernardin, 1989), suggesting selection for police work may present unusual difficulties.

Maintaining and improving Assessment centre validity

The nature of the AC method makes it especially vulnerable to loss of validity by slipshod practice. Schmitt, Schneider & Cohen (1990) analyse data from ACs for school administrators, centrally planned, but locally implemented in 16 separate sites. A VGA across the sites found true residual variance, showing validity was higher in ACs that served several school districts rather than just one, but lower where assessors had worked with the candidates—both results suggesting impartiality improves validity. Jones et al (1991) discuss ways of improving the validity of the Admiralty Interview Board. They reduced eight dimensions to four; they required assessors to announce ratings for specific dimensions before announcing their overall suitability rating; they introduced nine point ratings with indications what percentage of ratings should fall in each category. They introduced an 'evidence organiser', a form with headings for relevant evidence, and an indication of the relative importance of evidence. The changes improved prediction of *voluntary turnover* but not of training performance. Gaugler & Thornton (1989) confirm that using fewer dimensions gives more accurate ratings.

Assessment centres compared with other tests

Several studies show ACs achieve better validity than psychological tests. Vernon (1950) found CSSB's test battery had poor predictive validity. Similarly the British Admiralty Interview Board found tests alone gave poorer predictions (Gardner & Williams, 1973). American studies confirm British findings; in particular, the School and College Aptitude Test has been shown several times to have much poorer predictive validity than an AC (Bray & Campbell, 1968; Moses & Boehm, 1975).

But sometimes other methods are better than ACs. Campbell et al (1970) compared AC with a combination of ability test, personality and biodata, as predictors of managerial effectiveness in Standard Oil Company of New Jersey. The test and biodata package predicted advancement or effectiveness better than an AC, and was of course much cheaper. Hinrichs (1978) found assessments of management potential from personnel records had predictive validity as good as an AC. Rating potential from personnel records is very cheap, and can be done without the candidate knowing he/she is being assessed.

Reservations about assessment centre validity

Narrow database

While ACs have been used very widely in the USA, the published validity studies derive from relatively few organizations: AT&T, IBM, Union Carbide, SOHIO, Rohem & Haas, a few state governments, and some hospitals. In Britain, published validity data derive largely from the armed services and public sector employers.

Criterion contamination

This can be a blatant self-fulfilling prophecy: Mr Smith returns from the AC with a good rating (predictor) and so gets promoted (criterion). Or it can be subtler: candidates who have 'done well' at the AC are deemed suitable for more challenging tasks, so 'develop' more. Many ACs suffer from criterion contamination, because employers naturally want to act on the results of the assessment. Only two of the earlier American studies kept AC results secret until calculating the validity coefficient, thereby avoiding contamination: the original AT&T MPS, and AT&T's salesmen AC (Bray & Campbell, 1968). However, the VGA of Gaugler et al (1987) casts doubt on the extent of the criterion contamination problem. Criterion contamination will result in spuriously high validity coefficients, despite which the VGA found no evidence that criterion contamination increases validity. Criterion contamination may matter less in selection ACs, because rejection doesn't 'stick' to the candidate.

Ipsativity

One person's performance in a group exercise depends on how the others in the group behave. A fairly dominant person in a group of extremely dominant persons may look weak and ineffective by comparison. Gaugler & Rudolph (1992) show that how one candidate in a group is rated depends on how the others behave; candidates who performed poorly in an otherwise 'good' group got lower ratings than a poor candidate in a generally 'poor' group. Gaugler & Rudolph also find assessors' ratings more accurate when candidates differ a lot, suggesting assessors compare candidates with each other, not with an external standard. The *ipsativity* problem can be reduced to some extent by re-combining groups, and by introducing *normative* data from psychological tests. California Psychological Inventory scores can compare each candidate's dominance with people in general, as well as with the rest of the group.

'Face fits'

Critics comment on the "curious homogeneity in the criteria used for this [validity] research", namely "salary growth or progress (often corrected for starting salary), promotions above first level, management level achieved and supervisor's ratings of potential" (Klimoski & Strickland, 1977). These criteria "may have less to do with managerial effectiveness than managerial adaptation and survival". Klimoski & Strickland suggest ACs pick up the personal mannerisms that top management use in promotion, which may not have much to do with actual effectiveness. On this argument, ACs answer the question "does his/her face fit?" Klimoski & Strickland complain that few studies use less suspect criteria.

The review by Cohen, Moses & Byham (1974) finds AC ratings predicted *actual job performance* moderately well, but predicted *higher management ratings of management potential* much better (Table 9.2). A later study by Klimoski &

Strickland (1981, cited in Hunter & Hunter, 1984) reported that AC ratings predicted promotion and ratings of potential, but not good performance. On the other hand, later reviews by Schmitt et al and Gaugler et al find less difference between promotion/potential criteria and performance criteria. The review by Schmitt et al (1984) does strongly confirm Klimoski's argument that 'face fits' criteria are more popular for ACs. Twelve coefficients, based on 14 662 subjects, used status change and wages criteria, whereas only six coefficients, based on a mere 394 subjects, used performance ratings. In a sense, however, all these researches are irrelevant to Klimoski's criticism, because 'performance' criteria in AC research are still ratings, i.e. management's opinion of the candidate.

Klimoski is really addressing a much more fundamental problem in selection research—*the criterion*, discussed in Chapter 11. The general class of supervisor rating criterion can be viewed as answering the question: does Smith make a good impression on management? Klimoski argues the AC— more than other selection test—addresses the same question, which makes its high validity unsurprising, perhaps even trivial. The solution lies in validating ACs against 'objective' criteria, such as sales or output, not against different wordings ('potential'/'performance') of the general favourable-impression-on-management criterion.

Very few researches on ACs have used objective criteria. The meta-analysis by Gaugler et al distinguishes five broad classes and 12 narrower classes of criterion, all of which appear to involve somewhere management's opinion of the candidate. (For example, *training* is "performance of manager in training program", which is presumably rated by some higher-up manager.) McEvoy & Beatty (1989) report data for law enforcement agency managers, using conventional promotion and supervisor rating criteria, and *subordinate ratings*—a criterion rarely used in selection research. The three criteria were predicted equally well, suggesting either Klimoski's criticism is unfounded, or that the subordinate rating criterion is equally suspect. Russell & Domm (1990) use a net store profit criterion in an AC for retail store managers, and find it predicted as well (0.32) as a supervisor rating criterion (0.28).

Discriminant/convergent validity

The logic of the AC method implies assessors should rate candidates on *dimensions*; research suggests strongly, however, that assessors often rate them on *exercises*. Instead of rating influence, numerical ability, etc. as revealed in various exercises, assessors often rate overall performance in group discussion, overall performance in tray exercise, etc. Table 9.4 shows ratings of *different dimensions* made after the *same exercise* correlated very highly, in two of three organizations studied, whereas ratings of the *same trait in different exercises* hardly correlated at all (Sackett & Dreher, 1982). When the ratings

Table 9.4 Multi-trait multi-method analysis of three assessment centres (Sackett & Dreher, 1982)

	Organization		
	A	B	C
Number of traits rated	7	15	9
Number of exercises included	6	4	6
Average inter-correlation of ratings of:			
same trait across different exercises	0.07	0.11	0.51
different traits within same exercise	0.64	0.40	0.65

were factor-analysed, the factors clearly identified *exercises*, not *traits*. The ACs weren't measuring *general decisiveness* across a range of management tasks; they were measuring *general performance* on each of series of tasks. But if decisiveness in Task A doesn't generalize to decisiveness in Task B, how can one be sure it will generalize to decisiveness on the job? (In the third organization, ratings of the same trait in different exercises *did* correlate reasonably well, but only because there was pervasive 'halo' in all the ratings; all ratings, of any trait, on any exercise, correlated well.) Turnage & Muchinsky (1982) analysed ratings of over 2000 people, on eight traits, across five exercises, and found candidates were rated globally, so ratings of individual traits contributed little extra information. They also found that such limited differentiation as was recorded centred on *exercises* rather than *traits*, confirming Sackett & Dreher's results. Schneider & Schmitt (1992) find that the *form* of the exercise—leaderless group discussion or role play—accounts for the exercise effect; the *content* of the group discussion or role play is irrelevant.

Russell (1985) factor-analysed ratings on 16 assessment dimensions, covering four main areas—personal qualities, interpersonal skills, problem solving skills, and communication skills—so each assessor's ratings would ideally yield four corresponding factors. In practice, they didn't; five of the 10 assessors' ratings yielded only two or three factors. Furthermore, all 10 assessors' ratings yielded one very large factor, four times as big as any other, and identifiable variously as interpersonal skills, problem-solving skills or cognitive ability. Assessors didn't rate the four factors defined by the AC's planners, but defined their own individual categories.

Several attempts have been made to solve the discriminant—convergent validity problem. Silverman et al (1986) report that rating each exercise immediately after observing it encourages the global exercise effect, whereas waiting till the end of the AC—the AT&T method—encourages dimension-focused rating. Reilly, Henry & Smither (1990) used experienced assessors to generate check-lists of behaviour relevant to each dimension, and found these also increased dimension focused rating. On the other hand, changing the agenda of the assessors' conference to discuss candidates dimension by dimension, not exercise by exercise, didn't make any difference (Harris, Becker & Smith, in press).

Construct validity

Recently, researchers have sought to demonstrate the validity of AC ratings by correlating them with test data. Test scores make normative comparisons, and have known validity; they don't depend on making a favourable impression on management. Shore, Thornton & Shore (1990) report that AC ratings of *interpersonal style* correlate with 16PF scores, while ratings of *performance style* correlate with MA test scores. Crawley, Pinder & Herriot (1990), analysing ACs for accountants and supervisors, report mixed results: MA tests correlate with AC ratings for *problem solving* and *planning and organizing*, as they should, but also correlate with ratings of *assertion* and *oral communication*, which suggests *halo* at work. Scores for specific aptitudes, such as numerical and verbal reasoning, did not correlate with corresponding specific AC ratings. Of the personality tests used, some Myers Briggs Type Indicator correlations made sense; *Thinkers* were rated higher on *problem analysis* and *judgement*, whereas *Feelers* got higher ratings on *management control, subordinate development* and *business awareness*.

FAIRNESS AND THE ASSESSMENT CENTRE

The AC is often regarded as fair or even "Equal Employment Opportunities Commission-proof", meaning it creates no *adverse impact* on women or minorities. It has been recommended, or even ordered, by courts as an *alternative* to MA tests or educational requirements. Critics say ACs are most often used for management, at which level adverse impact on minorities is less of an issue.

The AC has high *face* or *content validity* (Chapters 11 and 12), which probably accounts for much of its popularity, and also probably does give it a measure of protection against claims of 'unfairness'. Presenting a speech, fighting one's case in a committee, chairing a meeting, answering an in-tray, or leading a squad, all have obvious, easily defended, job-relevance; they're almost work samples.

Gender

Schein (1975) argues most employers see successful managers as having characteristics, attitudes and temperaments more typical of males than females, which implies ACs may be biased against women. However, ACs don't seem to create *adverse impact*—as many women as men pass. A large scale follow-up of 1600 female entry-level managers in Bell Telephone found ratings of middle-management potential predicted achieved rank 7 years later as well as AT&T's study of male managers (Ritchie & Moses, 1983). Moses & Boehm (1975) report AC data from AT&T for 4846 women and 8885 men which showed no adverse impact at all; predictive validity was equally good for women and men. Walsh, Weinberg & Fairfield (1987) analysed data for 1035 applicants for financial services sales posts, and reports women got better assessments, but only from all male assessor panels, which suggests an inverted bias at work.

Race

An AC for white and non-white female supervisors created some *adverse impact*—fewer non-whites passed (Huck & Bray, 1976). Non-whites got poorer ratings for administrative skills, sensitivity and effective intelligence, but not for interpersonal effectiveness. However, AC results predicted job performance equally well for both non-white and white, and predicted rated potential for advancement for both non-white and white equally well; the method was proved valid despite adverse impact. In 'mixed' ACs—male, female, white, non-white—Schmitt & Hill (1977) found a very small tendency for non-white women to get poorer ratings on forcefulness, communications skills and for group exercises, if there were more white males present. Schmitt & Hill note the results are not really significant, either statistically or practically, but suggest the *possibility* of bias arising from group composition is sufficiently serious to merit further investigation.

Age

Assessment centre ratings sometimes show small negative correlations with age, which may create problems in the USA, where it's legally 'unfair' to discriminate against candidates over 40.

CONCLUSIONS

The AC is often referred to as the 'Rolls-Royce' of selection methods. It's certainly expensive, but is it worth the money?

Its advocates of course say it's very good value. Some argue ACs work precisely because they are expensive. They're expensive because they last a long time, because they typically employ six trained assessors, and because they include a wide range of different assessment methods. A range of assessors and assessment methods reduces bias, and gives candidates more chance to expose their strengths and weaknesses. Length gets behind candidates' fronts, to find out what they're really like or to pick those who can play the role of manager indefinitely.

Also ACs have the great virtue, these days, of being safe. They look 'fair'; they look plausible; they include samples of the job. They give people a chance to prove themselves. A selection method that's fair *and* accurate can be forgiven for being expensive.

Critics have argued ACs perpetuate the status quo, picking managers whose 'faces fit', filling the organization with carbon copies of top management, if not with yes-men and sycophants. This may be a problem, if top managers are out of date or incompetent. On the hand, this criticism could be interpreted as praise; selecting carbon copies of present management is better than selecting at random, which is all some methods can achieve.

Other critics might complain ACs are an elaborate charade. The WOSB started life as a cover plan to get the British Army to use MA tests, but military perversity, and Cook's Law, ensured all the elaborate, time-wasting elements survived, or even prospered. Perhaps ability tests contribute most of the AC's predictive validity (although several studies prove otherwise). Or perhaps the cheaper, less elaborate elements of the AC are what makes it work.

The fact is that psychologists still don't know why ACs work so well. It's an increasingly derided tradition to conclude every research paper by saying "more research is needed". But sometimes more research really *is* needed: analysis of AC validity is a prime candidate. If selectors knew which elements of the AC contribute to its success, they could improve its predictive accuracy still further, *or* reduce the AC's length and expense, or perhaps achieve both at once.

10 Work Samples and Other Methods

Education, physique and self-ratings

There are six classes of miscellaneous selection 'test' that don't fit neatly into any other main category: work sample tests, in-tray exercises, education, training and experience ratings, self-assessments, and physical tests.

WORK SAMPLE TESTS

Work sample tests used not to be very highly thought of. Guion's (1965a) book on personnel testing devoted just over three pages to them. They have become very much more popular since. McClelland (1973) argues the case for work samples: "If you want to know how well a person can drive a car, sample his ability to do so by giving him a driver's test".

Work sample tests are justified by *behavioural consistency* theory, which states two principles: "past behaviour is the best predictor of future behaviour", and "like predicts like". Asher & Sciarrino (1974) argue that "point-to-point correspondence between predictor and criterion" will ensure higher validity, and—perhaps more important these days—less scope for legal challenge. Mental ability (MA) tests assess the applicant's *general* suitability and make an intermediate inference—this person is intelligent so he/she will be good at widget-stamping. Testing the employee with a real or simulated widget-stamper makes no such inference (nor is widget-stamping ability quite such an emotive issue as general MA.)

Campion (1972) devised a work sample test for maintenance mechanics. After a thorough job analysis, he selected four tasks: installing pulleys and belts, disassembling and repairing a gear box, installing and aligning a motor, pressing a bush into a sprocket and reaming it to fit a shaft. Campion compared the work sample test with a battery of paper-and-pencil tests: Bennett Mechanical Comprehension, Wonderlic, and Short Employment Tests (Verbal, Numerical and Clerical Aptitude). The work samples predicted three supervisor rating criteria fairly well, whereas the paper-and-pencil tests predicted very poorly.

Campion describes a classic work sample test, of the type used in Europe and Britain in the 1920s and 1930s, and applied on a large scale in wartime testing programmes. The meaning of 'work sample' has been widened somewhat in the last 15–20 years. Robertson & Kandola (1982) distinguish four classes of 'work sample':

Psychomotor:	typing, sewing, using tools.
Individual decision making:	in-tray exercise (see below).
Job-related information tests	
Group discussions/decisions.	

The *psychomotor* category covers the classic work sample. *In trays* and *group exercises* extend the principle to jobs which don't need motor skills. 'Job-related information test' is another name for *trade* or *job knowledge* test, and hasn't much in common with a true work sample. Calling a trade test a 'work sample' has the possible advantage of making it more acceptable.

Cascio & Phillips (1979) describe 21 work samples for municipal employees in Miami Beach, covering a wide range of manual, clerical and administrative jobs, from electrician's helper (mate) to parking meter technician, from library assistant to concession attendant. Applicants for concession attendant were tested on site, out of hours: counting cash, giving change, completing revenue reports, making announcements and dealing with irate customers. Cascio & Philips argue the tests were very convincing to the applicants. If applicants for electrician had completed the wiring test correctly, the lights lit up; if the wiring wasn't correct, the bulbs didn't light, and the applicant couldn't deny he/she had made a mistake. Some tests had *realistic job preview* (Chapter 2) built in; quite a few applicants for the post of sewer mechanic withdrew after being tested in an underground sewage chamber. Gordon & Kleiman (1976) claim applicants tested by work sample are better motivated to accept the job than ones tested by MA tests. Cascio & Phillips took the unusual step, for psychologists, of working out how much their tests cost, and arrived at an average figure of $675 to plan each one, and $262 to test a batch of applicants. The US military also favour work samples, called *hands-on performance tests* (Carey, 1991), but sometimes use them as *criterion*, as well as using them as *predictor*.

Asher & Sciarrino's (1974) review finds work samples better than MA and personality tests. Schmitt et al (1984) report a *true validity* (corrected for sampling error only) of 0.38, one of the higher true validities they report. Dunnette's (1972) analysis of tests in the American petroleum industry found work samples achieved similar validities for operating and processing, maintenance, and clerical jobs. Hunter & Hunter (1984) find work samples the best test (0.54) by a short lead, for promotion decisions, for which, however, all tests give fairly good results.

Robertson & Kandola (1982) review validity of work samples from a wider body of research, taking in US wartime researches, and British research. Median validity for *psychomotor* work samples is quite good (0.39), with, however, a very wide range. Robertson & Kandola don't calculate a validity generalization analysis (VGA), nor do they appear to have corrected for any source of error, so their median is likely to be an underestimate of *true validity*. Median validities for job knowledge tests, group exercises and in-tray exercises are comparable to *psychomotor* work samples, although *job knowledge tests* predict training grades much better than job performance.

True work samples can only be used if the person has already mastered the job's skills; it's clearly pointless giving a typing test to someone who can't type (whereas in-tray and group exercises don't presuppose any special knowledge, skill, or experience). *Trainability tests* are a sub-type of work sample, assessing how well the applicant can *learn* a new skill. Trainability tests are widely used in Skillcentres run by the (British) Manpower Services Commission (Robertson & Downs, 1979). The instructor gives standardized instructions and a demonstration, then rates the trainee's efforts, using a check-list (Table 10.1). Robertson & Downs report good results for bricklaying, carpentry, welding, machine sewing, forklift truck driving, fitting, machining and even dentistry.

Table 10.1 Part of check-list for trainability test for centre lathe operation (Robertson & Downs, 1979) (Reproduced by permission)

Doesn't tighten chuck sufficiently

Doesn't select correct tool

Doesn't use coolant

Doesn't set calibrations to zero

Doesn't mark lengths on slide

Similar American research on *miniature training and evaluations* shows subjects how to do something, gives them a chance to practise, then tests them (Siegel, 1978). Siegel's validity data, on small samples, are unimpressive, but he finds the procedure popular with subjects: "Gave me a chance to prove that I could do some things with my hands, not just my head". Reilly & Israelski (1988) used trainability tests, called *minicourses*, to select staff for AT&T's new technology training, and report good correlations with training performance (0.55) and job performance (0.50), correcting for criterion reliability. A meta-analysis of trainability test validity (Robertson & Downs, 1989) finds they predict training success much better (0.39–0.57, uncorrected) than job performance (0.20–0.24); the high correlation with training success almost certainly reflects the similarity between test and criterion. Robertson & Downs (1989) also report that trainability test validity falls off over time quite markedly.

People doing trainability tests can assess their own performance, even though they aren't told the results. Applicants for machine sewing jobs in effect selected themselves for the job (Figure 10.1). Scores on a sewing machine trainability test weren't used to select, but high scorers took up sewing jobs, while low scorers generally did not (Downs, Farr & Colbeck, 1978).

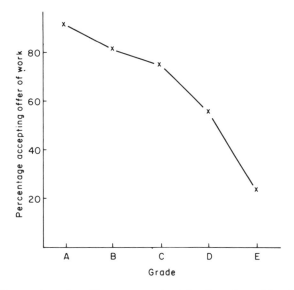

Figure 10.1   Proportion of applicants accepting job offer, after taking trainability test, for each applicant's grade obtained on the test. N.B. They were not told the test scores, nor were the test scores used to decide who to make offers to. Data from Downs, Farr & Colbeck (1978)

Critics (Barrett, 1992) argue that work sample tests are profoundly uninformative, unlikely to retain validity over time, and difficult to modify to regain lost validity. A motor mechanic work sample "may combine knowledge of carburettors, skill in using small tools, and ... reasoning ability". The work sample doesn't separate these abilities. If car engines change, e.g. adopting fuel injection, the work sample loses validity; but once devised, the work sample is difficult to modify because there is no information about the contribution of different elements to the whole (whereas paper-and-pencil tests can be analysed item by item, and items that change meaning can be omitted or changed). The same difficulty arises if the work sample creates adverse impact; the test's users don't know what to alter to eliminate the adverse impact. Barrett also disagrees with McClelland's optimistic view of official driving tests, as accurate work sample tests of driving ability, pointing out they fail to predict either accidents or road traffic convictions.

Fairness and work sample test

Work samples are currently popular because they're 'alternatives' to legally risky MA tests. Are work samples really 'fairer'? Cascio & Phillips's Miami Beach work samples passed as many blacks and Hispanics as whites. Other studies (Gordon & Kleiman, 1976) similarly report work samples create less adverse impact than MA tests. The 'work samples' in question appear to be paper-and-pencil job knowledge tests. Work samples also create less adverse impact than trade tests; Schmidt et al think trade tests create more adverse impact because they rely more on verbal ability. However, the samples studied are often small: Schmidt et al (1977) compared work sample and trade test for 58 white and 29 non-white metal trades apprentices. Chapter 7 emphasizes how risky it is to draw firm conclusions from small numbers. One study, using a large sample ($N = 450$), did find adverse impact on non-whites (Schoenfeldt, Acker & Perlson, 1976).

IN-TRAY EXERCISES

Candidates deal with a set of letters, memos, notes, reports and phone messages (Figure 10.2). Candidates are instructed to *act on* the items, not *write about* them, but are limited to written replies by the assumption it's Sunday, and they depart shortly for a week's holiday or business trip abroad. The in-tray is a management work sample—but doesn't need mastery of specific skills, so can be used for graduate recruitment. In-tray content can be varied to suit the job. The candidate's performance is usually rated (a) overall and (b) item by item. The overall evaluation checks whether the candidate sorts the items into high and low priority, and notices any connections between items. Some scoring methods are more or less objective, e.g. counting how many decisions the candidate makes; others require judgments by the scorer, and focus on stylistic aspects. The "in tray" was devised in 1957 by Frederiksen, Saunders & Wand (1957) as part of a *training* programme for US Air Force officers, was later adopted by AT&T, and now features in most assessment centres.

In-tray exercises can be scored with acceptable reliability by trained assessors (Schippman, Prien & Katz, 1990). In-tray exercises also achieve reasonable validity. AT&T's Management Progress Study found in-tray performance predicted salary level 5 years later. Wollowick & McNamara (1969) report similar results from the IBM assessment programme. In-tray performance predicts supervisory effectiveness moderately well (0.24–0.34) (Brass & Oldham, 1976). Robertson & Kandola (1982) summarize 53 validity coefficients for 'individual, decision making' tests, which include an unspecified number of in trays. Median validity, apparently uncorrected for restricted range or limited reliability, was 0.28. Schippmann, Prien & Katz (1990)

IBT/1

From: V Wordy MICE CEMH FIME (Engineering Director)

To: [Prior (Asst Gen Mgr)

I am in receipt of your memorandum of 15th November concerning the necessity for more rapid progress on the revised layout of Number 4 component assembly area and am fully cognisant of the urgency of this matter myself. My strenuous efforts in this respect are not however being assisted by the calibre of some of the personnel allocated to myself for this purpose. A particular obstacle with which I am currently faced lies in the persistent absenteeism of certain members of the workforce who appear to have little interest in contributing an effort commensurate to their present rates of pay. The designated complement of shop floor workers for Assembly Area 4 under the new establishment of 5th October is just adequate for the Area's requisites *on the strict understanding that the full complement are in fact present and available for work* as opposed for example to reading newspapers in the works canteen or absenting themselves for lengthy smoking breaks in the male toilet facilities. Efforts on the part of myself and my foremen to instill a sense of purpose and discipline into a workforce sadly lacking any semblance of either have not so far I am sorry to say received what I would consider adequate backing from the management. I would like to bring to your attention *for your immediate executive action* a particularly blatant case which fully merits in my estimation the immediate dismissal of the employee concerned. Yesterday our revised November schedule calls for us to be securing the transfer of Number III lathe from its former position to its new location.

Figure 10.2 A sample item from an "in-tray" test

reviewed 22 validity studies, which they concluded were too diverse to permit a meta-analysis; they also concluded criterion validity was generally good enough to justify using in trays. Several studies (Bray & Grant, 1966; Wollowick & McNamara, 1969) report that in-tray tests have *incremental validity*—they add new information, and don't just cover the same ground as tests of verbal or general MA. Lopez (1966) compared trainees and experienced AT&T managers; trainees were wordier, grasped fewer implications for the organization, were less considerate to others, and less alert to important issues. Trainees' decisions were poorer; they *either* reached a final decision too soon without getting all the facts, *or* they delegated decisions entirely to others, without any follow-up. Brannick, Michaels & Baker, (1989), however, report that in-tray exercises show the same feature as the assessment centres they often form part of; factor analysis of scores yields exercise-based factors, not factors corresponding to the dimensions the exercise is supposed to be assessing.

The in tray's main shortcomings arise from the 'Sunday afternoon' assumption; writing replies in a deserted office may be quite unlike dealing with the same issues face to face or by telephone on a hectic Monday morning. Attempts to add telephones to in-tray tests haven't really caught on. Tests that require people to *write* things they normally *say* to others have been criticized by fair employment agencies both sides of the Atlantic.

EDUCATION

Employers in Britain often specify so many 'O' and 'A' level passes; professional training schemes almost always do. American employers used to require high school graduation, but most no longer do so. Booth, McNally & Berry (1978) suggest people who do well at school are more able, mature and more highly motivated, so they fit into work more easily. It's a lot easier and cheaper to ask how well someone did at school, than to try to assess ability, maturity and motivation. It's important to distinguish *duration* of education from *achievement*; staying at school or college a long time proves less than passing exams or getting good grades.

Amount of education doesn't predict productivity very well. Research in the American petroleum industry concludes mere duration of education has zero predictive validity (Dunnette, 1972). However, duration of education does predict survival in recruits to the US Navy. American college grade-point averages (marks from exams and course work) correlate moderately with training grades, but hardly at all with supervisor ratings (O'Leary, 1980). Education predicts performance ratings in the American armed services very moderately, whereas it predicts 'suitability' ratings better (Vineberg & Joyner, 1982); this suggests better educated individuals make a better impression but don't necessarily perform any better.

Reilly & Chao (1982) summarize research on predictive validity of educational *achievement*, usually grade-point average in school or college. Achievement predicted supervisor ratings relatively poorly (0.14). Educational achievement predicted 'adjusted compensation' better (0.27). Baird (1985) finds low positive correlations between school or college achievements and various indices of occupational success, such as scientific output, performance as a physician or success in management. Humphreys (1986) offers an explanation: "[educational] credentials are easier to obtain than generally acknowledged"; this implies high school diplomas and college degrees have shared the same fate as the letter of reference—they fail to predict because they never say anything unkind about people.

Education tests have fallen foul of American fair employment laws, in a big way. Some US minorities do poorly at school, so far more of them fail to complete high school. Minimum education requirements may have the effect, perhaps sometimes even the intention, of excluding non-whites. The employer then has to prove the job really needs the educational level or qualifications specified. This has usually proved difficult. Meritt-Haston & Wexley's (1983) review of 83 US court cases found educational requirements were generally ruled unlawful for skilled or craft jobs, supervisors and management trainees, but were accepted for the police and for professors (academics). American universities can still, legally, require their teaching staff to have degrees.

TRAINING AND EXPERIENCE RATINGS

These are also known as T & E ratings, Traex exam or unassembled examination. A rating which seeks to quantify applicants' training and experience, instead of relying on possibly arbitrary judgements of the applicant's background, training, qualifications, etc., T & E ratings are widely used in the public sector in the USA, especially for jobs requiring specialized backgrounds such as engineering, scientific, and research. Training and experience ratings would be useful for selecting academics, but aren't used in Britain. T & E ratings are also useful for trade jobs, where written tests unfairly weight verbal skills. They are not suitable for entry-level jobs where no prior training and skill are required. Several systems are used; applications are assigned points for years of training/education, or else applicants are asked for self-ratings of the amount and quality of their experience. In the *behavioural consistency* method, areas that reveal the biggest differences between good and poor workers are identified by *critical incident technique* (Chapter 3). Applicants describe their major achievements in these areas, and their accounts are rated by the selectors using *Behaviourally Anchored Rating Scales* (Chapter 5).

Hunter & Hunter's (1984) VGA included 65 validity coefficients for T & E ratings, and reported a mean true validity of 0.13. McDaniel, Schmidt & Hunter (1988) confirm that T & E ratings achieve overall fairly low validity— 0.09. However, it's arguably more appropriate to compare the validity of T & E ratings with the 'validity' of sifting applications haphazardly, which is likely to be near zero. McDaniel et al also conclude that some types of T & E ratings achieve higher validity than others; the *behavioural consistency* method does best—0.25. The ratings may create adverse impact on women and non-whites who lack training and experience, but otherwise are rarely the subject of fair employment complaints.

Hough, Keyes & Dunnette (1983) develop the conventional application form or CV into the *accomplishment record*, in which the applicant describes his/her achievements, giving "a general statement of what was accomplished, a detailed description of exactly what was done, the time period over which the accomplishment was carried out, any formal recognition gained as a result of the achievement (e.g., awards, citations, etc.), and name and address of a person who could verify the information provided". So far, just a typical CV, but with two important differences: (a) the applicant describes accomplishments in eight job areas derived from *critical incidents* (Chapter 3), and (b) the *accomplishment record* is rated on *Behaviourally Anchored Rating Scales*. The *accomplishment record* was written by Hough et al for lawyers: a high score for *researching/investigating* was given to:

> I assumed major responsibility for conducting an industry wide investigation of the industry and for preparation of a memorandum in support of complaint against the three largest members of the industry .... I obtained statistical data from every large and medium industry in the US and from a selection of small .... I deposed [got statements from] *many* employees of [deleted] manufacturers and renters. I received a Meritorious Service award.

A low score on *researching/investigating* went to:

> My research involved checking reference books, LEXIS, and telephone interviews with various people—individuals, state officials etc.

The ratings were highly reliable, and correlated very highly with criterion ratings.

SELF-ASSESSMENTS

Allport once said "If you want to know about someone, why not ask him? He might tell you." Self-assessments ask people for a direct estimate of their potential. The California Psychological Inventory Dominance scale infers dominance from the answers people give to 30-odd questions; a self assessment gets straight to the point: "How dominant are you?"—on a seven-point scale. A typing test takes half an hour to test typing skill; a self-assessment simply asks "How good a typist are you?"

Ash (1980) compared a standard typing test with typists' ratings of their own skill. Ash's best result (0.59) suggested Allport was right; people are quite good judges of their own abilities. However, Ash's other correlations, for typing letters, tables, figures and revisions, were nowhere near so promising. Levine, Flory & Ash (1977) found self-assessments of spelling, reading speed, comprehension, grammar, etc., correlated poorly with supervisor rating. DeNisi & Shaw (1977) measured 10 cognitive abilities—mechanical comprehension, spatial orientation, visual pursuit, etc.—and compared test scores with self-assessments; correlations were very low, suggesting self-assessments couldn't be substituted for tests. Self-assessments have also been used in a battery of tests for bus drivers; the self-assessments studied by Baehr (unpublished, see Reilly & Chao, 1982) were much more elaborate: 72 items, based on a job analysis, and factored down to 13 scores. Baehr described the self-assessment as one of the two best predictors.

Reilly & Chao's (1982) analysis found the overall validity of self assessments very low (0.15). Mabe & West (1982) analysed 43 studies, and reported a much higher mean *true validity* (0.42), partly because they correct for predictor and criterion reliability. They concluded self-assessments had highest validity when given anonymously—not a lot of use to the selector—or when subjects were told self-assessments would be compared with objective tests—which means either giving a test or lying to the candidates. Self-assessments also worked better when subjects were accustomed to them, or when subjects were comparing themselves with fellow workers, which again tends to make them impractical for selection.

While self-assessments have been shown to predict performance quite well, hardly anyone has used them for 'real' decisions (Shrauger & Osberg, 1981). Levine, Flory & Ash (1977) think self-assessments aren't used, because employers suppose people can't or won't give accurate estimates of their abilities. They tested the faking hypothesis by comparing self-assessments of people who knew their typing ability would be tested, with people who had no such expectation. The two sets of self-assessment didn't differ, implying people weren't faking. Other studies however (Ash, 1980) found people overestimated their abilities. Fox & Dinur (1988) tried telling subjects their self-assessments would be checked against other data; predictive accuracy was not affected.

PHYSICAL TESTS

Some jobs require strength, agility, or endurance. Some jobs require, or are felt to require, physical size. Some jobs require dexterity. For some jobs attractive appearance is, explicitly or implicitly, a requirement.

Strength

Tests of physique or strength are used in Britain, usually in an arbitrary, haphazard way. Fire brigades require applicants to climb a ladder carrying a weight. Other employers rely on the company medical checkup, or an 'eyeball' test by personnel manager or supervisor.

Some North American employers use physical tests much more systematically. Armco Inc. use a battery of physical work sample tests for labourers, and have extensive data on norms, correlations and sex differences (Arnold et al, 1982). The Du Pont corporation also use physical tests for production workers. AT&T have developed a battery of three tests for pole-climbing—an essential part of many AT&T jobs (Reilly, Zedeck & Tenopyr, 1979); employees with good balance, adequate 'static strength' (pulling on a rope) and higher body density (less fat, more muscle) did better in training, and were more likely to survive at least 6 months. The US Army loses 9% of recruits during basic training because they aren't up to it physically; more specialized arms, like US

Navy underwater bomb disposal, lose over 50% (Hogan, 1985). Hogan finds three tests—1 mile run, sit and reach test, and arm ergometer muscle endurance—reduce wastage in bomb disposal training considerably.

Measures of physique and physical performance often inter-correlate very highly; Reilly et al started with 14, and found only three necessary. Fleishman & Mumford (1991) factor-analysed a very wide range of physical tasks and concluded there are nine factors (Note 1, in Chapter 3) underlying physical proficiency (Table 10.2). Fleishman developed *Physical Abilities Analysis*, a profile of the physical abilities needed for a job. Subsequently Hogan (1991a) re-analysed data on physical requirements of work, and tests of physical proficiency, and concluded three factors, instead of nine, underlie all types of work studied; the three factors are *strength*, *endurance* and *movement quality* (flexibility, balance and co-ordination). Arvey et al (1992) carried out a detailed analysis of the physical requirements of police work, and found

Table 10.2   The nine factors underlying human physical ability, according to Fleishman (1979)

Dynamic strength	Ability to exert muscular force repeatedly or continuously. Useful for: doing push-ups, climbing a rope.
Trunk strength	Ability to exert muscular force repeatedly or continuously using trunk or abdominal muscles. Useful for: leg-lifts or sit-ups.
Static strength	The force the individual can exert against external objects, for a brief period. Useful for: lifting heavy objects, pulling heavy equipment.
Explosive strength	Ability to expend a maximum of energy in one act or a series of acts. Useful for: long jump, high jump, 50 metre race.
Extent flexibility	Ability to flex or extend trunk and back muscles as far as possible in any direction. Useful for: reaching, stretching, bending.
Dynamic flexibility	Ability to flex or extend trunk and back repeatedly. Useful for: continual bending, reaching, stretching.
Gross body co-ordination	Also known as agility.
Balance	Ability to stand or walk on narrow ledges.
Stamina	Or cardiovascular endurance, the ability to make prolonged, maximum exertion. Useful for: long-distance running.

strength and *endurance* needed, but not *movement quality*. Some US organizations employ work physiologists to measure the *oxygen uptake* each job demands, and select people whose aerobic (oxygen uptake) capacity, measured by treadmill, exercise bicycle or step test, is adequate (Campion, 1983).

Schmitt et al (1984) report a VGA of tests of physique, which yields a true validity of 0.32. Of 22 validities analysed, 15 were for unskilled labourers, six for skilled labour and one for managers. Unfortunately, Schmitt et al don't reveal who thinks what aspect of managers' physique important. Hogan (1991b) reviews 13 studies, and reports corrected validities for strength and endurance, against training (0.23, 0.30) and work sample (0.82, 0.37) criteria. Chaffin (cited in Campion, 1983) finds the greater the discrepancy between a worker's strength and the physical demands of the job, the more likely the worker is to suffer a back injury—a notorious source of lost output in industry. Furthermore, the relation is continuous and linear, and doesn't have a threshold, so an employer who wants to minimize the risk of back injury should choose the strongest applicant, other things being equal.

Physical tests create very substantial *adverse impact* on women, who are lighter and less strong on average than men. Nevertheless, physical tests can survive legal scrutiny, if they are carefully validated. AT&T's pole-climbing tests rejected 10% of male applicants, and 50% of female applicants, without being 'unfair', because AT&T proved conclusively strength is essential in linemen. Arvey et al (1992), however, report that female applicants for police work did as well as males on *endurance* measures, even though they performed less well on *strength* measures.

Height

'Common sense' says police officers need to be big, to overcome violent offenders, and command respect. British police forces still specify minimum heights. American police forces used to set minimum heights, but have been challenged frequently under fair employment legislation. Women are less tall on average than men, and some ethnic minorities have smaller average builds than white Americans, so minimum height tests create *adverse impact* (Chapter 12) by excluding most women and some minorities. Therefore minimum height tests must be proved *job-related*. 'Common sense' is surprised to learn American research has been unable to prove a link between height and any criterion of effectiveness in police officers (Arvey, 1979b). Perhaps American police officers don't need height, bulk or brute force because they are armed. British police forces have always set a separate, lower minimum height for women, so the only group with a possible grievance are shortish men, who might argue that if a 5'6" woman can do the job, so could a 5'6" man.

Dexterity

Dexterity divides into *arm and hand* or *gross* dexterity, and *finger and wrist* or *fine* dexterity. Dexterity is needed for assembly work, which is generally semi-skilled or unskilled. It's also needed for some professional jobs, notably dentistry and surgery. Standardized tests of dexterity have been available for many years, e.g. Stromberg Dexterity, Bennett Hand Tool Test, Saville & Holdsworth Ltd's MANDEX (*gross* dexterity), O'Connor Finger and Tweezer Test, Crawford Small Parts Dexterity Test, SHL's FINDEX (*fine* dexterity), but don't appear to have been used very widely; at any rate the published validation information is thin. The General Aptitude Test Battery (GATB) (Chapter 7) includes both gross and fine dexterity tests; GATB is very widely used in the USA. Many work sample and trainability tests assess dexterity.

Ghiselli's meta-analysis reported moderate validities of dexterity tests for vehicle operation, trades and crafts, and industrial work. Re-analysis of the GATB database (Hunter, 1986) showed that the less complex the job, the more important dexterity becomes. Hartigan & Wigdor (1989) suggest the GATB data actually show that dexterity predicts success only at the lowest of five levels of complexity: cannery worker, shrimp picker, cornhusking machine operator, etc.

Appearance and attractiveness

Wallace & Travers (1938) describe how door-to-door salesmen were selected by a British company in the 1930s. The managing director and his personnel manager "were both more or less convinced that small dark men are the best", because "Both of these able gentlemen are small dark men". Wallace & Travers introduced a more scientific assessment of physique, classifying the salesmen as "gorillas, orang-utans, chimpanzees, baboons, or mixed anthropoids". This, and other clues, suggest Wallace & Travers had a low opinion of salesmen.

Attractiveness used to be dismissed as irrelevant, because "beauty is in the eye of the beholder". Extensive research of physical attractiveness since 1970 reaches different conclusions. There is broad consensus about who is and isn't attractive; attractiveness is an important individual difference, and not just in sexual encounters. Research on interviewing (Chapter 4) shows that appearance and attractiveness often affect selectors' decisions; Dipboye, Arvey & Terpstra (1977) showed that being physically attractive was worth on average two places in a rank order of order of 12 when applying for a job. But is appearance or attractiveness a *legitimate* part of the *person specification* for many jobs? For acting and modelling, certainly. Appearance or attractiveness is often an implicit requirement for receptionists; many advertisements specify "smart appearance", "pleasant manner", etc. Appearance, shading into 'charisma', is probably also important for selling, persuading and influencing jobs.

CONCLUSIONS

Educational qualifications These have surprisingly poor validity. Surprising not so much because education is a very widely used test; being in general use certainly doesn't guarantee a test's validity. Surprising because education reflects both ability and personality (effort, motivation, co-operativeness), and because Booth, McNally & Berry made a fair case for education's construct validity as a selection test.

Training and experience ratings These take some of the subjectivity out of application sifting, and the more successful versions achieve a moderate degree of validity.

Self-assessments Because they allow the subject to speak for him/herself, self-assessments appeal to some. They appeal to others because they're very simple, hence very cheap. Self-assessments have limited validity which, one suspects, might vanish altogether if self-assessments were used for real decisions, not just research.

Work samples These have generally very good validity but are cumbersome and usually local. Transportable tests are obviously cheaper than ones that have to be developed for every new job. True work samples can only be used for motor tasks, which means they can't select for jobs that are very varied, or involve dealing with people rather than things. Work samples have two major advantages. They measure how well applicants can do the job, so they measure every attribute needed for the job—strength, dexterity, eye sight, as well as intellectual abilities. Some work samples also measure aspects of interests and even personality (but work samples probably won't be so good at predicting long-term satisfaction, absence, turnover etc). Work sample tests are very safe. Fair employment legislation favours tests that resemble the job as closely as possible. Work samples can be *content-valid*, which means many legal problems are avoided (Chapters 11 and 12).

Physical tests If a job needs strength, it needs strength. Even American courts have admitted this, although a physical test has to be properly validated. On the other hand, if a job is thought to need height, research suggests it probably doesn't, so height tests aren't useful. Research on attractiveness in other fields suggests it may be very important in selection, but there's not a lot of direct evidence at present.

11 Validity and Criteria of Productivity

"We don't know what we're doing, but we are doing it very carefully and hope you are pleased with our unintelligent diligence" [Wherry, 1957]

What's the difference between a party game like "Trivial Pursuits" and a test of verbal ability? What distinguishes Problem Puzzles on a matchbox from a numerical ability test? What's the difference between a magazine's "Are You a Good Lover" quiz and a personality test?—*validity*. Joke tests are fun to do, but tell you nothing. True psychological tests can be used to make decisions, about who will be productive, and who won't.

A *valid* test is one that works, that measures what it claims to measure, that predicts something useful. Dunnette (1966) defines validity more elaborately as learning more about the meaning of a test. A valid test is backed by research and development. Anyone can string together a few dozen questions about assertiveness; it takes years of patient research, studying large groups of people, collecting follow-up data, to turn the list of questions into a valid psychological test.

The earliest psychological tests were validated against external criteria. Binet's intelligence test used teacher ratings, and age (the average 10-year-old can solve problems the average 6-year-old can't). Woodworth's Personal Data Sheet selected its questions from psychiatric texts and cases, and checked them against diagnostic status. Since then, validating tests has become a major industry, subject to intense legal scrutiny (Chapter 12). The American Psychological Association's (APA's) Division of Industrial/Organisational Psychology have published their *Principles for the Validation and Use of Personnel Selection Procedures*.

TYPES OF VALIDITY

1. Faith validity

"The person who sold me the test was very plausible."

The layperson is easily impressed by well-presented tests, smooth-talking salespersons and sub-psychodynamic nonsense. But plausibility doesn't guarantee validity, and money spent on glossy presentation and well-dressed sales staff is all too often money not spent on research and development.

2. Face validity

"The test looks plausible."

Some people are persuaded a test measures dominance if it's called "Dominance Test" or if the questions all concern behaving dominantly. Early personality inventories mostly relied on *face validity*. Allport's A(scendance)-S(ubmission) Reaction Study asks questions about rebuking queue-jumpers, asking the first question at seminars, avoiding bossy people, etc. Early research showed that face validity is never sufficient in itself. Face validity is useful, to the extent it makes the test more acceptable to employer and employee.

3. Content validity

"The test looks plausible to experts."

Experts analyse the job, choose relevant questions, and put together the test. The St Louis Fire brigade used 'a' (i.e. one) professional outside consultant, who conducted interviews with 27 fire captains to identify every component of the job and its importance. (The resulting test wasn't a great success—see Chapter 12). A *content valid* test is almost always face valid, but a face valid test isn't necessarily content valid. Content validity depends on *job analysis* (Chapter 3). Content validation was borrowed from educational testing, where it makes sense to ask if a test covers the curriculum, and to seek answers from *subject matter experts*. Content validation regards test items as *samples*, of things workers need to know, not as *signs* of what else workers might be able to do.

Content validation was poorly thought of, before the law started taking such a keen interest in selection. Dunnette (1966) said "this armchair approach to test validation is, at best, only a starting point". Guion (1978) describes the APA's own official policy statements on content validation as "filled with contradiction and confusion", because it was written by a committee (of which Guion was a dissenting member).

Be that as it may, selectors in the USA often have to use content validation, or nothing. The APA's *Principles* describe standards for good content validation: "(a) a test developer should define a job content domain, (b) ... the definition should be given in terms of tasks, activities, or responsibilities, or perhaps job knowledge, (c) ... the sample should include all important aspects of the domain, and (d) ... the qualifications of people who make the various kinds of judgments in the process should be duly recorded." Carrier, Dalessio & Brown (1990) report that managers' estimates of the content validity of structured interview items show 'modest' correlations with their empirical validity.

Distefano, Pryer & Erffmeyer (1983) describe four stages in content-validating a test for psychiatric aides.

1. Psychiatric aides, nurses and psychologists write an initial pool of basic work behaviour items.
2. Personnel, training staff, and nurses review and modify the items to ensure they deal with observable behaviour, and apply to all six hospitals.
3. Items are rated by 20 psychiatric aides and 18 aide supervisors on two scales:
   (a) essential (for effective performance of the job)/useful but not essential/not necessary,
   (b) task performed every day/several times a week/once a week/less than once a week/never.
4. The 78 surviving items are re-written in Behaviourally Anchored Rating Scale (BARS) format (Chapter 5):

   Physically assists patients with bathing, dressing, grooming, and related personal hygiene tasks as needed.
   (a) Seldom performs correctly according standards expected, and requires constant supervision,
   (b) Performs below acceptable level, below standards expected, and requires frequent instructions
   ...
   (e) Performs consistently above acceptable level, greatly exceeds standards expected, and almost never requires instructions.

Lawshe (1975) outlines a formal procedure for establishing content validity. A *content evaluation panel*, composed of workers and supervisors, rate test items as essential/useful/unnecessary. Their ratings are used to calculate a *content validity ratio* (CVR) for each test item. Lawshe supplies a table for deciding whether CVR is acceptable or not. Finally the *content validity index* is calculated—the mean CVR of the items retained in the final form of the test.

The (US) Equal Employment Opportunity Commission's (EEOC) *Guidelines* on selection procedures say

> a selection procedure based upon inferences about mental processes cannot be supported solely or primarily on the basis of content validity. Thus a content strategy is not appropriate for demonstrating the validity of selection procedures which purport to measure traits or constructs, such as intelligence, aptitude, personality, commonsense, judgment, leadership, and spatial ability.

This ought to limit content validation to work sample tests; but employers desperate to find fair and valid tests (Chapter 12) sometimes try to stretch content validation to "traits and constructs". Content valid tests take a long time to write, and are themselves often immensely long. They commonly achieve no greater *predictive* validity than a set of four or five standard, all-purpose aptitude tests (Tenopyr, 1977).

4. Criterion validity

"The test predicts productivity."

People who score highly on the test are more productive—no matter what the test is called, what the questions are, how plausible the test looks or how plausible the test's author sounds. What matters is the *criterion*—productivity. Criterion validity has three forms: *predictive, concurrent* and *retrospective*.

(a) Predictive validity

"The test predicts who will produce more."

Predictive validity is the most convincing demonstration of a test's validity, because it parallels real life selection: select *today*, find out *later* if you made the right choice. The same time-lag makes predictive validation slow and expensive. It is also referred to as *follow-up* or *longitudinal* validity.

(b) Concurrent validity

"The test 'predicts' who is producing more."

Test and criterion data are collected at the same time, i. e. concurrently. This makes concurrent validity quicker and easier to determine than predictive validity. Concurrent validity is also referred to as *present-employee* or *cross-sectional* validity.

(c) Retrospective validity

"Past tests 'predict' present productivity."

Retrospective validity is also known as *shelf research*, because employers trying to validate tests use data obtained when employees were recruited, but not necessarily collected for selection purposes. Retrospective studies are usually untidy, because the research has to be fitted to the data, not the data to the research.

(d) Some technicalities

Researchers usually report *correlations*, which can be misleading, if the relation between predictor and criterion isn't *linear*, or isn't *homoscedastic*. Figure 11.1 illustrates a *non-linear* relationship between predictor and criterion: very dull subjects make poor bottle-washers; fairly bright people make good bottle-washers; very bright people are as poor at bottle-washing as the very dull. The example is *fictional*; reliable examples of non-linear relations between predictor and criterion are scarce. Brown & Ghiselli (1953) found tests of arithmetic and reaction time had a curvilinear relationship with turnover in taxi drivers. Lack of *homoscedasticity* means variability of scores differs in different parts of the distribution. Figure 6.5 (page 100) illustrates a *non-homoscedastic* relationship; low scores on the American insurance industry's Aptitude Index Battery (Chapter 6), predict failure, but high scores don't predict success.

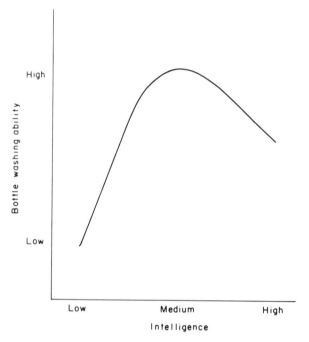

Figure 11.1   A fictional non-linear relationship between a predictor (intelligence) and productivity (bottle-washing)

A *scatterplot* (Figure 11.2) identifies non-linear or non-homoscedastic data, and also identifies *leverage*, where an apparently large and highly significant correlation turns out to result largely from a single *outlier*, one subject whose scores on predictor and criterion deviate from everyone else's. The larger the data set, the less problem outliers cause (Orr, Sackett & Dubois, 1991).

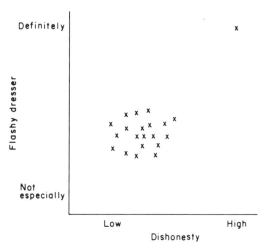

Figure 11.2 A fictional scatterplot of relationship between two variables (being a flashy dresser and being dishonest) in occupational psychologists, illustrating an "outlier" (top right) that could create a spuriously high correlation and cause people to think *all* smartly dressed psychologists are dishonest

Sorenson (1966) reports finding a *suppressor variable,* when selecting motor mechanics with Bennett Mechanical Comprehension Test (MCT), Survey of Mechanical Insight (SMI) and a Background Survey Questionnaire (BSQ). None of the tests predicted supervisor ratings very well; the Bennett MCT didn't predict at all. Nevertheless Sorenson thought MCT could help select motor mechanics, and included it in his regression equation:

Supervisor rating = 866 + (10 × SMI) − (6 × TMC) + (17 × BSQ).

The MCT test correlates fairly well with general intelligence, whereas the SMI is more of a 'nuts and bolts' test, which, however, also measures an irrelevant element of general intellectual ability. Some mechanics do well on SMI because they're generally bright, not because they're good mechanics. So 'suppressing' the general intelligence element, by subtracting MCT score, improves selection of mechanics. In practice, according to Wiggins (1973), suppressor variables very rarely prove useful.

5. Construct validity

"The test measures something meaningful."

Construct validity can focus on a *test*, or on a *trait or ability*.

(a) Test-centred construct validity

Cronbach (1984) discusses the construct validity of the Bennett MCT.

> *Experience*   The MCT assumes subjects have seen, used, or even repaired machinery, so it's unsuitable for people in developing countries. Women tend to get lower scores on MCT, perhaps because they have less experience with machinery.

> *Education*   People who have studied physics get higher MCT scores.

> *General ability*   Scores from MCTs correlate well with general intelligence.

> *Specific knowledge*   Cronbach once hypothesized that MCT measured knowledge of a few specific mechanic principles—gears, levers, etc. When he tested his hypothesis, he found it incorrect; MCT does measure *general* acquaintance with mechanical principles.

> *Dexterity*   Scores from MCTs correlate poorly with manual dexterity and motor mechanic work sample tests.

The Bennett test reflects general intelligence more than being good *with one's hands*, or with real machinery. On the other hand, Bennett scores are influenced by experience and education in ways not found in pure tests of general intelligence.

(b) Trait/ability-centred construct validity

Need for achievement is what made America and the West get where they are today, according to McClelland (1971). Need for achievement, abbreviated to "nAch", is *ambition*, to make money and build a business empire (Cook, 1993). Research on the construct validation of nAch follows seven main lines (Fineman, 1977):

> *Different measures*   Need for achievement is measured by inventory, and by projective tests: Thematic Apperception Test, TAT, doodles, preference for different tartans, even designs on pottery. Different measures inter-correlate poorly, which throws some doubt on the very existence of the construct of need for achievement.

> *Reliability*   Measures of nAch, especially projective tests, often have poor reliability, which casts further doubt on the existence of the construct.

Performance   Measures of nAch predict who will perform better on a task, because ambitious people are more efficient.

Level of aspiration   Achievement motivation predicts who chooses more difficult tasks, suggesting ambitious people welcome a challenge. Research on both level of aspiration and performance is disappointingly inconsistent, and effects, when found, are often very small. (Fineman's is a narrative review, making no corrections, so may underestimate true effect size.)

Upbringing   McClelland reports research on children building castles with toy bricks, while parents watched their efforts. Parents of high achievers are warm and encouraging, and physically affectionate; parents of low achievers keep finding fault and telling the child what to do next.

Psycho-history   McClelland presents some very challenging data, showing for example that literature full of achievement themes preceded, and therefore possibly *caused*, expansion of ancient Greek trade, as measured by the dispersion throughout the Mediterranean of Greek wine jars.

Creating an achieving society   McClelland thinks both upbringing and culture shape achievement motivation, so changing both should make a whole society achieve more. McClelland went to India, and tried to do just that, with mixed results.

Opinions differ widely about construct validation. Guion (1978) argues all test validation necessarily is construct validation, because the test writer always has a theory about what he/she is trying to measure. Consider 'scrap rate' — a very concrete measure. If high scrap rate is a sign of carelessness, workers whose scrap rate is high may be too irresponsible to make good foremen. To test this hypothesis, the tester needs other measures of carelessness. On the other hand, if scrap rate reflects clumsiness, it may not be a bar to promotion, and one seeks tests of physical co-ordination. Taking this broad view of construct validation, it becomes virtually synonymous with validation as a whole.

Ebel (1977) takes a much narrower view; constructs are "a few internal forces of personality", which he thinks don't exist anyway. So "why do we continue to talk about construct validation as if it were something we all understand and have found useful?" Certainly examples of constructs, in Ebel's narrow sense, are hard to find. There is some evidence that aggressiveness operates as an internal force, present in the aggressive person but not always directly affecting his/her behaviour (Cook, 1993). Otherwise evidence of 'internal forces' in personality remains sketchy and inconsistent.

6. Factorial validity

"The test measures two things but gives them 16 different labels."

Factor analysis is a useful component of validation, but insufficient in itself. Knowing *how many* factors a test measures doesn't tell you *what* they are, nor what they can predict.

7. Synthetic validity

"The test measures component traits and abilities that predict productivity."

The employer tells the psychologist "I need people who are good with figures, who are sociable and outgoing, and who can type". The psychologist uses tests of numerical ability, extraversion and typing skill, the validities of which have been *separately* proved. The separate validities of the three tests are *synthesized* to yield a compound validity. Lawshe (1952) defined synthetic validation as "the inferring of validity from a logical analysis of jobs into their elements, a definition of test validity for these elements, and combination of elemental validities into a whole". Synthetic validity is also known as *job component validity*.

Synthetic validation employs two principles. The first is familiar—*job analysis* to identify underlying themes in diverse jobs and select tests corresponding to each theme. The second principle holds that validity, once demonstrated for a combination of theme × test across the workforce as a whole, can be inferred for sub sets of the workers, *including sets too small for a conventional validation exercise*. Table 11.1 illustrates the principle with *fictional* data. A city employs 1500 persons in 300 different jobs. Some jobs, for example local tax clerk, employ enough people to calculate a conventional validity coefficient. Other jobs, for example refuse collection supervisor, employ too few to make a conventional local validity study worth undertaking. Some jobs, by their very nature, employ only one person, rendering any statistical analysis impossible. Job analysis identifies a number of themes underlying all 300 jobs, and suitable tests for each theme are introduced. Validity of the Dominance scale of the California Psychological Inventory (CPI) for the 25 refuse collection supervisors is inferred from its validity for the 430 persons throughout the workforce whose work requires *ability to influence others*. It's even possible to prove the validity of CPI Responsibility scale for the one and only crematorium attendant, by pooling his predictor and criterion data with the 520 others for whom *attention to detail* is important.

Guion (1965b) reported a case study of synthetic validity in a small electrical wholesalers, employing 48 employees, where the largest number of persons doing the same job was three. Guion identified seven elements in the company's work; the company's management rank-ordered staff on each

Table 11.1 Illustration of synthetic validation in a local authority (city) workforce of 1500

		Dimension			
	N	Ability to influence	Attention to detail	Numeracy	etc. ...
Test		CPI-Do	CPI-Re	GMA-N	etc. ...
Job					
Local tax clerk	150	—	XX	—	
Refuse collection supervisor	25	XX	XX	XX	
Crematorium attendant	1	XX	XX	—	
etc.					
...					
N involved		430	520	350	
Validity		0.30	0.25	0.27	

CPI—California Psychological Inventory; Do—dominance; Re—responsibility; GMA-N—Graduate and Managerial Assessment – Numerical.

element (omitting those for whom it wasn't relevant). The seven criterion rank orders were then correlated with the Guilford Zimmerman Temperament Survey (GZTS), Graves Design Judgment Test, and some ability tests, to find which different set of scores predicted each criterion.

The combination of Position Analysis Question (PAQ) (Chapter 3) and General Aptitude Test Battery (GATB) (Chapter 7) is well suited to synthetic validation. McCormick, Jeanneret & Mecham (1972) has shown that PAQ scores correlate with GATB *scores* very well, and with GATB *validity* fairly well. This implies PAQ job analysis can predict what profile of GATB scores will be found in people doing a job *successfully*.

Mossholder & Arvey (1984) review these, and several other, approaches to synthetic validation, and reach the rather melancholy conclusion that 35 years of research has only shown that synthetic validation is "feasible" but "has not done so in a completely convincing manner". The public expect personnel psychologists to deliver selection systems that work now, not blueprints for what someone (else) might one day achieve.

ASPECTS OF VALIDATION

Predictive vs concurrent validity

Received wisdom from 1946 held predictive validity superior to concurrent validity. Guion (1965a) even said the "present employee method is clearly a violation of scientific principles". Why?

1. Missing persons   In *concurrent* studies, people who were rejected, or who left, or who were dismissed aren't available for study. Nor are people who proved so good they have been promoted. In concurrent validation, both ends of the distribution of productivity may be missing, so *range is restricted*.

2. Unrepresentative samples   Present employees may not be typical of applicants—actual or possible. The applicant sample is often younger than the employee sample. The workforce may be all white and/or all male, when applicants include, or ought to include, women and non-whites.

3. Direction of cause   Present employees have changed to meet the job's demands. They have often been *trained* to meet the job's demands. So it's trivial to find successful managers are dominant, because managers learn to command influence and respect, whereas showing dominant applicants *become* good managers is useful.

4. Faking   Present employees are less likely to fake personality inventories than applicants, because they've already got the job.

The first two arguments imply concurrent validation will yield smaller validity coefficients. But reviews of research on mental ability testing conclude the two methods of measuring validity give much the same results (Bemis, 1968; Lent, Aurbach & Levin, 1971; Barrett, Phillips & Alexander, 1981). In an *ideal* predictive validity study there is no restriction of range, because every applicant is employed. In reality this rarely happens because the employer uses the test data to select. Even if the employer doesn't use the test to select, whatever selection method the employer does use may correlate with the test being validated, which creates *indirect* restriction of range. (Suppose staff are selected by educational level, and suppose an ability test is being predictively validated: educational level and ability test correlate, so the educational requirement excludes more applicants with low ability scores, which indirectly restricts range on the ability test.) Bemis (1968) found no difference in GATB score variance between predictive and concurrent validation samples, showing range hadn't in fact been restricted.

Concurrent validity also presents *direction of cause* problems. Suppose a concurrent study shows unsuccessful teachers are anxious. Are they poor teachers because they're anxious, or are they anxious because they're beginning to realize they're poor teachers? Brousseau & Prince (1981) tested 176 employees twice with GZTS at average intervals of 7 years, and found *changes* in GZTS scores correlated with aspects of their work measured by the Job Diagnostic Survey. People doing work with high *task identity*—doing a job from start to finish with a visible outcome—increased their scores on seven GZTS scales. People doing jobs with high *task significance*—impact on lives and work of others—increased their scores on eight scales. Brousseau & Prince's data show how work can cause systematic changes in personality, and suggest doubts about concurrent validation of personality inventories may be justified.

The *direction of cause* argument implies concurrent validity coefficients for personality measures will be lower. If people change to adapt to their work, their personality profiles will become more similar, which will reduce variance in personality scores, and lower the correlation. Comparisons of predictive and concurrent validation of personality tests could logically report three results: predictive validity higher, concurrent validity higher, or no difference between the two. Two meta-analyses between them do report all three results:

- predictive validity *higher* than concurrent validity (Tett, Jackson & Rothstein , 1991)
- predictive validity *lower* than concurrent validity, for honesty tests on employee samples (Ones et al, undated)
- predictive validity *not different* from concurrent validity, for honesty tests in applicant samples (Ones et al, undated).

These results are hard to explain very readily, but suggest caution when using concurrent validation with personality tests.

Is direction of cause a problem with ability tests? Reviewers assume not. The layperson sees it as self-evident that a year spent working with figures will improve performance on a numerical test. The tester cites high re-test reliabilities as proof mental abilities are stable, even fixed. (But subjects in re-test reliability studies don't have intensive practice between their two tests.) In their review, Barrett, Phillips & Alexander (1981) could only find two studies proving that mental ability test scores are "probably resistant to the effects of work experience". Anastasi (1981) reviews research on practice and coaching effects on ability tests, and concludes they exist but are small enough to be disregarded. However, the research all deals with coaching and practice for school tests, like the American Scholastic Aptitude Test or the British "11 plus", and doesn't address the question of the effects of long experience.

Cross-validation

This means checking the validity of a test a second time, on a second sample. Cross-validation is always desirable and becomes absolutely essential when keys are empirically constructed, when regression equations are calculated, or when multiple cut-offs are used, because these methods are particularly likely to capitalize on chance. Locke (1961) gives a very striking demonstration of the hazards of not cross-validating; he found students with long surnames (7+ letters) were less charming, stimulating, gay, happy-go-lucky and impulsive, liked vodka, but didn't smoke, and had more fillings in their teeth. Locke's results sound quite plausible, in places, but needless to say they completely failed to *cross-validate*. Tests that aren't cross-validated lead to *fold-back error*, calculating scoring weights from a sample, then applying them to the same sample as if it were independent. Cureton (1950) has a ruder name for keys and regressions that are not cross-validated—'baloney coefficients'.

Murphy (1984) notes that most researches published in *Personnel Psychology* and *Journal of Applied Psychology* in the late 1970s did cross-validate—usually by splitting a single sample into two, and calculating validity within each. Murphy considers this pointless; researchers can calculate the stability of validity coefficients or regression equations, using formulae based on sample size and number of predictors used. In fact cross-validation serves two different purposes; (a) it checks the sample size is large enough, and (b) it checks whether observed effects are robust enough to survive the move to a new sample, a new job or a new location.

Stability of validity over time

Most people assume validity is *stable over time*, so that a test that predicts performance after 1 year in the job will predict performance after 3 years equally well. Utility analyses explicitly assume test validity remains constant over 7 years (representing the average length of time a typical employee stays with one employer). Barrett, Caldwell & Alexander (1985) searched literature published between 1914 and 1984, and found 12 studies where the same criterion was used on two more occasions; 5.8% of the 480 pairs of validity coefficients were different—as many as would be expected by chance. Recently, however, the stability of validity has been questioned. Hulin, Henry & Noon (1990) conclude the relationship between predictive validity and time lapse between test and outcome is strongly negative (– 0.80). This implies an initially valid test will rapidly lose its validity. Critics (Barrett, 1992; Barrett, Alexander & Doverspike, 1992) note that nearly all the evidence of Hulin et al derives from narrow experimental measures, or baseball records, or flight-simulators, or educational achievement; only one study, of 31 described, uses an ability test to predict actual job performance. Schmidt et al (1988) report validity of mental ability tests for US Military Occupational Specialities does remain stable over 5 years. On the other hand, research on a large sample of sewing machinists (Deadrick & Madigan, 1990) found the predictive validity of mental ability tests *increased* over time, the predictive validity of experience *decreased*, while the predictive validity of dexterity tests stayed the same.

The 'advantage' of small samples

If two small (N = 10) samples are compared, the difference between them must be large to achieve significance—nearly one whole SD between the means

(Dunnette, 1966). If the samples are large (*N* = 1000), a very small average difference can achieve significance (one corresponding to 0.09 SDs). This follows logically from the way significance of mean difference is calculated. Dunnette argued a sample should be large enough to detect true relationships, but small enough not to detect trivial ones. A difference between means equivalent to only 0.09 SDs may interest researchers, but isn't likely to be much use to selectors. Dunnette suggests 50–60 is the ideal range (which just happened to be the sample size of the typical local validation study). Chapter 7 outlined modern arguments why 50–60 is nowhere near large enough to give reliable results. It's important to show a difference or a correlation is large enough to be cost-effective, but there are better ways of deciding than using samples that are too small to give reliable results; researchers should either calculate effect size, for example by squaring the correlation (page 53), or use *utility theory* (Chapter 13).

Is validation always essential?

Critics often think psychologists are obsessed with validity; some even claim excessive concern with statistics is a sign of an anal personality. Other experts don't keep measuring themselves, and announcing to the world that most of their decisions are unreliable or incorrect. Other scientists don't constantly demand proof of the validity of measures. Ebel (1977) cites the example of the Babcock test of butterfat in cream (in which the fat is dissolved by sulphuric acid, then centrifuged into the neck of the bottle, and measured). No one demands proof that the Babcock test is valid, that it 'really' measures butterfat in cream. As Ebel says, the Babcock test has 'self-evident' validity. Why can't psychological tests be accepted in the same way?

Ebel's argument is of course deliberately ingenuous. Butterfat is real; you can eat it (but not after dissolving it in sulphuric acid!). Intelligence is a *construct*, something inferred from behaviour. The inferential leap from psychological test to productivity is far greater than from centrifuge to fat content. And if ability tests measured something as uncontroversial as fat content, they might easily achieve the same unthinking acceptance.

THE CRITERION

Seventy years ago Bingham & Freyd (1926) said:

> the successful employee ... does more work, does it better, with less supervision, with less interruption through absence ... He makes fewer mistakes and has fewer accidents ... He ordinarily learns more quickly, is promoted more rapidly, and stays with the company.

The basic validation paradigm compares a *predictor*, meaning a selection test, with a *criterion*, meaning an index of the worker's success. The *criterion* side of the paradigm presents far greater problems than the *predictor* side. The predictor is simply any test that predicts who will do better work. The criterion by contrast requires researchers to define and measure 'success in work'. This soon gets very complicated (Austin & Villanova, 1992). Is success better measured 'objectively', by counting units produced, or better measured subjectively, by informed opinion? Is success at work uni-dimensional or multi-dimensional? Who decides whether work is successful? Different supervisors may not agree. Management and workers may not agree. The organization and its customers may not agree. The organization and the general public may not agree.

The quickest way to discredit a validation study is to discredit its criterion. A good criterion should be:

1. Reliable, meaning either stable (over time) or consistent (between observers). Ratings, the favourite criterion, have limited reliability. It's often assumed that objective criteria are automatically 100% reliable. They may be no more reliable than ratings; Hunter, Schmidt & Judiesch (1990) report an average reliability of 0.55 for weekly production records.

2. Relevant i. e. 'valid'. In one sense this is a tautology; the criterion *defines* success. But criteria have often been attacked as irrelevant, especially in fair employment cases.

3. Uncontaminated. If the person who makes the criterion rating knows the predictor score, the criterion is *contaminated*, and clearly invalid.

4. Practical. Information can be obtained at reasonable cost, by procedures management and workers accept.

It is axiomatic that an unreliable measure cannot be valid, because a measure that doesn't correlate with itself can't correlate with anything else. Nevertheless, in a Korean War study of bomber crews, the impossible apparently happened (Hemphill & Sechrest, 1952). The 'circular error' criterion (a photo showing whether the bomb hit the target) had zero reliability; photos of successive bombing runs showed no consistency at all in bombing accuracy. Nevertheless 'circular error' correlated well with supervisor ratings of the crews' bombing skills. How? By criterion contamination; the supervisors saw the photos, didn't grasp the fact that they were meaningless, but based their ratings on them.

Critics like to pick some occupation where the notion of a criterion seems particularly silly or inappropriate. Some choose university teachers (college professors); Farh, Werbel & Bedeian (1988) propose five criteria for academics: output of refereed publications, conference papers, student evaluations, committees attended and head of department ratings. Other critics choose ministers of religion. How can one possibly find a sensible criterion? (This side of the Day of Judgement?) Umeda & Frey (1974) used five objective criteria: number of baptisms a year, congregation size, status of job title, number of paid supervisees, and time devoted to professional reading, and five subjective criteria: ratings *by the minister him/herself* of job satisfaction, job success, human relations skills, public speaking ability and counselling skill. (It's unusual to use self-ratings as a criterion, for fear of less than total frankness, but ministers of religion are probably a special case.) Either the criteria really were unsatisfactory, or the sample wasn't large enough; the attempt to devise a biodata inventory for ministers failed.

Crites (1969) analyses criteria used by over 500 validation studies reported by Dorcus & Jones (1950), for the period 1914–1950.

Global ratings by supervisor	60%
Output criteria	16%
Sales	5%
Earnings	5%
Accidents	4%
Job level	4%
Survival	3%
Work sample	3%
Promotion	1%

Twenty years later, the review by Lent, Aurbach & Levin (1971) review found 879 of 1506 criteria (58%) were supervisor evaluations. The global supervisor rating is clearly the favourite criterion in validation research.

Subjective criteria

In the First World War, the US Army devised a system of rating officers for physical qualities, intelligence, leadership, personal qualities and general value to service. In the USA today, virtually all employees are rated, by supervisors and managers, usually annually, on a set of job-related dimensions. The ratings determine salary, promotions, even 'retention', and are subject to fair employment scrutiny, so they are usually made carefully. Numerous variations in rating formats have been devised, in the search for a system that will maximize reliability, and minimize halo and bias: BARS (described in Chapter 5), *behavioral observation scales, behavioral expectation scales*, etc. The supervisor rating criterion is very convenient to psychologists researching on selection—so long as they don't read any of the work of colleagues researching the very same ratings under the heading of *performance appraisal*. Their colleagues' efforts document the many problems of performance appraisal ratings: poor reliability, halo, leniency, bias and politicking (down-rating dangerous competitors, favouring safe mediocrities, hanging onto good steady workers, 'outplacing' problem individuals, etc).

Supervisor ratings have poor *reliability*; two supervisors' ratings of the same set of workers agree very imperfectly. Recently Rothstein (1990) plotted reliability against length of acquaintance, and found it only reaches 0.60 after 20 years. This implies the 0.60 value, widely cited for supervisor rating reliability and used in *validity generalization analyses*, is an *over*estimate.

All ratings exhibit *halo*. All ratings intercorrelate strongly, even though the scales aren't logically related; the person who is rated polite is likely also to be rated well adjusted, intelligent, highly motivated, etc. This is a pervasive feature of all ratings made by human observers, and was first noted as long ago as 1907. Halo is a serious problem in *appraisal* ratings, because appraisal is meant to identify where the worker is performing well and where he/she could do better. For this reason it's usually assumed halo is undesirable, and efforts are made to limit it. Halo is less of a problem when ratings are used as *criterion*; the researcher often prefers a single, global estimate of worth to the organization. Nathan & Tippins (1990) report that halo in supervisor ratings of clerical workers is associated with higher test validity.

Supervisor ratings may exhibit racial *bias*; Kraiger & Ford (1985) report a meta-analysis of 74 studies, and find a small but consistent *own-race bias*, accounting for 5% of variance in ratings. Project A data, from 1000 black and 2000 white subjects, confirm the *own-race bias*, but find it even smaller, accounting for only 1% of the variance in ratings (Oppler et al, 1992). Another type of bias is *leniency*; ratings made in appraisal schemes tend to be more *lenient* than ratings made especially for use in selection research (Landy & Farr, 1980).

Supervisor ratings are rarely criticized on grounds of their *validity*. Specially developed criteria often attract critical comment; everyone thinks they can devise surefire ways of assessing good workers, and everyone likes telling psychologists how to do their job. In contrast, supervisor ratings, for all their flaws, have a satisfying finality about them. How do you know X is better than Y? —because the supervisor says so. This is just as well, because attempts to validate supervisor ratings tend to fall into circularity. One strategy is to compare supervisor ratings with 'true' ratings produced by an 'expert' panel, but if one expert panel doesn't agree with another, which has given the 'true' ratings? Sometimes the supervisor rating criterion doesn't work well, because the supervisor sees little of the rated's work. Hirsch, Northrop & Schmidt (1986) think this may be why validation studies for police work get poor results. Fairly early on, research suggested that rating criteria didn't correlate well with other criteria (Severin, 1952). More recently, meta-analysis confirms that supervisor ratings correlate at best 0.27 with objective criteria, even correcting for error of measurement (Heneman, 1986).

Supervisor rating validity is also suspect, when it reflects behaviours that *please management*, rather than good job performance.

1. Ingratiation. The Measure of Ingratiatory Behaviors in Organisational Settings (MIBOS) identifies many ways to please management (besides doing good work): tell them about your successes, compliment them on their successes, listen sympathetically to their problems, laugh at their unfunny jokes, help them find somewhere to live, run errands for them, etc. (Kumar & Beyerlein, 1991).

2. 'Organizational citizenship'. Many employees do work that falls outside their job description, to help out colleagues or keep things running smoothly. 'Organizational citizenship' naturally pleases management, and attracts more favourable supervisor ratings (Orr, Sackett & Mercer, 1989).

3. Organizational fads and chairman's whims. In the 1890s, the Royal Navy valued 'spit and polish' so highly that some ship's captains were said to try to avoid gunnery practice in case the powder smoke spoiled their paintwork.

4. First World War mentality. Organizations occasionally exist in which subordinates gain credit for pushing ahead with management plans that are absurdly wrong, in pursuit of aims which are completely pointless, stifling criticism of either purpose or method with cries of "commitment" and "loyalty".

In many organizations supervisors rate *reputation*; a good reputation can be earned by good work, but many features of large organizations make it easy to earn one in other ways.

1. Social reality. A company that manufactures gearboxes has its success defined externally, and unambiguously, by its sales figures. A university by contrast constructs its own *social reality*. A consensus of academics decides what issues are worth researching and teaching, and by implication whose work has merit. Where success is defined by the organization and its staff, greater scope exists for creating undeserved reputations.

2. Attributability problem. Complex organizations and long time-scales mean it's often hard to assign true responsibility for successes or failures, which opens the door for fast operators to steal the credit for successes, dodge the blame for failures, and build an undeserved reputation.

3. Empire-building. In many organizations, success is defined in terms of increasing the size of one's department or budget. Services are provided for the sake of justifying the organization's expansion.

4. Re-organizations. Besides blurring responsibility for successes and failures, re-organizations create a perfect form of pseudo-work, divorced from external standards. The efforts of dozens, even hundreds of workers, are centred for months on something that has no end-product, and serves no useful purpose, but is an ideal environment for the person who seeks to build a reputation.

5. Cover your back. In cautious organizations a good reputation is built largely by *not* doing things: not making controversial decisions, not attracting complaints, not getting bad publicity, etc.

6. It's who you know, not what you know. This is a widely voiced observation, which implies one's time may be better spent creating a network of allies and contacts than doing any actual work.

7. The non-working day. Only part of an academic's day is spent doing core job-description activities—teaching students and conducting research. The rest of the day gets filled up by chattering, drinking coffee, tidying up, meetings, pointless paperwork, etc. The more of the working day is filled by non-work or semi-work, the more time there is to set about making oneself well thought of, without doing any good teaching or useful research.

The implication of these observations is that organizations that don't have clear objective criteria of good work are precisely those in which a subjective criterion is least likely to be valid.

Objective criteria

The first reported validation study (Link, 1918) used an objective criterion—munitions output over 4-week periods. *Output/production* criteria include: units produced, breakages, spoiled work, etc. Output can sometimes be measured by earnings, commission, bonus, etc. The *key-stroke* criterion, in word processing or supermarket checkouts, allows 'output' to be measured, precisely, continuously and cheaply (Sackett, Zedeck & Fogli, 1988). The key-stroke criterion is an exciting prospect for the personnel researcher, but a frightening intrusion to the workers and their representatives. Output criteria can also be used for sales work, and for scientific work: inventions patented, scientific papers published, etc. The quality of scientific research can be measured by the number of times the work is *cited* by other scientists. Output criteria can be misleading; sales figures often depend on how good the sales area is, production can depend on how well the machinery works. Scientists have been arguing for years whether publication and citation rates are good criteria of scientific output and creativity.

Objective criteria are many and various. Some are more objective than others; *training grades* often involve some subjective judgement in rating performance or written work. *Personnel* criteria include: advancement/promotion, length of service, turnover, punctuality, absence, disciplinary action, accidents, sickness. They are easy to collect but suffer several serious disadvantages: poor reliability, skewed distributions, poor intercorrelation. *Accident rate* has been used as a criterion in the transport industry, since Munsterburg's research on tram (streetcar) drivers. *Financial* criteria— salary/wages, bonus/commission—are also easy to collect, but may not necessarily reflect performance. The *gravitation/survival* criterion is used in the validation of Strong Interest Inventory (Chapter 8). It works on the principle that people gravitate to jobs that suit them and which they are good at, and survive in them. Survival in organizations that don't react to idleness or inefficiency isn't a good criterion. By contrast, survival is a very discriminating criterion for life insurance sales staff; only one in five last the first year.

Critics (Levin, 1988) also argue productivity depends on management and on how the work is organized; Levin cites a General Motors plant that used to have very low output, with very poor quality, until introducing 'Japanese' working practices transformed output and quality. Production workers are often interdependent, each worker's output regulated by the speed of the line, or socially by output norms (tacit agreements not to work harder than each other). This implies production rates may not be good measures of *individual* productivity.

Otis (1938) used *work samples* as criteria in research on sewing machinists, but until recently validation research rarely used them as criterion. Work samples are so expensive to develop that employers prefer to use them for selection. But a work sample used for selection can't be used again as criterion; a high correlation would be trivial. Recently, Project A (Landy & Rastegary, 1989; Campbell et al, 1990) has devised a set of ultimate 'hands-on', work sample criteria, designed to prove conclusively the Armed Services Vocational Aptitude Battery's (ASVAB's) validity in the face of Congressional criticism. Tank crews are observed minutely, in real life, in a real tank, repairing the radio, unjamming the gun and driving the tank from A to B. The research is staggeringly expensive by any but US military standards—with a budget of $40 million.

The work sample criteria can be used to validate less exacting, expensive and dangerous *walk-through* criteria, in which the soldier stands in a mock-up tank, and explains how to unjam the gun, or describes how the vehicle is driven (as opposed to actually doing it). Walk-through criterion performance correlates well (0.68) with work sample criterion performance (Hedge & Teachout, 1992).

Guion (1961) sees the ultimate criterion as "the total worth of a man to the company—in the final analysis", but this can't be measured until the employee's career is complete, which is usually too long to wait—although Anstey's 30-year follow up of the Civil Service Selection Board (CSSB) (Chapter 9) followed staff from selection almost to retirement.

MULTIPLE CRITERIA

Dunnette (1966) cites a hypothetical pair of salesmen, both successful, one diligent and persistent, the other persuasive and charismatic. He argues global criteria are over-simplified and misleading, because people succeed in so many different ways. Psychologists must understand the structure of success to predict it accurately. Therefore validation studies need multiple criteria. The textbook solution to understanding the structure of complex measures, such as criteria of productivity, is *factor analysis* (see Note 1 in Chapter 3). The first factor analysis of multiple criteria was reported in 1941; 12 supervisor ratings reduced to two or three factors, including one very large general factor of 'ability to do present job' (Ewart, Seashore & Tiffin, 1941). Other studies report similar results. Petrie & Powell (1951) used 18 criterion ratings in their study of nurse selection, but found the average intercorrelation between ratings so high that they summed the ratings to give a single overall criterion. Crites (1969) reviews factor analytic studies of ratings of vocational success, and finds they yield between three and 15 factors, of the 'drive and efficiency' and 'sales ability' type. Many studies found large halo effects, which might be an artefact in the ratings or might mean that success is genuinely unitary. More recent research has used BARS, or variations on the BARS theme, to try to reduce halo. Dunnette (1976) isolated four main criterion factors in sales and technical jobs: *initiative and persistence, personal commitment, knowledge utilization*, and *planning, organizing and handling detail*. These four factors had low intercorrelations, indicating absence of halo.

Other researchers have factor-analysed *objective criteria*, with much more mixed results. Richard et al (1965) factor analysed 80 criteria of success in doctors, and extracted up to 30 factors. Both individual criteria and the resulting factors were very specific; for example age, rank, experience, committee membership and journal editorships defined the *academic seniority* factor. Some factors were decidedly odd: *rejection of actual practice, ease of scheduling research interview*. Richard et al's research doesn't throw a lot of light on success in the medical profession.

An earlier British study makes more sense of criteria for bus conductors (the second of a crew of two, who collected the fares). Six criteria yield two factors (Table 11.2). The first factor is clearly *value to employer*; the second factor has loadings on disciplinary action, shortages (in takings) and lateness, and can be identified as a *responsibility* factor (Heron, 1954).

Table 11.2 Intercorrelation and factor analysis of six measures of productivity in bus conductors (Heron, 1954) (Reproduced by permission)

		GE	CS	AB	DA	LA	Factor I	Factor II
(Poor) supervisor rating	(SR)	0.31	0.51	0.38	0.13	0.49	0.70	0.03
(Low) gross earnings	(GE)		0.10	0.41	0.06	0.24	0.44	−0.42
Cash shortages	(CS)			0.27	0.23	0.45	0.61	0.32
Absence	(AB)				0.02	0.37	0.28	0.27
Disciplinary action	(DA)					0.27	0.28	0.27
Lateness	(LA)						0.70	0.14

Similar research (Ronan, 1963) factor-analysed objective criteria for skilled trades apprentices and journeymen. Factor I is clearly a *safe worker* factor, with loadings on *injury index* and *time lost through accidents*. Factor II has loadings on *school rating* and *maths grade*, which makes it the *successful school work* factor. Ronan calls Factor III, with loadings on *promotions* and *supervisory rating*, *supervisory evaluation*; cynics might call it the 'face fits' criterion. Factor IV is an *adjustment* factor, with large loadings on *absence index* and *personality disorder*, and smaller loadings on *shop rating* and *grievance*. Ronan suggests men with a lot of grievances 'can't get along with anybody'—a suggestion that might not appeal to unions. Another study factor-analysed a mixture of objective and subjective criteria (sales figures and supervisor ratings), and got three factors, one contributed almost entirely by sales figures, the others by ratings, suggesting the two types of criteria don't mix well (Rush, 1953).

Crites (1969) suggests success may have a hierarchical structure, like intellectual ability (Figure 11.3). At the highest level is the *general factor— overall vocational success*. At the intermediate level are *group factors: administrative skills* and *drive and initiative*. At the level of *specific factors* are individual ratings such as *company loyalty*, and single objective criteria, such as *scrap*. It's tempting to argue global supervisory ratings measure accurately *overall vocational success*, but the concept as elaborated by Crites is much broader.

Figure 11.3 A hierarchical model of criteria of productivity, adapted from Crites (1969)

Composite or separate criteria?

Objective criteria don't intercorrelate very well, and even subjective criteria sometimes contain separable factors, which gives the selection researcher a choice of strategies: use separate criteria, or combine them in a single composite. American personnel researchers classically favoured separate criteria, each reflecting a different aspect of behaviour at work. Multiple separate criteria have more promise of increasing scientific understanding of success at work, but they cost more and can make validation very confusing. If 20 selection tests are used to predict five criteria, 100 validity coefficients result (several hundred if the researcher corrects for restricted range, unreliability, etc.). Experience suggests the resulting 100 coefficients won't present a very tidy picture. There's more at stake here than neat, publishable results for the researcher; the employer may have to fight a fair employment case on the results (Chapter 12). Combining multiple criteria into a single composite makes the results easier to follow, and easier to defend in court.

As long ago as 1931, Bird proposed an *efficiency index*, based on salary, tenure, salary increase, promotion and supervisor rating. Toops (1944) describes the *Kelly Bid* system for developing weighted multiple criterion; Umeda & Frey (1974) used three raters—Catholic priest, Seventh Day Adventist, Baptist—to assign 100 points or *bids* among 10 criterion elements, to determine the relative importance of each in the composite. Some composite criteria are not very successful; Merrihue & Katzell (1955) devised the *Employee Relations Index* (ERI), a composite criterion for managers, based on eight personnel indices: absence rate, resignation, dispensary visits, dismissal, suggestions submitted, disciplinary suspensions, grievances, etc. The ERI proved a poor criterion, because most of its components were largely outside the manager's control. No doubt a very bad manager could drive more workers to the dispensary, but most visits reflect a real need. A simpler, and more logical, system is the *Laurent Success Index*, based on salary in relation to age (Laurent, 1970). Laurent claims his Success Index is an absolute criterion "independent of any particular group of individuals or company or currency"—so long as the employer's appraisal system is efficient, and closely linked to employees' salary. Project A uses composite criteria—five in all: *technical proficiency, general soldiering proficiency, effort and leadership, personal discipline, physical fitness and military bearing* (Campbell et al, 1990). The composite criteria derive from archive data, BARS, job-knowledge tests, work samples and ratings.

Opponents of composite criteria say they're bound to be unsatisfactory because one can't equate *units produced* with *days off*, or *employee satisfaction* with *scrap rate*. Brogden & Taylor (1950) disagree, and say all criteria can be measured on a common scale—the dollar. A good worker is one who is *worth more* to the employer; all criteria reduce to dollar or pound value of output. The composite 'accountant's criterion' is used widely in recent American research, especially since *Rational Estimate* techniques have made it easier to calculate. Schmidt & Hunter use a single criterion in all their meta-analyses (Chapter 7); if the original research used multiple criteria, Schmidt & Hunter combine them into a single composite.

Structural models of predictor–criterion relationships

Earlier researches using multiple predictors and multiple criteria presented their results in large, generally very confusing, correlation tables. Nathan & Alexander (1988) report a *validity generalization analysis* for five criteria of clerical proficiency: supervisor rating, supervisor ranking, work samples, production quantity and production quality. Mental ability tests correlated best with supervisor ranking (0.66), work sample (0.60), then with supervisor rating (0.44) and production quantity (0.35), but not at all with quality.

Several recent analyses of large sets of military adopt a more illuminating approach, using computer packages to construct models of predictor—criterion relationships. Vance (Vance et al, 1988; 1989) analysed four predictors and three criteria for US Air Force jet engine mechanics. The criteria were supervisor, peer and self ratings and a *walk through*, scored for time and correctness. The predictors were ASVAB, experience, level of support from supervisor and training grades. The complex relations between these seven variables were analysed for each of three tasks: inspecting engines, installing components in the engine and filling in the forms afterwards. For installing components, ASVAB scores predicted training grades well, and proficiency ratings moderately well. The ASVAB only related to walk-through time by way of training grades. Experience predicted both proficiency ratings and walk-through time very well. Supervisor support failed to relate to any other variable. Similarly the walk-through performance criterion wasn't related to any predictor. The walk-through and rating criteria were unrelated.

A similar analysis for nine Military Occupational Specialities (Borman et al, 1991) included personality tests (Assessment of Background and Life Experience, ABLE) and personnel records as well as ASVAB, and job knowledge and work sample tests, and found a complex network of paths (Figure 11.4). In ABLE, Achievement predicts awards for good work and supervisor rating, but not job knowledge nor work sample. Similarly, ABLE Dependability predicts (absence of) discipline problems and good supervisor rating, but neither job knowledge nor work sample. Performance is multidimensional; different aspects of performance are predicted by different measures.

Work quality

Critics often complain the criteria used in most selection research favour quantity, not *quality*. Three recent researches that did include quality criteria

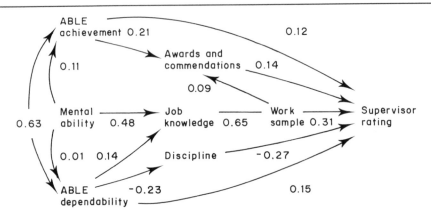

Figure 11.4 Paths between Assessment of Background and Life Experience (ABLE), mental ability awards and commendations, discipline records, job knowledge test, work sample test and supervisor rating, for nine Military Occupational Specialities. (Reprinted by permission from Borman et al, 1991, *J. Appl. Psychol.*, **64**, 410–21. Copyright 1991 by the American Psychological Association)

got worryingly poor results. Hoffman, Nathan & Holden (1991) assessed quality in gas appliance repair work, using an inspector's error count, done 'blind'; quality didn't correlate at all with mental ability or job knowledge test scores, which did, however, predict the more usual output and supervisor rating criteria. Dubois, Sackett & Zedeck (in press) obtain similar results for supermarket checkout operators; mental ability tests weren't related to accuracy, but did predict speed. Nathan's & Alexander's (1988) meta-analysis of clerical work found tests didn't correlate at all with quality.

CRITERION PROBLEMS

Dynamic criteria

Ghiselli & Haire (1960) used a battery of tests to predict dollar volume of fares collected by 56 taxi drivers over 18 weeks. Tests that predicted the criterion in the first 3 weeks didn't necessarily predict it in the last 3 weeks. Ghiselli called his paper "The validation of selection tests in the light of the dynamic nature of criteria". A *dynamic criterion* is one that changes over time; Ghiselli assumes that taxi driving after 18 weeks is somehow different from taxi-driving after 3 weeks, so a test that predicts one will not necessarily predict the other. Would-be selectors of taxi drivers must decide whether they want to predict productivity in the short term, or in the long term, because the same set of tests won't predict both. (A more parsimonious interpretation of Ghiselli's results says his sample was far too small.) Bass (1962) presented similar data for 99 wholesale food salesmen, showing correlations between peer assessments and criterion ratings declined from 0.30–0.40 at 6 months to 0.00–0.20 at 4 years. Correlations between ability tests and successive criterion ratings fluctuated around a very low mean.

On this modest empirical foundation, the theory of dynamic criteria rested unchallenged for some 25 years, until Barrett, Caldwell & Alexander (1985) argued there's no evidence criteria are 'dynamic'. Ghiselli & Haire found the first week's taxi fares correlated very poorly (0.19) with the 18th week's fares. Most researchers would call this an unreliable criterion, rather than a 'dynamic' one, and would increase their sample size, or average the criterion over enough weeks to achieve acceptable reliability. Barrett et al review 55 studies of criterion re-test reliability; only 24 of 276 correlations fail to achieve significance. Two more recent studies, of student ratings of faculty (university teachers) over 13 semesters (terms) (Hanges, Schneider & Niles, 1990), and of weekly output data of sewing machine operators (Deadrick & Madigan, 1990), report that the nearer in time two measures are, the greater the correlation between them—but even distant correlations are positive and significant. In their review of the literature, Hulin, Henry & Noon (1990) conclude initial and final performance are often poorly related, implying criteria are often unreliable—but many of the data they include don't derive from 'real' work. Barrett, Alexander & Doverspike (1992) conclude there's no evidence performance genuinely changes over time, which implies criteria aren't dynamic.

Murphy (1989) argues that performance (i.e. the criterion) has two stages: *transition* and *maintenance*. In the transition phase, the worker is still learning the job, whereas by the maintenance phase the job is very well learned and largely automatic. Mental ability tests predict performance during the transition phase, i.e. in the short term, but don't predict performance in the maintenance phase, i.e. in the long term. Critics argue that performance in 'real' jobs, as opposed to simple laboratory tasks, is always sufficiently complex to ensure that automatization doesn't happen.

CRITERIA, 'FAIRNESS', AND THE LAW

Criterion ratings face two problems. They may be accused of bias, or they may simply be ruled unsatisfactory. Bias in ratings means racial bias: bias against non-whites; bias in favour of non-whites ('bending over backwards'); even failure to discriminate *amongst* non-whites, so all non-whites get the same rating. Research (see above) finds a consistent, but small, *own-race bias* in supervisor ratings.

In the US, fair employment agencies may also find fault with ratings that are unreliable, subjective or too general. In the important *Albemarle* case (Chapter 12) criterion ratings were ruled unsatisfactory because they were vague and their basis unclear. In *Rowe* vs *General Motors*, supervisor ratings were again ruled unsatisfactory, because foremen had no written instructions about the requirements for promotion, and because standards were vague and subjective. In the case of *Wade* vs *Mississippi Cooperative Extension Service* the court ruled that supervisor ratings of attitude, personality, temperament and habits had to be job-related:

> a substantial portion of the evaluation rating relates to such general characteristics as leadership, public acceptance, attitudes toward people, appearance and grooming, personal contact, outlook on life, ethical habits, resourcefulness, capacity for growth, mental alertness and loyalty to organisation. As may be readily observed, these are traits which are susceptible to partiality and to the personal taste, whim or fancy of the evaluator.

Criterion ratings should not include generalized assessments of the worker's worth as a citizen or member of the human race; they should limit themselves to whether he/she does his/her work properly.

Nor are objective criteria free from challenge. An employer cannot simply say 'high turnover' and leave it at that; it may be necessary to prove that high turnover creates problems, costs money, or results from employees' restlessness and not from employer's behaviour. Fair employment legislation imposes a duty on the employer to make efforts to 'accommodate' employees: provide a crèche, allow time off for religious festivals, etc. An employer who hadn't 'accommodated' might not be able to defend (no) absence or (good) time-keeping as criteria.

CONCLUSIONS

Face validity isn't really validity at all, although plausibility is always worth having. Factorial validation has its uses but is only a small part of validation. Construct validation certainly has its place—in developing theories of individual differences, not in proving selection tests work. Synthetic validation is a promising idea, whose promise has yet to be fulfilled. Content validation has one main thing in its favour—it's legally acceptable in the USA.

This leaves *criterion* validation as the best test of selection. Personnel managers select today, and find out later if they've made the right choice. In theory, true *predictive* validation is best, but *concurrent* validation apparently gives the same results in practice and is easier to do. Concurrent validation, however, may not be so suitable where experience can change scores, which has been demonstrated for personality.

Validating selection procedures doesn't look as complicated in the 1990s, as it did in the 1960s. Over-interpretation of small samples caused psychologists then to suppose *curvilinearity, non-homoscedasticity* or *suppressor variables* were frequent occurrences; they now turn out to be very infrequent in practice. Chapter 7 shows that what validation research really needs is *numbers*. If the researcher's sample isn't big enough, *validity generalization* allows samples to be pooled, to achieve large enough numbers. When criterion validation uses large numbers, or pools studies, clear results emerge.

The criterion problem can be very simple, when work generates something that can be counted: widgets manufactured per day, or sales per week. The criterion problem can be *made* very simple, if the organization has an appraisal system whose ratings can be used. The supervisor rating criterion is often seized on with joy, because it's universal (in the US), because it's unitary, and because it's hard to argue with. On the other hand, the criterion problem can soon get very complex, if one wants to dig a bit deeper into what constitutes effective performance. Questions about the real nature of work, or the true purpose of organizations soon arise.

12 Minorities, "Fairness" and the Law

Getting the numbers right

> The House of Commons of the British Parliament numbers 650 Members of Parliament. Following the 1992 election, there are 60 female MPs, and four black MPs. The great majority of MPs are white and male.

Once upon time employers could 'hire at will, and fire at will'. They could employ only fair-haired men, or red-haired women, or Baptists, or syco- phants, or Freemasons, or football players. They could sack men who wore brown suits, or women who wore trousers. They might be forced out of business by more efficient competitors, who chose their staff more carefully, and treated them better, but they were in no danger from the law. Employers could also indulge any racial stereotypes they happened to have: don't employ Fantasians because they're all thick; don't employ Ruritanians because they're bone idle; Northerners are thieves; Southerners are sly; Easterners are smartasses, etc. Those bad old days are long past.

Fair employment legislation has shaped selection practices in the USA for a whole generation; in 1964, Title VII of the Civil Rights Act (CRA) prohibited discrimination in employment on grounds of race, colour, religion or national origin (Table 12.1). The CRA also prohibited discrimination on grounds of gender; Ash & Kroeker (1975) say the US Government didn't originally intend to include women a *protected minority*, and that the scope of CRA was broadened by hostile Senators who thought it would reduce the bill to an absurdity, and lead to its defeat. The CRA was joined in 1967 by the Age Discrimination in Employment Act which prohibited discrimination on grounds of age, between ages 40 and 70, and the Vocational Rehabilitation Act in 1973 which prohibited discrimination on grounds of handicap.

US government agencies were created to enforce the new laws: the Equal Employment Opportunities Commission (EEOC), the Office of Personnel Management (formerly the US Civil Service Commission) and the Office of Federal Contract Compliance Program. Many individual States have their own laws and enforcement agencies (which this chapter won't attempt to go into). The various agencies issued differing sets of guidelines, until eventually, in 1978, EEOC issued the *Uniform Guidelines on Employment Selection Procedures*.

Table 12.1 Key events in the development of "fair employment" legislation in the USA and UK

Year	USA	UK
1964	Civil Rights Act	
1967	Age Discrimination Act	
1970	First Guidelines published	
1971	*Griggs* vs *Duke Power Co.*	
1973	Vocational Rehabilitation Act	
1975	*Albermarle Paper Co* vs *Moody*	Sex Discrimination Act
1976		Race Relations Act
1978	*Uniform Guidelines* published	
1981	Professional & Administrative Career Examination	
1984		Commission for Racial Equality Code published
1985		Equal Opportunities Commission Code published
1988	*Watson* vs *Ft Worth Bank*	
1990	Americans with Disabilities Act	London Underground case
1991	Civil Rights Act	

In Britain the Race Relations Act (1976) set up the Commission for Racial Equality, which issued its *Code of Practice for the Elimination of Racial Discrimination and the Promotion of Equality of Opportunity in Employment* in 1984. The Sex Discrimination Act (1975) set up the Equal Opportunities Commission, which issued its *Code of Practice* in 1985. Both British codes of conduct are short documents, compared with the *Uniform Guidelines*, and don't give any very detailed instructions about selection. Note that race and sex discrimination are dealt with by separate laws and separate agencies in the UK. Discrimination on grounds of age isn't illegal in the UK. Nor is it illegal to discriminate against the handicapped, but there has been a 3% quota system since 1944.

Figure 12.1 shows how fair employment laws work in the USA; British agencies have followed the same general model, and adopted many of the key concepts. If selection (or promotion) excludes too many non-whites or women, it is said to create *adverse impact*. Adverse impact (AI) shifts the burden of proof (of no discrimination) onto the employer. The employer can remove AI by *quota hiring* to 'get the numbers right'. Or else the employer can argue the selection tests are *job related*. The employer who succeeds in proving tests *job related* faces one last hurdle—proving there's no *alternative test* that's equally valid but doesn't create AI.

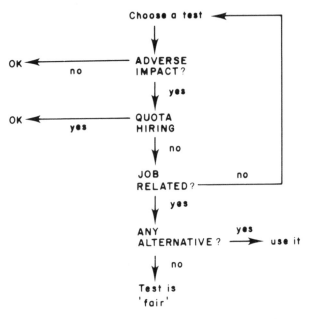

Figure 12.1   Stages in deciding if a test is "fair"

ADVERSE IMPACT

In Britain 4% of the population are non-white; half are female; so 2% are both female and non-white. If Members of Parliament were selected without regard to sex or race, Table 12.2 shows there would be approximately 325 women MPs, 26 non-white MPs, and 13 non-white women MPs.

Are there fewer women or non-whites in the House of Commons than one would expect? Psychologists immediately think of calculating the χ^2 statistic, which yields highly significant values for all three comparisons, confirming there aren't 'enough' female, non-white, or non-white female MPs. The problem with the χ^2 statistic is that it's almost impossible *not* to find a significant discrepancy when analysing large numbers. No employer is likely to have a perfect balance of race and sex throughout a large workforce. In the USA, *Uniform Guidelines* introduced the *four-fifths* rule. If the selection ratio (selected/applied) for a protected minority is less than four-fifths of the highest ratio for any group, a "presumption of discrimination" is established.

Table 12.2 Composition of the House of Commons after the 1992 election, and "expected" composition, assuming MPs are selected regardless of sex and race

	Actual	"Expected"	"Expected" (four-fifths)
Male, white	587	312	
Male, non-white	3	13	10
All males	590	325	
Female, white	59	312	250
Female, non-white	1	13	10
All females	60	325	260

The proportion of women in the Commons is obviously far less than four-fifths the number of men; the number of non-whites is significantly fewer than four-fifths of 4% of 650; and the number of non-white women significantly fewer than four-fifths of 4% of half of 650. 'Recruitment and selection' for the Commons creates *adverse impact* on both women and on non-whites.

Four-fifths is only a guideline, which doesn't apply to small numbers, where it mightn't achieve statistical significance, nor to very large numbers, such as national statistics on arrest records for Hispanic Americans.

Note that AI isn't quite what the layperson thinks of as 'discrimination'. It doesn't mean turning away minorities in order to keep the job open for white males, or otherwise deliberately treating minorities differently. Deliberate discrimination, in the USA, is called *disparate treatment*, and can be proved by the *McDonnell Douglas test*, which means essentially telling a suitably qualified minority person "the job's gone" then offering it to a majority person. Sharf (1988) argues the US Congress *never meant to create the AI principle*; it was created by the EEOC and the 'civil rights bar'. Administrators and lawyers saw their role as "promoting a workforce representative of the community", wrote this view into the 1970 EEOC Guidelines and into 'guidance' to employers, and finally got it accepted with the 1971 *Griggs* case.

Summarizing American experience up to 1979, Miner & Miner (1979) conclude that:

(a) Both non-whites *and* women are under-represented as: managers and officials, professionals, technicians and skilled craftsmen
(b) Non-whites *but not* women are under-represented as: sales workers, and office and clerical workers
(c) Women and non-whites are *over*-represented as unskilled workers and service workers.

This leaves only semi-skilled workers not in need of EEOC's services.

Which population?

Is the shortage of non-white faces in the Commons justified by saying there aren't any suitable candidates, or that most constituencies have no non-white voters? In America two Supreme Court cases—*Teamsters* vs *United States* and *Hazelwood School District* vs *United States*—ruled general population comparisons aren't always relevant; the populations should be those with 'necessary qualifications'. Comparing a district's teachers with its pupils, and finding non-whites *weren't* under-represented, was irrelevant, whereas finding non-whites under-represented as truck drivers was "probative", because almost anyone can learn to drive a truck. The easier the job, the greater the presumption of discrimination if a protected group is under-represented. So perhaps calculations of AI in the House of Commons ought to be based on the non-white middle classes, or non-whites who earn the same salary as MPs. In 1989, the *Wards Cove Packing Co. Inc.* vs *Antonio* case made it clear that the relevant population for testing AI was qualified individuals. Barrett (1990) hopes the decision will end the *aggregation fallacy*, in which AI calculations made from an entire workforce are applied to sections of it.

Sharf (1982)—a vocal critic of the EEOC—claims EEOC use a 'ratchet' tactic when calculating AI; they compare the proportion of non-whites employed by the targeted employer with the *highest* proportion employed by *any* employer, including ones who give preferential treatment to eliminate AI. "One employer's program of preferential treatment becomes another employer's potential liability"; once the expected proportion has gone up, it can't go back down.

If there's no AI, the case is dropped [or ought to be—Kleiman & Durham (1981) report some courts still go on to investigate promotion decisions even when they *don't* create AI]. But if AI is demonstrated, the burden of proof shifts to the employer to prove *good business reasons*, which essentially means proving the selection procedure is *valid*. (Good business reasons don't include saying customers won't like female/non-white staff, so the absence of non-white and female MPs couldn't be justified by claiming people wouldn't vote for them.) Employers whose 'numbers aren't right' are presumed guilty of discrimination until they succeed in proving their innocence.

Subjective tests and adverse impact

Until 1988 interviews and other 'subjective' tests were dealt with under the *disparate treatment* (deliberate discrimination) provisions of US employment law, not under adverse impact provisions. To prove discrimination in selection by interview, lawyers had to find evidence of bias in the questions asked, not evidence of imbalance in proportion of whites and non-whites accepted. Deliberate discrimination is much harder to prove than adverse impact—

which probably helps explain the continuing popularity of the interview in the USA. However, in *Watson* vs *Ft Worth Bank & Trust* the Supreme Court noted that insisting on the *disparate treatment* route for subjective assessments could open a big legal loophole because employers only needed include a subjective element in their assessment to avoid adverse impact claims (Barrett, 1990). The Court accordingly decided adverse impact claims could apply to subjective methods. (If Watson could claim AI, the burden of proof shifted, and the Bank had to prove its promotion assessments were valid; otherwise Watson had to prove they were invalid.)

QUOTA HIRING

Employers who can't prove good business reasons, or don't want to go to the trouble and expense of trying, must 'get their numbers right', by changing their selection criteria. They can adopt *affirmative action* (AA) programmes, which set targets for the proportion of non-whites or women in each grade of every job. The Office of Federal Contract Compliance requires any company that supplies the US Government to have an AA programme. Other companies adopt an AA programme to settle cases brought by EEOC, or to forestall them. Sharf (1982) describes quota hiring as the EEOC's "hidden agenda". Miner & Miner (1979) agree that many observers see hiring "on a random or quota basis" as "EEOC's ultimate goal". Quotas can be 'hard' or 'soft'. A hard quota requires every other new employee to be non-white; a soft quota tells the personnel manager in effect 'try to find more minorities'. London's Borough of Lambeth, noted for its very progressive policies, announced in 1986 a soft quota for disabled black women in its road-mending teams.

An AA programme doesn't always end the employer's problems. Employing non-whites implies not employing whites; employing women implies not employing men. White males have been known to resent being passed over in favour of apparently less well qualified or experienced members of protected groups. AT&T were sued by a male employee who saw a less suitable female promoted instead of him; even though AT&T were following AA policies agreed by a 'consent decree', they had to pay the man damages, though they didn't have to promote him. The Kaiser Corporation found employers couldn't introduce quotas for minorities *until* they had been sued for discrimination; voluntary introduction of a quota for non-whites discriminated against white employees. (This decision was later reversed by the Supreme Court.) Gottfredson (1988) argues only a minority of employers can run successful AA programmes, by snapping up all the non-white talent first; this makes AA more difficult, if not impossible, for the rest.

Schmidt, Mack & Hunter (1984) describe the *top-down quota* system; the employer decides what proportion of the workforce ought to be non-white (e.g. 10%), what proportion of the present intake shall be non-white (e.g. 15 out of 150), then selects the 15 non-whites with the highest selection test scores (although their scores may be lower than those of white applicants who aren't made an offer). Top-down quotas maximize productivity, while allowing for fair employment. Top-down quotas may have unforeseen long-term effects, however. The more places are 'reserved' for non-whites, the more highly selected will be the white employees, so the bigger will be the difference between them and the non-white quota.

Separate norms are another variation on the quota hiring principle. The VG-GATB (described in Chapter 7) used separate norms, euphemistically called 'within-group scoring'. A raw score on GATB of 308 placed a white American at the 50th percentile, but a black American at the 84th percentile. Prospective employers were only given the percentiles, *not* the raw scores. 'Within-group scoring' clearly gave black, and Hispanic, applicants a very large helping hand in job-seeking. In 1986 the Assistant Attorney General for Civil Rights challenged VG-GATB as discriminatory, and it was shelved (Hartigan & Wigdor, 1989). The CRA of 1991 prohibited separate norms. Separate norms are not viewed with favour in Britain either.

Critics (Gottfredson, 1988) say American politicians have ambivalent attitudes to quota hiring; it's what they really want, but they won't publicly demand it, and sometimes won't even publicly support it. While explicit quotas and separate norms are currently viewed as unacceptable, "surreptitious quota programmes" and "underground preferential treatment" are widespread. Hartigan & Wigdor imply the US Government finds it convenient to blame discrimination on psychological tests, and use testing's alleged deficiencies as a pretext for reverse discrimination. Tests don't create AI; they only reflect it.

JOB RELATED ASSESSMENT

The Tower Amendment to CRA specifically

> allows employers to give and to act upon the results of any professionally developed ability test provided that such test, its administration or action upon the results is not designed, intended or used to discriminate because of race, color, religion, sex or national origin.

For a while employers thought this allowed them to continue using psychological tests without hindrance. However, American agencies were very suspicious of any test that created AI. David Copus, former Director of National programs at EEOC, said:

> when an employer or union attempts to explain the absence of women or minorities from certain jobs by claiming that few if any women or minorities

possess the skills, abilities, or other qualifications which are required for the job, ... Title VII assumes that Anglo males, females, and minorities are equally qualified for all jobs.

Two events made the 1970s a very bad decade for selection in general, and psychological tests in particular: the 1971 Supreme Court ruling *Griggs* vs *Duke Power Co.*, and the EEOC's 1970 *Guidelines on Employee Selection Procedures*.

Griggs vs *Duke Power Company*

Before CRA, the Duke Power Co., in North Carolina, did not employ non-whites except as labourers. The very day CRA came into effect, the company changed its rules: non-labouring jobs needed a high school diploma or satisfactory scores on the Wonderlic Personnel and Bennett Mechanical Comprehension Tests. The cut-off point was set at national high school graduate average, which 58% white employees passed, but only 6% non-whites. In 1967, 13 black employees sued the company, and the case began its slow, expensive, progress through the American legal system, eventually reaching the Supreme Court in 1971.

The Supreme Court ruled that the company's new test discriminated—not necessarily intentionally. The Court's ruling attributed non-whites' low scores on Wonderlic and Bennett tests to inferior education in segregated schools. The Court said "The touchstone is business necessity. If an employment practice which operates to exclude negroes cannot be shown to be related to job performance, the practice is prohibited." High school education and high test scores *weren't* necessary, because existing white employees with neither continued to perform quite satisfactorily. The Court concluded by saying "any tests used must measure the person for the job and not the person in the abstract". The Court considered EEOC's 1970 *Guidelines* "entitled to great deference"—giving the legal seal of approval to a set of very demanding standards.

It's difficult to overemphasize the importance of the *Griggs* case.

(a) It established the principle of *indirect discrimination*. An employer could be proved guilty of discriminating, by setting standards that made no reference to race or sex, and that were often well-established, 'common sense' practice. *Griggs* objected to high school diplomas and ability tests. Another case, *Green* vs *Missouri Pacific Railroad*, ruled exclusion of applicants with criminal records discriminatory, because more non-whites had criminal records. Height, weight and strength tests for the police and fire brigade were also excluded. In Britain, some employers sift out applicants who have been unemployed for more than for example, 6 months, on the argument that such people will have lost the habit of working. The Commission for Racial Equality argues this creates AI, because unemployment is higher in ethnic minorities. Indirect discrimination can occur in quite unforeseen ways. Arvey et al (1975) compared employers who took a long time to fill vacancies (average of 76 days from closing date to interview) with ones who worked fast (average of 14 days), and found the long wait halved the number of non-white applicants who appeared for interview. The long wait creates AI, and isn't job-related, so it's almost certainly illegal discrimination.

(b)   *Griggs* objected to assessing people 'in the abstract', and insisted all assessment be job-related. This implicitly extended the scope of the act; employers can't demand employees be literate, or honest, or veterans (ex-servicemen), or good-looking, just because that's the sort of person they want working for them.

(c)   Tests of general mental ability clearly assess people 'in the abstract', so many employers stopped using them, the Tower Amendment notwithstanding.

1970 *Guidelines*

The EEOC's 1970 *Guidelines* set very high standards for validation studies—impossibly high according to critics. The result was most employers would find it very difficult to prove their selection procedures were 'job-related'.

The American Psychological Association's (APA) *Standards for Educational and Psychological Tests* distinguished three ways of proving selection procedures worked: content, criterion and construct validation. When the EEOC drew up the 1970 *Guidelines*, the APA persuaded them to recognize its *Standards*. It seemed a good idea at the time, but went badly wrong. The APA's *ideal standards* for validation became the EEOC's *minimum acceptable*. The EEOC and the courts misunderstood the idea of the three forms of validation, and regarded them as mutually exclusive, whereas most validation procedures contain elements of all three. And the 1970 *Guidelines* didn't accept content or construct validation, except "where criterion related studies are not feasible".

The 1970 *Guidelines* and *Griggs* both insisted a test must be *job-related*, if it has created AI. 'Job-related' means *valid*—something every occupational psychologist wants, and knows how to measure.

Albemarle Paper Co. vs *Moody*

Four years after *Griggs*, another case, *Albemarle Paper Co.* vs *Moody*, examined a "hastily assembled validation study that did not meet professional standards" (Cronbach, 1980), and didn't like it. The company used Wonderlic Personnel Test and a modern version of Army Beta, and validated them concurrently against supervisor ratings. The court made a number of criticisms of the study's methodology:

(a) The supervisor ratings were unsatisfactory: "there is no way of knowing precisely what criterion of job performance the supervisors were considering, whether each of the supervisors was considering the same criterion, or whether, indeed, any of the supervisors actually applied a focused and stable body of criteria of any kind".

(b) Only senior staff were rated, whereas the tests were being used to select for junior posts. "The fact that the best of those employees working near the top of a line of progression score well on a test does not necessarily mean that test, or some particular cut-off on the test, is a permissible measure of the minimal qualifications of new workers, entering lower level jobs."

(c) Only white staff were rated, whereas applicants included non-whites.

(d) Finally, the results were an "odd patchwork"; sometimes Form A of the Wonderlic test predicted, where the supposedly equivalent Form B did not. Local validation studies with smallish samples sizes usually get 'patchy' results. Occupational psychologists accept this; *Albemarle* showed outsiders expected tests to do better.

Albemarle created a "headwind" against aptitude testing in selection (Holt, 1977). Post *Albemarle*, "Many people [thought testing] just a gimmick to preserve discrimination. Many more people—maybe even most judges—suspect that it is some kind of mumbo-jumbo on a par with reading tea leaves and examining the entrails of birds".

An influential paper in the *Harvard Law Review* in 1969 quoted extensively from Ghiselli's (1966b) *Validity of Occupational Aptitude Tests*, and concluded that "the likelihood that scores on any particular aptitude test will correlate significantly with performance on any particular job is very slim indeed". Cooper & Sobol (1969) said the Wonderlic Personnel Test sometimes didn't predict performance at all, and that it sometimes even correlated negatively with performance. No one in 1969 had heard of *validity generalization* (Chapter 7), so no one knew any better. Given that American lawyers are more likely to read *Harvard Law Review* than *Journal of Applied Psychology*, many probably still know no better.

The EEOC published new, revised *Uniform Guidelines* in 1978. The new *Uniform Guidelines* made a number of important changes.

(a) They allow content, construct *or* criterion validity.

(b) They require the employer (not the employee) to search for alternative tests.

(c) They allow employers to use validity data collected elsewhere.

(d) They introduce the 'bottom line' concept of AI. Adverse impact is calculated from the ratio appointed/applied, not from particular parts of the selection. So could an employer use the Wonderlic test, which creates a very large AI, so long as enough non-whites got through the selection process as a whole? No—the agencies reserve the right to question particular tests that create AI.

Miner & Miner (1979) say EEOC commonly use an individual complaint of discrimination as an "opportunity to look into the whole range of an employer's personnel practices for evidence of barriers to equal opportunity". It's even been claimed "EEOC staff includes many bright young people who are out to change the world and [who] have little knowledge of or interest in how the business world operates" (Miner & Miner, 1979). But then the 1960s were a decade of great idealism, and full employment.

The US CRA of 1991 says that if a test creates AI, it must have "substantial and demonstrable relationship to effective job performance". The practical implications of this wording have yet to become apparent; it could represent a full return to the immediate post-*Griggs* position. "Substantial" relationship may mean only high validity coefficients are acceptable. "Performance" could exclude other criteria, such as absence, theft, turnover. "Effective performance" could imply a return to the misleading idea that employees are *either* satisfactory *or* unsatisfactory, not graded continuously from one extreme to the other. The 1991 Act apparently places the onus of proving validity back on the employer.

Criterion validation

The 1970 Guidelines expressed a preference for criterion validation. Miner & Miner (1979) describe an ideal criterion validation study. First test a large number of candidates, but don't use the test scores in deciding who to employ. Then wait for as long as necessary, and collect criterion data. Make sure you have a wide range of scores on the test. If you are using a battery of tests, it's advisable to cross-validate the results. Don't use the test scores to make your selection decisions before you have finished the validation study, or you will restrict range. Don't test existing employees and compare test data with criterion data collected at the same time, because existing employees may not be representative of applicants. It sounds quite easy—but there are five reasons why it's difficult, time-consuming and expensive, in practice.

1. Criterion   "[The criterion] Must represent major or critical work behaviour as revealed by careful job analysis" (1970 *Guidelines*). Rating criteria may be accused of bias, especially if non-whites or women get lower ratings. Behaviourally Anchored Rating Scale (BARS) formats (see Chapter 5) are more acceptable than vague graphic scales or highly generalized personality traits. Objective criteria must be justifiable; the employer may have to prove high turnover costs money and isn't the organization's fault. Training criteria are least likely to prove acceptable, and may themselves be ruled to need validation against job performance.

2. *Sample size* The correlation between predictor and criterion must be significant at the 5% level—yet the typical local validation study rarely has enough subjects to be sure of achieving this (Chapter 7). The EEOC help ensure the sample size is too small by insisting that differential validities for minorities be calculated, and by insisting every job be treated separately.

3. *Concurrent/predictive validity* The *Uniform Guidelines* favour predictive validity, which takes longer and costs more. An employer facing EEOC investigation may not have time to conduct a predictive validation study. (The wise employer doesn't wait to hear from the agencies before thinking about validation.)

4. *Representative sampling and differential validity* These are the "Catch 22" of the *Guidelines*. A 'representative' sample contains the right proportion of non-whites and women. The hypothesis of *differential validity* postulates that tests can be valid for whites or males, but not for non-whites or females. An employer with an all-white and/or all-male workforce can't prove there's no differential validity, without employing women and/or non-whites. Miner & Miner say the "Catch" was included on purpose: "the concept was devised by the governmental enforcement agencies in order to pressure companies into hiring more minority group members and women". Research during the 1970s proved fairly conclusively that differential validity does not exist; tests that are valid for white males are equally valid for women and non-whites.

5. *Adverse impact* Mental ability tests create so much AI on some minorities that the agencies, the courts and the minorities are unlikely ever to accept them, no matter what proof of their predictive validity is produced. Ledvinka (1982) agrees: "Many employers suspect that, even if they were to select their employees with unassailably valid tests, the government would find a way to harass them if their hiring practices had an AI". Ability tests create most AI on blacks, some AI on Hispanics and native Americans, but none on women. Americans of Chinese or Japanese ancestry score better on ability tests than white Americans (Vernon, 1982). Adverse impact of mental ability tests has been documented in Israel, on Israelis of non-European origin (Zeidner, 1988). Otherwise, little is known about AI created by mental ability tests in Britain, Europe and the rest of the world.

Kleiman & Faley (1985) review 12 court cases on criterion validity, since publication of the *Uniform Guidelines* in 1978. Their review isn't very encouraging for any employers thinking of relying on proving that their selection procedures actually predict productivity.

1. Courts often appear to suppose some tests had been completely discredited, and can't ever be valid—notably the Wonderlic Personnel Test; Dunnette's (1972) meta-analysis concluded the Wonderlic test has good average predictive validity.
2. Courts often examine item content or format, even though this is irrelevant when assessing predictive validity.
3. Courts often object to coefficients being corrected for restricted range as 'misleading'.
4. Courts' decisions are inconsistent and unpredictable.
5. Courts often ignore or avoid technical issues, and take a 'common sense' approach—to issues like sample size where 'common sense' is generally wrong.
6. Only five of the 12 employers won their cases.

Critics may say psychologists have just been hoist with their own petard. They always claimed their tests were the best way to select staff. They were always ready to dismiss other people's methods as completely invalid. They always insisted validating tests was a highly technical business best left to the experts. But when fair employment agencies took them at their word, the psychologists couldn't deliver an acceptable validity study. Their 50-year-old bluff had been called.

In fact fair employment legislation has done occupational psychologists a service, forcing them to prove more thoroughly that tests are valid and worth using, by *validity generalization analysis* (Chapter 6), *utility analysis* (Chapter 1 and 13), and *differential validity* research (see later). But it takes a long time to get new ideas accepted, especially when the old ones "have been virtually set in concrete in the ... Uniform Guidelines" (Schmidt, Hunter & Pearlman, 1981).

Content validation

In 1964, when the CRA was passed, *content* validity was virtually unheard of, and not very highly regarded. Guion (1965b) said:

> Content validity is of extremely limited utility as a concept for employment tests .... [it] comes uncomfortably close to the idea of face validity unless judges are especially precise in their judgements ... evidence has accumulated to show that face validity, like content validity, is not an adequate substitute for empirical determination of predictive power.

Content validation improves on *face* validation to the extent of using experts to analyse the job, analyse the test, and conclude the latter relevant to the former. But content validation is clearly inferior to criterion validation; proving a measure *does* predict performance is a lot better than finding experts who say it *ought to*.

Guion (1977) later said content validation was added to the 1970 *Guidelines* as an afterthought, for occasions when criterion validation wasn't feasible. A whole generation of psychologists and lawyers have earned a comfortable living from that afterthought. Content validation became the favourite validation strategy after the *Guidelines* and the *Griggs* case. Criterion validation was impossibly difficult (see earlier), and the courts couldn't understand construct validation (see later). (Quite a few psychologists admit to finding it a rather nebulous idea.) Content validation has four big advantages:

1. No criterion is required, so it can't be unsatisfactory. The test is its own justification.
2. There's no time interval between testing and validation. The test is 'validated' before it's used.
3. Differential validity can't exist, because there's no criterion.
4. Content valid tests are easy to defend in court. Every item of the test is clearly relevant to the job. The psychologist doesn't get tied in knots trying to explain the connection between *knowing the opposite of 'big'*, and being able to sell potato crisps (one of 130 items of the AH4 test of general mental ability, which has some predictive validity for retail food salesmen).

Content validation requires careful job analysis, to prove the test "is a representative sample of the content of the job" (*Uniform Guidelines*). Test content must reflect *every* aspect of the job, in the *correct proportions*; if 10% of the job consists of writing reports, report writing mustn't account for 50% of the test. It's easy to prove job-relatedness for simple 'concrete' jobs, such as typing tests for typists. Content validation is much more difficult when the job is complex, yet the demands of the *Guidelines* caused many American employers to try content validation, where the problem really needed criterion or construct validation. The public sector in the US, especially police and fire brigades, have repeatedly developed content valid selection procedures and seen them ruled unfair. For example, the St Louis Fire Brigade devised a set of promotion tests, misleadingly described as an assessment centre. In one test, firefighters viewed slides of fires, and *wrote* the commands they would give, which was ruled to overemphasize verbal ability. Nearly half the fire captain's job is supervision, which the tests didn't cover at all. (The Brigade planned to assess supervisory ability during a subsequent probationary period.) After a series of court hearings and appeals, lasting until 1981, the tests were ruled unfair (Bersoff, 1981).

Construct validation

"A demonstration that (a) a selection procedure measures a construct (something believed to be an underlying human trait or characteristic, such as honesty) and (b) the construct is important for successful job performance" (*Uniform Guidelines*). Cronbach (1980) gives the example of high school graduation. A narrow approach usually concludes employees don't need to write essays or do sums or even to be able to read, so the 'test' isn't job-related. The broader construct validity approach argues it's a reasonable supposition that people who do well at school differ from those who don't in more than just academic ability or even intelligence. Cronbach calls the something 'motivation' and 'dependability'. So an employer who doesn't want lazy, undependable employees could exclude them by requiring a high school diploma.

Cronbach's example shows very clearly why construct validation isn't a promising approach. The constructs 'motivation' and 'dependability' are exactly the sort of abstractions that are difficult to define, difficult to measure, and impossible to defend in court. The two links—test-to-construct and construct-to-job—are usually both fairly tenuous: "seminar room abstractions" (Cronbach, 1980). Miner & Miner (1979) say equal employment opportunities agencies won't accept construct validation unless it includes criterion validation—which makes construct validation superfluous. American experience shows general education requirements are rarely accepted by the courts (Chapter 10).

The fate of PACE

Ironically, fair employment legislation created the biggest problems for State and Federal Governments, because they must appoint *by merit*. Private employers could, before CRA, select who they liked, how they liked; the public sector had to advertise every post, check every application, use the same tests for every candidate, and select the best. The weight of numbers made written tests essential. The US public sector still has to select the best, but has also to 'get its numbers right': so many women, so many non-whites, so many non-white women, etc. After all if the government doesn't set an example, why should private employers spend time and money to ensure fairness.

PACE (Professional & Administrative Career Examination) was used to select college level entrants to fill 118 varied US Federal Government occupations: internal revenue officer, customs inspector, personnel manager, international relations analyst, criminal investigator, even archeologist. It consisted primarily of an ability test (Test 500), with bonus points for special experience or achievements. It was validated against five criteria, for *four* of the 118 jobs, and achieved a composite validity coefficient of 0.60 (Olian & Wilcox, 1982); PACE had both content and criterion validity.

However, PACE created massive AI on blacks and Hispanics. Applicants had to achieve a score of 70 on PACE to be eligible for selection; 42% of whites, but only 5% blacks and 13% Hispanics scored over 70. Also, PACE illustrates well the principle that the higher the score required on an ability test, the greater the resulting AI. If the 'passmark' were set at 90, 8.5% of whites, but only 0.3% of blacks and 1.5% of Hispanics would be accepted. No AI for women was created by PACE. [*Hirings* based on PACE did create AI for women, because preference was given to veterans (ex-servicemen) who were mostly male.]

In 1979, PACE was challenged because:

1. only 27 occupations of the 118 were included in the job analysis, and only four in the validation study,
2. validation was concurrent, not predictive,
3. test fairness wasn't investigated,
4. the Office of Personnel Management (OPM) hadn't tried to find an alternative test that didn't create AI.

The OPM were prepared to fight the case by:

(a) citing *validity generalization* research (Chapter 7), to answer point 1,
(b) citing reviews showing concurrent validities don't differ from predictive validities, to answer point 2 (Chapter 11),
(c) citing *differential validity* research (see later), to answer point 3,
(d) by reviewing every possible alternative test, to answer point 4, (and concluding PACE was the most cost-effective, and had the highest validity).

The case never came to court; in 1981 the Government agreed to abandon PACE over a 3-year period, and to develop alternative tests that create no AI. What these alternative tests might be, and whether they can achieve a predictive validity of 0.60, remains to be seen.

Validity generalization analysis

Validity generalization analyses (VGAs) for mental ability tests imply that local validity studies are pointless, that differential validity probably doesn't exist, and that mental ability tests are valid predictors for every type of work. Accepting these conclusions would leave little or no scope for fair employment cases involving MA tests—so it isn't surprising that American civil rights lawyers aren't keen to accept VGA (Seymour, 1988). In *EEOC* vs *Atlas Paper Box Co.*, Hunter, as expert witness, argued the Wonderlic Personnel test is a test of

'g', that 'g' predicts proficiency in all work, so that the Wonderlic tests will predict proficiency in the Atlas plant. Hunter had never visited the plant, and hadn't carried out a job analysis, since VGA implies neither could serve any useful purpose. The case is still being fought (Goldstein & Patterson, 1988).

Cut-off scores

Despite the arbitrary nature of many test cut-off scores, they have created surprisingly little difficulty in the normally litigious USA (Cascio, Alexander & Barrett, 1988; Maurer & Alexander, 1992). Cut-offs are accepted, sometimes but not always, at levels that exclude a proportion of the existing workforce, on the grounds that not all existing employees are necessarily competent, or that the employer can seek to raise standards. American courts frequently refer to "unacceptable standards" or "safe and efficient" performance, apparently subscribing to the simplistic view that performance is good or bad, not distributed on a continuum. Distribution based cut-offs, e.g. take no one who scores more than 1 SD below the mean, have been objected to occasionally, on the grounds that a particular intake might be exceptionally good, in which case it's unfair to reject applicants just because they score in that intake's lowest 15%.

Risk

'Business necessity' allows some employers to use selection methods creating AI without having to prove their validity exhaustively, if "the risks involved in hiring an unqualified applicant are staggering". The case of *Spurlock* vs *United Airlines* showed America's enthusiasm for equality stopped short of being flown by inexperienced pilots; the court even agreed pilots must be graduates "to cope with the initial training program and the unending series of refresher courses". (Presumably no one told them airline pilots in other countries, including Britain, don't have to be college graduates and often aren't.)

Bona fide occupational qualification (BFOQ)

This is known in Britain as *genuine* OQ. When Congress was debating CRA, Congressmen and women waxed lyrical about a hypothetical elderly woman who wanted a *female* nurse—white, black, oriental—but female, so they added the concept of the BFOQ: that for some jobs being male, or female, is essential. The agencies interpreted BFOQs very narrowly. Early on, airlines found they couldn't insist flight attendants be female, as a BFOQ. Nor would the elderly woman have been allowed to insist on her female nurse. The scope of the BFOQ is limited in practice to actors and lavatory attendants.

ALTERNATIVE TESTS

The 1970 *Guidelines* required employers to prove no alternative test existed that *didn't* create AI, before they used valid tests that *did* create AI. *Albemarle Paper Company* vs *Moody* over-ruled this in 1975, on the grounds employers couldn't prove a negative and said: "it remains open to the complaining party to show that other tests or selection devices, without a similarly undesirable racial effect, would also serve the employer's legitimate interest in 'efficient and trustworthy workmanship'". In 1978 the *Uniform Guidelines* placed the obligation to prove a negative back on the employer. Sharf quotes a former head of EEOC: "There is not any way in which black people tomorrow as a group are going to, no matter what kind of test you give them, score the same way that white people score ... I can't live with that. I think employers can. And I think test validation gives them an A-1 out, because if you validate your tests you don't have to worry about exclusion of minorities and women any longer ... Thus I think that by giving alternatives, we relieve especially minorities of the frustration they inevitably find in taking validated tests."

Culture-free tests

Some ability tests are very obviously culture bound. The *Information* sub-test of the Wechsler Adult Intelligence Scale has 29 items, of which nine must be altered before the test can be used in Britain; few people in Britain, bright or dull, know when Thanksgiving Day is or the distance from Denver to Dallas. If an American test has to be altered before it can be used in Britain, perhaps it needs alteration before it can be used for non-white Americans. Many attempts have been made to find tests that can be used equally validly on white, non-white, middle-class, working-class, American, British, German, Gurkha, Hottentot—any member of the human race. Some use shapes, some use mazes, some seek universals of human experience. Can culture-free tests reduce or even eliminate AI? No—in fact culture-free tests may *increase* AI (Arvey, 1972).

Reilly & Chao (1982) and Hunter & Hunter (1984) review a range of *alternative* tests. None achieve the same validity for selection as ability tests, except biodata and job tryouts. Biodata inventories are fundamentally arbitrary, so are unlikely to impress the public or the courts as acceptable ways of choosing staff. Job tryouts can only be used where applicants have been trained for the job. But for promotion a range of alternative tests are as valid as ability tests: work samples, peer ratings, job knowledge tests and assessment centres.

Adverse impact of 'alternative' tests

'Test' to a psychologist means a psychological test, but the EEOC gives it a much wider meaning: "background requirements, educational or work history requirements, scored interviews, biographical information blanks, interviewer's rating scales, scored application forms," —and in case they'd overlooked anything—"etc". *Any* selection procedure is a 'test', so any selection procedure can be judged by the same rules as ability tests. (Although 'subjective' tests, such as interviews, have generally been treated differently; see pages 228–9.) In practice, the main focus has been on ability tests, because they create most AI, and because Jensen (1969) had drawn everyone's attention to the fact. But most other tests have come under legal scrutiny in the USA at some time; Ledvinka (1982) lists ones found to create AI and (sometimes) rejected: education, experience, height and weight, physical agility, (no) criminal record, good credit record, (not) being an unmarried mother, honourable discharge from forces, or (no) dishonourable discharge.

Sharf (1982) detects another EEOC 'ratchet' at work here; EEOC have licensed themselves to declare a selection procedure discriminatory in employer B, if they've previously decided it's discriminatory in employer A. If height or weight or no-arrest record has been declared 'not job-related' in organization A, the presumption exists it's not job-related in organization B (whereas, Sharf notes, "the employer who wants to transport validity evidence ... finds seven paragraphs of restrictive conditions").

Arvey summarizes evidence on AI of different methods (Table 12.3). Every method excludes too many of one protected group or another, usually in at least one way no one can do much about. The law can't make women as tall and strong as men; the EEOC can't prevent intellectual efficiency falling off with age; 25 years of controversy hasn't closed the gap in test scores and educational achievement between white and non-white Americans. On the other hand, Table 12.3 does suggest discrimination against women should be fairly easy to avoid for most jobs. Bias against women mostly emerges in the interview, from which it could be removed by careful practice.

Table 12.3 Summary of AI on five classes of selection test on four minorities. (Arvey, 1979b)

	Blacks	Females	Elderly	Handicapped
Intelligence and verbal tests	AI	+	ai	?
Work samples	+	NE	NE	NE
Interview	+	AI	ai	ai
Educational requirement	AI	+	ai	?
Physical tests	+	AI	?	AI

AI—established evidence of AI; ai—some evidence of AI; ?—no proof of AI, but likely to exist, for some tests, or some persons; +—evidence the minority does as well or better than majority on this test; NE—no evidence.

'Sex plus' discrimination

The EEOC and the courts looked very critically at employers who said things like "no women with pre-school children" or "no wives of students". Such 'tests' don't exclude women as such, but sub-sets of women, hence the name *sex plus*. Such requirements are clearly discriminatory, because employers don't say "no men with pre-school children" or "no students' husbands". Validity isn't a defence; it's no use the employer proving women with pre-school children take more time off.

UK PRACTICE

The Commission for Racial Equality's (CRE) *Code* recommends employers to keep detailed records with which to compare actual and ideal composition of applicant pool and workforce. They have adopted the adverse impact principle, sometimes referred to as *disproportionate effect*, and offer the four-fifths principle as 'guidance', while admitting it has no statutory force. The CRE *Code* recommends that "selection criteria and tests are examined to ensure that they are related to job requirements and are not unlawfully discriminatory" (Para 1.13). The Equal Opportunity Commission's (EOC) *Code* similarly says "selection tests ... should specifically relate to job requirements". The CRE's *Code* is particularly concerned that employers don't require better command of English or higher educational qualifications than the job needs. To promote drivers and conductors to inspectors, Bradford buses used a home-made essay test of interest in the job, knowledge of local geography, etc. The CRE (1983) objected to this test, because Asian candidates found it more difficult, and because it wasn't job-related. The CRE later objected to a similar home-made essay test used to select factory foremen, because foremen only needed to write short notes about fairly specific matters (CRE, 1984b).

The CRE's earlier formal *Inquiries* dealt with employers sufficiently ignorant or unsubtle to say things like "[we don't employ West Indians because they are] too slow, too sly, too much mouth and they skive off" (CRE, 1984a), then with employers whose recruitment methods appeared to keep out minorities—usually by recruiting through existing staff. The CRE's *Enquiries* into alleged discrimination have dealt with taxi-drivers, milkmen, bakery shop assistants, factory workers, foremen and apprentices, bus drivers, conductors and inspectors, clerical workers, hospital cleaners—jobs for which selection procedures in Britain are minimal and unsystematic. The EOC has concerned itself more with *sex-plus* discrimination, and with *maximum* entry age limits (because raising a family means women often enter a career later than men).

Towards the end of the 1980s, however, the first cases involving psychological tests began to appear. London Underground (subway) appointed 160 middle managers, in such a rush that they didn't have time to include all the tests psychologists had recommended, or to pre-test the ones they did use (CRE, 1990). The tests used, numerical and verbal reasoning, and an interview, created adverse impact on Asian and West Indian applicants. Race was confounded with age and education, however; the West Indian applicants were much older than the white applicants, and had less formal education.

In 1990, another case involving tests came to trial—the 'Paddington Guards' case. British Rail guards seeking promotion to driver were tested with verbal reasoning, numerical reasoning, and clerical speed and accuracy tests. A group of guards of Asian origin alleged unfair discrimination, because the tests weren't clearly job-related, but were harder for people whose first language wasn't English. The case was settled out of court, so no judgment concerning tests was recorded.

These cases inspired the CRE to issue a series of recommendations about psychological tests (CRE, 1992). Some are sound: conduct a job analysis and use it to choose selection tests, allow candidates enough time to absorb the instructions and do the practice examples, avoid English language tests on candidates whose first language isn't English. Some are unrealistic: do not use time limits. (Most MA tests are timed, and cannot be used untimed without being re-standardized.) Other recommendations seek to send British personnel managers and psychologists down paths already travelled in the USA: if the test creates adverse impact do not use it, or else validate it on at least 100 persons in each minority group; do not assume a test proved valid for one job will be valid for another. Current thinking in the USA, based on 30 years of research, sees local validity studies as a waste of time (Chapter 7), because validity of mental ability tests generalizes widely, and sees differential validity as non-existent (see below).

Fair employment laws haven't had the impact in Britain they had in the USA. English law doesn't provide for *class actions*, in which one person's test case can be used to enforce the rights of a whole class of others, e.g. female employees. The British government hasn't introduced *contract compliance*, although some local authorities have. British courts enforce the letter of the law, not what they perceive to be its spirit. Britain has far fewer lawyers, and they aren't allowed to start cases on a 'no win, no fee' basis.

DIFFERENTIAL VALIDITY

Critics often claim tests are valid for the white majority, but not for non-whites. There are two linked hypotheses:

1. *single group validity*—tests are valid for one group but not (at all) for others;
2. *differential validity*—tests are valid for both groups, but more valid for one group than the other.

Critics generally assume tests have lower (or no) validity for non-whites, because their culture, education etc. differs. The issue gets complex statistically.

Some people naively suppose it sufficient to show the test's validity coefficient achieves significance for whites, but not for non-whites. The correlations should be compared with each other, not with zero.

Data of Kirkpatrick et al (1968) data on the Pre-Nursing & Guidance Examination were often cited as proof that tests aren't fair for minorities. Validity coefficients for whites tended to be higher, or more statistically significant, than those for non-whites. Kirkpatrick et al reported a *local validation* study, which isn't capable of demonstrating differential validity. Many of the samples, white or non-white, were too small to prove anything. In most comparisons the minority sample is smaller than the white sample, so the correlation is more likely to be insignificant.

Single studies of differential validity will always prove inconclusive, because the samples will be too small. Suppose true validities of a test for a job are 0.50 for whites, and 0.30 for non-whites, and suppose criterion reliability is 0.70 but that range isn't restricted at all, then each sample needs to number 528, to have a reasonable chance (90%) of detecting the difference (Schmidt, Pearlman & Hunter, 1980). Pooling the results of many researches, through meta-analysis, is needed to give conclusive answers.

Meta-analysis

Schmidt, Berner & Hunter (1973) reviewed 410 pairs of non-white/white validity coefficients. In 75 pairs the correlation was significant for whites but not for non-whites, while in 34 pairs it was significant for non-whites but not for whites. At first sight this is weak confirmation of the hypothesis that tests are more likely to be valid for whites than for non-whites. However, the average non-white sample was only half the size ($N = 49$) of the average white sample ($N = 100$), so non-white correlations are less likely to achieve significance. Schmidt et al calculated how often the patterns—white significant and non-white insignificant, and white insignificant and non-white significant— would appear by chance, given the sample sizes. The values calculated—76 and 37—were almost identical to those observed. Schmidt et al conclude that single group validity is "probably illusory", a "pseudoproblem".

If white and non-white sample sizes are the same, the pattern of white-correlation-significant but black-correlation-insignificant ought to occur as often as white-insignificant but black-significant. O'Connor, Wexley & Alexander (1975) actually found 25 white-significant and black-insignificant pairs and 17 white-insignificant and black-significant pairs—which doesn't prove a trend.

Other early meta-analyses also found no evidence of differential validity.

Boehm (1972) found only seven pairs of correlations from a total of 160 showed differential validity; most pairs showed the test failed to predict significantly for white *or* non-white. Boehm (1977) later analysed 538 pairs of white and non-white validities, and found differential validity in only 8%. Boehm concluded differential validity was more likely to be 'found' by methodologically inferior studies; neither single group validity nor differential validity was found by any study where both white and non-white samples exceeded 100.

Sets of correlations

Boehm's (1977) analysis may be misleading. Most validation studies use more than one test and more than one criterion. The tests usually intercorrelate to some degree; so do the criteria. Therefore each correlation between test and criterion is not an independent observation. Suppose a validation study used Forms A and B of the Watson Glaser Critical Thinking Appraisal (CTA), and found both correlated well with ratings of intellectual effectiveness and of originality (Figure 12.2). Does the study report four relationships, or two, or only one? Hunter & Schmidt argue that including all 538 pairs of correlations in Boehm's calculation is conceptually the same as including the same correlation ten times—it makes the results look more consistent and more significant than they really are.

Katzell & Dyer (1977) analysed the same 31 studies, but first identified *sets* of correlated predictors and criteria like the one illustrated in Figure 12.3, then chose *one* pair of correlations at random from each set, so each of the 64 pairs was an independent observation. Ten of the 64 (19%) showed a significant white vs non-white difference. A second random sample of correlation pairs found 31% yielded a significant white vs non-white difference. Katzell & Dyer's re-analysis implies Boehm had allowed true differential validity to be masked, by including pairs of correlations that found no differential validity over and over again under different names.

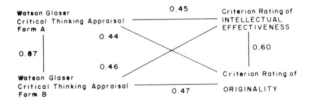

Figure 12.2 Fictional "set" of predictor–criterion relationships, showing fictional correlations between criterion relations, actual correlation between Forms A and B of the Watson Glaser Critical Thinking Appraisal (WGCTA) and fictional correlations between WGCTA and criterion ratings

Exclude insignificant correlations?

Hunter & Schmidt (1978) argue *both* analyses, by Boehm and Katzell & Dyer, are seriously flawed. Katzell & Dyer excluded pairs in which neither observed validity coefficient was as large as 0.20. Katzell & Dyer and Boehm excluded pairs where neither correlation was significant—on the grounds that a test that failed to predict for either race can't demonstrate differential validity. Hunter & Schmidt argue this was a mistake. Validity coefficients often fail to achieve significance because the sample is too small, or range is restricted, or the criterion is unreliable (Chapter 7). So excluding pairs where the correlations were small or insignificant excludes some pairs where there was true validity, and also excludes some pairs where white and non-white validities were identical. Three recent studies that avoid this error find differential validity occurring at chance levels. Bartlett et al (1978) analyse 1190 pairs of black and white validity coefficients and found 6.8% differ, at the 5% level of significance. Hunter, Schmidt & Hunter (1979) analyse 712 pairs, and find 6% significantly different. Schmidt et al (1980) analyse data for Hispanic Americans from 19 studies, and found only 6% of pairs of validity coefficients significantly different. However, more recently, Hartigan & Wigdor (1989) point to 72 studies using the General Aptitude Test Battery (GATB) with at least 50 black and 50 white subjects, in which GATB's composite validity was lower for blacks (0.12) than for whites (0.19).

On balance, the hypothesis of differential validity has been disproved. Ability tests can be used equally validly for white and non-white Americans. Humphreys (1973) suggests reversing perspective in a way he thinks many psychologists will find hard to accept: the hypothesis of differential validity implies "Minorities probably do not belong to the same biological species as the majority; but if they do, the environmental differences have been so profound and have produced such huge cultural differences that the same principles of human behaviour do not apply to both groups".

Test fairness

Critics often claim tests aren't fair, meaning non-whites don't score as well as whites. In the technical sense of the word, *unfair* means the test doesn't predict the minority's productivity as accurately as it predicts majority productivity. Several models of test fairness have been proposed; the most widely accepted is Cleary & Hilton's (1986) model, based on regression lines. EEOC now accepts Cleary & Hilton's model of test fairness, which implies American courts ought to.

Figure 12.3 shows the first type of unfair test, where there is true differential validity. When regression lines are fitted to the majority and minority distributions, the *slopes* of the lines differ. A *slope* difference means the test predicts

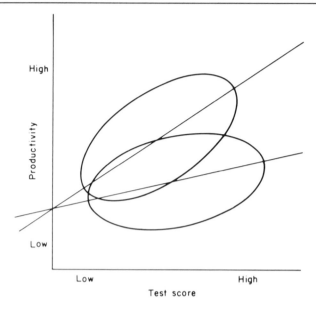

Figure 12.3 An "unfair" test, showing a *slope* difference; the correlation between test and productivity is higher for majority than for minority applicants

productivity more accurately for one group than the other. This chapter has already concluded there's no evidence differential validity exists, which implies there's no evidence slope differences do either. Bartlett et al's (1978) review finds black vs white difference in slope occur at chance frequency; Schmidt, Pearlman & Hunter (1980) find the same for Hispanic Americans.

Figure 12.4 shows the second type of unfair test. Minority and majority differ in test score, but don't differ in productivity. When regression lines are fitted to the majority and minority distributions, they *intercept* the vertical axis at different points—so-called *intercept* differences which indicate bias. Of course the lines rarely have exactly the same intercept in practice, but where intercepts differ, they often 'over-predict' minority productivity. In Ruch's unpublished review (see Schmidt, Pearlman & Hunter, 1980), nine out of 20 studies found tests *over*-predicted non-white productivity. Far from being 'unfair' to non-whites, tests may actually favour them.

Figure 12.5 shows a test which is fair, even though majority and minority averages differ. A regression line fitted to the two distributions has the same slope, and the same intercept, which means it's one continuous straight line. Test scores predict productivity, regardless of minority or majority group membership. Schmidt, Pearlman & Hunter (1980) review eight studies that show tests don't under-predict non-whites' productivity.

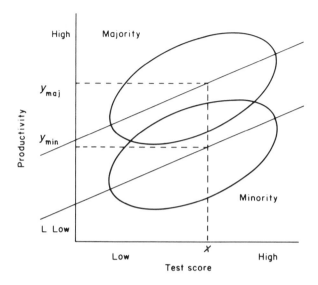

Figure 12.4 An "unfair" test, showing an *intercept* difference; A given test score (x) predicts lower productivity (y_{min}) for minority applicants than for majority applicants (y_{maj})

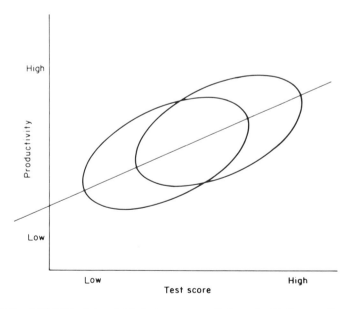

Figure 12.5 A "fair" test, in which test scores predict productivity equally accurately for minority and majority applicants

Schmidt, Pearlman & Hunter (1980) think future revisions of the *Uniform Guidelines* should drop the requirement for differential validation by race. Schmidt & Hunter (1981) suggest everyone accepts that tests are fair: "that average ability and cognitive skill differences between groups are directly reflected in test performance and thus are *real*. We do not know what all the causes of these differences are, how long they will persist, or how best to eliminate them". They conclude "it is not intellectually honest, in the face of empirical evidence to the contrary, to postulate that the problem [of AI] is biased and/or unfair employment tests".

Virtually all the research on differential validity is American; there are few or no British or European data on the issue. Psychologists cannot automatically extrapolate from North America to Europe and argue that if there is no differential validity in the USA, there will be none in Europe, because the ethnic minorities in Europe aren't the same ones as in North America, because culture and educational systems vary, etc. This implies that collecting enough evidence on differential validity to give a conclusive view, one way or the other, should be a high priority for British and European psychologists.

CONCLUSIONS

The *Uniform Guidelines* have been a great burden to American employers. They are rigid and inflexible. They stifle new developments in selection. They force employers to waste time and effort adapting effective methods to meet unrealistic requirements. They give administrators and lawyers power to make decisions about complex technical disputes they often don't understand. The *Guidelines* are misnamed: they don't provide guidance; they create confusion and uncertainty.

The Civil Rights Act has often, only half-jokingly, been called "the occupational psychologists' charter". Lawyers too have done well from it. But fair employment legislation wasn't meant to benefit psychologists and lawyers; it was intended to help minorities. According to Ledvinka (1982), it hasn't; the disparity between white and non-white, in wages, prospects, status, being employed at all, got bigger during the 1970s, not smaller.

If American fair employment agencies are really trying to abolish selection tests, they are doing quite well. In 1963, 90% of American employers used psychological tests in selection; by 1976, only 42% still used them (Miner & Miner, 1979). Some of the USA's largest employers stopped testing. General Electric dropped all aptitude tests in the early 1970s to 'get their numbers right', then realized in the late 1970s that "a large percentage of the people hired under the new selection standards were not promotable. General Electric had merely transferred the adverse impact from the hiring stage to the promotion stage" (Schmidt & Hunter, 1981). Similarly, US Steel stopped testing apprentices, except to exclude the very dull, with the result that "(a) scores on mastery tests given during training declined markedly, (b) the flunk-out [failure] and drop-out rates increased dramatically, (c) average training time and training cost for those who *did* make it through the program increased substantially, and (d) average ratings of later performance on the job declined". Schmidt & Hunter wonder aloud if these trends contributed to America's declining national productivity during the 1970s.

13 The Value of Good Selection

Calculating the cost of smugness

We find everywhere a type of organization (administrative, commercial, or academic) in which the higher officials are plodding and dull, those less senior are active only in intrigue ... and the junior men are frustrated and frivolous. Little is being attempted, nothing is being achieved.

[C. Northcote Parkinson, 1958]

Sometimes choosing the wrong person has visibly disastrous results: a train crash, a battle lost, the organization disgraced or discredited. Sometimes the results are less striking but still visible: lost customers, minor accidents, frequent absences, damaged equipment, ill feeling, mysterious illnesses—for as long as it takes the employer to realize a mistake has been made. In Britain, employees start acquiring employment protection rights after 6 months' employment, so mistakes become increasingly difficult and expensive to rectify. Another cost of poor selection is more easily overlooked: the good people the organization rejects go and work for its competitors. The scarcer the skill, the bigger the resulting loss.

In some organizations the costs of selecting ineffective staff mount indefinitely, because the organization lacks the mechanism, or the will, to dispense with their services. Some employers tolerate inefficient staff for ever. Naturally, morale in such organizations suffers, driving out the remaining efficient workers, until only the incompetent remain, creating the state of terminal sickness so graphically described by Northcote Parkinson. Staff wander aimlessly about "giggling feebly", losing important documents, coming alive only to block the advancement of anyone more able, "until the central administration gradually fills up with people stupider than the chairman". Other diagnostics include surly porters and telephonists, out-of-order lifts, a proliferation of out-of-date notices, and *smugness*, especially smugness. The organization is doing a good job, in its own modest way; anyone who disagrees is a troublemaker who would probably be happier somewhere else. Parkinson advises that *smugness* is most easily diagnosed in the organization's refectory. The terminally smug don't just consume an "uneatable, nameless mess"; they congratulate themselves on having catering staff who can provide it at such reasonable cost—"smugness made absolute".

Personnel selectors often see their task as avoiding mistakes, minimizing error. They bring in psychologists as the final check that the candidate is 'safe'. So long as the year's gone by with no obvious disasters and no complaints, personnel have done their job. This negative approach to selection is wrong. Chapter 1 showed productivity is normally distributed. There is a continuous distribution of productivity from the very best to the very worst; selection isn't as simple as avoiding mistakes—not employing a small minority of obvious incompetents or troublemakers. The employer who succeeds in employing *average* staff hasn't succeeded in employing *good* staff; the employer who finds *good* staff hasn't found *excellent* staff. To take the argument to its logical limit, any employer who hasn't got the world's 100 best programmers filling 100 programmer vacancies hasn't maximized productivity. The world's 100 best programmers clearly isn't a realistic target, but programmers in the top 15% perhaps might be, at least for some employers.

HOW TO SELECT

There are five criteria for judging selection tests.

1. *Validity* is the most important criterion. Unless a test can predict productivity, there's little point using it.
2. *Cost* tends to be accorded far too much weight by selectors. Cost isn't an important consideration, so long as the test has *validity*. A valid test, even the most elaborate and expensive, is almost always worth using.
3. *Practicality* is a negative criterion, a reason for *not* using a test.
4. *Generality* simply means how many types of employees the test can be used for.
5. *Legality* is another negative criterion—a reason for *not* using something. It's often hard to evaluate, as the legal position on many tests is obscure or confused.

Meta-analysis makes some sense of the confused literature on selection tests, but much remains unclear. Table 13.1 collates the results of five meta-analyses, but should be treated with some caution, as there's insufficient information about some analyses. Hunter & Hunter's analyses are somewhat sketchily described by *Psychological Bulletin* standards; they do not say where they got their information, nor how they analysed it. It's not at all clear how independent are the analyses in Table 13.1. Dunnette's (1972) derives entirely from the American petroleum industry, Vineberg & Joyner's (1982) entirely from the American armed services, so these two are independent. The analysis by Schmidt et al (1984) derives entirely from studies published in *Personnel Psychology* and *Journal of Applied Psychology*, whereas Hunter & Hunter (1984)

Table 13.1 Summary of meta-analyses of selection test validity. All correlations, except those marked with an asterisk, have been corrected for restricted range, etc.

	Dunnette (1972)	Reilly & Chao (1982)	Vineberg & Joyner (1982)	Hunter & Hunter (1982)	Schmitt et al (1984)	Other
Chapter 2 graphology			'None'			0.21/zero[1]
Chapter 4 interview	0.16	0.23		0.14		0.47[2]
unstructured						0.31[2]
structured						0.62[2]
Chapter 5 reference		0.17		0.26		
peer ratings				0.49	0.43	
Chapter 6 biodata	0.34	0.38	0.24	0.37	0.24	
Chapter 7 general	0.45			0.53	0.25	
perceptual	0.34					
psychomotor	0.35					
aptitude			0.28		0.27	
Chapter 8 interest	0.03					
personality	0.08		0.13	0.10	0.15	0.24[3] 0.08*
honesty						0.18[3] 0.08*
conscientiousness						0.22[5] 0.41[6]
projective		'Little'				
Chapter 9 assessment centre				0.43	0.41	0.37[7]

Table 13.1 (Continued)

	Dunnettte (1972)	Reilly & Chao (1982)	Vineberg & Joyner (1982)	Hunter & Hunter (1982)	Schmitt et al (1984)	Other
Chapter 10						
education	0.00			0.10		
academic		0.17	0.25	0.11		
T & E rate				0.13		0.09[8]
work sample				0.54	0.38	0.39*[9]
trainability						0.20–0.26[10]*
job knowledge	0.51			0.48		
job tryout	0.44			[0.44]		
self assessment			'Some'			
physical					0.32	

[1] Neter & Ben-Shakhar (1989).
[2] Wiesner & Cronshaw (1988).
[3] Tett, Jackson & Rothstein (1991).
[4] Hough (in press).
[5] Barrick & Mount (1991).
[6] Ones et al. (undated).
[7] Gaugler et al (1987).
[8] McDaniel, Schmidt & Hunter (1988).
[9] Robertson & Kandola (1982).
[10] Robertson & Downs (1989).

mostly use unpublished US Government data. The biggest overlap appears to be between the meta-analyses of Reilly & Chao (1982) and Hunter & Hunter. Other meta-analyses of validity, for graphology, interviewing, personality testing, assessment centres, T & E ratings, work sample and trainability tests, generally confirm the conclusions of the original five meta-analyses, with two exceptions. Recent research on interviewing indicates *structured* interviewing achieves far higher validity than interviewing in general. Research on personality tests confirms they generally predict job proficiency poorly, but that they can predict honesty and conscientiousness more successfully.

With these cautions in mind, one may try to draw some preliminary conclusions, aided by Hunter & Hunter's two 'league tables' of selection tests. The first league table is for *selection* tests; the second table is for *promotion* tests (Figure 13.1). (Hunter & Hunter classify assessment centres as promotion tests, but they can be used for selection too.) Figure 13.1 shows *selection* is much more difficult than *promotion*. Promotion tests all have fairly good average validity quotients, so personnel managers can choose on the basis of cost, convenience, legal problems or the type of staff involved. Promotion should be easier than selection because the employer is dealing with a known

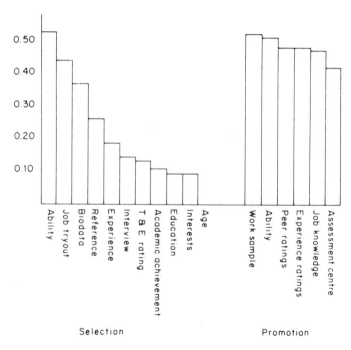

Figure 13.1   Estimates of the validity of various selection and promotion tests. Data from Hunter & Hunter (1984)

quantity; employers have more, and better, information about existing staff, assuming they have a good appraisal system and good records. (Although three of the six promotion tests in Figure 13.1 are not 'historical'.) Selection tests have to be chosen much more carefully; their validity varies very widely, from a high point of 0.53 to a low point of zero. Figure 13.1 also shows the distribution of validity is *skewed* towards the low end; there are a lot of tests with very limited validity. Table 13.2 summarizes the relative merits of 10 selection methods, against the five criteria: validity, cost, practicality, generality and legality.

Interview costs are given as medium/low, because interviews vary so much, and because they're so much taken for granted that few estimates of their cost have been made. Structured interview costs are high, because the system has to be tailor made and requires a full job analysis. Biodata costs are given as medium, on the assumption the inventory will have to be specially written for the employer; a 'ready-made' biodata inventory would be as cheap as ability or personality tests.

A *practical* test is one that isn't difficult to introduce, because it fits in easily or because no one objects to it. Ability tests are very practical because they can be given when candidates come for interview. References are very practical because everyone is used to giving them. Assessment centres are only fairly practical, because they need a lot of organizing and they don't fit into the conventional timetable of selection procedures. Personality tests are only fairly practical, because management and candidates are suspicious of them. Peer assessments are highly impractical because they require applicants to spend a long time with each other, and because people often object strongly to making them. Structured interviews may have limited practicality, because personnel and line managers are likely to resist the loss of autonomy involved.

Legality is rated on American experience; no selection test has fallen seriously foul of the law in Britain yet, but Chapter 12 argued that UK fair employment agencies model themselves on American practice, so American experience may be a useful guide to the shape of things to come in Britain.

Most selection tests can be used for any category of worker, but true work samples and job knowledge tests can only be used where there's a specific body of knowledge to test, which in practice means skilled manual jobs. Peer ratings can only be used in the armed services. Personality tests are usually only used for white-collar workers. So too are assessment centres, although they have been used for police officers and enlisted personnel (non-commissioned ranks) in the armed services.

Taking *validity* as the over-riding consideration, there are six classes of test with high *validity*: peer ratings, biodata, ability tests, assessment centres, work sample tests and job knowledge tests. Three of these have very limited *generality*, which leaves biodata, ability tests and assessment centres.

Table 13.2 Summary of 11 selection tests by five criteria

	Validity	Cost	Practicality	Generality	Legality
Interview	Low	Medium/high	High	High	Untested
Structured interview	High	High	?Limited	High	No problems
References	Moderate	Very low	High	High	A few doubts
Peer ratings	High	Very low	Very limited	? uniformed services	Untested
Biodata	High	Medium	High	High	Some doubts
Ability	High	Low	High	High	Major doubts
Personality	Variable	Low	Fair	High	Untested
Assessment centre	High	Very high	Fair	Fairly high	No problems
Work sample	High	High	High	Blue collar	No problems
Job knowledge	High	Low	High	Blue collar	Some doubts
Education	Low	Low	High	High	Major doubts

1. *Biodata* don't achieve quite such good validity as ability tests, and aren't as transportable, which makes them more expensive.

2. *Ability tests* have excellent validity, can be used for all sorts of job, are readily transportable, are cheap and easy to use, but fall foul of the law in the USA.

3. *Assessment centres* have excellent validity, can be used for most grades of staff, are legally fairly safe, but are difficult to install and expensive.

4. *Work samples* have excellent *validity*, are easy to use, are generally quite safe legally, but are expensive, because they are necessarily specific to the job. Much the same considerations apply to job knowledge tests, except they're cheaper because they're commercially available, and they're more likely to cause legal problems because they're usually paper-and-pencil tests.

Most other tests in Tables 13.1 and 13.2 have lower *validity*—but not zero validity. Tests with validities below 0.20–0.30 are commonly written off as a waste of time, but in fact can be worth using, if they're cheap, or if they contribute new information. Hence the only test in Table 13.1 that can be definitely dismissed as never worth using is graphology.

Personality inventories achieve poor validity for predicting job proficiency, but can prove more useful for predicting how well the individual will conform to the job's norms and rules.

References have only moderate validity, but are cheap, easy and fairly safe to use.

Incremental validity The big gap in present knowledge is the validity of *combinations* of tests. Chapter 8 shows that personality tests do contribute incremental validity, when used with mental ability tests. Chapter 10 shows that in-tray exercises contribute incremental validity to tests of mental ability. On the other hand, tests of mental ability are unlikely to add a lot to tests of job knowledge. There remain, however, a large number of possible combinations of selection methods, where no information about incremental validity is available. Does biodata improve on structured interviewing? Do good reference checks improve on personality inventories? Is there anything to be gained adding peer ratings to work samples and mental ability tests? What combination of the methods listed in Tables 13.1 and 13.2 will give the best results, and how good will that 'best' be?

CALCULATING THE RETURN ON SELECTION

It's fairly easy to calculate the cost of selection, although most employers only think of doing so when asked to introduce *new* methods; they rarely work out how much *existing* methods, such as day-long panel interviews, cost. It's more difficult to calculate the *return* on selection. The formula was first stated by Brogden in 1946, but for many years had only academic interest because a crucial term in it couldn't be measured—SD_y, the standard deviation of employee productivity. Until *Rational Estimate* and *Superior Equivalents* techniques (Chapter 1) were devised, there was no way of measuring how much more good employees are worth.

Brogden's equation states:

$$\text{SAVING per EMPLOYEE per YEAR} = (r \times SD_y \times Z) - (C/P),$$

where: r is the validity of the selection procedure (expressed as a correlation coefficient),

         SD_y is the standard deviation of employee productivity in pounds or dollars,

         Z is the calibre of recruits (expressed as their standard score on the selection test used),

         C is the cost of selection per applicant,

         P is the proportion of applicants selected.

Or to put it in plain English, the amount an employer can save, per employee recruited, per year, is:

VALIDITY of the test *times* CALIBRE of recruits *times* SD_y

minus

COST of selection *divided by* PROPORTION of applicants selected.

Here is a worked example:

1. The employer is recruiting in the salary range £20 000 p.a., so SD_y can be estimated—by the 70% 'rule of thumb'—at £14 000. (Or SD_y can be measured by Rational Estimate or Superior Equivalents techniques).

2. The employer is using a test of high level mental ability whose proven validity is 0.45, so r is 0.45.

3. The people recruited score on average 1 SD above the mean for the ability test, so Z is 1. This assumes the employer succeeds in recruiting high calibre people.

4. The employer uses a consultancy, who charge £480 per candidate.

5. Of 10 applicants, four are appointed, so P is 0.40.

The SAVING per employee per year:

= $(0.45 \times £14\,000 \times 1) - (£480/0.40)$
= £6300 − £1200
= £5100.

Each employee selected is worth over £5000 a year more to the employer than one recruited at random. The four employees recruited will be worth in all £20 400 more to the employer, *each year*. The larger the organization, the greater the total sum that can be saved by effective selection, hence the estimate given in Chapter 1 of $18 million for the Philadelphia police force, with 5000 employees.
    Selection pays off better:

- when the *calibre* of recruits is high,
- where employees differ a lot in worth to the organization, i. e. when SD_y is high,
- where selection procedure has high validity.

Selection pays off less well:

- when recruits are uniformly mediocre,
- when SD_y is low,
- when selection procedure has low validity.

Employers should have no difficulty attracting good recruits in periods of high unemployment (unless the pay or conditions are poor). Chapter 1 showed SD_y is rarely low. But the third condition—zero validity—is all too likely to apply; many selection methods have zero, or near zero, validity. But if any of the three terms are zero, their product—the value of selection—is necessarily zero too. Only the right-hand side of the equation—the cost of selection—is never zero.
    In the worked example, even using a fairly expensive selection procedure, the cost per employee selected is only a fifth of the increased value per employee per year, giving the lie to the oft-heard claim that elaborate selection methods, or psychological assessment, aren't worthwhile. In this example, selection pays for itself six times over in the first year. Failure to select the right employee by contrast goes on costing the employer money, *year after year*.

Return on selection is a *linear function of validity*; the higher the validity, the greater the return. The Brogden formula means selection tests can be worth using, even when validity is low—if their cost is also low. Table 13.3 gives three examples.

Table 13.3 Three examples of utility analyses of selection procedures

	1. CP–Dominance	2. EPI (pilot training)	3. Panel interview
r	0.25	0.15	0.14
SD_y	£14 000	£14 000	£14 000
z	0.50	0.50	0.50
Saving	£1400	£1050	£980
C	£25	£1	£200
P	0.20	0.01	0.20
Cost	£125	£100	£1000
Return	£1275	£950	− £20

CPI—California Psychological Inventory; EPI—Eysenck Personality Inventory

In example 1, the employer uses the Dominance scale of the California Psychological Inventory (CPI) to select managers. Assume the scale has a validity of $r = 0.25$, and that recruits have an average dominance half a SD above the mean, so $Z = 0.50$. A validity of $r = 0.25$ is often dismissed as useless, sometimes on the grounds that it accounts for only 6% of the variance in selection ($0.25^2 = 0.0625$). Example 1 shows that CPI Dominance would, on the assumptions made, have a worthwhile return for the employer, saving £1275 per employee selected, per year.

Example 2 is inspired by Bartram & Dale's (1982) work, using the Eysenck Personality Inventory (EPI) to select military pilots. EPI's validity was generally low, around $r = 0.15$, a value so low many would automatically dismiss the test. However the EPI is extremely cheap to use—a nominal £1 per candidate is entered in Table 13.3. (On the other hand, the Royal Air Force selects very few applicants; Table 13.3 assumes only 1 in 100, so testing costs aren't negligible.) Overall the EPI proves to be worth using. (Especially as Table 13.3 doesn't take account of training costs, which run into six-figure sums per pilot.)

Example 3 shows another selection procedure with low validity—the interview—and illustrates how a selection procedure with low validity can actually waste money. The interview achieves the same potential saving per candidate as the EPI, having the same validity, but costs a lot more. In fact the gain in productivity, for the first year, doesn't cover the cost of selection. Example 3 assumes a panel of 10 interviewers, taking an hour per candidate, and values the interviewers' time at £15 per hour, on the accountant's assumption that if they weren't interviewing they could be doing something useful. The other £50 covers cost of secretaries, porters, etc. (If a 10-person interview board sounds preposterously wasteful, reflect that some employers use panels of 25 or more.)

Utility analysis in practice

Boudreau (1983a) points out that some of Schmidt & Hunter's (1981) estimates of savings achieved by good selection are over optimistic. The value of the increased productivity isn't all 'money in the bank'. Increased production means increased costs: raw materials, overheads, commission, etc. It also means increased taxes. Moreover the *costs* of selection are incurred before the *savings* are made, so interest charges need to be included. Correcting for these omissions reduces estimates of savings by 67%.

On the other hand, Boudreau (1983b) thinks Schmidt & Hunter also *underestimate* the savings good selection can achieve, because they only analyse one batch of new recruits. In the real world employers are constantly hiring new staff. Boudreau analyses the return on selection over 25 years, by the end of which time *everyone* has been selected by a test with high validity. Boudreau takes the examples of computer programmers, selected with the Programmer Aptitude Test (Chapter 7), which has very high validity (0.76). Selection ratio is 0.50. Calibre of recruit is good, representing a Z value of 0.80. Programmers stay with the employer on average for 10 years, so after 10 years the programmer workforce has been completely replaced. Each year the employer recruits 618 new programmers. The return, in increased productivity, increases steadily, until year 10, when the whole workforce has been selected by the test. In year 10, the gain is nearly $8 million, allowing for increased costs, taxes and interest.

Critics of utility theory in general (Vance & Colella, 1990) note that no follow-up studies have been reported that actually demonstrate any of the predicted savings. They also comment that utility theory makes the simplistic assumption that every worker works in isolation, whereas in reality much work is done by teams, where superhumans performing at the 95% percentile will be held back by slower mortals performing at the 50th percentile.

CONCLUSIONS

The illusion of selection

Bad selection isn't just a waste of time; it costs employers a lot of money, year after year. Bad selection methods include the unstructured interview, which is a very time-wasting procedure, for candidate and interviewer alike. Yet bad selection methods are still very popular, especially the unstructured interview. The interview has survived 60 years of mounting criticism from psychologists, while ability tests, which are very good predictors of productivity, have been practically forced out of business in the USA. Why?

'Summing other people up' is an activity people like to think they are good at, like driving a car, holding their liquor or making love. Hence people aren't receptive to the suggestion their task could be done quicker and better by ability test, or biodata inventory. One wonders if the popularity of assessment centres derives as much from the elaborate opportunities they give to 'sum people up', as from their high validity.

Incompetence + Jealousy = 'Injelitance'?

The discussion has assumed that all employers genuinely want the best applicants; Northcote Parkinson thinks this very naive: "if the head of an organisation is second rate, he will see to it that his immediate staff are all third rate: and they will, in turn, see to it that their subordinates are fourth rate". Such organizations suffer *injelitance*—"a disease of induced inferiority", compounded equally of *incompetence* and *jealousy*. The 'injelitant' organization doesn't fill up with stupid people accidentally—dull smug people at its core deliberately recruit even duller smugger people, to protect their own positions. And what better way is there to perpetuate incompetence than the traditional interview? Mediocrities can be selected and promoted, using the code words "soundness", "teamwork" and "judgement". And what greater threat to injelitant organizations can there be than objective tests of ability? which might introduce unwelcome, disruptive 'clever' people. Parkinson thinks injelitance a terminal illness of organizations, which can only be cured by dismissing all the staff, and burning the buildings to the ground; he does suggest, however, that "infected personnel" might be "dispatched with a warm testimonial to such rival institutions as are regarded with particular hostility".

Cook's Law

An important principle of selection, stated on page 67: the more important the decision, the more time must be spent making it, and *the more time must be seen to be spent making it*. Work samples and simple aptitude tests are good enough for shop-floor workers. Clerical tests are good enough for lowly office workers. But selecting anyone 'important' requires longer, more elaborate selection procedures, taking many man hours. Panel interviews in the British public sector show Cook's Law to advantage: a panel of 10 spends all day interviewing candidates, at vast expense. But usually all the time is spent interviewing—the *visible* part of selection—while far too little time is spent in preparation and analysis.

Cook's Law has a corollary, which is very comforting to occupational psychologists: the more important the selection, the more the employer is willing to pay. It's no more difficult nor time-consuming to assess a potential Managing Director (Company President) than to assess a line manager, but most consultancies charge more, and most employers pay willingly.

Creating an underclass?

An employer who succeeds in recruiting able, productive workers needs fewer of them. If all employers use highly accurate tests to select productive workers, the number of jobs will shrink, creating more unemployment. If every employer uses highly accurate tests, people of low ability will find it hard to get work. If employers started exchanging information, the ungifted will find themselves never even being short-listed. The result will be a steadily growing, unemployed, disillusioned, and resentful *underclass*. This isn't a new idea; Cattell saw it coming 50 years ago (Cattell, 1936).

Burning the candle at both ends?

At the other end of the distribution of ability, a shrinking workforce, of more able people, works harder and longer to maximize productivity. In the process, they wear themselves out, and have no time left to enjoy life. Many managers already see this happening to themselves. If fewer and fewer people produce more and more, who is going to buy it? How are they going to pay for it?

Is productivity the only end?

This book started life as a title in a series on *Psychology and Productivity*, so it reviews what psychologists know about selecting people who produce more. This doesn't mean psychologists think all employers ought to work like that all the time. A world run by cost accountants would be a very dreary place.

Work serves other purposes besides producing goods/services. Work fulfils workers; work absorbs unemployment; work is good for people; work keeps people out of bars; work fills up the day; work brings people together; work prevents urban riots.

References

Allport, G. W. (1937) *Personality: a psychological interpretation.* Holt, New York.

Altink, W. M. M., Roe, R. A. and Greuter, M. A. M. (1991) Recruitment and selection in the Netherlands. *European Review of Applied Psychology,* **41**, 35–43.

Amir, Y., Kovarsky, Y. and Sharan, S. (1970) Peer nominations as a predictor of multistage promotions in a ramified organisation. *Journal of Applied Psychology,* **54**, 462–469.

Anastasi, A. (1981) Coaching, test sophistication, and developed abilities. *American Psychologist,* **36**, 1086–1093.

Anderson, C. W. (1960) The relation between speaking times and decision in the employment interview. *Journal of Applied Psychology,* **44**, 267–268.

Anderson, V. V. (1929) *Psychiatry in industry.* Holt, New York.

Anderson, N. and Shackleton, V. (1990) Decision making in the graduate selection interview: a field study. *Journal of Occupational Psychology* **63**, 63–76.

Andrews, L. G. (1922) A grading system for picking men. *Sales Management,* **4**, 143–144.

Anstey, E. (1966) The Civil Service Administrative Class and the Diplomatic Service: a follow up. *Occupational Psychology,* **40**, 139–151.

Anstey, E. (1977) A 30-year follow-up of the CSSB procedure, with lessons for the future. *Journal of Occupational Psychology,* **50**, 149–159.

Arnold, J. D., Rauschenberger, J. M., Soubel, W. G. and Guion, R. G. (1982) Validation and utility of a strength test for selecting steelworkers. *Journal of Applied Psychology,* **67**, 588–604.

Arthur, W., Barrett, G. V. and Doverspike, D. (1990) Validation of an information-processing-based test battery for the prediction of handling accidents among petro-leum-product transport drivers. *Journal of Applied Psychology,* **75**, 621–628.

Arvey, R. D. (1972) Some comments on culture fair tests. *Personnel Psychology,* **25**, 433–448.

Arvey, R. D. (1979a) Unfair discrimination in the employment interview: legal and psychological aspects. *Psychological Bulletin,* **86**, 736–765.

Arvey, R. D. (1979b) *Fairness in selecting employees.* Addison Wesley, Reading, Mass.

Arvey, R. D. and Begalla, M. E. (1975) Analysing the homemaker job using the Position Analysis Questionnaire (PAQ). *Journal of Applied Psychology,* **60**, 513–517.

Arvey, R. D., Gordon, M., Massengil, D. P. and Mussio, S. (1975) Differential dropout rates of minority and majority job candidates due to 'time lags' between selection procedures. *Personnel Psychology,* **28**, 175–180.

Arvey, R. D., McGowen, S. and Horgan, D. (1981) The use of experience requirements in selecting employees. (Unpublished.)

Arvey, R. D., Miller, H. E., Gould, R. and Burch, P. (1987) Interview validity for selecting sales clerks. *Personnel Psychology,* **40**, 1–12.

Arvey, R. D., Landon, T. E., Nutting, S. M. and Maxwell, S. E. (1992) Development of physical ability tests for police officers: a construct validation approach. *Journal of Applied Psychology,* **77**, 996–1009.

Ash, P. and Kroeker, L. P. (1975) Personnel selection, classification, and placement.

Annual Review of Psychology, **26**, 481–507.

Ash, P., Slora, K. B., and Britton, C. F. (1990) Police agency officer selection practices. *Journal of Police Science and Administration,* **17**, 258–269.

Ash, R. A. (1980) Self-assessments of five types of typing ability. *Personnel Psychology,* **33**, 273–282.

Asher, J. J. and Sciarrino, J. A. (1974) Realistic work sample tests: a review. *Personnel Psychology,* **27**, 519–533.

Ashworth, S. D., Osburn, H. G., Callender, J. C. and Boyle, K. A. (1992) The effects of unrepresented studies on the robustness of validity generalisation results. *Personnel Psychology,* **45**, 341–361.

Austin, J. T. and Villanova, P. (1992) The criterion problem: 1917–1992. *Journal of Applied Psychology,* **77**, 836–874.

Avolio, B. J. and Barrett, G. V. (1987) Effects of age stereotyping in a simulated interview. *Psychology and Aging,* **2**, 56–63.

Baehr, M. E. and Orban, J. A. (1989) The role of intellectual abilities and personality characteristics in determining success in higher-level positions. *Journal of Vocational Behavior,* **35**, 270–287.

Baird, L. L. (1985) Do grades and tests predict adult accomplishment? *Research in Higher Education,* **23**, 3–85.

Banks, M. H., Jackson, P. R., Stafford, E. M. and Warr, P. B. (1983) The Job Components Inventory and the analysis of jobs requiring limited skill. *Personnel Psychology,* **36**, 57–66.

Baron, R. A. (1983) "Sweet smell of success"? The impact of pleasant artificial scents on evaluations of job applicants. *Journal of Applied Psychology,* **68**, 709–713.

Barrett, G. V. (1990) Personnel selection after Watson, Hopkins, Atonio, and Martin (WHAM). *Forensic Reports,* **3**, 179–203.

Barrett, G. V. (1992) Clarifying construct validity: definitions, processes, and models. *Human Performance,* **5**, 13–58.

Barrett, G. V. and Depinet, R. L. (1991) A reconsideration of testing for competence rather than for intelligence. *American Psychologist,* **46**, 1012–1024.

Barrett, G. V., Phillips, J. S. and Alexander, R. A. (1981) Concurrent and predictive validity designs: a critical reanalysis. *Journal of Applied Psychology,* **66**, 1–6.

Barrett, G. V., Caldwell, M. S. and Alexander, R. A. (1985) The concept of dynamic criteria: a critical reanalysis. *Personnel Psychology,* **38**, 41–56.

Barrett, G. V., Alexander, R. A. and Doverspike, D. (1992) The implications for personnel selection of apparent declines in predictive validities over time: a critique of Hulin, Henry and Noon. *Personnel Psychology,* **45**, 601–617.

Barrick, M. R. and Mount, M. K. (1991) The big five personality dimensions and job performance: a meta-analysis. *Personnel Psychology,* **44**, 1–26.

Bartlett, C. J., Bobko, P., Mosier, S. B. and Hannan, R. (1978) Testing for fairness with a modified multiple regression strategy: an alternative to differential analysis. *Personnel Psychology,* **31**, 233–241.

Bartram, D. and Dale, H. C. A. (1982) The Eysenck Personality Inventory as a selection test for military pilots. *Journal of Occupational Psychology,* **55**, 287–296.

Bass, B. M. (1962) Further evidence on the dynamic character of criteria. *Personnel Psychology,* **15**, 93–98.

Baxter, J. C., Brock, B., Hill, P. C. and Rozelle, R. M. (1981) Letters of recommendation: a question of value. *Journal of Applied Psychology,* **66**, 296–301.

Bayne, R. (1982) Palmistry: a critical review. In Mackenzie Davey, D. and Harris, M. (eds) *Judging people,* McGraw Hill, London.

Becker, T. E. and Colquitt, A. L. (1992) Potential versus actual faking of a biodata form:

an analysis along several dimensions of item type. *Personnel Psychology*, **45**, 389–406.

Bemis, S. E. (1968) Occupational validity of the General Aptitude Test Battery. *Journal of Applied Psychology*, **52**, 240–244.

Bender, W. R. G. and Loveless, H. E. (1958) Validation studies involving successive classes of trainee stenographers. *Personnel Psychology*, **11**, 491–508.

Bernardin, H. J. (1977) The relationship of personality variables to organisational withdrawal. *Personnel Psychology*, **30**, 17–27.

Bersoff, D. N. (1981) Testing and the law. *American Psychologist*, **36**, 1047–1056.

Bingham, W. V. and Freyd, M. (1926) *Procedures in employment psychology*. Shaw, Chicago.

Bobko, P. and Karren, R. (1982) The estimation of standard deviation in utility analysis. *Proceedings of the Academy of Management*, **42**, 272–276.

Bobko, P., Karren, R. and Parkington, J. J. (1983) Estimation of standard deviations in utility analyses: an empirical test. *Journal of Applied Psychology*, **68**, 170–176.

Bobko, P., Shetzer, L. and Russell, C. (1991) Estimating the standard deviation of professors' worth: the effects of frame and presentation order in utility analysis. *Journal of Occupational Psychology*, **64**, 179–188.

Boehm, V. R. (1972) Negro–white differences in validity of employment and training selection procedures: summary of research evidence. *Journal of Applied Psychology*, **56**, 33–39.

Boehm, V. R. (1977) Differential prediction: a methodological artifact. *Journal of Applied Psychology*, **62**, 146–154.

Booth, R. F., McNally, M. S. and Berry, N. H. (1978) Predicting performance effectiveness in paramedical occupations. *Personnel Psychology*, **31**, 581–593.

Borman, W. C. (1979) Format and training effects on rating accuracy and rater errors. *Journal of Applied Psychology*, **64**, 410–421.

Borman, W. C., White, L. A., Pulakos, E. D. and Oppler, S. H. (1991) Models of supervisory job performance ratings. *Journal of Applied Psychology*, **76**, 863–872.

Boudreau, J. W. (1983a) Economic considerations in estimating the utility of human resource productivity improvement programs. *Personnel Psychology*, **36**, 551–576.

Boudreau, J. W. (1983b) Effects of employee flows on utility analysis of human resource productivity improvement programs. *Journal of Applied Psychology*, **68**, 396–406.

Brannick, M. T., Michaels, C. E. and Baker, D. P. (1989) Construct validity of in-basket scores. *Journal of Applied Psychology*, **74**, 957–963.

Brass, D. J. and Oldham, G. R. (1976) Validating an In-Basket test using an alternative set of leadership scoring dimensions. *Journal of Applied Psychology*, **61**, 652–657.

Bray, D. W. and Campbell, R. J. (1968) Selection of salesmen by means of an assessment center. *Journal of Applied Psychology*, **52**, 36–41.

Bray, D. W. and Grant, D. L. (1966) The assessment center in the measurement of potential for business management. *Psychological Monographs*, **80**, (17, whole No. 625).

Breaugh, J. A. and Mann, R. B. (1984) Recruiting source effects: a test of two alternative explanations. *Journal of Occupational Psychology*, **57**, 261–267.

British Psychological Society (1985) The use of tests by psychologists: report on a survey of the members of the British Psychological Society. BPS, Leicester.

Brogden, H. E. (1950) When testing pays off. *Personnel Psychology*, **2**, 171–183.

Brogden, H. E. and Taylor, E. K. (1950) A theory and classification of criterion bias. *Educational and Psychological Measurement*, **10**, 159–186.

Brousseau, K. R. and Prince, J. B. (1981) Job–person dynamics: an extension of longitudinal research. *Journal of Applied Psychology*, **66**, 59–62.

Brown, S. H. (1978) Long-term validity of a personal history item scoring procedure.

Journal of Applied Psychology, **63**, 673–676.

Brown, S. H. (1979) Validity distortions associated with a test in use. *Journal of Applied Psychology*, **64**, 460–462.

Brown, S. H. (1981) Validity generalisation and situational moderation in the life insurance industry. *Journal of Applied Psychology*, **66**, 664–670.

Brown, C. W. and Ghiselli, E. E. (1953) The prediction of proficiency of taxicab-drivers. *Journal of Applied Psychology*, **37**, 437–439.

Browning, R. C. (1968) Validity of reference ratings from previous employers. *Personnel Psychology*, **21**, 389–393.

Bruchon-Schweitzer, M. and Ferrieux, D. (1991) Une enquete sur le recrutement en France. *European Review of Applied Psychology*, **41**, 9–17.

Brush, D. H. and Owens, W. A. (1979) Implementation and evaluation of an assessment classification model for manpower utilisation. *Personnel Psychology*, **32**, 369–383.

Buckley, M. R. and Eder, R. W. (1988) B. M. Springbett and the notion of the "snap decision" in the interview. *Journal of Management*, **14**, 59–67.

Buel, W. D. (1964) Voluntary female clerical turnover: the concurrent and predictive validity of a weighted application blank. *Journal of Applied Psychology*, **48**, 180–182.

Bureau of National Affairs (1979) *Recruitment policies and methods*. BNA, Washington DC.

Burke, M. J. (1984) Validity generalisation: a review and critique of the correlation model. *Personnel Psychology*, **37**, 93–115.

Burke, M. J. and Frederick, J. T. (1984) Two modified procedures for estimating standard deviations in utility analyses. *Journal of Applied Psychology*, **69**, 482–489.

Buros, O. K. (1970) *Personality tests and reviews*. Gryphon Press, Highland Park NJ.

Burrington, D. D. (1982) A review of state government employment application forms for suspect inquiries. *Public Personnel Management Journal*, **11**, 55–60.

Byham, W. C. (1971) The assessment center as an aid in management development. *Training and Development Journal*, **25**, 10–22.

Caldwell, D. F. and O'Reilly, C. A. (1990) Measuring person–job fit with a profile-comparison process. *Journal of Applied Psychology*, **75**, 648–657.

Callan, J. P. (1972) An attempt to use the MMPI as a predictor of failure in military training. *British Journal of Psychiatry*, **121**, 553–557.

Callender, J. C. and Osburn, H. G. (1980) Development and test of a new model for validity generalisation. *Journal of Applied Psychology*, **65**, 543–558.

Callender, J. C. and Osburn, H. G. (1981) Testing the constancy of validity with computer-generated sampling distributions of the multiplicative model variance estimate: results for petroleum industry validation research. *Journal of Applied Psychology*, **66**, 274–281.

Campbell, C. C., Ford, P., Rumsey, M. G., Pulakos, E. D., Borman, W. C., Felker, D. B., de Vera, M. V. and Riegelhaupt, B. J. (1990) Development of multiple job performance measures in a representative sample of jobs. *Personnel Psychology*, **43**, 277–300.

Campbell, J. P., Dunnette, M. D., Lawler, E. E. and Weick, K. E. (1970) *Managerial behavior, performance, and effectiveness*. McGraw Hill, New York.

Campbell, R. J. and Bray, D. W. (1967) Assessment centers: an aid in management selection. *Personnel Administration*, **30**, 6–13.

Campion, J. E. (1972) Work sampling for personnel selection. *Journal of Applied Psychology*, **56**, 40–44.

Campion, M. A. (1983) Personnel selection for physically demanding jobs: review and recommendations. *Personnel Psychology*, **36**, 527–550.

Campion, M. A. and Campion, J. E. (1987) Evaluation of an interviewee skills training program in a natural field experiment. *Personnel Psychology*, **40**, 675–691.

Campion, M. A., Pursell, E. D. and Brown, B. K. (1988) Structured interviewing: raising the psychometric qualities of the employment interview. *Personnel Psychology*, **41**, 25–42.

Carey, N. B. (1991) Setting standards and diagnosing training needs with surrogate job performance measures. *Military Psychology*, **3**, 135–150.

Carlson, R. E. (1967) Selection interview decisions: the effect of interviewer experience, relative quota situation, and applicant sample on interviewer decisions. *Personnel Psychology*, **20**, 259–280.

Carrier, M. R., Dalessio, A. T., and Brown, S. H. (1990) Correspondence between estimates of content and criterion-related validity values. *Personnel Psychology*, **43**, 85–100.

Carroll, S. J. and Nash, A. N. (1972) Effectiveness of a forced-choice reference check. *Personnel Administration*, **35**, 42–146.

Cascio, W. F. (1975) Accuracy of verifiable biographical information blank responses. *Journal of Applied Psychology*, **60**, 767–769.

Cascio, W. F. (1976) Turnover, biographical data, and fair employment practice. *Journal of Applied Psychology*, **61**, 576–580.

Cascio, W. F. (1982) *Costing human resources: the financial impact of behavior in organisations*. Kent, Boston MA.

Cascio, W. F. and Phillips, N. F. (1979) Performance testing: a rose among thorns? *Personnel Psychology*, **32**, 751–766.

Cascio, W. F., Alexander, R. A. and Barrett, G. V. (1988) Setting cutoff scores: legal, psychometric, and professional issues and guidelines. *Personnel Psychology*, **41**, 1–24.

Cash, T. F., Gillen, B. and Burns, D. S. (1977) Sexism and "beautyism" in personnel consultant decision making. *Journal of Applied Psychology*, **62**, 301–310.

Cattell, R. B. (1936) *The fight for our national intelligence*. P. S. King, London.

Cattell, R. B. (1965) *The scientific analysis of personality*. Penguin, Harmondsworth, Middx.

Cattell, R. B. (1986) The 16PF in personnel work. Seminar at Independent Assessment and Research Centre, London, June 1986.

Cattell, R. B., Eber, H. W. and Tatsuoka, M. M. (1970) *Handbook for the 16PF questionnaire*. IPAT, Champaign, IL.

Cecil, E. A., Paul, R. J. and Olins, R. A. (1973) Perceived importance of selected variables used to evaluate male and female job applicants. *Personnel Psychology*, **26**, 397–404.

Cleary, T. A. and Hilton, T. I. (1986) Test bias: prediction of grades of Negro and white students in integrated colleges. *Journal of Educational Measurement*, **5**, 115–124.

Clark, J. G. and Owens, W. A. (1954) A validation study of the Worthington Personal History Blank. *Journal of Applied Psychology*, **38**, 85–88.

Cline, V. B. (1964) Interpersonal perception. In Maher, B. A. (ed.) *Progress in experimental personality research Vol. 1*. Academic Press, New York.

Cohen, B. M. Moses, J. L. and Byham, W. C. (1974) *The validity of assessment centers: a literature review*. Development Dimensions Press, Pittsburgh.

Cohen, S. L. (1978) Standardisation of assessment center technology: some critical concerns. *Journal of Assessment Center Technology*, **1**, 1–10.

Cohen, S. L. and Sands, L. (1978) The effects of order of exercise presentation on assesment center performance: one standardisation concern. *Personnel Psychology*, **31**, 35–46.

Collins, R. (1979) *The credential society: an historical sociology of educational stratification*. Academic Press, New York.

Commission for Racial Equality (1983) *The West Yorkshire Passenger Transport Executive (Bradford Metro): report of a formal investigation*. CRE, London.

Commission for Racial Equality (1984a) *St Chads' Hospital: report of a formal investigation.* CRE, London.

Commission for Racial Equality (1984b) *Dunlop Ltd, Leicester: report of a formal investigation.* CRE, London.

Commission for Racial Equality (1990) *Lines of progress: an enquiry into selection and equal opportunities in London Underground.* CRE, London.

Commission for Racial Equality (1992) *Psychometric tests and racial equality.* CRE, London.

Cook, M. (1979) *Perceiving others: the psychology of interpersonal perception.* Methuen, London.

Cook, M. (1992) An evaluation of the DISC/Personal Profile Analysis. *Selection and Development Review,* **8,** 3–6.

Cook, M. (1993) *Levels of personality.* 2nd Edition. Cassell, London.

Cooper, G. and Sobol, R. B. (1969) Seniority and testing under fair employment laws. *Harvard Law Review,* **82,** 1598–1679.

Cooper, R. and Payne, R. (1967) Extraversion and some aspects of work behavior. *Personnel Psychology,* **20,** 45–57.

Cooper, W. H. (1981) Ubiquitous halo. *Psychological Bulletin,* **90,** 218–244.

Cornelius, E. T., DeNisi, A. S. and Blencoe, A. G. (1984) Expert and naive raters using the PAQ: does it matter? *Personnel Psychology,* **37,** 453–464.

Cox, J. A. and Krumboltz, J. D. (1958) Racial bias in peer ratings of basic airmen. *Sociometry,* **21,** 292–299.

Coward, W. M. and Sackett, P. R. (1990) Linearity of ability–performance relationships: a reconfirmation. *Journal of Applied Psychology,* **75,** 297–300.

Crawley, B., Pinder, R. and Herriot, P. (1990) Assessment centre dimensions, personality and aptitudes. *Journal of Occupational Psychology,* **63,** 211–216.

Crites, J. O. (1969) *Vocational psychology.* McGraw Hill, New York.

Cronbach, L. J. (1980) Selection theory for a political world. *Public Personnel Management Journal,* **9,** 37–50.

Cronbach, L. J. (1984) *Essentials of psychological testing.* 4th Edition. Harper and Row, New York.

Cronbach, L. J. and Gleser, G. C. (1965) *Psychological tests and personnel decisions.* University of Illinois Press, Urbana, IL.

Culpin, M. and Smith, M. (1930) *The nervous temperament.* Medical Research Council, Industrial Health Research Board, London.

Cunningham, J. W., Boese, R. R., Neeb, R. W. and Pass, J. J. (1983) Systematically derived work dimensions: factor analyses of the Occupation Analysis Inventory. *Journal of Applied Psychology,* **68,** 232–252.

Cureton, E. E. (1950) Validity, reliability, and baloney. *Educational and Psychological Measurement,* **10,** 94–96.

Darlington, R. B. and Stauffer, G. F. (1966) A method for choosing a cutting point on a test. *Journal of Applied Psychology,* **50,** 229–231.

Dawes, R. M. (1971) A case study of graduate admissions: application of three principles of human decision making. *American Psychologist,* **26,** 180–188.

Deadrick, D. L. and Madigan, R. M. (1990) Dynamic criteria revisited: a longitudinal study of performance stability and predictive validity. *Personnel Psychology,* **43,** 717–744.

Dedrick, E. J. and Dobbins, G. H. (1991) The influence of subordinate age on managerial actions—an attributional analysis. *Journal of Organisational Behavior,* **12,** 367–377.

De Nisi, A. S. and Shaw, J. B. (1977) Investigation of the uses of self-reports of abilities. *Journal of Applied Psychology,* **62,** 641–644.

Dickey-Bryant, L., Lautenschlager, G. J., Mendoza, J. L. and Abrahams, N. (1986) Facial attractiveness and its relation to occupational success. *Journal of Applied Psychology*, **71**, 16–19.

Dipboye, R. L., Arvey, R. D. and Terpstra, D. E. (1977) Sex and physical attractiveness of raters and applicants as determinants of résumé evaluation. *Journal of Applied Psychology*, **62**, 288–294.

Distefano, M. K., Pryer, M. W. and Erffmeyer, R. C. (1983) Application of content validity methods to the development of a job-related performance rating criterion. *Personnel Psychology*, **36**, 621–631.

Dobson, P. and Williams, A. (1989) The validation of the selection of male British Army officers. *Journal of Occupational Psychology*, **62**, 313–325.

Dorcus, R. M. and Jones, M. H. (1950) *Handbook of employee selection*, McGraw Hill, New York.

Dougherty, T. W., Ebert, R. J. and Callender, J. C. (1986) Policy capturing in the employment interview. *Journal of Applied Psychology*, **71**, 9–15.

Downs, S., Farr, R. M. and Colbeck, L. (1978) Self-appraisal: a convergence of selection and guidance. *Journal of Occupational Psychology*, **51**, 271–278.

Drakeley, R. J. Herriot, P. and Jones, A. (1988) Biographical data, training success and turnover. *Journal of Occupational Psychology*, **61**, 145–152.

Dreher, G. F., Ash, R. A. and Hancock, P. (1988) The role of the traditional research design in underestimating the validity of the employment interview. *Personnel Psychology*, **41**, 315–327.

Dubois, C. L. Z., Sackett, P. R., Zedeck, S. and Fogli, L. (in press) Further exploration of typical and maximum performance criteria: definitional issues, prediction and white–black differences. *Journal of Applied Psychology*.

Dulewicz, S. V. and Keenay, G. A. (1979) A practically oriented and objective method for classifying and assigning senior jobs. *Journal of Occupational Psychology*, **52**, 155–166.

Dunnette, M. D. (1966) *Personnel selection and placement*. Tavistock, London.

Dunnette, M. D. (1972) *Validity study results for jobs relevant to the petroleum refining industry*. American Petroleum Institute.

Dunnette, M. D. (1976) Aptitudes, abilities, and skills. In Dunette, M. D. (ed.) *Handbook of industrial and organisational psychology*. Rand McNally, Chicago.

Dunnette, M. D. (1982) *Development and validation of an industry wide electricity power plant operator selection system*. Personnel Decisions Research Institute, Minneapolis, MN.

Dunnette, M. D. and Kirchner, W. K. (1959) A check list for differentiating different kinds of sales jobs. *Personnel Psychology*, **12**, 421–429.

Dunnette, M. D. and Maetzold, J. (1955) Use of a weighted application blank in hiring seasonal employees. *Journal of Applied Psychology*, **39**, 308–310.

Dunnette, M. D., McCartney, J., Carlson, H. C. and Kirchner, W. K. (1962) A study of faking behavior on a forced-choice self-description checklist. *Personnel Psychology*, **15**, 13–24.

Eaton, N. K., Wing, H. and Mitchell, K. J. (1985) Alternate methods of estimating the dollar value of performance. *Personnel Psychology*, **38**, 27–40.

Ebel, R. L. (1977) Comments on some problems of employment testing. *Personnel Psychology*, **30**, 55–63.

Elliott, A. G. P. (1981) Some implications of lie scale scores in real-life selection. *Journal of Occupational Psychology*, **54**, 9–16.

Ellis, A. and Conrad, H. S. (1948) The validity of personality inventories in military practice. *Psychological Bulletin*, **45**, 385–426.

Epstein, S. (1979) The stability of behavior: I. On predicting most of the people much of the time. *Journal of Personality and Social Psychology*, **37**, 1097–1126.

Ewart, E., Seashore, S. E. and Tiffin, J. (1941) A factor analysis of an industrial merit rating scale. *Journal of Applied Psychology*, **25**, 481–486.

Eysenck, H. J. (1953) *The structure of human personality*. Methuen, London.

Farh, J., Werbel, J. D. and Bedeian, A. G. (198) An empirical investigation of self-appraisal-based performance evaluation. *Personnel Psychology*, **41**, 141–156.

Farr, J. L. (1973) Response requirements and primacy–recency effects in a simulated selection interview. *Journal of Applied Psychology*, **57**, 228–233.

Feltham, R. (1988a) Validity of a police assessment centre: a 1–19-year follow-up. *Journal of Occupational Psychology*, **61**, 129–144.

Feltham, R. (1988b) Assesment centre decision making: judgemental vs. mechanical. *Journal of Occupational Psychology*, **61**, 237–241.

Fineman, S. (1977) The achievement motive construct and its measurement: where are we now? *British Journal of Psychology*, **68**, 1–22.

Flanagan, J. C. (1946) The experimental validation of a selection procedure. *Educational and Psychological Measurement*, **6**, 445–466.

Flanagan, J. C. (1954) The critical incident technique. *Psychological Bulletin*, **51**, 327–358.

Fleishman, E. A. (1979) Evaluating physical abilities required by jobs. *Personnel Administrator*, **24**, 82–92.

Fleishman, E. A. and Mumford, M. D. (1991) Evaluating classifications of job behavior: a construct validation of the ability requirement scales. *Personnel Psychology*, **44**, 523–575.

Forsythe, S., Drake, M. F. and Cox, C. E. (1985) Influence of applicant's dress on interviewer's selection decisions. *Journal of Applied Psychology*, **70**, 374–378.

Fowler, R. D. (1985) Landmarks in computer-assisted psychological assessment. *Journal of Consulting and Clinical Psychology*, **53**, 748–759.

Fox, S. and Dinur, Y. (1988) Validity of self-assessment: a field evaluation. *Personnel Psychology*, **41**, 581–592.

Frederiksen, N., Saunders, D. R. and Wand, B. (1957) The In-Basket test. *Psychological Monographs*, **71**, (whole No. 438).

Gandy, J. A., Outerbridge, A. N., Sharf, J. C. and Dye, D. A. (1989) *Development and initial validation of the Individual Achievement Record*. Office of Personnel Management, Washington DC.

Gardner, K. E. and Williams, A. P. O. (1973) A twenty-five year follow-up of an extended interview selection procedure in the Royal Navy. *Occupational Psychology*, **47**, 1–13.

Garwood, M. K., Anderson, L. E. and Greengart, B. J. (1991) Determining job groups: application of hierarchical agglomerative cluster analysis in different job analysis situations. *Personnel Psychology*, **44**, 743–762.

Gatewood, R., Thornton, G. C. and Hennessey, H. W. (1990) Reliability of exercise ratings in the leaderless group discussion. *Journal of Occupational Psychology*, **63**, 331–342.

Gaugler, B. B. and Rudolph, A. S. (1992) The influence of assessee performance variation on assessors' judgements. *Personnel Psychology*, **45**, 77–98.

Gaugler, B. B. and Thornton, G. C. (1989) Number of assessment center dimensions as a determinant of assessor accuracy. *Journal of Applied Psychology*, **74**, 611–618.

Gaugler, B. B., Rosenthal, D. B., Thornton, G. C. and Bentson, C. (1987) Meta-analysis of assessment center validity. *Journal of Applied Psychology*, **72**, 493–511.

Ghiselli, E. E. (1959) The development of processes for indirect or synthetic validity (a symposium). 2. The generalisation of validity. *Personnel Psychology*, **12**, 397–402.

Ghiselli, E. E. (1966a) The validity of a personnel interview. *Personnel Psychology*, **19**, 389–394.

Ghiselli, E. E. (1966b) *The validity of occupational aptitude tests*, Wiley, New York.

Ghiselli, E. E. (1973) The validity of aptitude tests in personnel selection. *Personnel Psychology*, **26**, 461–477.

Ghiselli, E. E. and Haire, M. (1960) The validation of selection tests in the light of the dynamic character of criteria. *Personnel Psychology*, **13**, 225–231.

Gifford, R., Ng, C. F. and Wilkinson, M. (1985) Nonverbal cues in the employment interview: links between applicant qualities and interviewer judgements. *Journal of Applied Psychology*, **70**, 729–736.

Glass, G. V. (1976) Primary, secondary, and meta-analysis of research. *Educational Researcher*, **5**, 3–8.

Glennon, J. R., Albright, L. E. and Owens, W. A. (1963) *A catalog of life history items*. American Psychological Association, Chicago.

Goldsmith, D. B. (1922) The use of a personal history blank as a salesmanship test. *Journal of Applied Psychology*, **6**, 149–155.

Goldstein, I. L. (1971) The application blank: how honest are the responses? *Journal of Applied Psychology*, **55**, 491–492.

Goldstein, B. (1975) *Screening for emotional and psychological fitness in correctional officer hiring*. Resource Center on Correctional Law and Legal Services, Washington DC.

Goldstein, B. L. and Patterson, P. O. (1988) Turning back the Title VII clock: the resegregation of the American work force through validity generalisation. *Journal of Vocational Behavior*, **33**, 452–462.

Gordon, H. W. and Leighty, R. (1988) Importance of specialised cognitive functions in the selection of military pilots. *Journal of Applied Psychology*, **73**, 38–45.

Gordon, M. E. and Fitzgibbons, W. J. (1982) Empirical test of the validity of seniority as a factor in staffing decisions. *Journal of Applied Psychology*, **67**, 311–319.

Gordon, M. E. and Kleiman, L. S. (1976) The prediction of trainability using a work-sample test and an aptitude test: a direct comparison. *Personnel Psychology*, **29**, 243–253.

Gottfredson, L. S. (1988) Reconsidering fairness: a matter of social and ethical priorities. *Journal of Vocational Behavior*, **33**, 293–319.

Gough, H. G. (1962) Clinical vs statistical prediction in psychology. In Postman, L. (ed.) *Psychology in the making*. Knopf, New York.

Gough, H. G. (1969) *Manual for the California Psychological Inventory*. Consulting Psychologists Press, Palo Alto.

Grant, D. L. and Bray, D. W. (1969) Contributions of the interview to assessment of management potential. *Journal of Applied Psychology*, **53**, 24–34.

Graves, L. M. and Karren, R. J. (1992) Interviewer decision processes and effectiveness: an experimental policy-capturing investigation. *Personnel Psychology*, **45**, 313–340.

Graves, L. M. and Powell, G. N. (1988) An investigation of sex discrimination in recruiters' evaluations of actual applicants. *Journal of Applied Psychology*, **73**, 20–29.

Grimsley, G. and Jarrett, H. F. (1973) The relationship of past management achievement to test measures obtained in the employment situation: methodology and results. *Personnel Psychology*, **26**, 31–48.

Guastello, S. J. (1992) Drugs test results and workforce productivity: review of premises and findings. (Unpublished.)

Guastello, S. J. and Rieke, M. L. (1991) A review and critique of honesty test research. *Behavioral Sciences and the Law*, **9**, 501–523.

Guilford, J. P. (1959) *Personality*. McGraw-Hill, New York.

Guilford, J. P. (1967) *The nature of human intelligence*. McGraw-Hill, New York.

Guion, R. M. (1961) Criterion measurement and personnel judgement. *Personnel Psychology*, **14**, 141–149.

Guion, R. M. (1965a) *Personnel testing*. McGraw-Hill, New York.

Guion, R. M. (1965b) Synthetic validity in a small company: a demonstration. *Personnel Psychology*, **18**, 49–63.

Guion, R. M. (1977) Content validity—the source of my discontent. *Applied Psychological Measurement*, **1**, 1–10.

Guion, R. M. (1978) "Content validity" in moderation. *Personnel Psychology*, **31**, 205–213.

Guion, R. M. and Gottier, R. F. (1965) Validity of personality measures in personnel selection. *Personnel Psychology*, **18**, 135–164.

Gustad, J. W. (1956) Psychological test reviews: Edwards Personal Preference Schedule. *Journal of Consulting and Clinical Psychology*, **20**, 322–324.

Hakel, M. D. (1982) The employment interview. In Rowland, K. M. and Ferris, G. R. (eds.) *Personnel management*, Allyn and Bacon, Boston.

Hakel, M. D., Dobmeyer, T. W. and Dunnette, M. D. (1970) Relative importance of three content dimensions in overall suitability ratings of job applicants' resumés. *Journal of Applied Psychology*, **54**, 65–71.

Hall, W. B. and MacKinnon, D. W. (1969) Personality inventory correlates of creativity among architects. *Journal of Applied Psychology*, **53**, 322–326.

Hanges, P. J., Schneider, B. and Niles, K. (1990) Stability of performance: an interactionist perspective. *Journal of Applied Psychology*, **75**, 658–667.

Hansen, J. C. (1976) Exploring new directions for Strong Campbell Interest Inventory occupational scale construction. *Journal of Vocational Behavior*, **9**, 147–160.

Hargrave, G. E. and Hiatt, D. (1989) Use of the California Psychological Inventory in law enforcement officer selection. *Journal of Personality Assessment*, **53**, 267–277.

Harrell, T. W. (1972) High earning MBAs. *Personnel Psychology*, **25**, 523–530.

Harrell, T. W. and Harrell, M. S. (1945) Army General Classification Test scores for civilian occupations. *Educational and Psychological Measurement*, **5**, 229–239.

Harris, M. M. (1989) Reconsidering the employment interview: a review of recent literature and suggestions for future research. *Personnel Psychology*, **42**, 691–726.

Harris, M. M., Becker, A. and Smith, D. E. (in press) Does the assessment center scoring method affect the dimensionality of ratings? *Journal of Applied Psychology*.

Hartigan, J. A. and Wigdor, A. K. (1989) *Fairness in employment testing*. National Academy Press, Washington DC.

Hartshorne, H. and May, M. A. (1928) *Studies in the nature of character. Vol 1. Studies in deceit*. MacMillan, New York.

Harvey, R. J., Friedman, L., Hakel, M. and Cornelius, E. T. (1988) Dimensionality of the Job Element Inventory, a simplified worker-oriented job analysis questionnaire. *Journal of Applied Psychology*, **73**, 639–646.

Hawk, J. A. (1970) Linearity of criterion-GATB aptitude relationships. *Measurement and Evaluation in Guidance*, **2**, 249–251.

Hedge, J. W. and Teachout, M. S. (1992) An interview approach to work sample criterion measurement. *Journal of Applied Psychology*, **77**, 453–456.

Helmreich, R. L., Sawin, L. L. and Carsrud, A. L. (1986) The honeymoon effect in job performance: temporal increases in the predictive power of achievement motivation. *Journal of Applied Psychology*, **71**, 185–188.

Helson, R. and Moane, G. (1987) Personality change in women from college to midlife. *Journal of Personality and Social Psychology*, **53**, 176–186.

Hemphill, J. K. and Sechrest, L. B. (1952) A comparison of three criteria of aircrew effectiveness in combat over Korea. *Journal of Applied Psychology*, **36**, 323–327.

Heneman, R. L. (1986) The relationship between supervisory ratings and results-oriented measures of performance: a meta-analysis. *Personnel Psychology*, **39**, 811–826.

Heron, A. (1954) Satisfaction and satisfactoriness: complementary aspects of occupational adjustment. *Occupational Psychology*, **28**, 140–153.

Herriot, P. and Rothwell, C. (1983) Expectations and impressions in the graduate selection interview. *Journal of Occupational Psychology*, **56**, 303–314.

Herriot, P. and Wingrove, J. (1984) Decision processes in graduate pre-selection. *Journal of Occupational Psychology*, **57**, 269–275.

Herrnstein, R. J. (1973) *IQ in the meritocracy*. Allen Lane, London.

Herzberg, F. (1954) Temperament measures in industrial selection. *Journal of Applied Psychology*, **38**, 81–84.

Hinrichs, J. R. (1978) An eight year follow-up of a management assessment center. *Journal of Applied Psychology*, **63**, 596–601.

Hinrichs, J. R. and Haanpera, S. (1976) Reliability of measurement in situational exercises: an assessment of the assessment center method. *Personnel Psychology*, **29**, 31–40.

Hirsch, H. R., Northrop, L. C. and Schmidt, F. L. (1986) Validity generalisation results for law enforcement occupations. *Personnel Psychology*, **39**, 399–420.

Hitt, M. A. and Barr, S. H. (1989) Managerial selection decision models: examination of configural cue processing. *Journal of Applied Psychology*, **74**, 53–61.

Hoffman, C. C., Nathan, B. R. and Holden, L. M. (1991) A comparison of validation criteria: objective versus subjective performance and self versus supervisor ratings. *Personnel Psychology*, **44**, 601–619.

Hogan, J. (1985) Tests for success in diver training. *Journal of Applied Psychology*, **70**, 219–224.

Hogan, J. (1991a) Structure of physical performance in occupational tasks. *Journal of Applied Psychology*, **76**, 495–507.

Hogan, J. (1991b) Physical abilities. In Dunnette, M. D. and Hough, L. M. (eds) *Handbook of industrial–organisational psychology*, Consulting Psychologists Press, Palo Alto.

Hogan, J. and Hogan, R. (1989) How to measure employee reliability. *Journal of Applied Psychology*, **74**, 273–279.

Hoiberg, A. and Pugh, W. M. (1978) Predicting Navy effectiveness: expectations, motivation, personality, aptitude, and background variables. *Personnel Psychology*, **31**, 841–852.

Hollander, E. P. (1965) Validity of peer nominations in predicting a distant performance criterion. *Journal of Applied Psychology*, **49**, 434–438.

Hollingworth, H. H. (1922) *Vocational Psychology*, Appleton Century Crofts, New York.

Hollman, T. D. (1972) Employment interviewers' errors in processing positive and negative information. *Journal of Applied Psychology*, **56**, 130–134.

Holt, T. (1977) A view from Albemarle. *Personnel Psychology*, **30**, 65–80.

Hough, L. M. (1988) Personality assessment for selection and placement decisions. Paper presented at Third Annual Conference of the Society for Industrial and Organisational Psychology, Dallas, TX, April 21 1988.

Hough, L. M. (in press) The "big five" personality variables—construct confusion: description versus prediction. *Human Performance*.

Hough, L. M., Keyes, M. A., and Dunnette, M. D. (1983) An evaluation of three "alternative" selection procedures. *Personnel Psychology*, **36**, 261–276.

Hough, L. M., Eaton, N. K., Dunnette, M. D., Kamp, J. D. and McCloy, R. A. (1990) Criterion-related validities of personality constructs and the effect of response distortion on those validities. *Journal of Applied Psychology*, **75**, 581–595.

Hovland, C. I. and Wonderlic, E. F. (1939) Prediction of success by a standardised interview. *Journal of Applied Psychology*, **23**, 537–546.

Huck, J. R. and Bray, D. W. (1976) Management assessment center evaluations and subsequent job performance of white and black females. *Personnel Psychology*, **29**, 13–30.

Hughes, J. F., Dunn, J. F. and Baxter, B. (1956) The validity of selection instruments under operating conditions. *Personnel Psychology*, **9**, 321–423.

Hulin, C. L., Henry, R. A. and Noon, S. L. (1990) Adding a dimension: time as factor in the generalisability of predictive relationships. *Psychological Bulletin*, **107**, 328–340.

Hull, C. L. (1928) *Aptitude testing*. Harrap, London.

Humphreys, L. G. (1973) Statistical definitions of test validity for minority groups. *Journal of Applied Psychology*, **58**, 1–4.

Humphreys, L. G. (1986) Commentary. *Journal of Applied Psychology*, **29**, 421–437.

Hunter, J. E. (1983) A causal analysis of cognitive ability, job knowledge, and supervisory ratings. In Landy, F., Zedeck, S. and Cleveland, J. (eds) *Performance measurement and theory*. Erlbaum, Hillsdale, HJ.

Hunter, J. E. (1986) Cognitive ability, cognitive aptitudes, job knowledge, and job performance. *Journal of Vocational Behavior*, **29**, 340–362.

Hunter, J. E. and Hunter, R. F. (1984) Validity and utility of alternate predictors of job performance. *Psychological Bulletin*, **96**, 72–98.

Hunter, J. E. and Schmidt, F. L. (1978) Differential and single-group validity of employment tests by race: a critical analysis of three recent studies. *Journal of Applied Psychology*, **63**, 1–11.

Hunter, J. E., Schmidt, F. L. and Rauschenberger, J. M. (1977) Fairness of psychological tests: implications of four definitions for selection utility and minority hiring, *Journal of Applied Psychology*, **62**, 245–260.

Hunter, J. E., Schmidt, J. E. and Hunter, R. (1979) Differential validity of employment tests by race: a comprehensive review and analysis. *Psychological Bulletin*, **86**, 721–735.

Hunter, J. E., Schmidt, F. L. and Pearlman, K. (1982) History and accuracy of validity generalisation equations: a response to the Callender and Osburn reply. *Journal of Applied Psychology*, **67**, 853–858.

Hunter, J. E., Schmidt, F. L. and Judiesch, M. K. (1990) Individual differences in output variability as a function of job complexity. *Journal of Applied Psychology*, **75**, 28–42.

Iles, P. A. and Robertson, I. T. (1989) The impact of personnel selection procedures on candidates. In Herriot, P. (ed.) *Handbook of assessment in organisations*. Wiley, Chichester.

Imada, A. S. and Hakel, M. D. (1977) Influence of nonverbal communication and rater proximity on impressions and decisions in simulated employment interviews. *Journal of Applied Psychology*, **62**, 295–300.

Jackson, D. N., Peacock, A. C. and Holden, R. R. (1982) Professional interviewers' trait inferential structures for diverse occupational groups. *Organisational Behavior and Human Performance*, **29**, 1–20.

Jagacinski, C. M. (1991) Personnel decision making: the impact of missing information. *Journal of Applied Psychology*, **76**, 19–30.

James, L. R., Demaree, R. G., Mulaik, S. A. and Ladd, R. T. (1992) Validity generalisation in the context of situational models. *Journal of Applied Psychology*, **77**, 3–14.

Janz, T. (1982) Initial comparisons of patterned behavior description interviews versus unstructured interviews. *Journal of Applied Psychology*, **67**, 577–580.

Jensen, A. R. (1969) *Genetics and education*. Methuen, London.

Johnson, C. D., Messe, L. A. and Crano, W. D. (1984) Predicting job performance of low income workers: the Work Opinion Questionnaire. *Personnel Psychology*, **37**, 291–299.

Johnson, C. E., Wood, R., and Blinkhorn, S. F. (1988) Spiriouser and spiriouser: the use of ipsative personality tests, *Journal of Occupational Psychology*, **61**, 153–162.

Jones, A. (1981) Inter-rater reliability in the assessment of group exercises at a UK assessment centre. *Journal of Occupational Psychology*, **54**, 79–86.

Jones, A. and Harrison, E. (1982) Prediction of performance in initial officer training using reference reports. *Journal of Occupational Psychology*, **55**, 35–42.

Jones, A., Herriot, P., Long, B. and Drakeley, R. (1991) Attempting to improve the validity of a well-established assessment centre. *Journal of Psychology*, **64**, 1–21.

Judiesch, M. K., Schmidt, F. L. and Mount, M. K. (1992) Estimates of the dollar value of employee output in utility analyses: an empirical test of two theories. *Journal of Applied Psychology*, **77**, 234–250.

Kane, J. S. and Lawler, E. E. (1978) Methods of peer assessment. *Psychological Bulletin*, **85**, 555–586.

Katzell, R. A. and Dyer, F. J. (1977) Differential validity revived. *Journal of Applied Psychology*, **62**, 137–145.

Kaufman, G. G. and Johnson, J. C. (1974) Scaling peer ratings: an examination of the differential validities of positive and negative nominations. *Journal of Applied Psychology*, **59**, 302–306.

Keating, E., Patterson, D. G. and Stones, C. H. (1950) Validity of work histories obtained by interview. *Journal of Applied Psychology*, **34**, 6–11.

Keenan, A. and Wedderburn, A. A. I. (1980) Putting the boot on the other foot: candidates' descriptions of interviewers. *Journal of Occupational Psychology*, **53**, 81–89.

Keller, L. M., Bouchard, T. J., Arvey, R. D., Segal, N. L. and Dawis, R. V. (1992) Work values: genetic and environmental influences. *Journal of Applied Psychology*, **77**, 79–88.

Kelly, G. A. (1955) *The psychology of personal constructs*. Norton, New York.

Kelly, E. L. and Fiske, D. W. (1951) *The prediction of performance in clinical psychology*, University of Michigan Press, Ann Arbor.

Kenny, D. A. and Zaccaro, S. J. (1983) An estimate of variance due to traits in leadership. *Journal of Applied Psychology*, **68**, 678–685.

Kinicki, A. J., Lockwood, C. A., Hom, P. W. and Griffeth, R. W. (1990) Interviewer predictions of applicant qualifications and interviewer validity: aggregate and individual analyses. *Journal of Applied Psychology*, **75**, 477–486.

Kinslinger, H. J. (1966) Application of projective techniques in personnel psychology since 1940. *Psychological Bulletin*, **66**, 134–150.

Kirkpatrick, J. J., Ewen, R. B., Barrett, R. S. and Katzell, R. A. (1968) *Testing and fair employment*. New York University Press, New York.

Kirnan, J. P., Farley, J. A. and Geisinger, K. F. (1989) The relationship between recruiting source, applicant quality, and hire performance: an analysis by sex, ethnicity and age. *Personnel Psychology*, **44**, 293–308.

Kleiman, L. S. and Durham, R. L. (1981) Performance appraisal, promotion and the courts: a critical review. *Personnel Psychology*, **34**, 103–121.

Kleiman, L. S. and Faley, R. H. (1985) The implications of professional and legal guidelines for court decisions involving criterion-related validity: a review and analysis. *Personnel Psychology*, **38**, 803–833.

Kleiman, L. S. and Faley, R. H. (1990) A comparative analysis of the empirical validity of past- and present-oriented biographical items. *Journal of Business and Psychology*, **4**, 431–437.

Klein, S. P. and Owens, W. A. (1965) Faking of a scored life history blank as a function of criterion objectivity. *Journal of Applied Psychology*, **49**, 452–454.

Klimoski, R. J. and Rafaeli, A. (1983) Inferring personal qualities through handwriting analysis. *Journal of Occupational Psychology*, **56**, 191–202.

Klimoski, R. J. and Strickland, W. J. (1977) Assessment centers—valid or merely precient? *Personnel Psychology*, **30**, 353–361.

Kline, P. (1976) *The psychology of vocational guidance*. Batsford, London.

Kluger, A. N., Reilly, R. R., and Russell, C. J. (1991) Faking biodata tests: are option-keyed instruments more resistant? *Journal of Applied Psychology*, **76**, 889–896.

Knatz, H. F. and Inwald, R. E. (1983) A process for screning out law enforcement candidates who might break under stress. *Criminal Justice Journal*, **2**, 1–5.

Kraiger, K. and Ford, J. K. (1985) A meta-analysis of ratee race effects in performance ratings. *Journal of Applied Psychology*, **70**, 56–65.

Kraut, A. I. (1975) Prediction of managerial success by peer and training-staff ratings. *Journal of Applied Psychology*, **60**, 14–19.

Krzystofiak, F., Newman, J. M. and Anderson, G. (1979) A quantified approach to measurement of job content: procedures and payoffs. *Personnel Psychology*, **32**, 341–357.

Kumar, K. and Beyerlein, M. (1991) Construction and validation of an instrument for measuring ingratiatory behaviors in organisational settings. *Journal of Applied Psychology*, **76**, 619–627.

Landy, F. J. and Farr, J. L. (1980) Performance rating. *Psychological Bulletin*, **87**, 72–107.

Landy, F. J. and Rastegary, H. (1989) Criteria for selection. In Smith, M. and Robertson, I. T. (eds) *Advances in selection and assessment*. Wiley, Chichester.

Landy, F. J. and Vasey, J. (1991) Job analysis: the composition of SME samples. *Personnel Psychology*, **44**, 27–50.

Latham, G. P., Saari, L. M., Pursell, E. D. and Campion, M. A. (1980) The situational interview. *Journal of Applied Psychology*, **65**, 422–427.

Laurent, H. (1962) Early identification of management talent. *Management Record*, **24**, 33–38.

Laurent, H. (1970) Cross-cultural cross-validation of empirically validated tests. *Journal of Applied Psychology*, **54**, 417–423.

Lawshe, C. H. (1952) What can industrial psychology do for small business (a symposium). 2. Employee selection. *Personnel Psychology*, **5**, 31–34.

Lawshe, C. H. (1975) A quantitative approach to content validity. *Personnel Psychology*, **28**, 563–575.

Ledvinka, J. (1982) *Federal regulation of personnel and human resource management*. Van Nostrand Reinhold, New York.

Ledvinka, J. and Simonet, J. K. (1983) *The dollar values of JEPS at Life of Georgia*. Working Paper 83-134, College of Business Administration, University of Georgia.

Lent, R. H., Aurbach, H. A. and Levin, L. S. (1971) Predictors, criteria, and significant results. *Personnel Psychology*, **24**, 519–533.

Levin, H. M. (1988) Issues of agreement and contention in employment testing. *Journal of Vocational Behavior*, **33**, 398–403.

Levine, E. L. and Rudolph, S. M. (1977) *Reference checking for personnel selection: the state of the art*. American Society for Personnel Administration, Washington DC.

Levine, E. L., Flory, A. and Ash, R. A. (1977) Self-assessment in personnel selection. *Journal of Applied Psychology*, **62**, 428–435.

Levine, E. L., Ash, R. A., Hall, H. and Sistrunk, F. (1983) Evaluation of job analysis methods by experienced job analysts. *Academy of Management Journal*, **26**, 339–348.

Lewin, A. Y. and Zwany, A. (1976) Peer nominations: a model, literature critique and a paradigm for research. *Personnel Psychology*, **29**, 423–447.

Lilienthal, R. A. and Pearlman, K. (1983) *The validity of Federal selection tests for aid/technicians in the health, science and engineering fields*. US Office of Personnel Management, Washington DC.

Link, H. C. (1918) An experiment in employment psychology. *Psychological Review*, **25**,

116–127.

Linn, R. L., Harnisch, D. L. and Dunbar, S. B. (1981) Validity generalisation and situational specificity: an analysis of the prediction of first-year grades in law school. *Applied Psychological Measurement*, **5**, 281–289.

Locke, E. L. (1961) What's in a name? *American Psychologist*, **16**, 607.

Lopez, F. M. (1966) *Evaluating executive decision making: the in-basket technique.* American Management Association, New York.

Love, K. G. (1981) Comparison of peer assessment methods: reliability, validity, friendship bias, and user reaction. *Journal of Applied Psychology*, **66**, 451–457.

McBain, W. N. (1970) Arousal, monotony and accidents in line driving. *Journal of Applied Psychology*, **54**, 509–519.

McClelland, D. C. (1971) *The achieving society.* Van Nostrand, Princeton, NJ.

McLelland, D. C. (1973) Testing for competence rather than for "intelligence". *American Psychologist*, **28**, 1–14.

McCormick, E. J., Jeanneret, P. R. and Mecham, R. C. (1972) Study of job characteristics and job dimensions as based on the Position Analysis Questionnaire (PAQ). *Journal of Applied Psychology*, **56**, 347–368.

McCormick, E. J., DeNisi, A. S., and Shaw, J. B. (1979) Use of the Position Analysis Questionnaire for establishing the job component validity of tests. *Journal of Applied Psychology*, **64**, 51–56.

McDaniel, M. A., Whetzel, D. L., Schmidt, F. L., Hunter, J. E., Maurer, S. & Russell, J. (1987) *The validity of employment interviews: a review and meta-analysis.* (Unpublished.)

McDaniel, M. A., Schmidt, F. L. and Hunter, J. E. (1988) A meta-analysis of the validity of methods for rating training and education in personnel selection. *Personnel Psychology*, **41**, 283–314.

McDonald, T. and Hakel, M. D. (1985) Effects of applicant race, sex, suitability and answers on interviewer's questioning strategy and ratings. *Personnel Psychology*, **38**, 321–334.

McEvoy, G. M. and Beatty, R. W. (1989) Assessment centers and subordinate appraisals of managers: a seven-year examination of predictive validity. *Personnel Psychology*, **42**, 37–52.

McEvoy, G. M. and Buller, P. F. (1987) User acceptance of peer appraisals in an industrial setting. *Personnel Psychology*, **40**, 785–797.

McHenry, J. J., Hough, L. M., Toquam, J. L., Hanson, M. A. and Ashworth, S. (1990) Project A validity results: the relationship between predictor and criterion domains. *Personnel Psychology*, **43**, 335–354.

McMurray, R. N. (1947) Validating the patterned interview. *Personnel*, **23**, 263–272.

Mabe, P. A. and West, S. G. (1982) Validity of self-evaluation of ability: a review and meta-analysis. *Journal of Applied Psychology*, **67**, 280–296.

Mackinnon, D. W. (1977) From selecting spies to selecting managers. In Moses, J. L. and Byham, W. C. (eds.) *Applying the assessment center method.* Pergamon Press, New York.

Mael, F. A. (1991) A conceptual rationale for the domain and attributes of biodata. *Personnel Psychology*, **44**, 763–792.

Mael, F. A. and Schwartz, A. C. (1991) *Capturing temperament constructs with objective biodata.* Technical report No. 939. United States Army Research Institute for the Behavioral and Social Sciences, Alexandria, Virginia.

Mahoney, T. A., Jerdee, T. H. and Nash, A. N. (1960) Predicting managerial effectiveness. *Personnel Psychology*, **13**, 147–163.

Martin, S. L. and Terris, W. (1991) Predicting infrequent behavior: clarifying the impact on false-positive rates. *Journal of Applied Psychology*, **76**, 484–487.

Matarazzo, J. D. (1972) *Wechsler's measurement and appraisal of intelligence*, 5th Edition. Williams and Wilkins, Baltimore.

Matarazzo, J. D. (1992) Psychological testing and assessment in the 21st century. *American Psychologist*, **47**, 1007–1018.

Mathieu, J. E. and Tannenbaum, S. I. (1989) A process-tracing approach toward understanding supervisors' SD$_y$ estimates: results from five job classes. *Journal of Occupational Psychology*, **62**, 249–256.

Matteson, M. T. (1978) An alternative approach to using biographical data for predicting job success. *Journal of Occupational Psychology*, **51**, 155–162.

Maurer, S. D. and Alexander, R. A. (1992) Methods of improving employment test critical scores derived by judging test content: a review and critique. *Personnel Psychology*, **45**, 727–762.

Maurer, S. D. and Fay, C. (1988) Effect of situational interviews, conventional structured interviews, and training on interview rating agreement: an experimental analysis. *Personnel Psychology*, **41**, 329–344.

Mayfield, E. C. (1964) The selection interview—a re-evaluation of published research. *Personnel Psychology*, **17**, 239–260.

Mayfield, E. C. (1970) Management selection: buddy nominations revisited. *Personnel Psychology*, **23**, 377–391.

Mayfield, E. C. and Carlson, R. E. (1966) Selection interview decisions: first results from a long-term research project. *Personnel Psychology*, **19**, 41–53.

Meehl, P. E. (1954) *Clinical vs statistical prediction*. University of Minnesota Press.

Meehl, P. E. (1978) Theoretical risks and tabular asterisks: Sir Karl, Sir Ronald and the slow progress of soft psychology. *Journal of Consulting and Clinical Psychology*, **46**, 806–834.

Megargee, E. I. (1972) *The California Psychological Inventory handbook*. Jossey Bass, San Francisco.

Meier, S. T. (1984) The construct validity of burnout. *Journal of Occupational Psychology*, **57**, 211–219.

Merrihue, W. V. and Katzell, R. A. (1955) ERI—yardstick of employee relations. *Harvard Business Review*, **33**, 91–99.

Meritt-Haston, R. and Wexley, K. N. (1983) Educational requirements: legality and validity. *Personnel Psychology*, **36**, 743–753.

Miller, K. (1976) Personality assessment. In Ungerson, B. (ed.) *Recruitment handbook*. Gower Press: Aldershot.

Miner, J. B. (1970) Executive and personnel interviews as predictors of consulting success. *Personnel Psychology*, **23**, 521–538.

Miner, J. C. (1971) Personality tests as predictors of consulting success. *Personnel Psychology*, **24**, 191–204.

Miner, J. C. (1978) The Miner Sentence Completion Scale: a reappraisal. *Academy of Management Journal*, **21**, 283–294.

Miner, M. G. and Miner, J. B. (1979) *Employee selection within the law*. Bureau of National Affairs: Washington DC.

Mischel, W. (1968) *Personality and assessment*. Wiley: New York.

Mitchell, T. W. and Klimoski, R. J. (1982) Is it rational to be empirical? A test of methods for scoring biographical data. *Journal of Applied Psychology*, **67**, 411–418.

Mls, J. (1935) Intelligenz und fahigkeit zum kraftwagenlenken. Proceedings of the Eighth International Conference of Psychotechnics, Prague, pp. 278–284.

Moore, H. (1942) *Psychology for business and industry*. McGraw Hill, New York.

Morris, B. S. (1949) Officer selection in the British Army 1942–1945. *Occupational Psychology*, **23**, 219–234.

Morrow, P. C., McElroy, J. C., Stamper, B. G. and Wilson, M. A. (1990) The effects of physical attractiveness and other demographic characteristics on promotion decisons. *Journal of Management*, **16**, 723–736.

Mosel, J. N. (1952) Prediction of department store sales performance from personal data. *Journal of Applied Psychology*, **36**, 8–10.

Mosel, J. N. and Goheen, H. W. (1958) The validity of the Employment Recommendation Questionnaire in personnel selection. I. Skilled trades. *Personnel Psychology*, **11**, 481–490.

Mosel, J. N. and Goheen, H. W. (1959) The validity of the Employment Recommendation Questionnaire. III. Validity of different types of references. *Personnel Psychology*, **12**, 469–477.

Moses, J. L. (1973) The development of an assessment center for the early identification of supervisory talent. *Personnel Psychology*, **26**, 569–580.

Moses, J. L. and Boehm, V. R. (1975) Relationship of assessment center performance to management progress of women. *Journal of Applied Psychology*, **60**, 527–529.

Mossholder, K. W. and Arvey, R. D. (1984) Synthetic validity: a conceptual and comparative review. *Journal of Applied Psychology*, **69**, 322–333.

Motowidlo, S. J., Carter, G. W., Dunnette, M. D., Tippins, N., Werner, S., Burnett, J. R., Vaughan, M. J. (1992) Studies of the structured behavioural interview. *Journal of Applied Psychology*, **77**, 571–587.

Muchinsky, P. M. (1979) The use of reference reports in personnel selection: a review and evaluation. *Journal of Occupational Psychology*, **52**, 287–297.

Muchinsky, P. M. and Tuttle, M. L. (1979) Employee turnover: an empirical and methodological assessment. *Journal of Vocational Behavior*, **14**, 43–77.

Mumford, M. D. (1983) Social comparison theory and the evaluation of peer evaluations: a review and some applied implications. *Personnel Psychology*, **36**, 867–881.

Murphy, K. R. (1984) Cost–benefit considerations in choosing among cross-validation methods. *Personnel Psychology*, **37**, 15–22.

Murphy, K. R. (1989) Is the relationship between cognitive ability and job performance stable over time? *Human Performance*, **2**, 183–200.

Murphy, K. R., Thornton, G. C., and Prue, K. (1991) Influence of job characteristics on the acceptability of employee drug testing. *Journal of Applied Psychology*, **76**, 447–453.

Nathan, B. R. and Alexander, R. A. (1988) A comparison of criteria for test validation: a meta-analytic investigation. *Personnel Psychology*, **41**, 517–535.

Nathan, B. R. and Tippins, N. (1990) The consequences of "halo error" in performance ratings: a field study of the moderating effect of halo on test validation results. *Journal of Applied Psychology*, **75**, 290–296.

Neter, E. and Ben-Shakhar, G. (1989) The predictive validity of graphological inferences: a meta-analytic approach. *Personality and Individual Differences*, **10**, 737–745.

Nevo, B. (1976) Using biographical information to predict success of men and women in the army. *Journal of Applied Psychology*, **61**, 106–108.

Normand, J., Salyards, S. D. and Mahoney, J. J. (1990) An evaluation of preemployment drug testing. *Journal of Applied Psychology*, **75**, 629–639.

Northrop, L. C. (1985) *Validity generalisation results for apprentice occupations*, US Office of Personnel Management, Washington DC.

O'Connor, E. J., Wexley, K. N. and Alexander, R. A. (1975) Single-group validity: fact or fallacy? *Journal of Applied Psychology*, **60**, 352–355.

O'Leary, B. S. (1980) *College grade point average as an indicator of occupational success: an update*, US Office of Personnel Management, Washington DC.

Olian, J. D. and Wilcox, J. C. (1982) The controversy over PACE: an examination of the evidence and implications of the Luevano consent decree for employment testing.

Personnel Psychology, **35**, 659–676.

Olian, J. D., Schwab, D. P. and Haberfeld, Y. (1988) The impact of applicant gender compared to qualifications on hiring recommendations: a meta-analysis of experimental studies. *Organisational Behavior and Human Decision Processes*, **41**, 180–195.

Ones, D. S., Viswesvaran, C. and Schmidt, F. L. (undated) *Meta-analysis of integrity test validities: findings and implications for personnel selection and theories of job performance.* Department of Management and Organisation, University of Iowa.

Ones, D. S., Mount, M. K., Barrick, M. R. and Hunter, J. E. (in press) Personality and job performance: a critique of the Tett, Jackson & Rothstein (1991) meta-analysis. *Personnel Psychology*.

Oppler, S. H., Campbell, J. P., Pulakos, E. D. and Borman, W. C. (1992) Three approaches to the investigation of subgroup bias in performance measurement: review, results, and conclusions. *Journal of Applied Psychology*, **77**, 201–217.

Orpen, C. (1985) Patterned behavior description interviews versus unstructured interviews: a comparative validity study. *Journal of Applied Psychology*, **70**, 774–776.

Orr, J. M., Sackett, P. R. and Mercer, M. (1989) The role of prescribed and nonprescribed behavior in estimating the dollar value of performance. *Journal of Applied Psychology*, **75**, 34–40.

Orr, J. M. Sackett, P. R. and Dubois, C. L. Z. (1991) Outlier detection and treatment in I/O psychology: a survey of researcher beliefs and an empirical illustration. *Personnel Psychology*, **44**, 473–486.

Otis, J. L. (1938) The prediction of success in power sewing machine operating. *Journal of Applied Psychology*, **22**, 350–366.

Owens, W. A. (1976) Background data. In Dunnette, M. D. (ed.) *Handbook of industrial and organisational psychology*. Rand McNally, Chicago.

Owens, W. A. and Schoenfeldt, L. F. (1979) Toward a classification of persons. *Journal of Applied Psychology*, **65**, 569–607.

Pace, L. A. and Schoenfeldt, L. F. (1977) Legal concerns in the use of weighted applications. *Personnel Psychology*, **30**, 159–166.

Parkinson, C. N. (1958) *Parkinson's law*. John Murray, London.

Parry, J. (1959) The place of personality appraisal in vocational selection. *Occupational Psychology*, **33**, 149–156.

Pearlman, K. (1984) *Validity generalisation*. Proceedings of the 92nd Annual Convention of the American Psychological Association.

Pearlman, K., Schmidt, F. L. and Hunter, J. E. (1980) Validity generalisation results for tests used to predict job proficiency and training success in clerical occupations. *Journal of Applied Psychology*, **65**, 373–406.

Peres, S. H. and Garcia, J. R. (1962) Validity and dimensions of descriptive adjectives used in reference letters for engineering applicants. *Personnel Psychology*, **15**, 279–286.

Petrie, A. and Powell, M. B. (1951) The selection of nurses in England. *Journal of Applied Psychology*, **35**, 281–285.

Power, R. P. and MacRae, K. D. (1971) Detectability of items in the Eysenck Personality Inventory. *British Journal of Psychology*, **62**, 395–401.

Primoff, E. S. (1959) Empirical validations of the J-coefficient. *Personnel Psychology*, **12**, 413–418.

Psychological Corporation (1978) *Summaries of court decisions on employment testing, 1968–1977*. Arthur, New York.

Pursell, E. D., Dossett, D. L. and Latham, G. P. (1980) Obtaining valid predictors by minimizing rating errors in the criterion. *Personnel Psychology*, **33**, 91–96.

Pynes, J. and Bernardin, H. J. (1989) Predictive validity of an entry-level police officer assessment center. *Journal of Applied Psychology*, **74**, 831–833.

Pynes, J., Bernardin, H. J., Benton, A. L. and McEvoy, G. M. (1988) Should assessment center ratings be mechanically derived? *Journal of Business and Psychology*, **2**, 217–227.

Rasmussen, K. G. (1984) Nonverbal behavior, verbal behavior, résumé credentials, and selection interview outcomes. *Journal of Applied Psychology*, **69**, 551–556.

Raza, S. M. and Carpenter, B. N. (1987) A model of hiring decisions in real employment interviews. *Journal of Applied Psychology*, **72**, 596–603.

Ree, M. J. and Earles, J. A. (1991) Predicting training success: not much more than *g*. *Personnel Psychology*, **44**, 321–332.

Reilly, R. R. and Chao, G. T. (1982) Validity and fairness of some alternative employee selection procedures. *Personnel Psychology*, **35**, 1–62.

Reilly, R. R. and Israelski, E. W. (1988) Development and validation of minicourses in the telecommunications industry. *Journal of Applied Psychology*, **73**, 721–726.

Reilly, R. R., Zedeck, S. and Tenopyr, M. L. (1979) Validity and fairness of physical ability tests for predicting performance in craft jobs. *Journal of Applied Psychology*, **64**, 262–274.

Reilly, R. R., Henry, S. and Smither, J. W. (1990) An examination of the effects of using behavior checklists on the construct validity of assesment center dimensions. *Personnel Psychology*, **43**, 71–84.

Richards, J. M., Taylor, C. W., Price, P. B. and Jacobsen, T. L. (1965) An investigation of the criterion problem for one group of medical specialists. *Journal of Applied Psychology*, **49**, 79–90.

Ritchie, R. J. and Boehm, V. R. (1977) Biographical data as a predictor of women's and men's management potential. *Journal of Vocational Behavior*, **11**, 363–368.

Ritchie, R. J. and Moses, J. L. (1983) Assessment center correlates of women's advancement into middle management: a 7-year longitudinal analysis. *Journal of Applied Psychology*, **68**, 227–231.

Roach, D. E. (1971) Double cross-validation of a weighted application blank over time. *Journal of Applied Psychology*, **55**, 157–160.

Roadman, H. E. (1964) An industrial use of peer ratings. *Journal of Applied Psychology*, **48**, 211–214.

Robertson, I. T. and Downs, S. (1979) Learning and the prediction of performance: Development of trainability testing in the United Kingdom. *Journal of Applied Psychology*, **64**, 42–50.

Robertson, I. T. and Downs, S. (1989) Work-sample tests of trainability: a meta-analysis. *Journal of Applied Psychology*, **74**, 402–410.

Robertson, I. T. and Kandola, R. S. (1982) Work sample tests: validity, adverse impact and applicant reaction. *Journal of Occupational Psychology*, **55**, 171–183.

Robertson, I. T. and Kinder, A. (1993) Personality and job competences: the criterion-related validity of some personality variables. *Journal of Organisational and Occupational Psychology*, in press.

Robertson, I. T. and Makin, P. J. (1986) Management selection in Britain: a survey and critique. *Journal of Occupational Psychology*, **59**, 45–57.

Robertson, I. T. and Smith, M. (1989). Personnel selection methods. In Smith, M. & Robertson, I. T. (eds), *Advances in selection and assessment*. John Wiley, Chichester.

Robinson, D. D. (1972) Prediction of clerical turnover in banks by means of a weighted application blank. *Journal of Applied Psychology*, **56**, 282.

Roche, W. J. (1965) A dollar criterion in fixed-treatment employee selection. In Cronbach, L. J. and Gleser, G. C. (eds), *Psychological tests and personnel decisions*. University of Illinois Press, Urbana, IL.

Rodger, D. A. (1959) Personality of the route salesman in a basic food industry. *Journal of Applied Psychology*, **43**, 235–239.

Ronan, W. W. (1963) A factor analysis of eleven performance measures. *Personnel Psychology*, **16**, 255–267.

Roose, J. E. and Dougherty, M. E. (1976) Judgement theory applied to the selection of life insurance salesmen. *Organisational Behavior and Human Performance*, **16**, 231–249.

Rosenbaum, R. W. (1976) Predictability of employee theft using weighted application blanks. *Journal of Applied Psychology*, **61**, 94–98.

Rothe, H. F. (1946) Output rates among butter wrappers: II. frequency distributions and an hypothesis regarding restriction of 'output'. *Journal of Applied Psychology*, **30**, 320–327.

Rothstein, H. R. (1990) Interrater reliability of job performance ratings: growth to asymptote level with increasing opportunity to observe. *Journal of Applied Psychology*, **75**, 322–327.

Rothstein, H. R., Schmidt, F. L., Erwin, F. W., Owens, W. A. and Sparks, C. P. (1990) Biographical data in employment selection: can validities be made generalisable? *Journal of Applied Psychology*, **75**, 175–184.

Rundquist, E. A. (1947) Development of an interview for selection purposes. In Kelly, G. A. (ed.) *New methods in applied psychology*. University of Maryland Press, College Park MD.

Rush, C. H. (1953) A factorial study of sales criteria. *Personnel Psychology*, **6**, 9–24.

Russell, C. J. (1985) Individual decision processes in an assessment center. *Journal of Applied Psychology*, **70**, 737–746.

Russell, C. J. and Domm, D. R. (1990) On the validity of role congruency-based assessment center procedures for predicting performance ratings, sales revenue, and profit. Presented at 50th annual meeting of the Academy of Management, San Francisco, CA.

Russell, C. J., Mattson, J., Devlin, S. E., and Atwater, D. (1990) Predictive validity of biodata items generated from retrospective life experience essays. *Journal of Applied Psychology*, **75**, 569–580.

Ryan, A. M. and Lasek, M. (1991) Negligent hiring and defamation: areas of liability related to pre-employment inquiries. *Personnel Psychology*, **44**, 293–319.

Rynes, S. and Gerhart, B. (1990) Interview assessments of applicant "fit": an exploratory investigation. *Personnel Psychology*, **43**, 13–35.

Sackett, P. R. and Dreher, G. F. (1982) Constructs and assessment center dimensions: some troubling empirical findings. *Journal of Applied Psychology*, **67**, 401–410.

Sackett, P. R. and Harris, M. M. (1984) Honesty testing for personnel selection: a review and critique. *Personnel Psychology*, **37**, 221–245.

Sackett, P. R. and Wilson, M. A. (1982) Factors affecting the consensus judgement process in managerial assessment centers. *Journal of Applied Psychology*, **67**, 10–17.

Sackett, P. R., Zedeck, S. and Fogli, L. (1988) Relations between typical and maximum job performance. *Journal of Applied Psychology*, **73**, 482–486.

Sands, W. A. (1978) Enlisted personnel selection for the U. S. Navy. *Personnel Psychology*, **31**, 63–70.

Sands, W. A. and Gade, P. A. (1983) An application of computerised adaptive testing in U. S. Army recruiting. *Journal of Computer-Based Instruction*, **10**, 87–89.

Saville and Holdsworth Ltd (1985) *Occupational Personality Questionnaire: manual*. SHL Ltd, Esher, Surrey.

Schein, V. A. (1975) Relationships between sex role stereotypes and requisite management characteristics among female managers. *Journal of Applied Psychology*, **60**, 340–344.

Schippmann, J. S., Prien, E. P. and Katz, J. A. (1990) Reliability and validity of in-basket measures. *Personnel Psychology*, **43**, 837–859.

Schmidt, F. L. and Hunter, J. E. (1977) Development of a general solution to the problem of validity generalisation. *Journal of Applied Psychology*, **62**, 529–540.

Schmidt, F. L. and Hunter, J. E. (1978) Moderator research and the law of small numbers. *Personnel Psychology*, **31**, 215–232.

Schmidt, F. L. and Hunter, J. E. (1981) Employment testing: old theories and new research findings. *American Psychologist*, **36**, 1128–1137.

Schmidt, F. L. and Hunter, J. F. (1983) Individual differences in productivity: an empirical test of estimates derived from studies of selection procedure utility. *Journal of Applied Psychology*, **68**, 407–414.

Schmidt, F. L. and Hunter, J. E. (1984) A within setting empirical test of the situational specificity hypothesis in personnel selection. *Personnel Psychology*, **37**, 317–326.

Schmidt, F. L. and Johnson, R. H. (1973) Effects of race on peer ratings in an industrial situation. *Journal of Applied Psychology*, **57**, 237–241.

Schmidt, F. L., Berner, J. G. and Hunter, J. E. (1973) Racial differences in validity of employment tests: reality or illusion? *Journal of Applied Psychology*, **58**, 5–9.

Schmidt, F. L., Greenthal, A. L., Hunter, J. E., Berner, J. G. and Seaton, F. W. (1977) Job sample vs. paper-and-pencil trades and technical tests: adverse impact and examinee attitudes. *Personnel Psychology*, **30**, 187–197.

Schmidt, F. L., Hunter, J. E., Pearlman, K. and Shane, G. S. (1979a) Further tests of the Schmidt–Hunter Bayesian validity generalisation procedure. *Personnel Psychology*, **32**, 257–281.

Schmidt, F. L., Hunter, J. E., McKenzie, R. C. and Muldrow, T. W. (1979b) Impact of valid selection procedures on work-force productivity. *Journal of Applied Psychology*, **64**, 609–626.

Schmidt, F. L., Gast-Rosenberg, I. and Hunter, J. E. (1980) Validity generalisation results for computer programmers. *Journal of Applied Psychology*, **65**, 643–661.

Schmidt, F. L., Pearlman, K. and Hunter, J. E. (1980) The validity and fairness of employment and educational tests for Hispanic Americans: a review and analysis. *Personnel Psychology*, **33**, 705–724.

Schmidt, F. L., Hunter, J. E. and Pearlman, K. (1981) Task differences as moderators of aptitude test validity in selection: a red herring. *Journal of Applied Psychology*, **66**, 166–185.

Schmidt, F. L., Hunter, J. E. and Pearlman, K. (1982) Assessing the economic impact of personnel programs on workforce productivity. *Personnel Psychology*, **35**, 333–347.

Schmidt, F. L., Hunter, J. E., Croll, P. R. and McKenzie, R. C. (1983) Estimation of employment test validities by expert judgement. *Journal of Applied Psychology*, **68**, 590–601.

Schmidt, F. L., Mack, M. J. and Hunter, J. E. (1984) Selection utility in the occupation of U.S. park ranger for three modes of test use. *Journal of Applied Psychology*, **69**, 490–497.

Schmidt, F. L., Hunter, J. E., Pearlman, K. and Hirsh, H. R. (1985a) Forty questions about validity generalisation and meta-analysis. *Personnel Psychology*, **38**, 697–798.

Schmidt, F. L., Ocasio, B. P., Hillery, J. M. and Hunter, J. E. (1985b) Further within-setting empirical tests of the situational specificity hypothesis in personnel selection. *Personnel Psychology*, **38**, 509–524.

Schmidt, F. L., Hunter, J. E. and Outerbridge, A. N. (1986) Impact of job experience and ability on job knowledge, work sample performance, and supervisory ratings of job performance. *Journal of Applied Psychology*, **71**, 432–439.

Schmidt, F. L., Hunter, J. E., Outerbridge, A. N. and Goff, S. (1988) Joint relation of experience and ability with job performance: test of three hypotheses. *Journal of Applied Psychology*, **73**, 46–57.

Schmidt, F. L., Ones, D. S. and Hunter, J. E. (1992) Personnel selection. *Annual Review* of Psychology, **43**, 627–670.

Schmitt, N. (1976) Social and situational determinants of interview decisions: implications for the employment interview. Personnel Psychology, **29**, 79–101.

Schmitt, N. (1977) Interrater agreement in dimensionality and combination of assessment center judgements. Journal of Applied Psychology, **62**, 171–176.

Schmitt, N. and Hill, T. E. (1977) Sex and race composition of assessment center groups as a determinant of peer and assessor ratings. Journal of Applied Psychology, **62**, 261–264.

Schmitt, N., Gooding, R. Z., Noe, R. A. and Kirsch, M. (1984) Meta-analysis of validity studies published between 1964 and 1982 and the investigation of study characteristics. Personnel Psychology, **37**, 407–422.

Schmitt, N., Schneider, J. R. and Cohen, S. A. (1990) Factors affecting validity of a regionally administered assessment center. Personnel Psychology, **43**, 1–12.

Schneider, J. R. and Schmitt, N. (1992) An exercise design approach to understanding assessment center dimension and exercise constructs. Journal of Applied Psychology, **77**, 32–41.

Schoenfeldt, L. F., Schoenfeldt, B. B., Acker, S. R. and Perlson, M. R. (1976) Content validity revisited: the development of a content-oriented test of industrial reading. Journal of Applied Psychology, **61**, 581–588.

Schrader, A. D. and Osburn, H. G. (1977) Biodata faking: effects of induced subtlety and position specificity. Personnel Psychology, **30**, 395–404.

Schuerger, J. M., Zarrella, K. L. and Hotz, A. S. (1989) Factors that influence the temporal stability of personality by questionnaire. Journal of Personality and Social Psychology, **56**, 777–783.

Schuler, H. (1989) Construct validity of a multimodal employment interview. In Fallon, B. J., Pfister, H. P. and Brebner, J. (eds) Advances in Industrial Organisational Psychology. Elsevier, North Holland.

Schuler, H., Frier, D. and Kauffmann, M. (1991) Use and evaluation of selection methods in German companies. European Review of Applied Psychology, **41**, 19–25.

Scott, R. D. and Johnson, R. W. (1967) Use of the weighted application blank in selecting unskilled employees. Journal of Applied Psychology, **51**, 393–395.

Severin, D. (1952) The predictability of various kinds of criteria. Personnel Psychology, **5**, 93–104.

Seymour, R. T. (1988) Why plaintiffs' counsel challenge tests, and how they can successfully challenge the theory of "validation generalisation". Journal of Vocational Behavior, **33**, 331–364.

Shackleton, V. and Newell, S. (1991) Management selection: a comparative survey of methods used in top British and French companies. Journal of Occupational Psychology, **64**, 23–36.

Shaffer, D. R., Mays, P. V. and Etheridge, K. (1976) Who shall be hired: a biassing effect of the Buckley amendment on employment practices. Journal of Applied Psychology, **61**, 571–575.

Shaffer, G. S., Saunders, V. and Owens, W. A. (1986) Additional evidence for the accuracy of biographical data: long-term retest and observer ratings. Personnel Psychology, **39**, 791–809.

Shapira, Z. and Shirom, A. (1980) New issues in the use of behaviorally anchored rating scales: level of analysis, the effects of incident frequency, and external validation. Journal of Applied Psychology, **65**, 517–523.

Sharf, J. C. (1982) Personnel testing and the law. In Rowland, K. M. and Ferris, G. R. (eds) Personnel Management. Allyn and Bacon, Boston.

Sharf, J. C. (1988) Litigating personnel measurement policy. Journal of Vocational

Behavior, **33**, 235–271.

Shore, T. H., Thornton, G. C. and Shore, L. M. (1990) Construct validity of two categories of assessment center dimension ratings. *Personnel Psychology*, **43**, 101–115.

Shrauger, S. J. and Osberg, T. M. (1981) The relative accuracy of self-prediction and judgements by others in psychological assessment. *Psychological Bulletin*, **90**, 322–351.

Siegel, A. I. (1978) Miniature job training and evaluation as a selection/classification device. *Human Factors*, **20**, 189–200.

Silver, E. M. and Bennett, C. (1987) Modification of the Minnesota Clerical Test to predict performance on video display terminals. *Journal of Applied Psychology*, **72**, 153–155.

Silverman, W. H., Dalessio, A., Woods, S. B. and Johnson, R. L. (1986) Influence of assessment center methods on assessors' ratings. *Personnel Psychology*, **39**, 565–578.

Smith, M. (1991) Recruitment and selection in the UK with some data on Norway. *European Review of Applied Psychology*, **41**, 27–34.

Smith, J. E. and Hakel, M. D. (1979) Convergence among data sources, response bias, and reliability and validity of a structured job analysis questionnaire. *Personnel Psychology*, **32**, 677–692.

Smith, W. J., Albright, L. E., Glennon, J. R. and Owens, W. A. (1961) The prediction of research competence and creativity from personal history. *Journal of Applied Psychology*, **45**, 59–62.

Snedden, D. (1930) Measuring general intelligence by interview. *Psychological Clinic*, **19**, 131–134.

Sorenson, W. W. (1966) Test of mechanical principles as a suppressor variable for the prediction of effectiveness on a mechanical repair job. *Journal of Applied Psychology*, **50**, 348–352.

Sparrow, J. (1989) The utility of PAQ in relating job behaviours to traits. *Journal of Occupational Psychology*, **62**, 151–162.

Sparrow, J., Patrick, J., Spurgeon, P. and Barwell, F. (1982) The use of job component analysis and related aptitudes in personnel selection. *Journal of Occupational Psychology*, **55**, 157–164.

Spencer, G. J. and Worthington, R. (1952) Validity of a projective technique in predicting sales effectiveness. *Personnel Psychology*, **5**, 125–144.

Spool, M. D. (1978) Training programs for observers of behavior: a review. *Personnel Psychology*, **31**, 853–888.

Springbett, B. M. (1958) Factors affecting the final decision in the employment interview. *Canadian Journal of Psychology*, **12**, 13–22.

Stagner, R. (1958) The gullibility of personnel managers. *Personnel Psychology*, **11**, 347–352.

Sterns, L., Alexander, R. A., Barrett, G. V. and Dambrot, F. H. (1983) The relationship of extraversion and neuroticism with job preferences and job satisfaction for clerical employees. *Journal of Occupational Psychology*, **56**, 145–153.

Stone, E. F., Stone, D. L. and Gueutal, H. G. (1990) Influence of cognitive ability on responses to questionnaire measures: measurement precision and missing response problems. *Journal of Applied Psychology*, **75**, 418–427.

Strong, E. K. (1926) An interest test for personnel managers. *Journal of Personnel Research*, **5**, 194–205.

Strong, E. K. (1955) *Vocational interests eighteen years after college*. University of Minnesota Press, Minneapolis.

Stumpf, S. A. and London, M. (1981) Capturing rater policies in evaluating candidates for promotion. *Academy of Management Journal*, **24**, 752–766.

Super, D. E. and Crites, J. O. (1962) *Appraising vocational fitness by means of psychological tests*. Harper and Row, New York.

Sydiaha, D. (1961) Bales' interaction process analysis of personnel selection interviews. *Journal of Applied Psychology*, **45**, 393–401.

Taylor, M. S. and Sniezek, J. A. (1984) The college recruitment interview: topical content and applicant reactions. *Journal of Occupational Psychology*, **57**, 157–168.

Tenopyr, M. L. (1977) Content-construct confusion. *Personnel Psychology*, **30**, 47–54.

Tett, R. P., Jackson, D. N. and Rothstein, M. (1991) Personality measures as predictors of job performance—a meta-analytic review. *Personnel Psychology*, **44**, 703–742.

Thayer, P. W. (1977) 'Somethings old, somethings new'. *Personnel Psychology*, **30**, 513–524.

Thorndike, R. L. (1986) The role of general ability in prediction. *Journal of Vocational Behavior*, **29**, 332–339.

Tiffin, J. (1943) *Industrial psychology*. Prentice Hall, New York.

Toplis, J. (1975) Group selection methods. In Ungerson, B. (ed.) *Recruitment handbook*. Gower Press, London.

Toops, H. A. (1944) The criterion. *Educational and Psychological Measurement*, **4**, 271–293.

Tosi, H. L. and Einbender, S. W. (1985) The effects of the type and amount of information in sex discrimination research: a meta-analysis. *Academy of Management Journal*, **28**, 712–723.

Trattner, M. H. (1985) *Estimating the validity of aptitude and ability tests for semiprofessional occupations using the Schmidt-Hunter interactive validity generalisation procedure*. U S Office of Personnel Management, Washington DC.

Travers, R. M. W. (1951) Rational hypotheses in the construction of tests. *Educational and Psychological Measurement*, **11**, 128–137.

Tucker, D. H. and Rowe, P. M. (1977) Consulting the application form prior to the interview: an essential step in the selection process. *Journal of Applied Psychology*, **62**, 283–287.

Tucker, M. F., Cline, V. B., and Schmitt, J. R. (1967) Prediction of creativity and other performance measures from biographical information among pharmaceutical scientists. *Journal of Applied Psychology*, **51**, 131–138.

Tullar, W. L. (1989) Relational control in the interview. *Journal of Applied Psychology*, **74**, 971–977.

Tullar, W. L., Mullins, T. W. and Caldwell, S. A. (1979) Effects of interview length and applicant quality on interview decision time. *Journal of Applied Psychology*, **64**, 669–674.

Turnage, J. J. and Muchinsky, P. M. (1982) Transsituational variability in human performance within assessment centers. *Organisational Behavior and Human Performance*, **30**, 174–200.

Tziner, A. and Dolan, S. (1982) Evaluation of a traditional selection system in predicting success of females in officer training. *Journal of Occupational Psychology*, **55**, 269–275.

Ulrich, L. and Trumbo, D. (1965) The selection interview since 1949. *Psychological Bulletin*, **63**, 100–116.

Umeda, J. K. and Frey, D. H. (1974) Life history correlates of ministerial success. *Journal of Vocational Behavior*, **4**, 319–324.

US Department of Labor (1970) *Manual for the USTES General Aptitude Test Battery. Section III, Development*. US Department of Labor, Washington DC.

Vale, C. D., Keller, L. S. and Bentz, V. J. (1986) Development and validation of a computerised interpretation system for personnel tests. *Personnel Psychology*, **39**, 525–542.

Valenzi, E. and Andrews, I. R. (1971) Individual differences in the decision process of employment interviewers. *Journal of Applied Psychology*, **58**, 49–53.

Vance, R. J. and Colella, A. (1990) The utility of utility analysis. *Human Performance*, **3**, 123–139.

Vance, R. J., MacCallum, R. C., Coovert, M. D., and Hedge, J. W. (1988) Construct validity of multiple job performance measures using confirmatory factor analysis. *Journal of Applied Psychology*, **73**, 74–80.

Vance, R. J., Coovert, M. D., MacCallum, R. C. and Hedge, J. W. (1989) Construct models of task performance. *Journal of Applied Psychology*, **74**, 447–455.

Vernon, P. E. (1950) The validation of Civil Service Selection Board procedures. *Occupational Psychology*, **24**, 75–95.

Vernon, P. E. (1982) *The abilities and achievements of Oriental North Americans.* Academic Press, New York.

Vernon, P. E. and Parry, J. B. (1949) *Personnel selection in the British forces.* University of London Press, London.

Vinchur, A. J., Schippman, J. S., Smalley, M. D. and Rothe, H. F. (1991) Productivity consistency of foundry chippers and grinders: a 6-year field study. *Journal of Applied Psychology*, **76**, 134–136.

Vineberg, R. and Joyner, J. N. (1982) *Prediction of job performance: a review of military studies.* Human Resources Research Organisation, Alexandria, VA.

Viteles, M. S. (1932) *Industrial psychology.* Norton, New York.

Wagner, R. (1949) The employment interview: a critical summary. *Personnel Psychology*, **2**, 17–46.

Waldman, D. A. and Avolio, B. J. (1989) Homogeneity of test validity. *Journal of Applied Psychology*, **74**, 371–374.

Wallace, N. and Travers, R. M. (1938) A psychometric sociological study of a group of speciality salesmen. *Annals of Eugenics*, **8**, 266–302.

Walsh, J. P., Weinberg, R. M. and Fairfield, M. L. (1987) The effects of gender on assessment centre evaluations. *Journal of Occupational Psychology*, **60**, 305–309.

Wanous, J. P. (1978) Realistic job previews: can a procedure to reduce turnover also influence the relationship between abilities and performance? *Personnel Psychology*, **31**, 249–258.

Warmke, D. L. and Billings, R. S. (1979) Comparison of training methods for improving the psychometric quality of experimental and administrative performance ratings. *Journal of Applied Psychology*, **64**, 124–131.

Waters, L. K. and Waters, C. W. (1970) Peer nominations as predictors of short-term sales performance. *Journal of Applied Psychology*, **54**, 42–44.

Weekley, J. A. and Gier, J. A. (1987) Reliability and validity of the situational interview for a sales position. *Journal of Applied Psychology*, **72**, 484–487.

Weekley, J. A., Frank, B., O'Connor, E. J. and Peters, L. H. (1985) A comparison of three methods of estimating the standard deviation of performance in dollars. *Journal of Applied Psychology*, **70**, 122–126.

Wexley, K. N., Yukl, G. A., Kovacs, S. Z. and Sanders, R. E. (1972) Importance of contrast effects in employment interviews. *Journal of Applied Psychology*, **56**, 45–48.

Wherry, R. J. (1957) The past and future of criterion evaluation. *Personnel Psychology*, **10**, 1–5.

Wiggins, J. S. (1973) *Personality and prediction.* Addison Wesley, Reading, MA.

Wiesner, W. H. and Cronshaw, S. F. (1988) A meta-analytic investigation of the impact of interview format and degree of structure on the validity of the employment interview. *Journal of Psychology*, **61**, 275–290.

Williams, S. B. and Leavitt, H. J. (1947) Group opinion as a predictor of military leadership. *Journal of Consulting Psychology*, **11**, 283–291.

Wilson, N. A. B. (1948) The work of the Civil Service Selection Board. *Occupational Psychology*, **22**, 204–212.

Wilson, M. A., Harvey, R. J., and Macy, B. A. (1990) Repeating items to estimate the test–retest reliability of task inventory ratings. *Journal of Applied Psychology*, **75**, 158–163.

Wingrove, J., Glendinning, R. and Herriot, P. (1984) Graduate pre-selection a research note. *Journal of Occupational Psychology*, **57**, 169–171.

Wollowick, H. B. and McNamara, W. J. (1969) Relationship of the components of an assessment center to management success. *Journal of Applied Psychology*, **53**, 348–352.

Wright, O. R. (1969) Summary of research on the selection interview since 1964. *Personnel Psychology*, **22**, 391–413.

Wright, O. R., Carter, J. L. and Fowler, E. P. (1967) A differential analysis of an oral interview program. *Public Personnel Review*, **28**, 242–246.

Zdep, S. M. and Weaver, H. B. (1967) The graphoanalytic approach to selecting life insurance salesmen. *Journal of Applied Psychology*, **51**, 295–299.

Zedeck, S., Tziner, A. and Middlestadt, S. E. (1983) Interviewer validity and reliability: an individual analysis approach. *Personnel Psychology*, **36**, 355–370.

Zeidner, M. (1988) Cultural fairness in aptitude testing revisited: a cross-cultural parallel. *Professional Psychology: Research and Practice*, **19**, 257–262.

Author Index

Subject Index